AF891879

NO MAMES

10:05 AM, La Lagunillla, Mexico City, some random day in 2019, a bunch of notifications on the iphone my friend Rafa gave me because mine died.

La luz se cuela por la orilla de tela que pusimos en la ventana, levanto un poco el cuello, Fer sigue dormido a lado de mi. Es un sentimiento similar al que tuve cuando Mayan pegó esos filtros de colores en la ventana de la sala para darle color a la luz, un trabajo super bonito. ¿Similar? Abro las notificaciones.

The picture we made of my embellished face by Karla while lying on the concrete floor of my apartment in the hood is now on the Instagram profile of Vogue Magazine. I'm completely speechless as I give Fer some forehead kisses trying to wake him up and tell him about the news.

La luz que me rodea es dorada, me siento de metal y la emoción me agrega brillo, algunas lágrimas calientes caen de mis ojos, al parecer nunca van a fraguar, porque ya mancharon mi cobija. Diría mi amiga Joan: "Tu cielo me cerró las puertas y ahora estoy en Vogue".

Mayan never told me this would happen. I like that about her and her work, there's always something unsaid and untold about the stories that she portrays.

Feelings and moods are crystal clear and you can actually stand at that moment, in the room. Protagonism and genius as we understand it from a white male gaze is absent, but the image is full of a personal approach where everyone involved is sharing time. You can't see her, but she's there, sometimes sitting on the mountain of clothes, others getting her feet wet after filling the tub with water. She's in the colors, in the light that fills the walls, in the subtle smile on my face.

*

1:00 PM, Barrio de Santo Domingo, Mexico City, another day of waking up cold in 2017.

Some months ago Ainé, Ano, and I moved here after leaving our homes for different reasons — trans-hate, family abuse — three sad trans tigers. Ainé hasn't come out of her room yet, I don't know why. It's also hard for me to focus on someone else's struggles while I'm jobless and my emotional stability depends on playing reggaeton blends and mixes all day long to numb our reality. Our reality: 90% of trans people in Mexico don't have access to a formal job because of discrimination. Sex workers and trans women in vulnerable and dangerous environments have a 35-year life expectancy and we're living here without paying rent and with a weird unstable arrangement.

> *Impresionante como cambia la vida, la vida que siempre es otra y nunca es la misma, ¿Cómo podría hablar del pasado sin hablar del otro pasado? Presente, pasado y futuro coexisten diario en mi ser y de otra manera no puede ser.*

Also tonight I'm playing Mami Slut, a party created by Jovan for the queer community in Mexico City. It's a space where I've found a home to develop myself as an artist and a trans person, can't wait!

*

6:00 PM, La Lagunilla, Mexico City, a nice morning in 2020, another text from Mayan!

(After a brief hi-hello conversation)

Mayan: I'm taking some pictures of couples and there's one that I would like to do with you and Fer, would you feel comfortable about it?

Havi: Sure! Let's just fix a date and time for it to happen.

Wow, honestly so excited. I could never imagine being in such a beautiful relationship as a trans woman. Years ago, I even went through one where we never established a physical connection because I could feel how he shrunk with fear whenever I touched him. Can you believe how that can make you feel as a human being? I don't think so. Love for trans women in Mexico is almost as rare as getting justice for being murdered as a woman, almost as rare as finding a place to rent where you won't be discriminated against for being LGBT+, almost as rare as walking down the streets without everyone staring. But it's happening, and I feel safer than I've ever felt before. We're working out a lot of things, obviously, but it's worth it.

Sus brazos me arrullan en las noches, está aprendiendo a mejorar su relación con los abrazos y los cuidados, me hace poemas, me da besos y me cuida cuando estoy enferma. En este punto ya pasamos el periodo de enamoramiento, estamos aprendiendo a platicar las cosas. Por mi parte, estoy superando muchos traumas que me dejó el abandono y la falta de amor real en mi otra relación. Al parecer a la gente no le gusta sólo estar conmigo por mi potencial y lo que les puedo dar.

*

10:00 PM, La Lagunilla, Mexico City, 2020. Mayan is outside our apartment with all her stuff, I need to come down and help her! Brb.

Lol I totally forgot to clean some stuff in the room but she's actually picking things up from the floor and telling me to try them on for the shoot, this girl is unreal, honestly this couldn't have happened in any other way.

*

3:00 PM, La Lagunilla, Mexico City, exciting 2020 day yeiii.

Mayan sent me some pictures of me and Fer
Oh
My
God

(posting them immediately, likes start raining, people start sharing)
Uhm…what???!! They got deleted from Instagram for "sexual misconduct"?

There's no fucking nipples showing
There's no nudity

Oh…right.
People can't stand seeing a trans girl being loved while them being cis-hetero can't find someone that thinks they are worth the world. Jealous bitches.

(months later my whole Instagram profile will be deleted for posting another picture of me and Fer, one year later it will happen again for the same reason, Instagram policies target trans people who are happy just to take away what they can from us)

*

7:00 AM, Friday, November 17, 2017. Lago Tanganica 67, Granada, Mexico City

I met Samantha and Adrian a few months ago, Sam and I are in the same modeling agency, something I always wanted to have. Adrian is starting to make fashion and editorial productions, there's something really simple but strong about what he's doing and I'm glad we get to know each other. Apparently for this Barragan runway Sam is also assisting Victor for some details on the shoes that…have, like…concrete? Will I be able to walk in that? We will find out, but they look amazing.

The fashion industry in Mexico City is starting to bloom in diversity of bodies, genders, races and backgrounds. People who were never even close to being in a fashion show, including myself, are now here, walking for the freshest ideas that have started to shake the status quo of a classist, racist and transphobic industry in the whole country. It feels like we're starting something important here.

No sé cómo describir esa sensación de que las cosas están cambiando, sin darle un sentido moral, solamente está pasando. Hay algo en el aire y en el suelo que me dice que somos una generación particular, me genera mucha esperanza. Estoy cansada, joven, drogadicta y flaca, pero siento como me estoy prendiendo en fuego, poquito a poco.

8:24 AM, October 5, 2021. Polanco, Mexico City

Cold sheer blankets and my bank account is almost empty but in a few hours I'll have bigger tits and I hope to look better than ever. A friend of mine wrote a text for a post to help me raise some funds for my recovery where they stated "gender reaffirming surgery", weird, I don't know what that means but cool...

The anesthesiologist just did his job and before i'm gone i'm texting Mayan and other people I know to help me boost the campaign so I can be economically
stable
during
my
recovery
....
(She's gone.)

*

12:00 PM, November 29, 2021, La Lagunilla, Mexico City

There's nothing covering the window in my room. I'm lying on the bed wearing a neon bikini and violet pants. Mayan wanted full natural light for the video we're shooting. She's sitting on a new carpet we bought and I can't stop smiling seeing her here again, it's been almost three years now of working together from my most vulnerable places, she can actually notice how I've grown and we're crying while remembering and talking about all the things that I've achieved, and for me it's actually a we.

She's holding the camera but she's not even looking through the lens. Apparently for her the most important lens is the one that goes deep into my soul: my two green olive eyes which I think she loves because they have a hint of yellow, just like hers.

El aire entra por la ventana, estoy cómoda, platicando, llorando, riendo, pensando. Tantas cosas que se hacen pocas y ya no es poco a poco, estoy ardiendo.

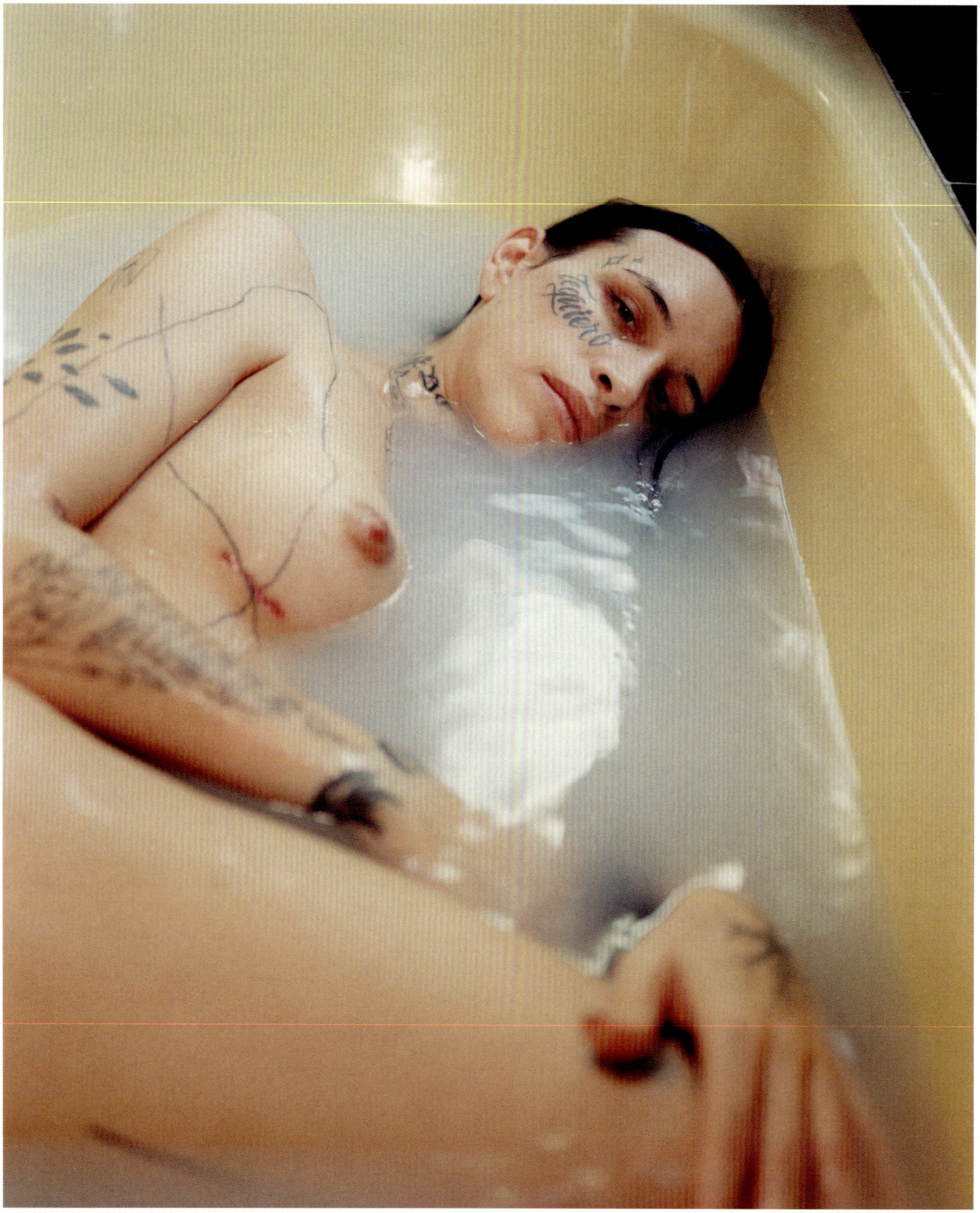

The next day:

I'm fucking naked, literally, this girl took me from cleaning the spiderwebs out of my emotions to having me fully topless, bottomless, and swimming in warm water mixed with milk. This is it, it feels like we've reached a mountain together at this point, the light is so beautiful, my body turns and contours the bathtub while she's waiting for precise moments to get what she wants, I'm conscious of that. We're so far from the first time we shot, she doesnt want my beauty anymore, she had it the first time. She wants my humanity, my naked trans body and my naked soul looking through the lens.

And I'll give it to her.

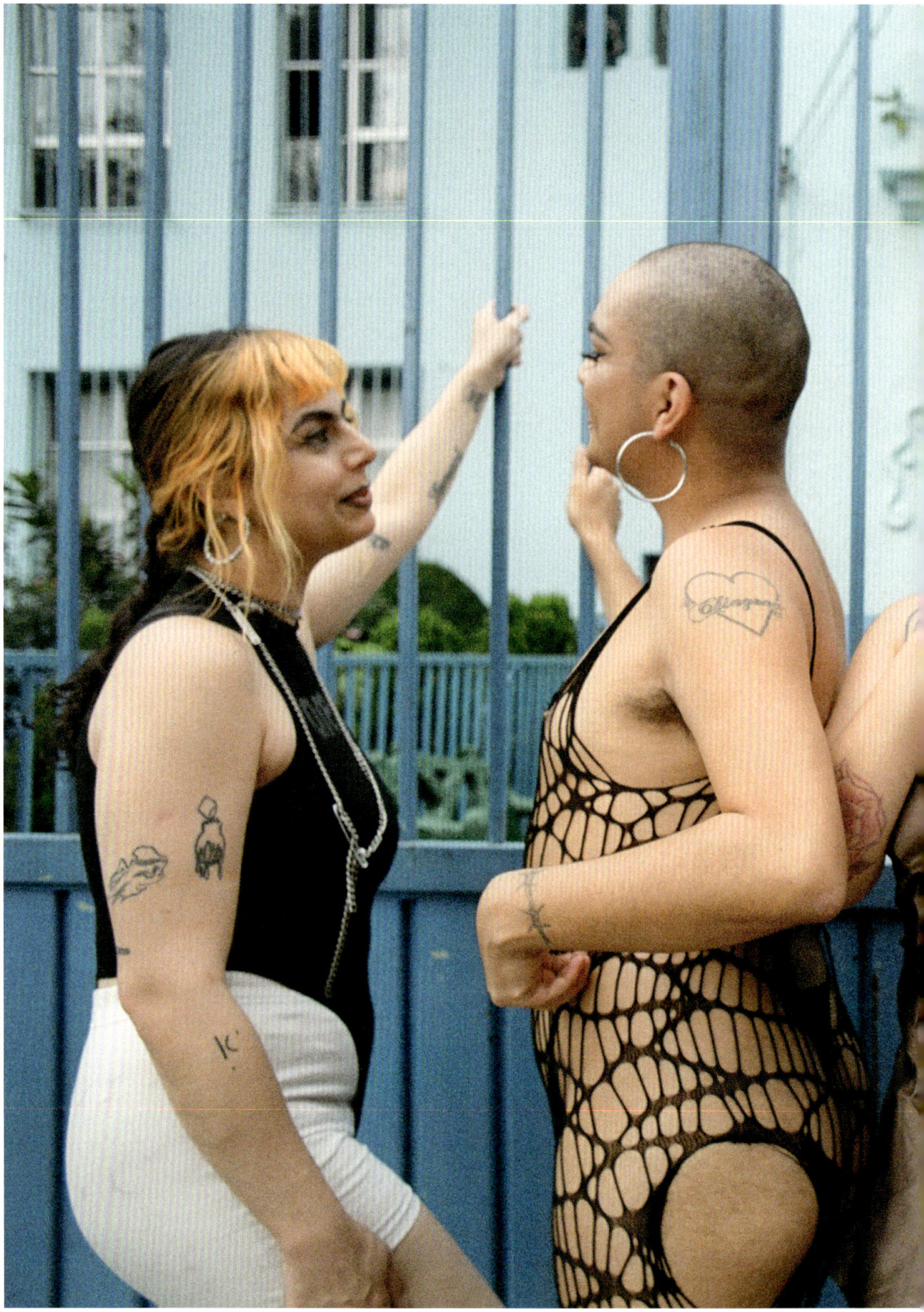

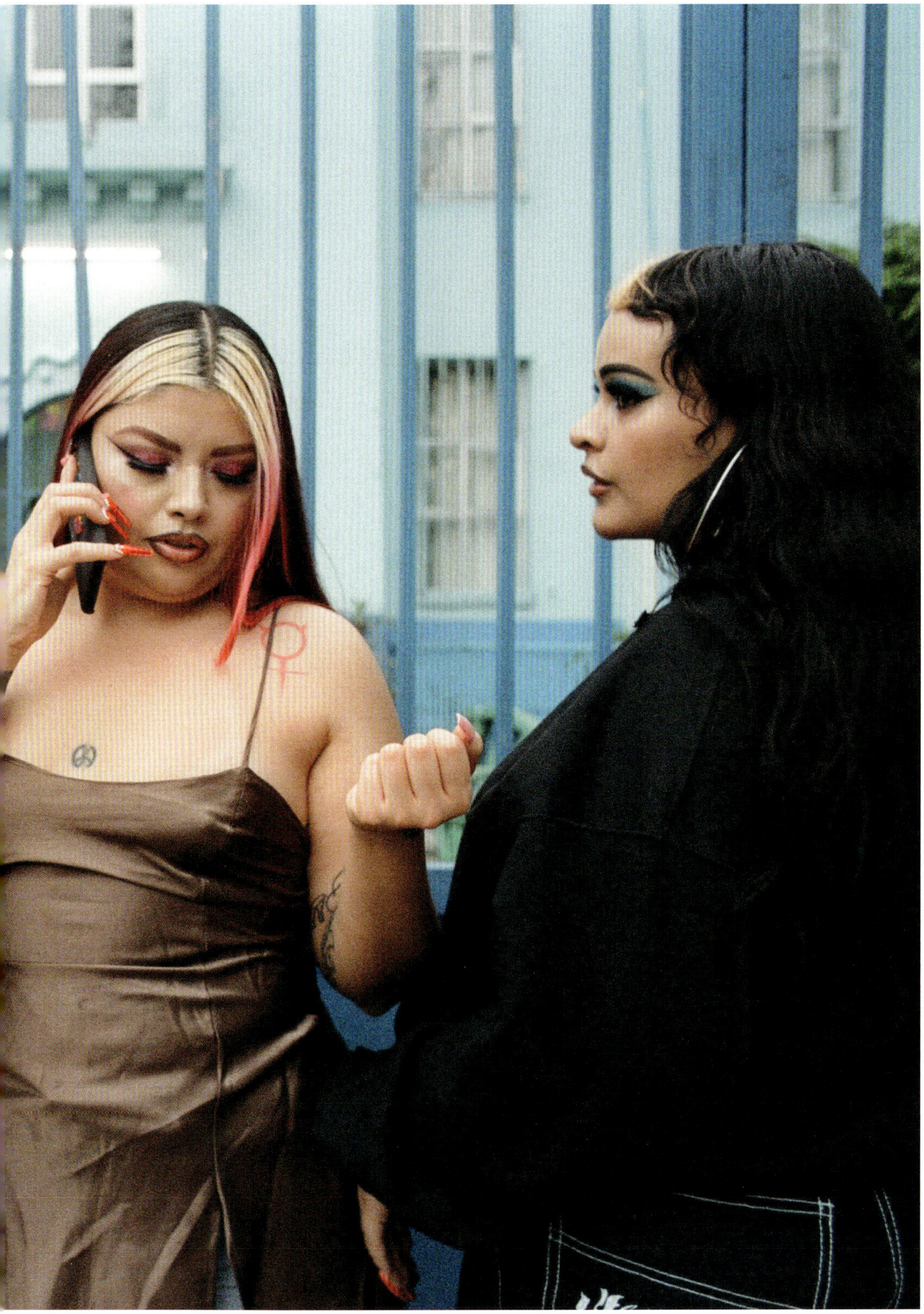

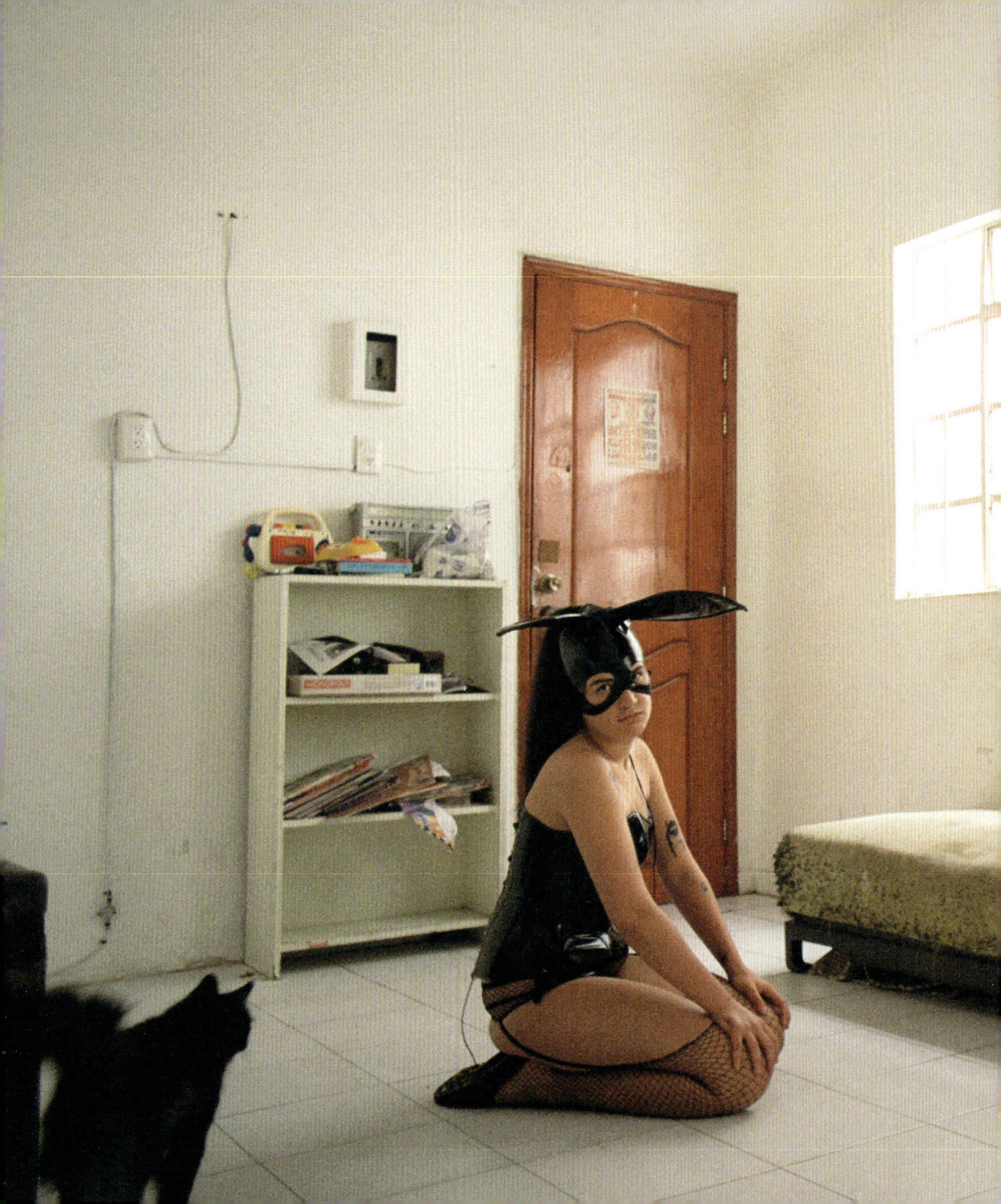

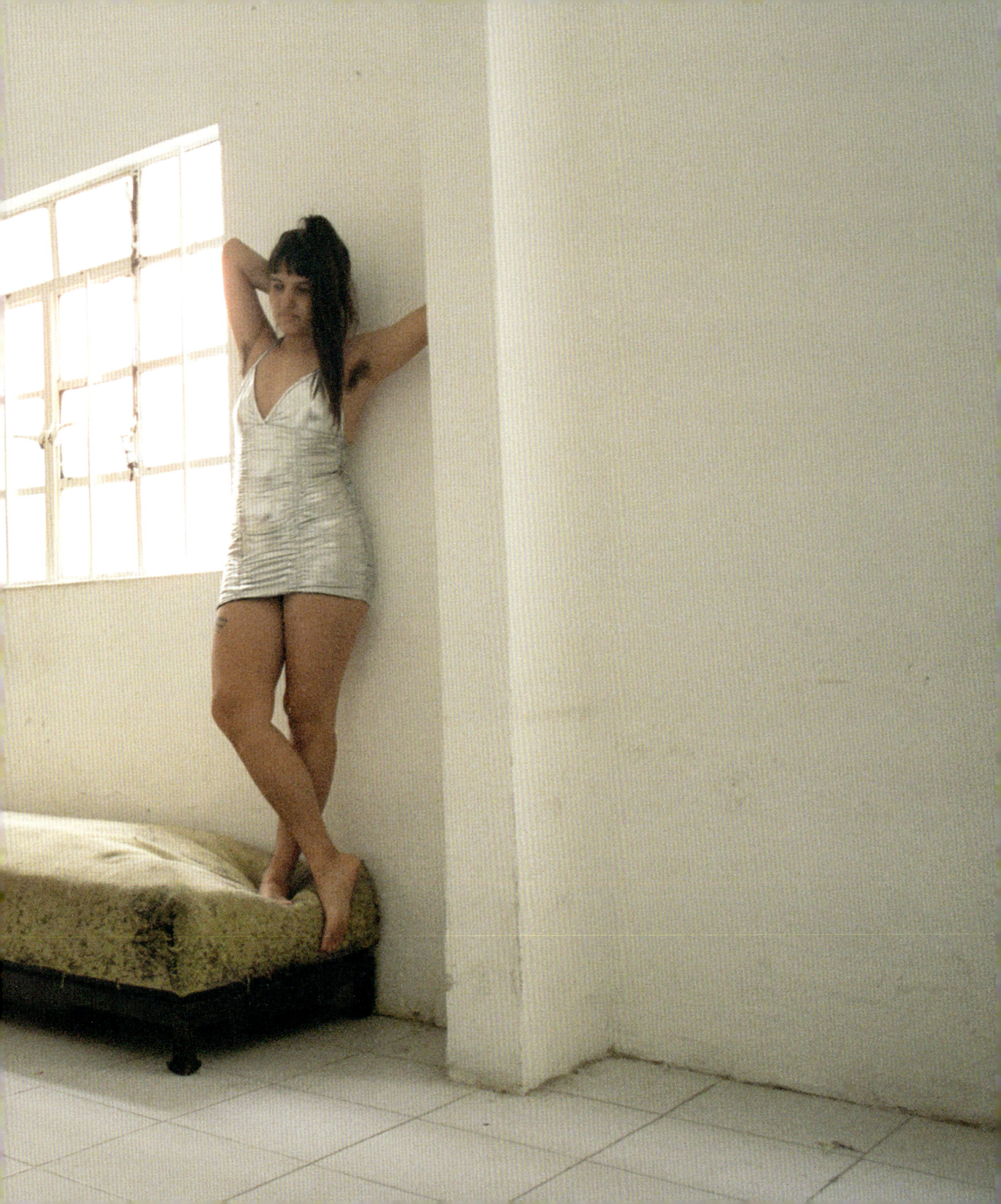

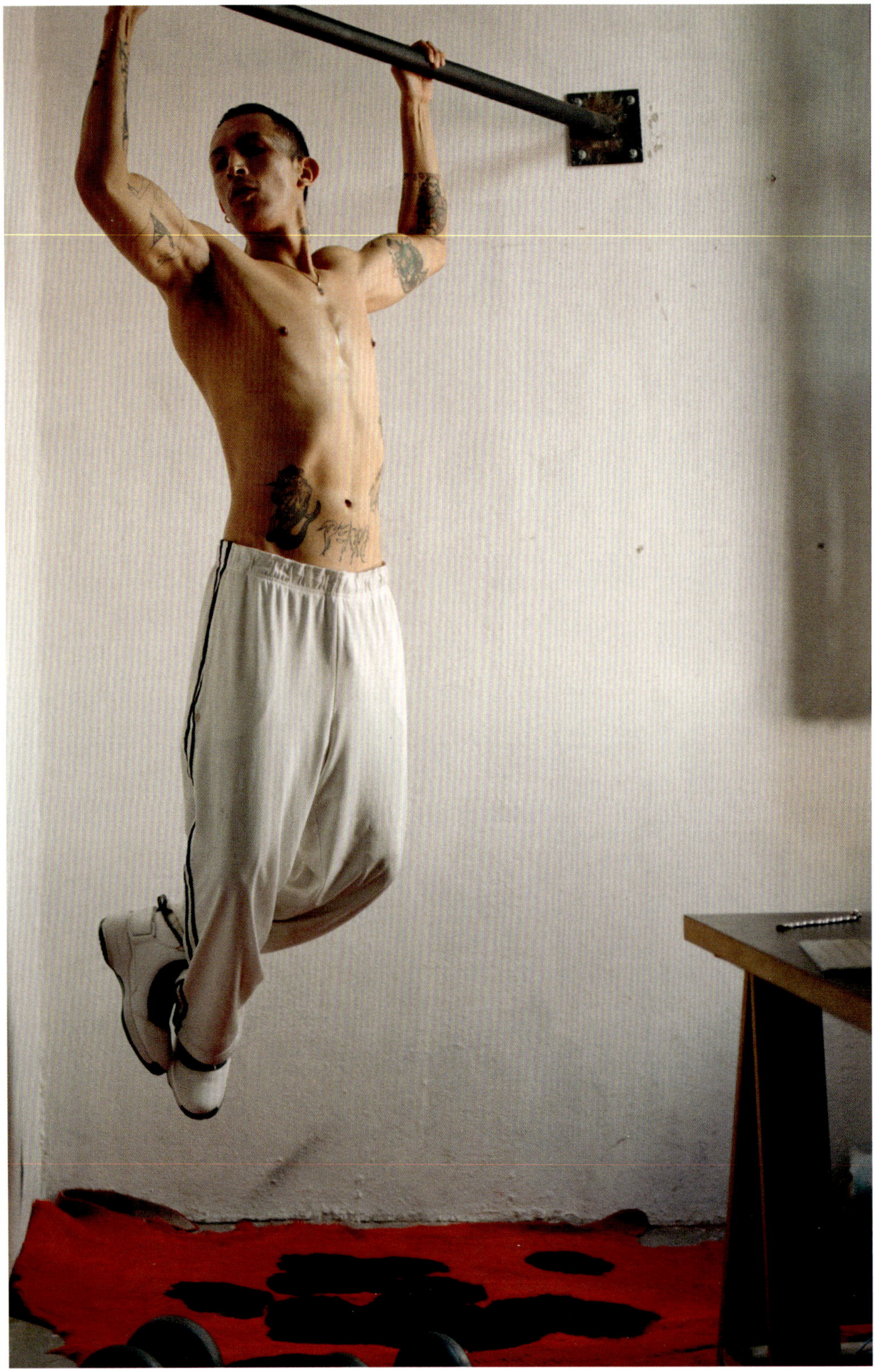

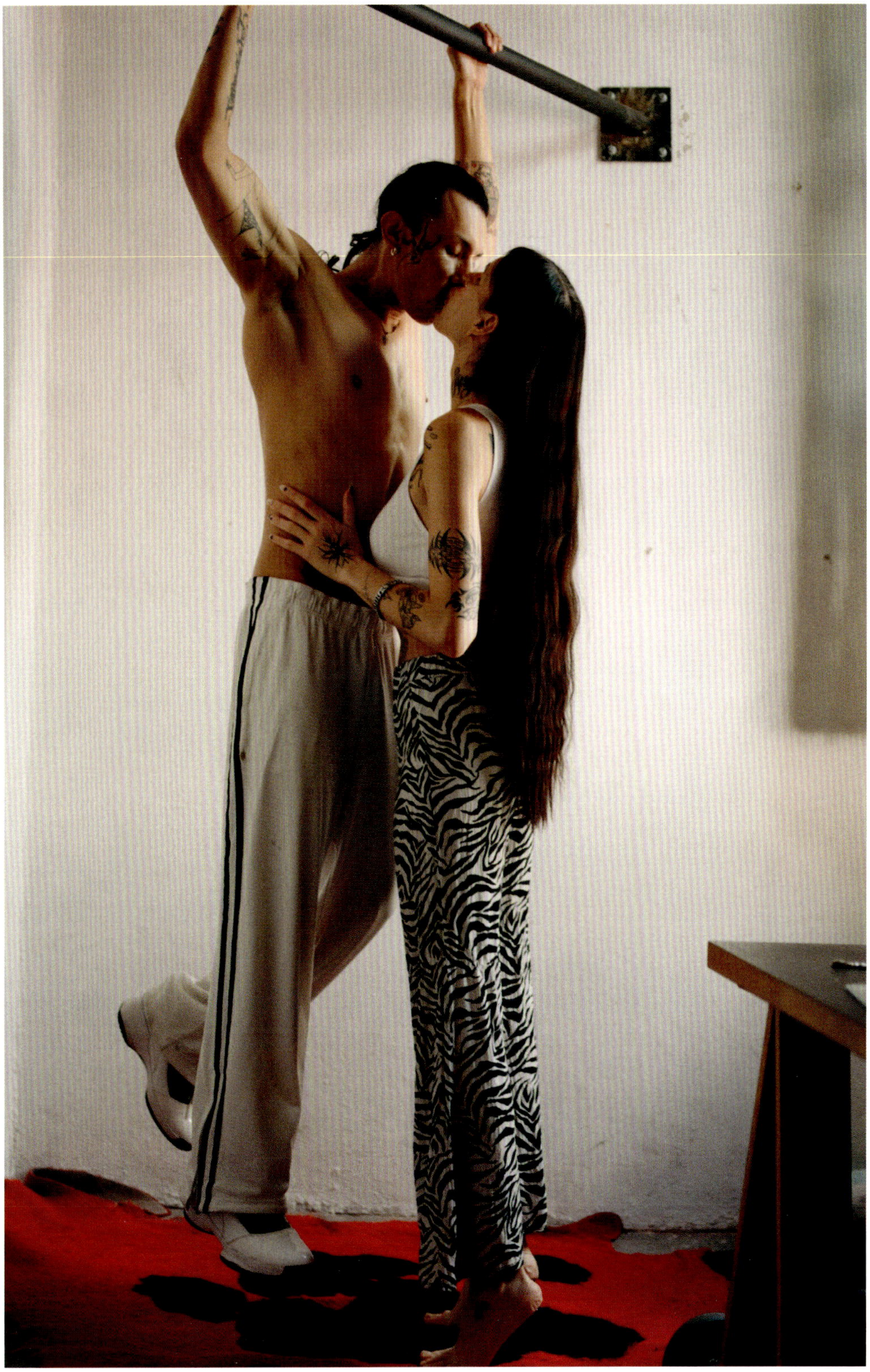

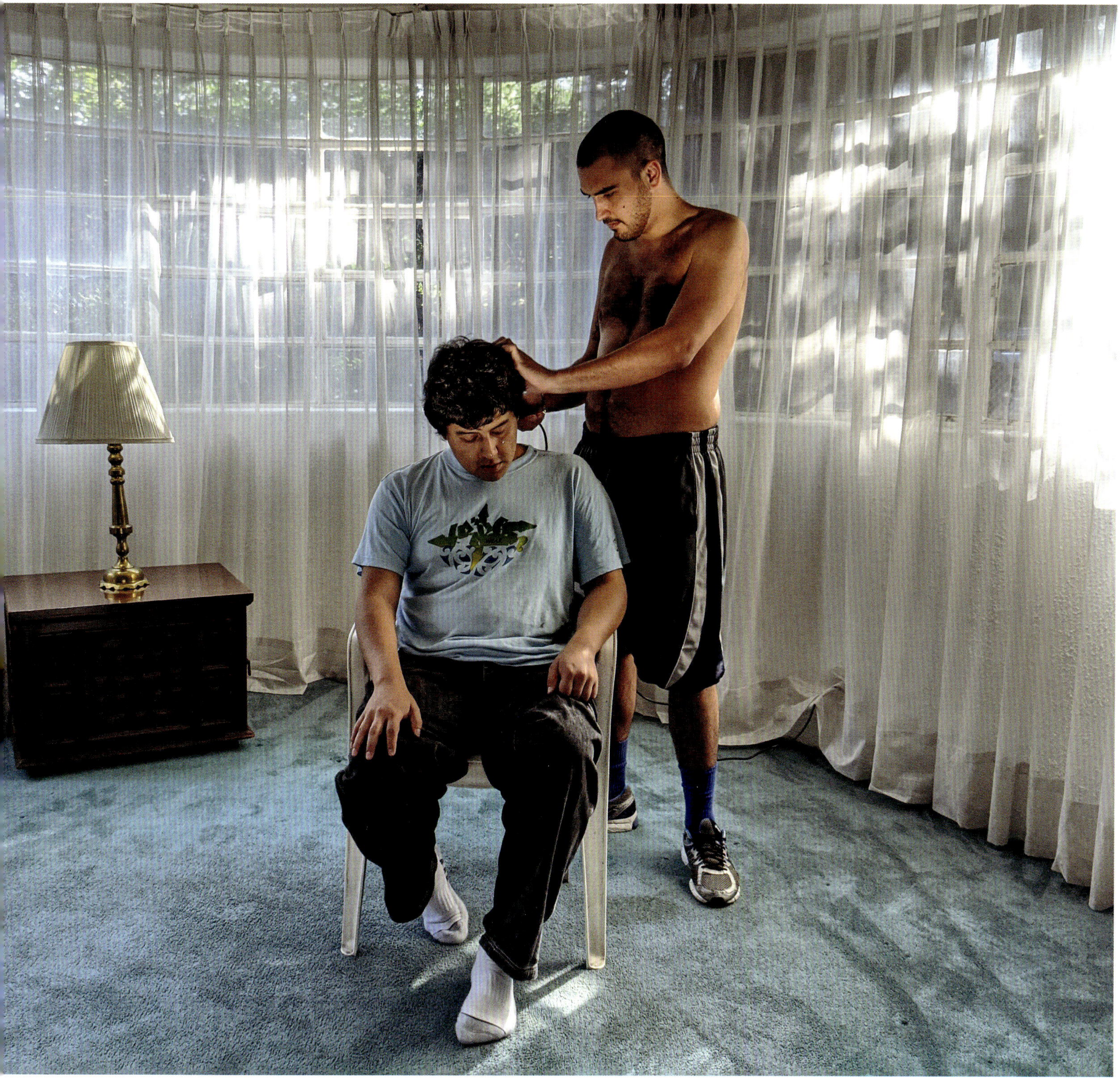

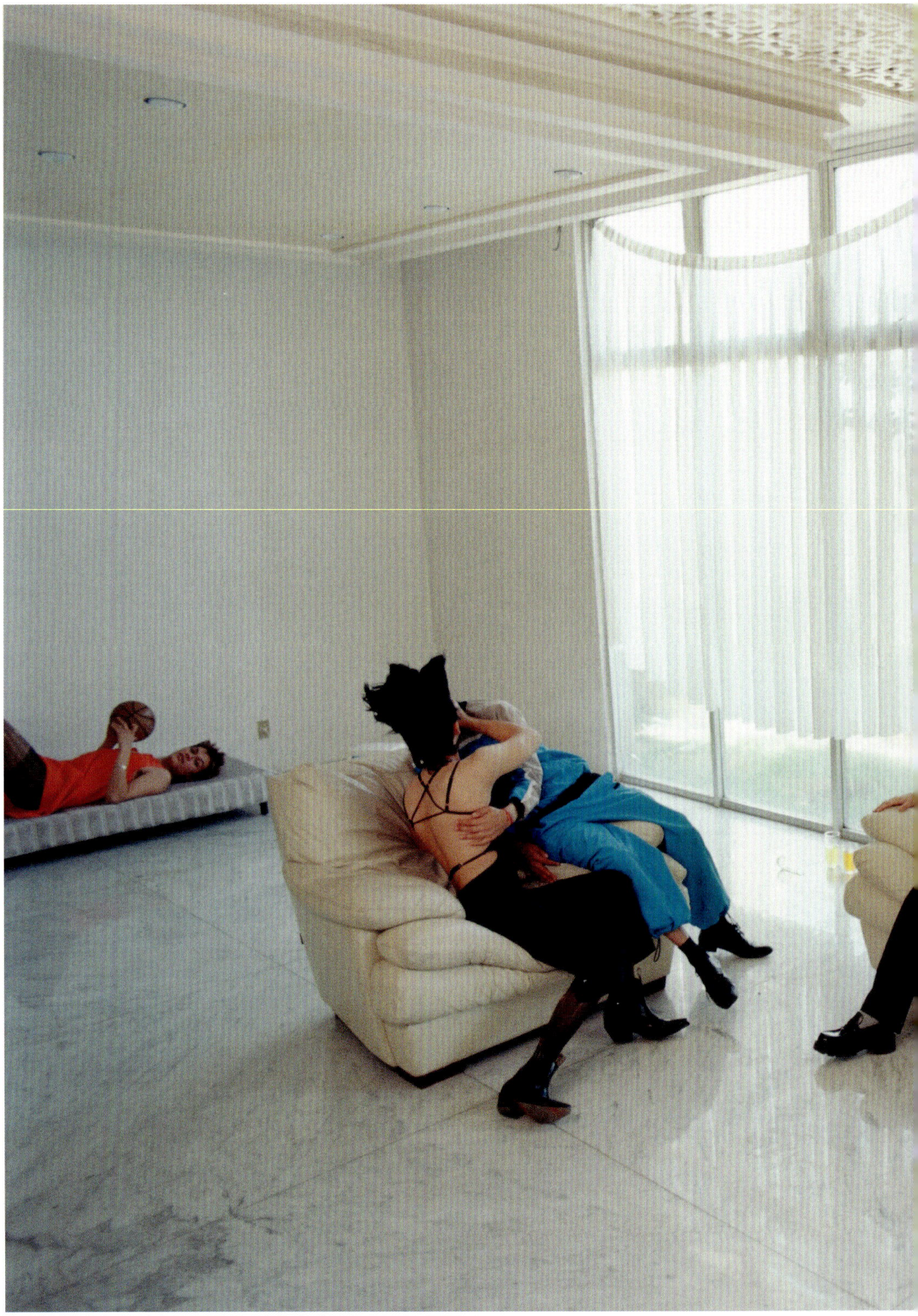

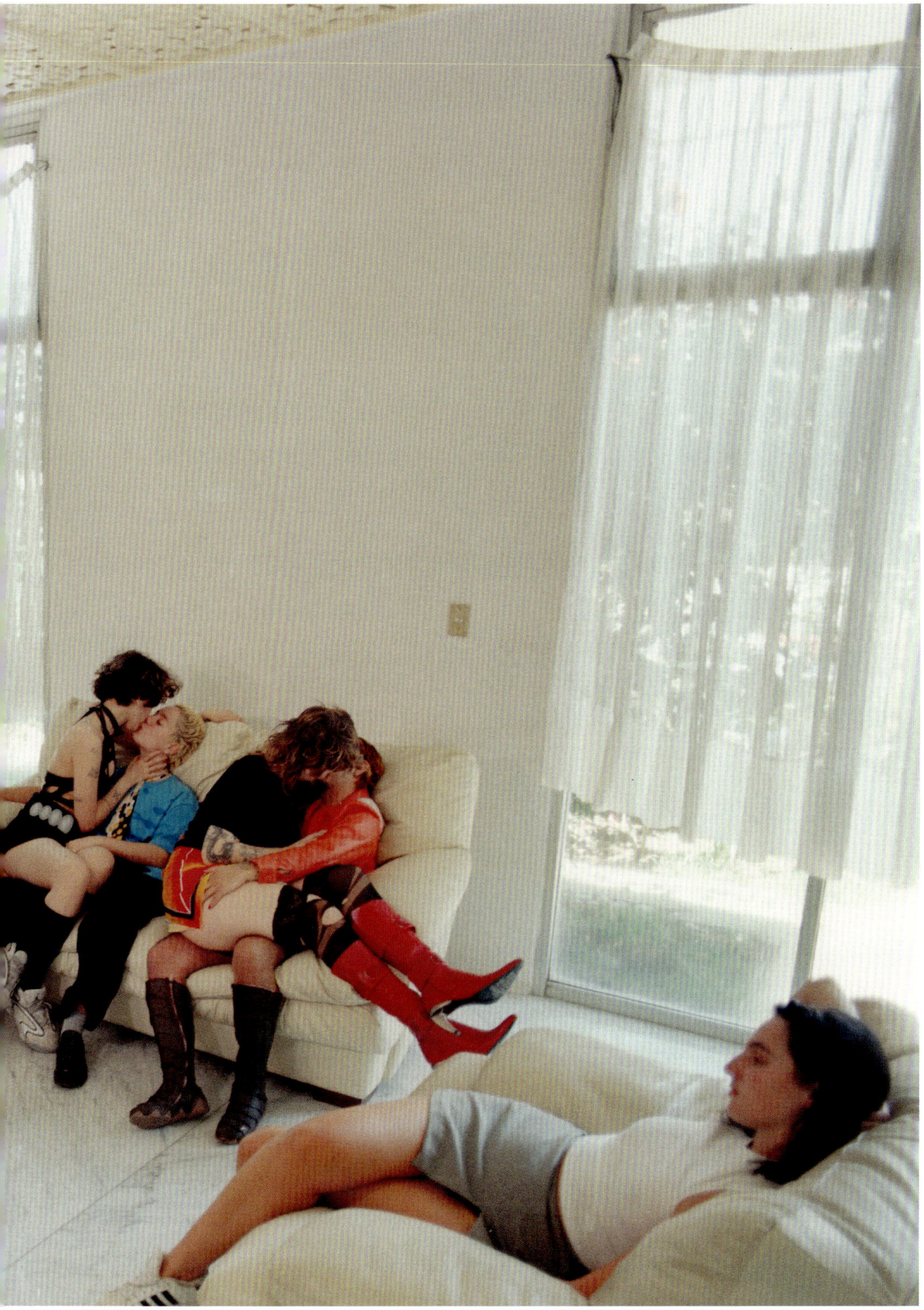

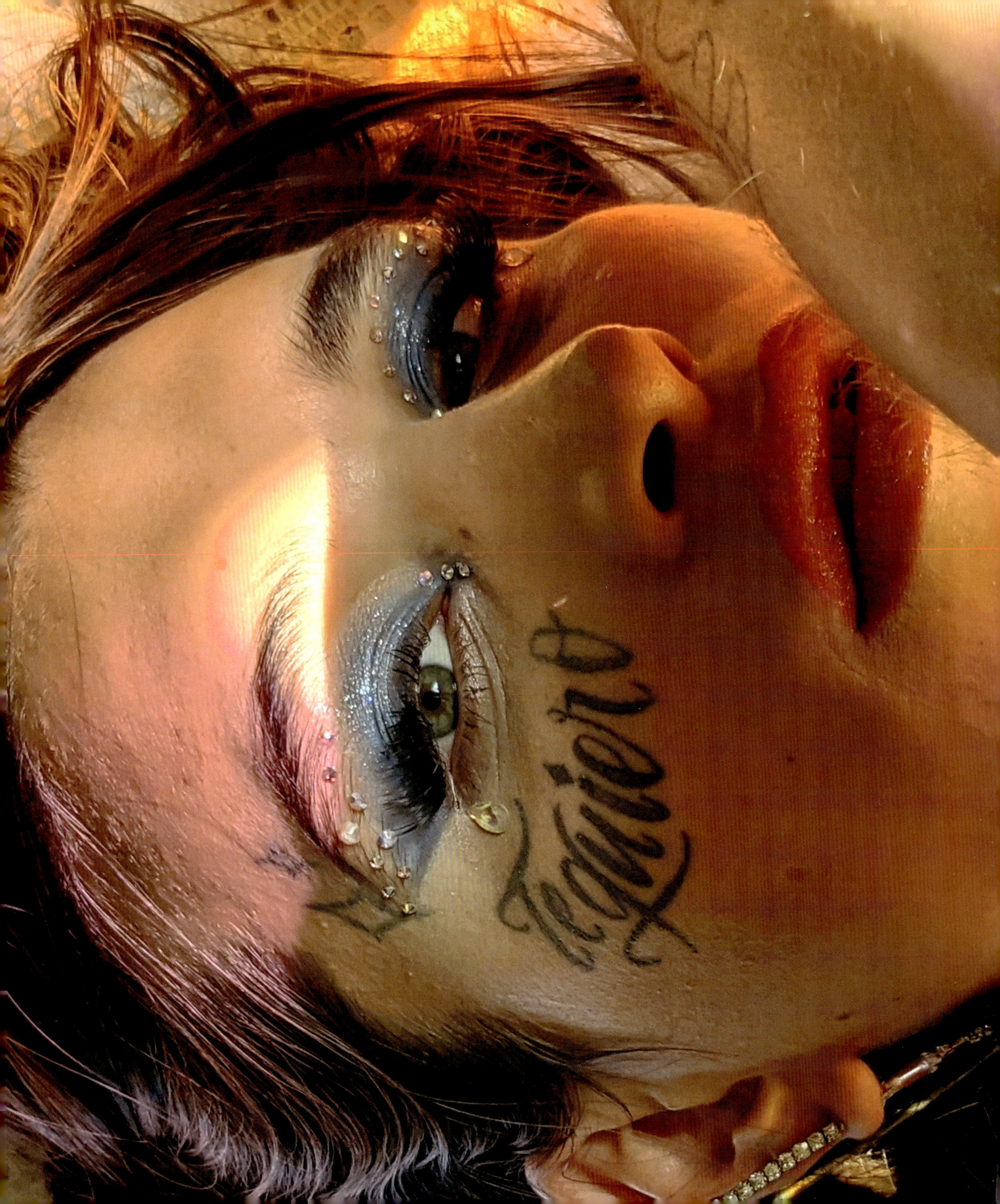

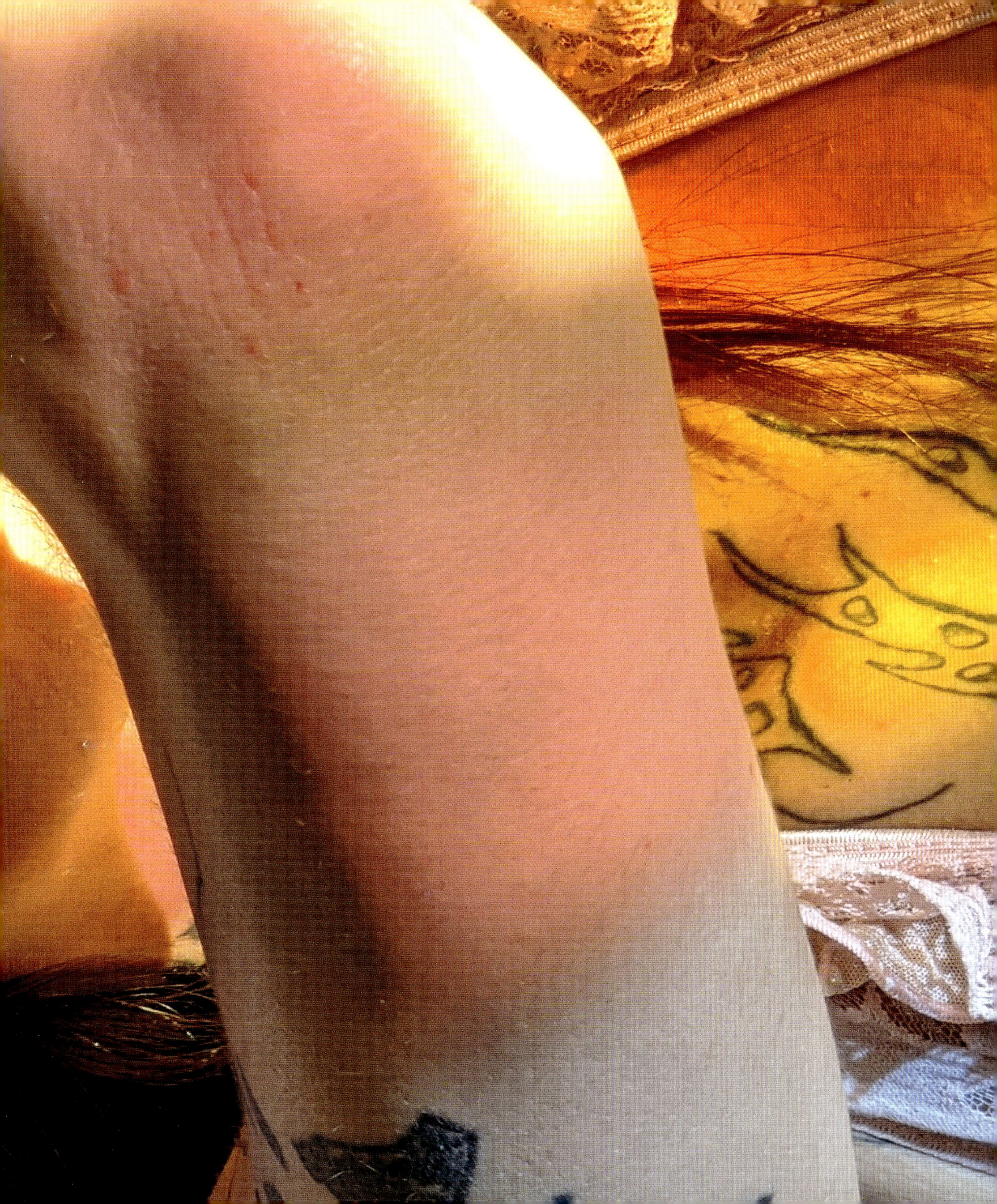

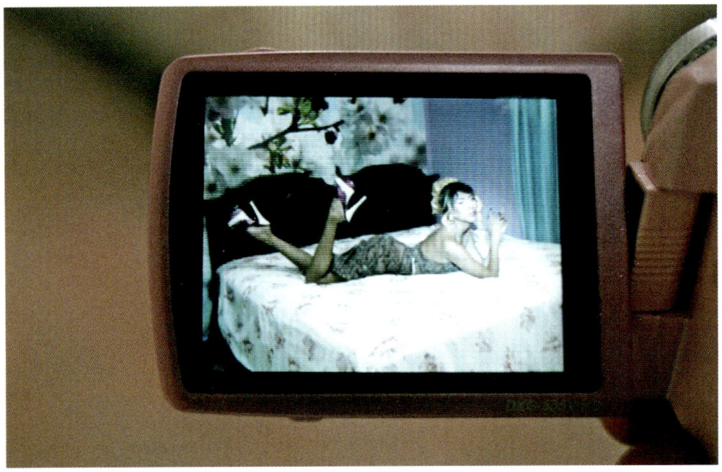

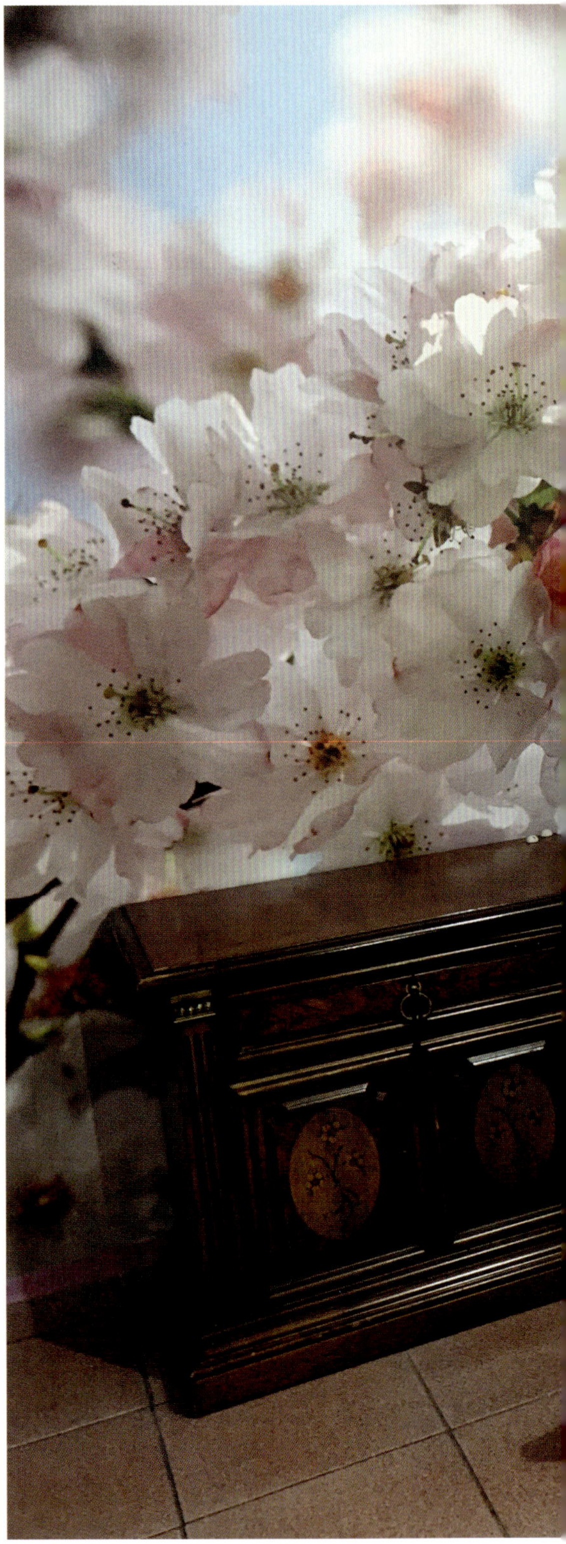

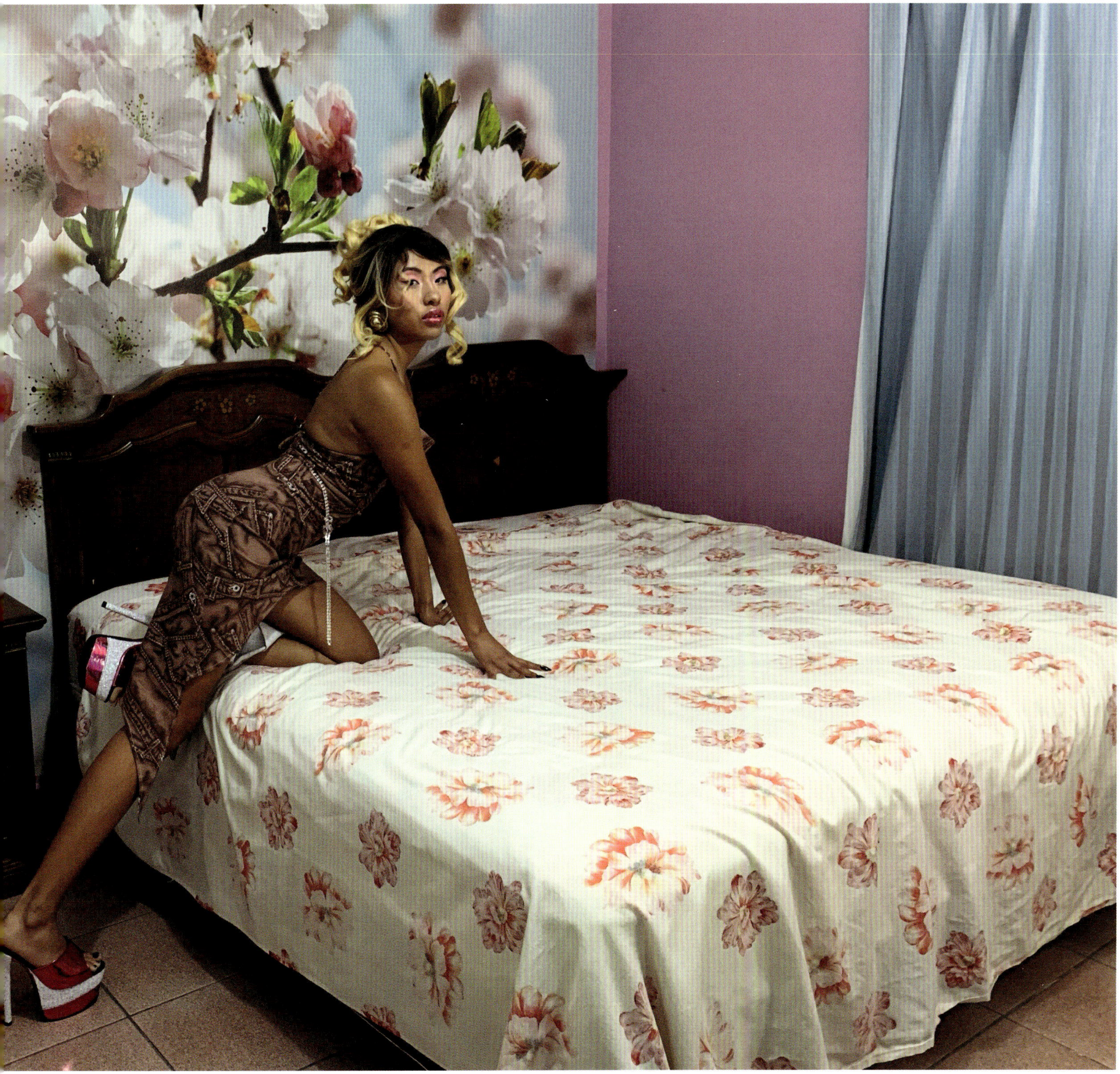

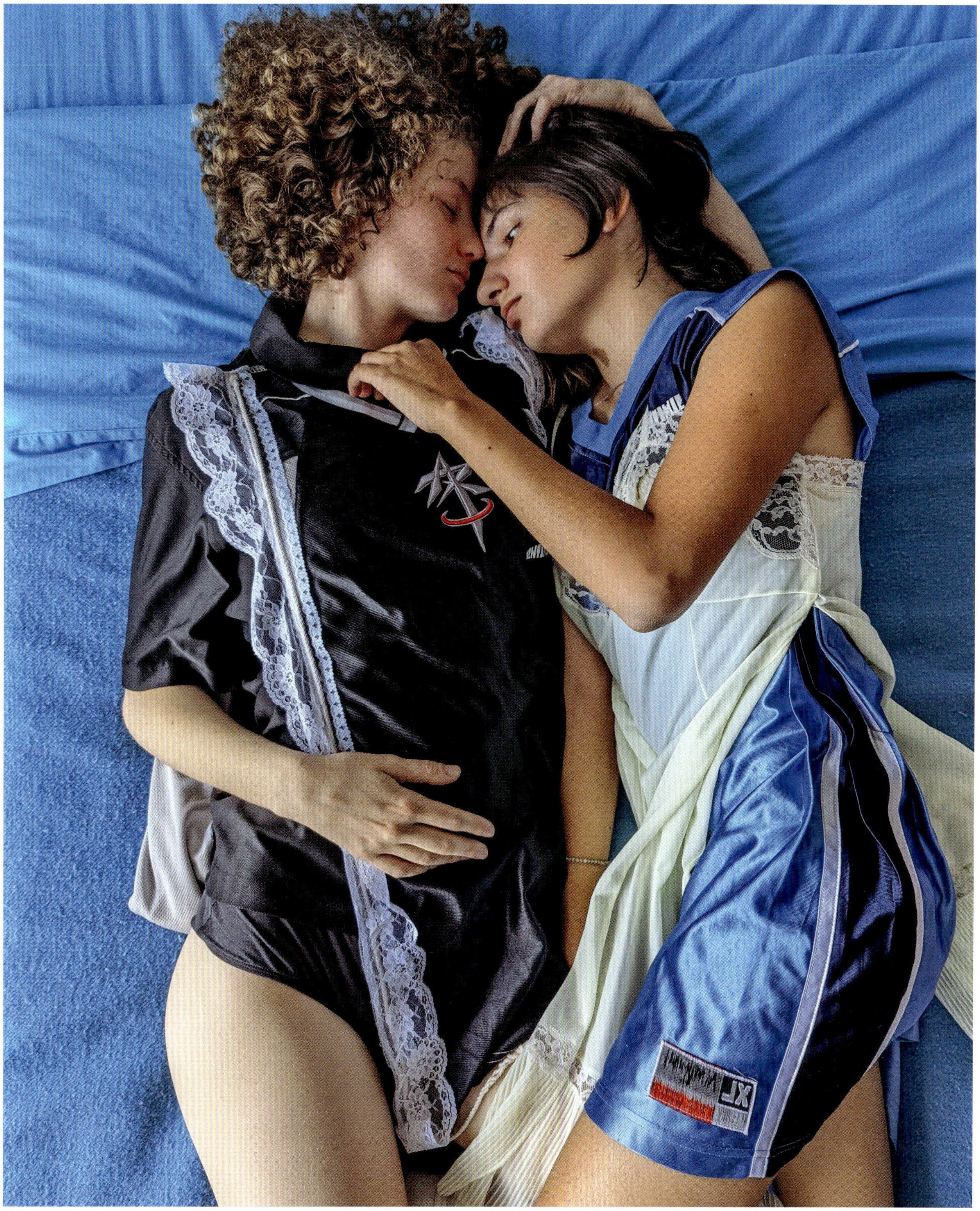

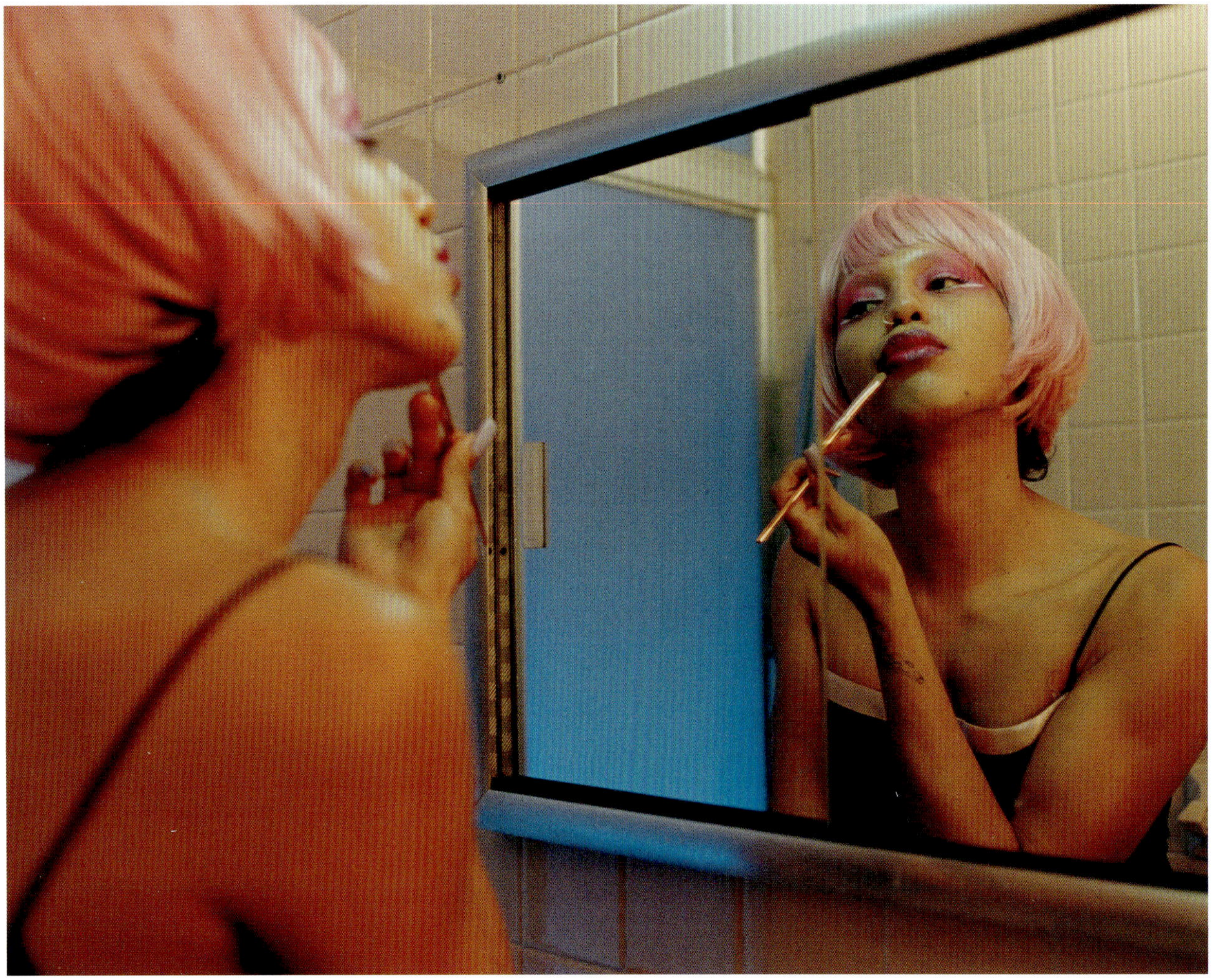

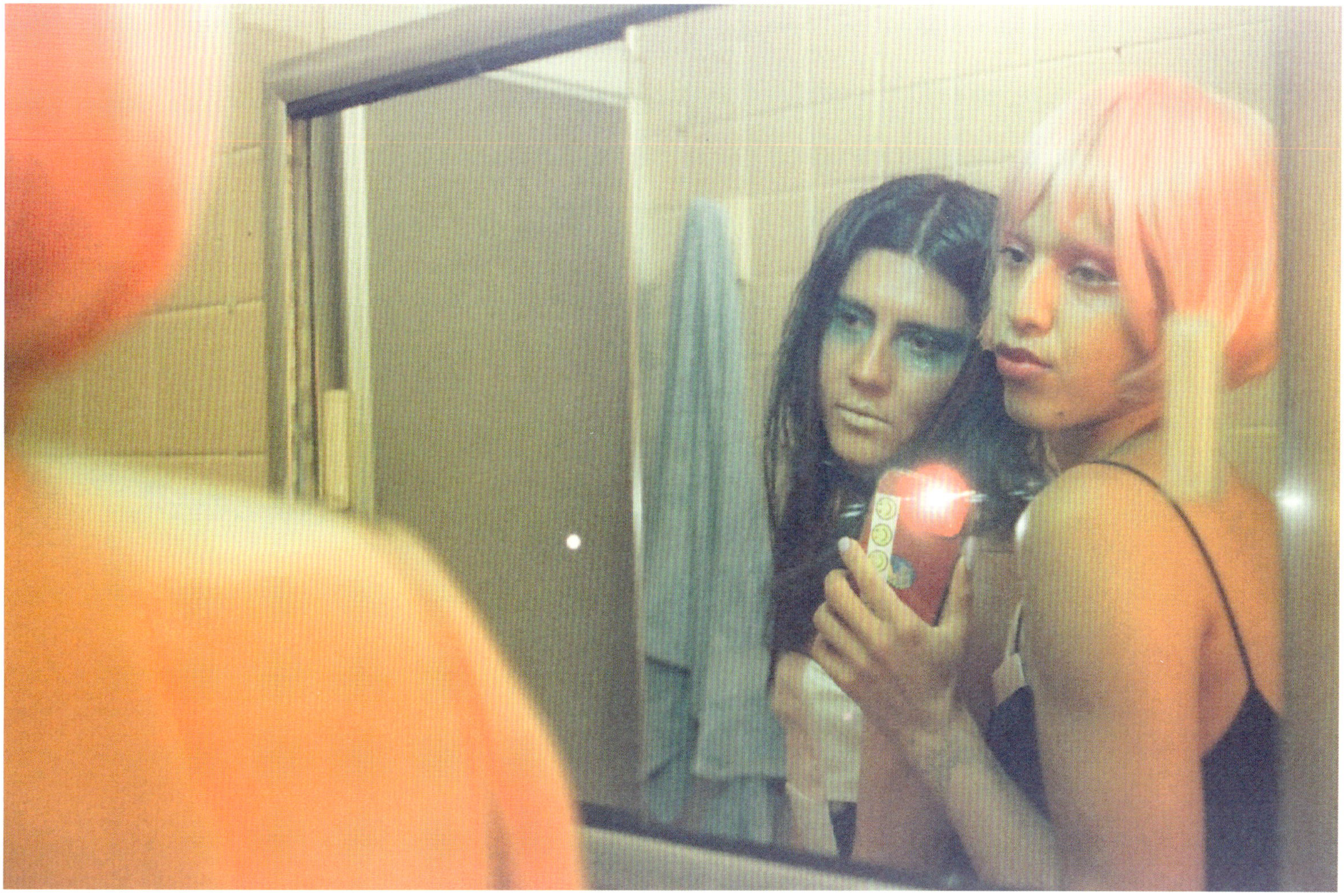

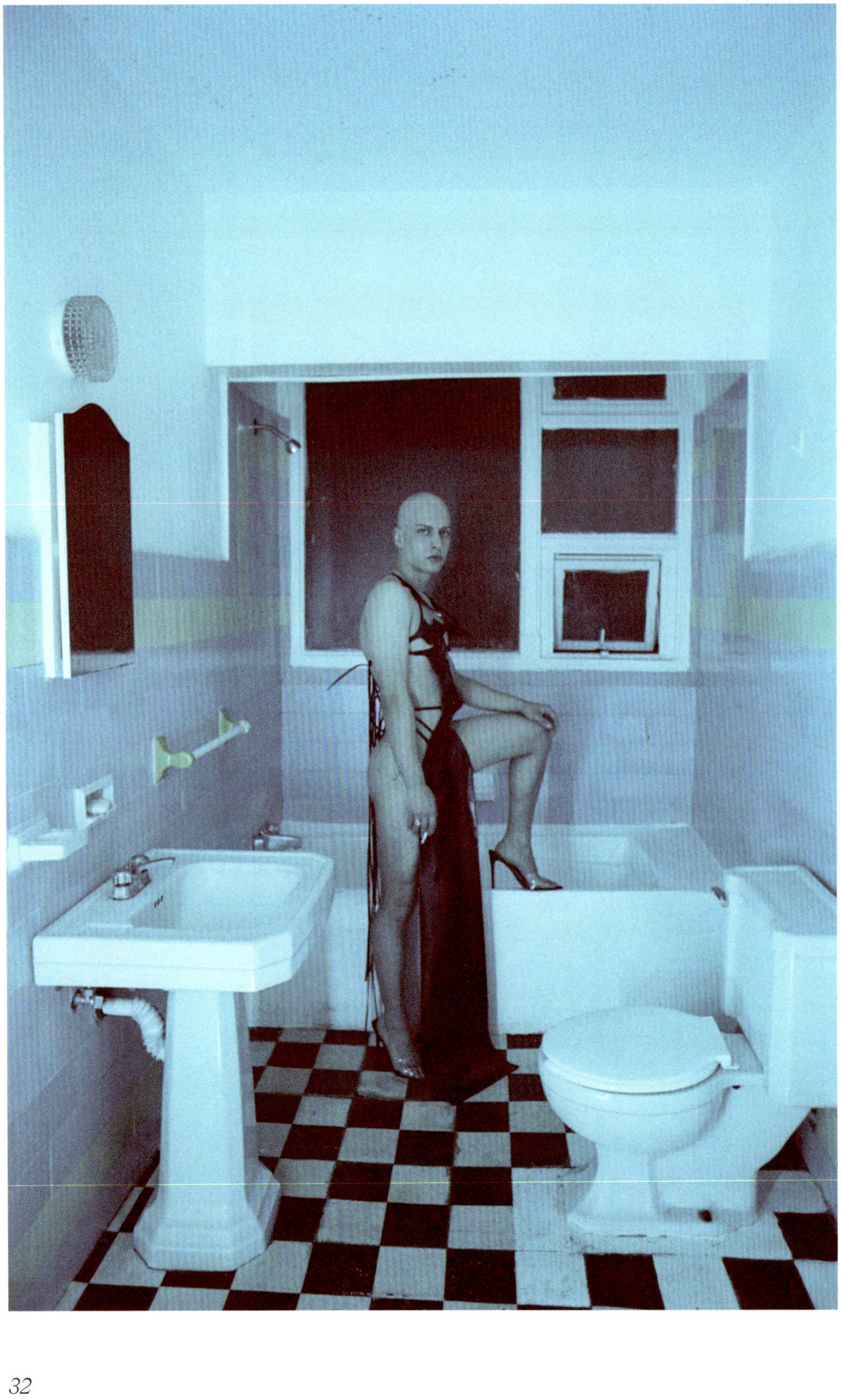

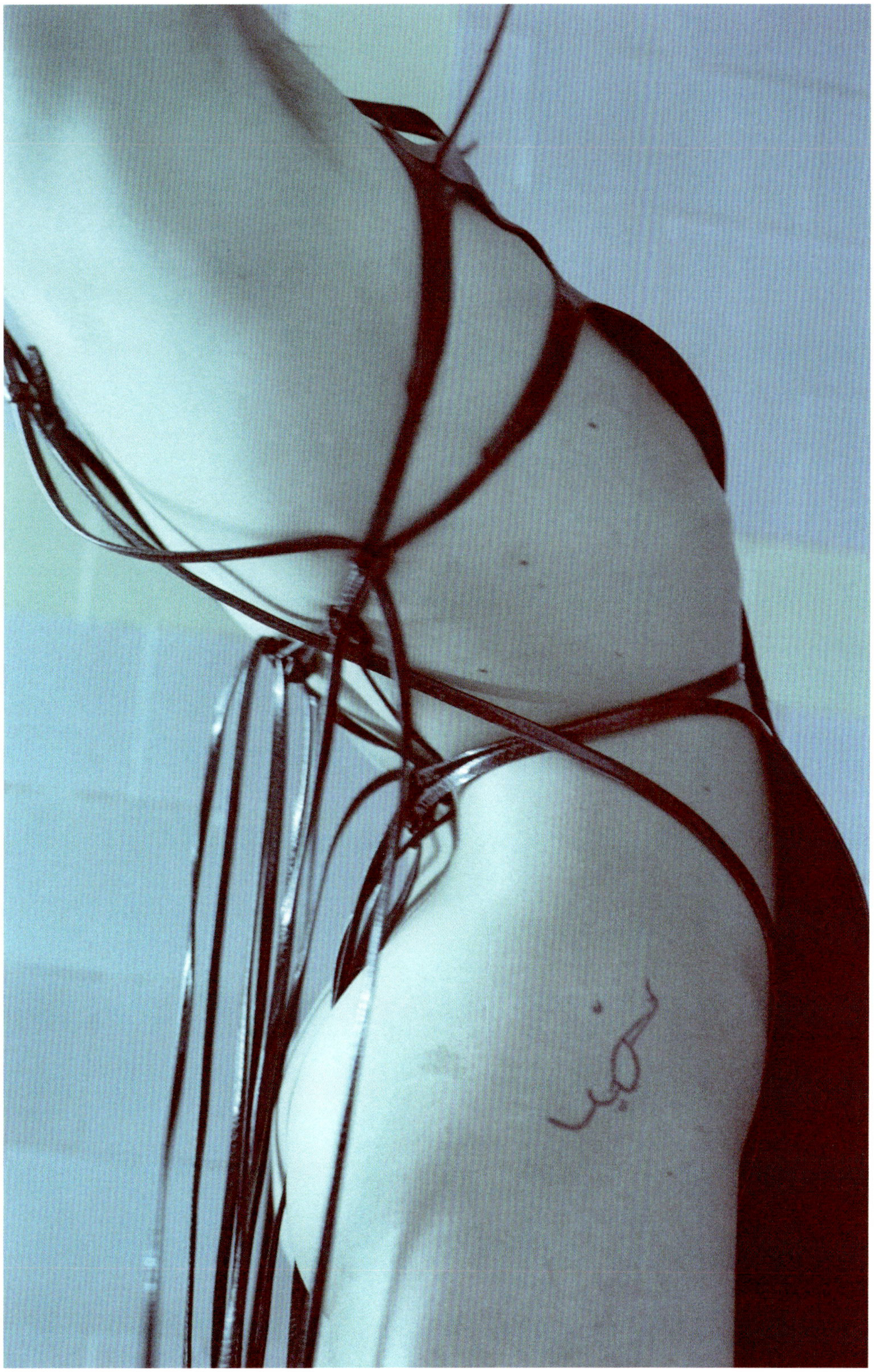

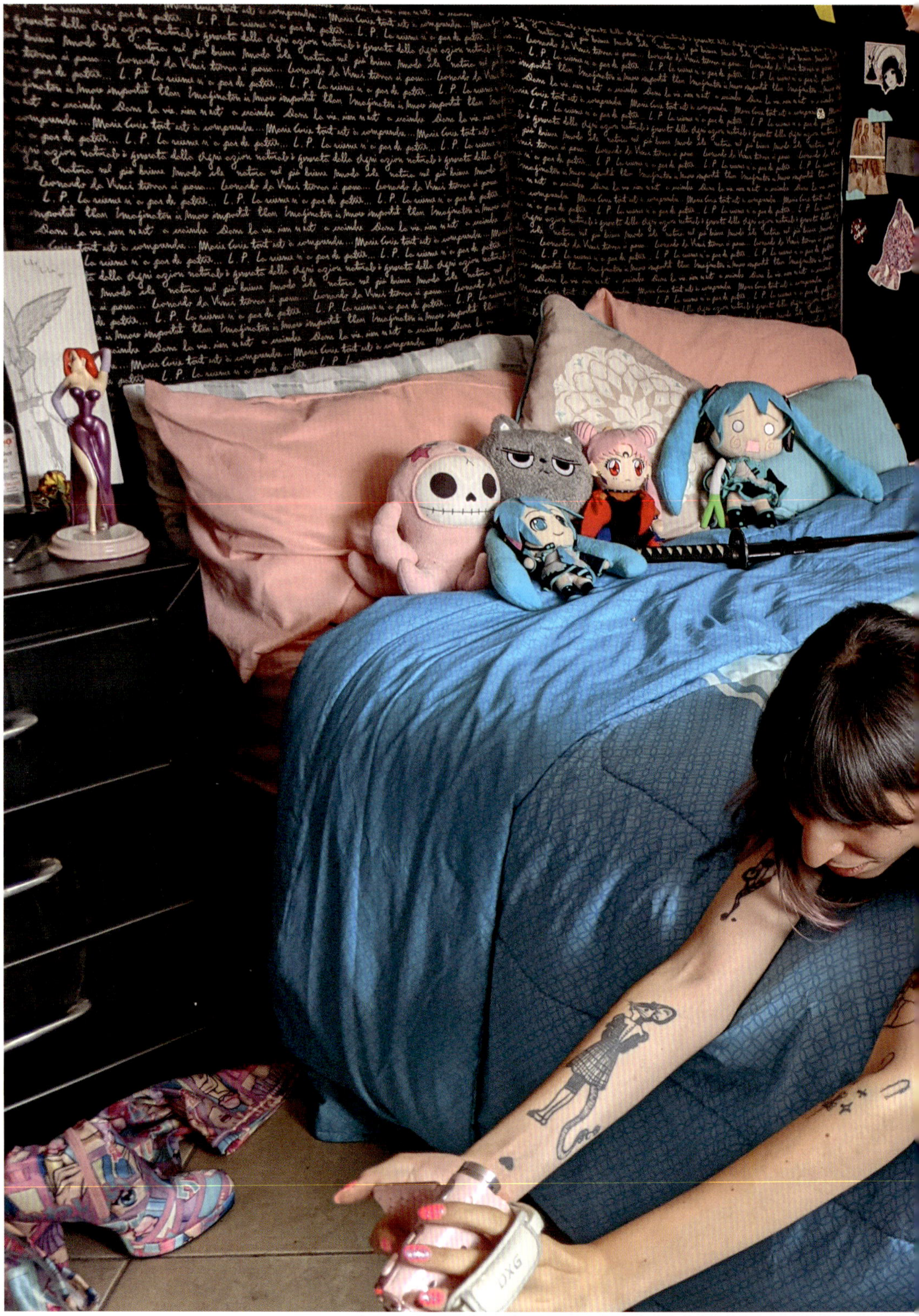

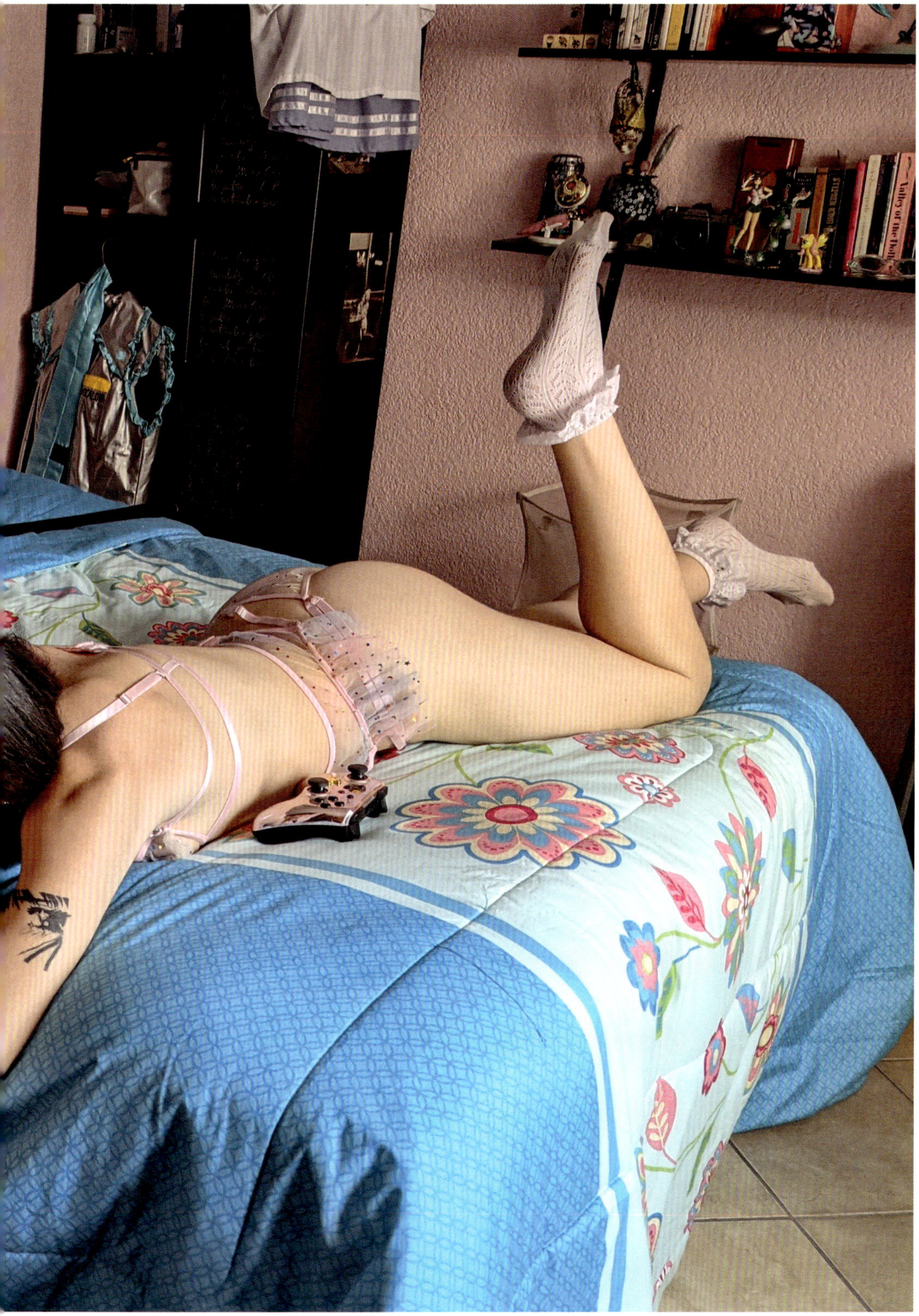

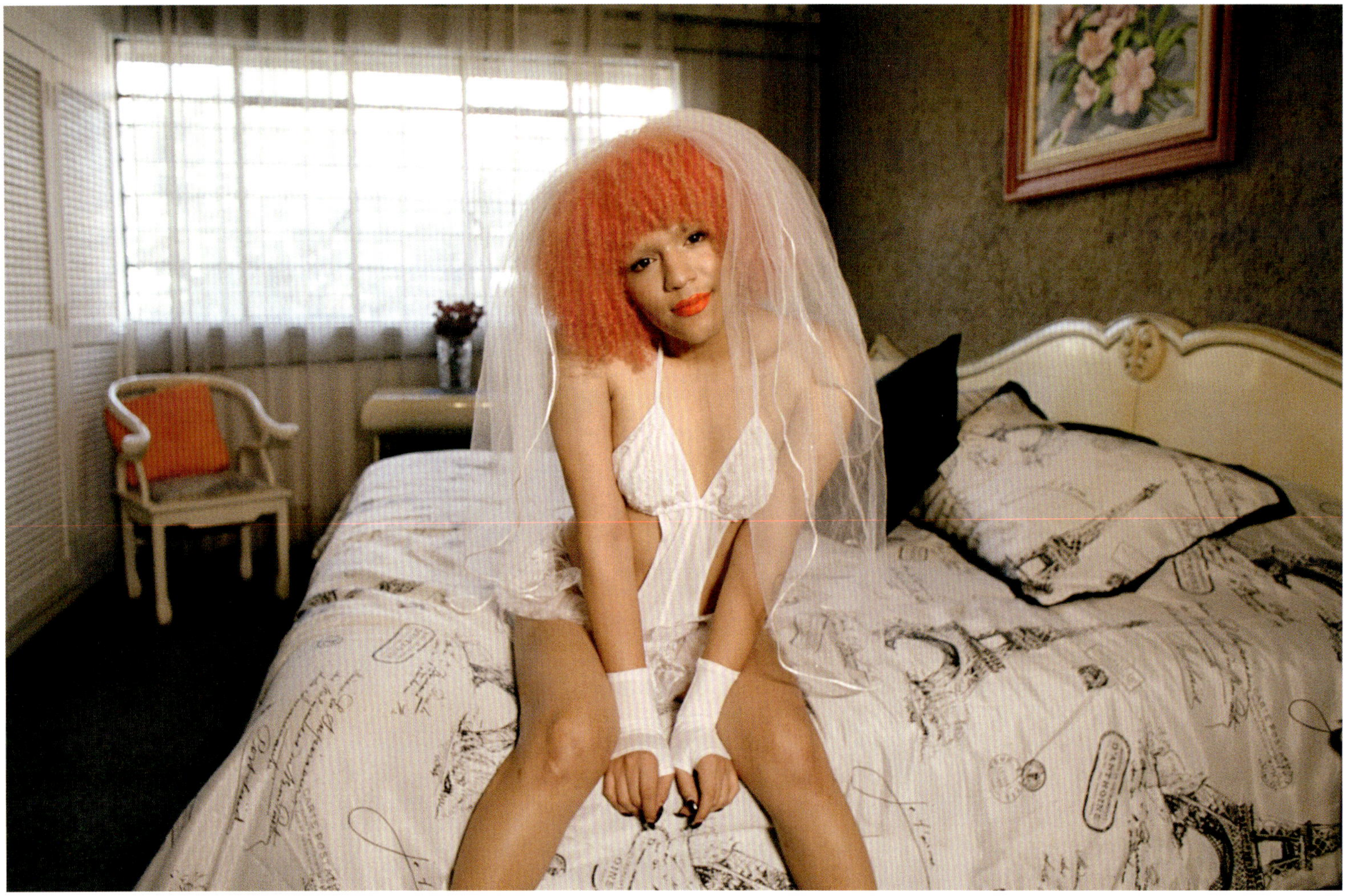

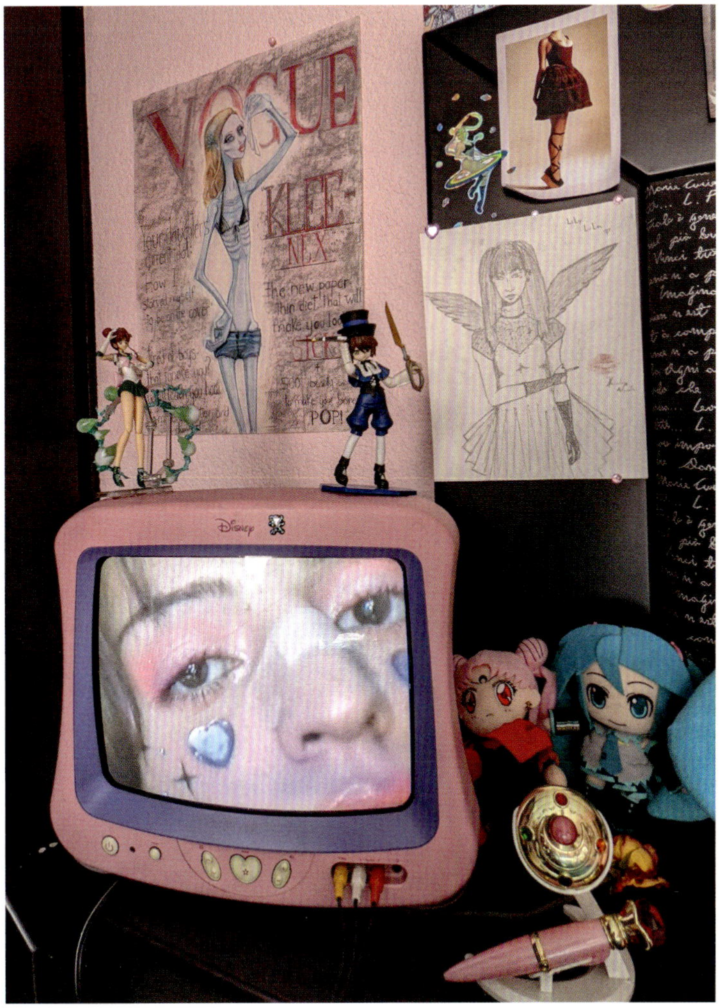
VOGUE
KLEE
NEX
Disney

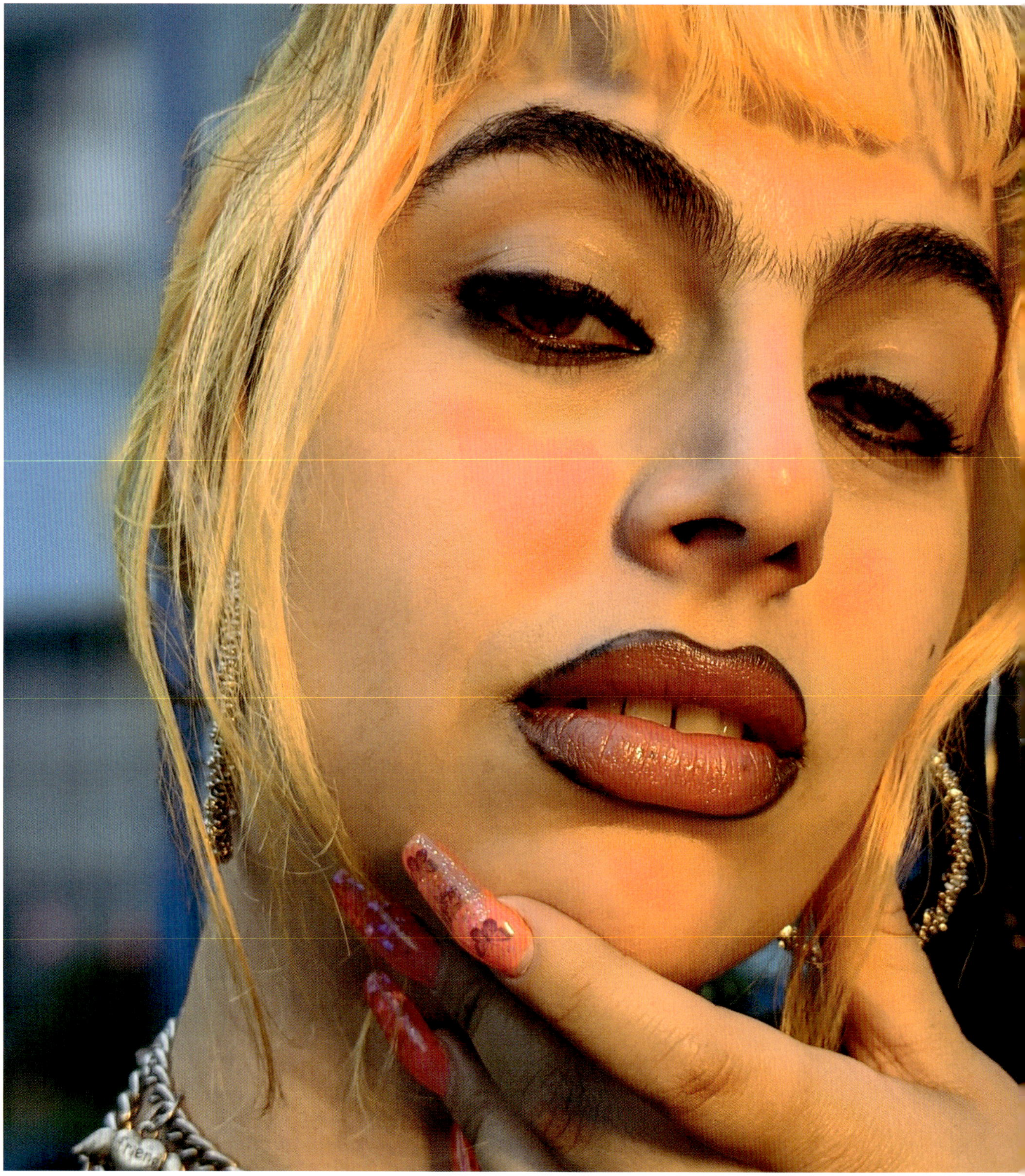

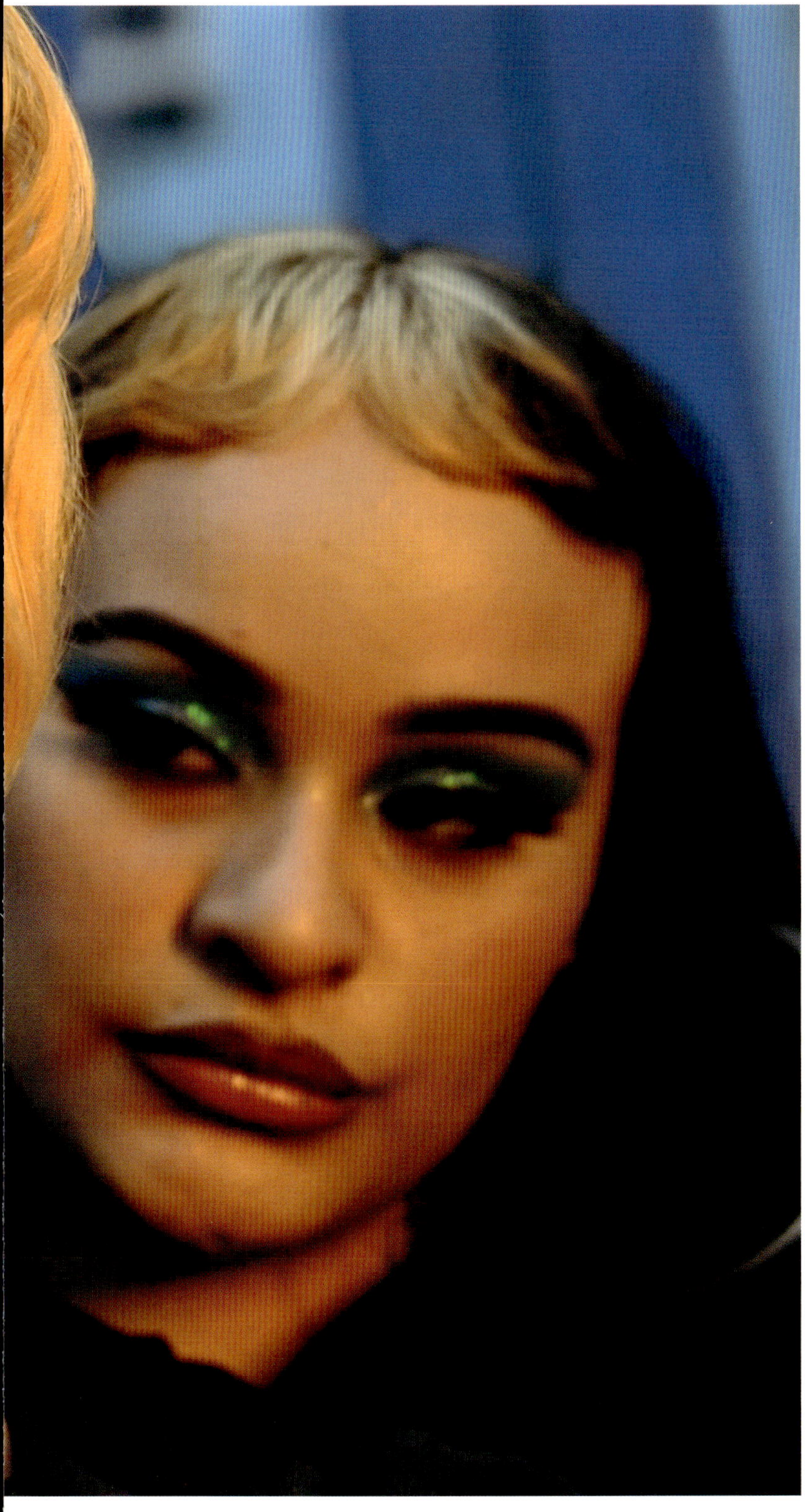

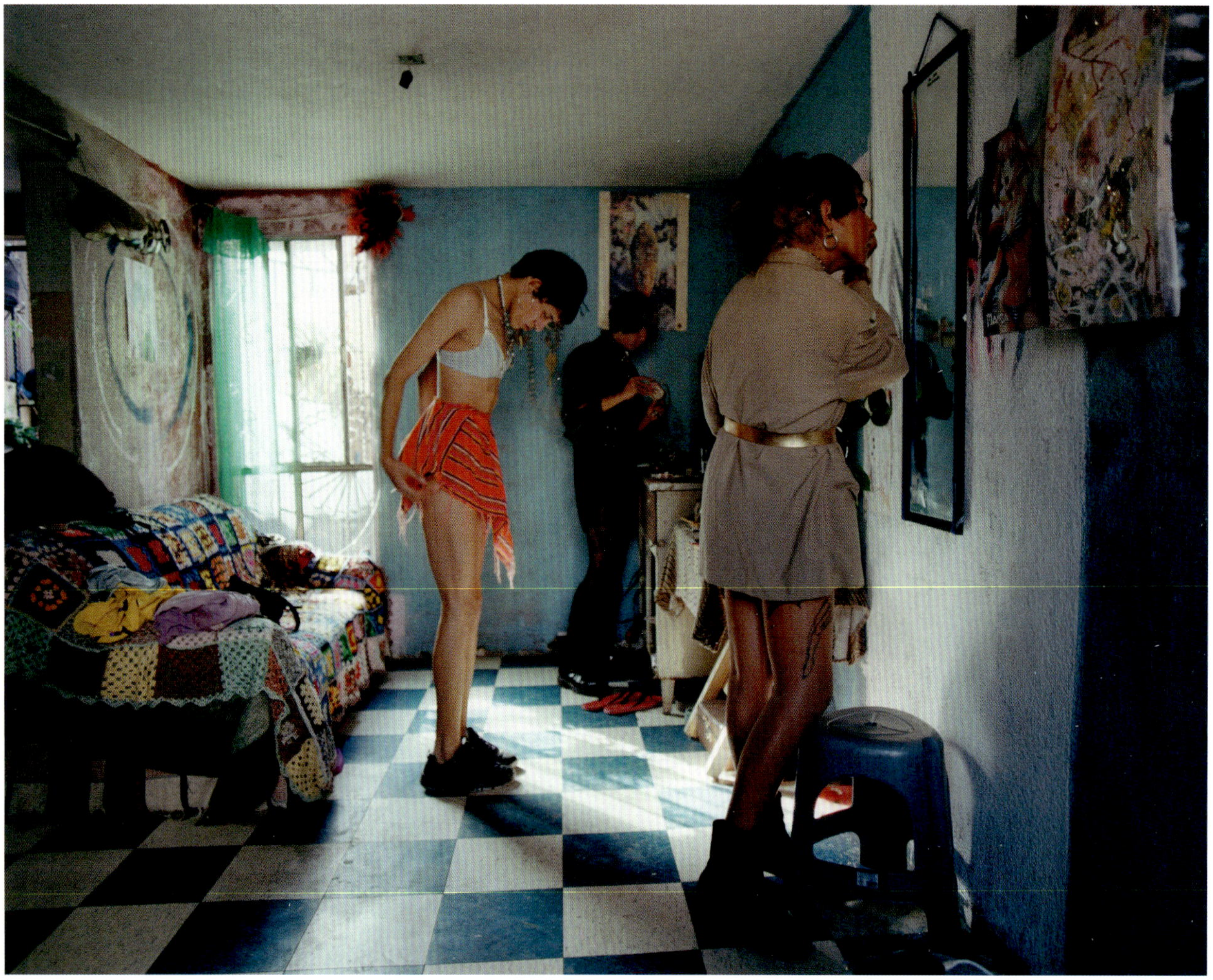

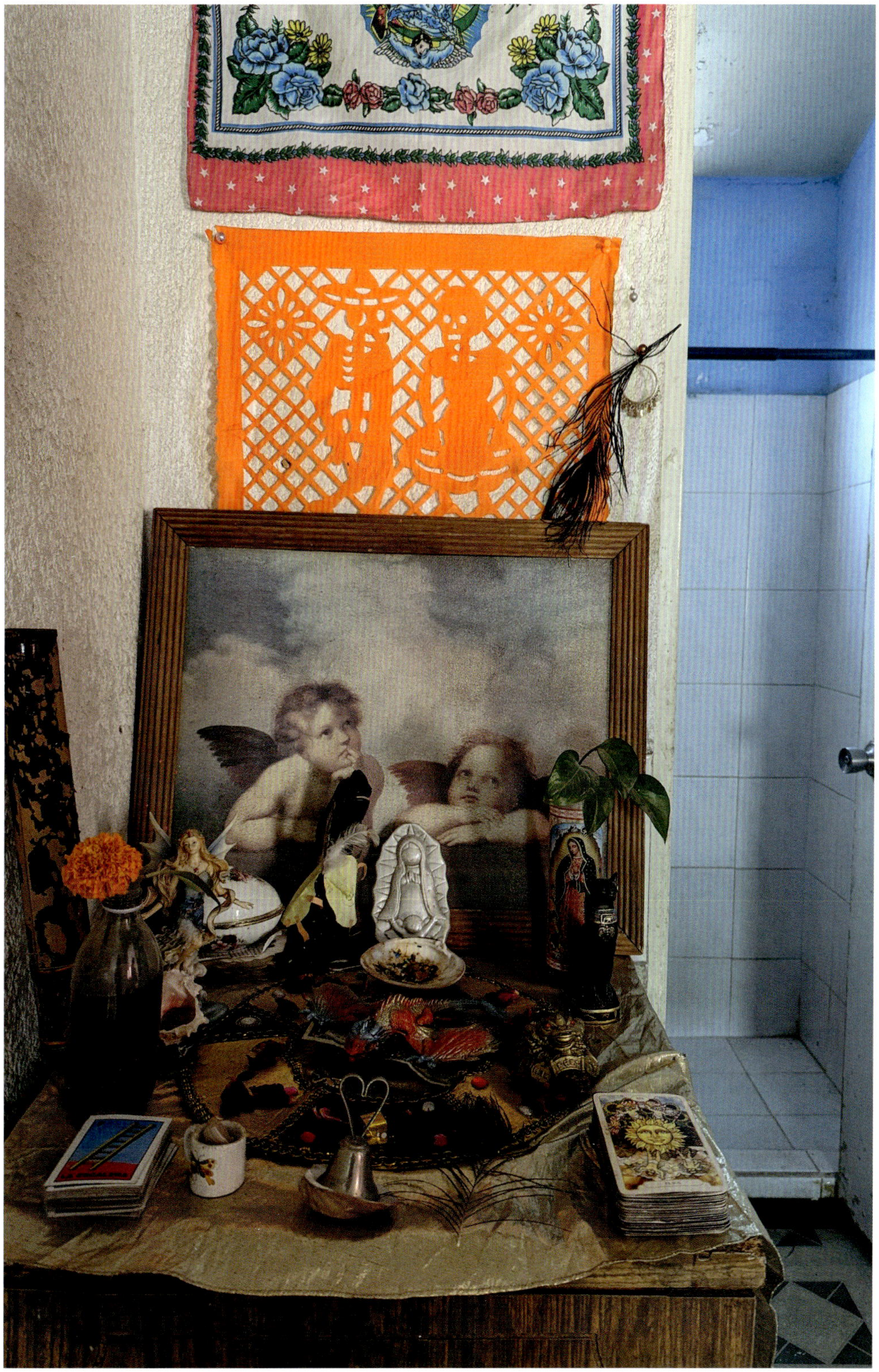

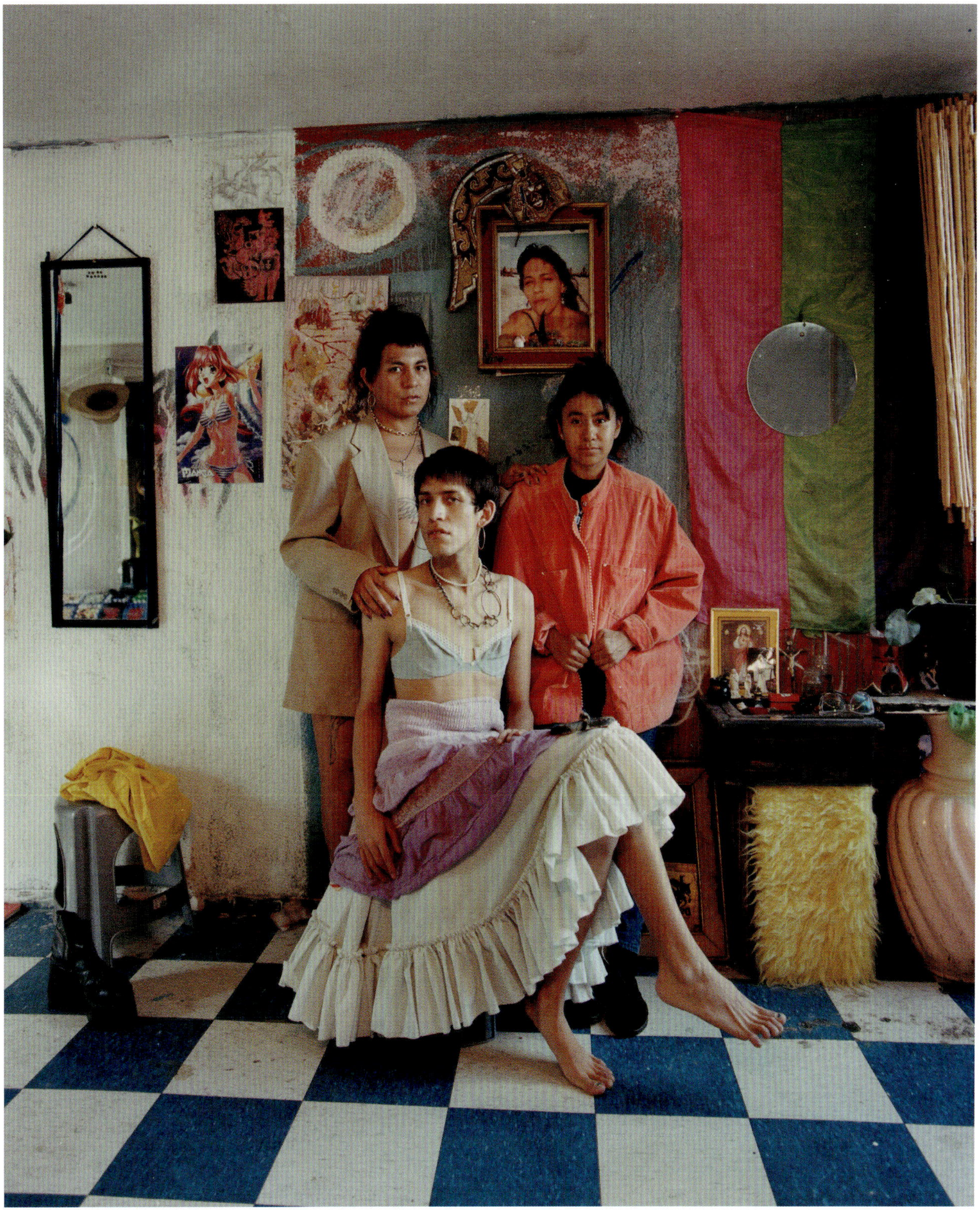

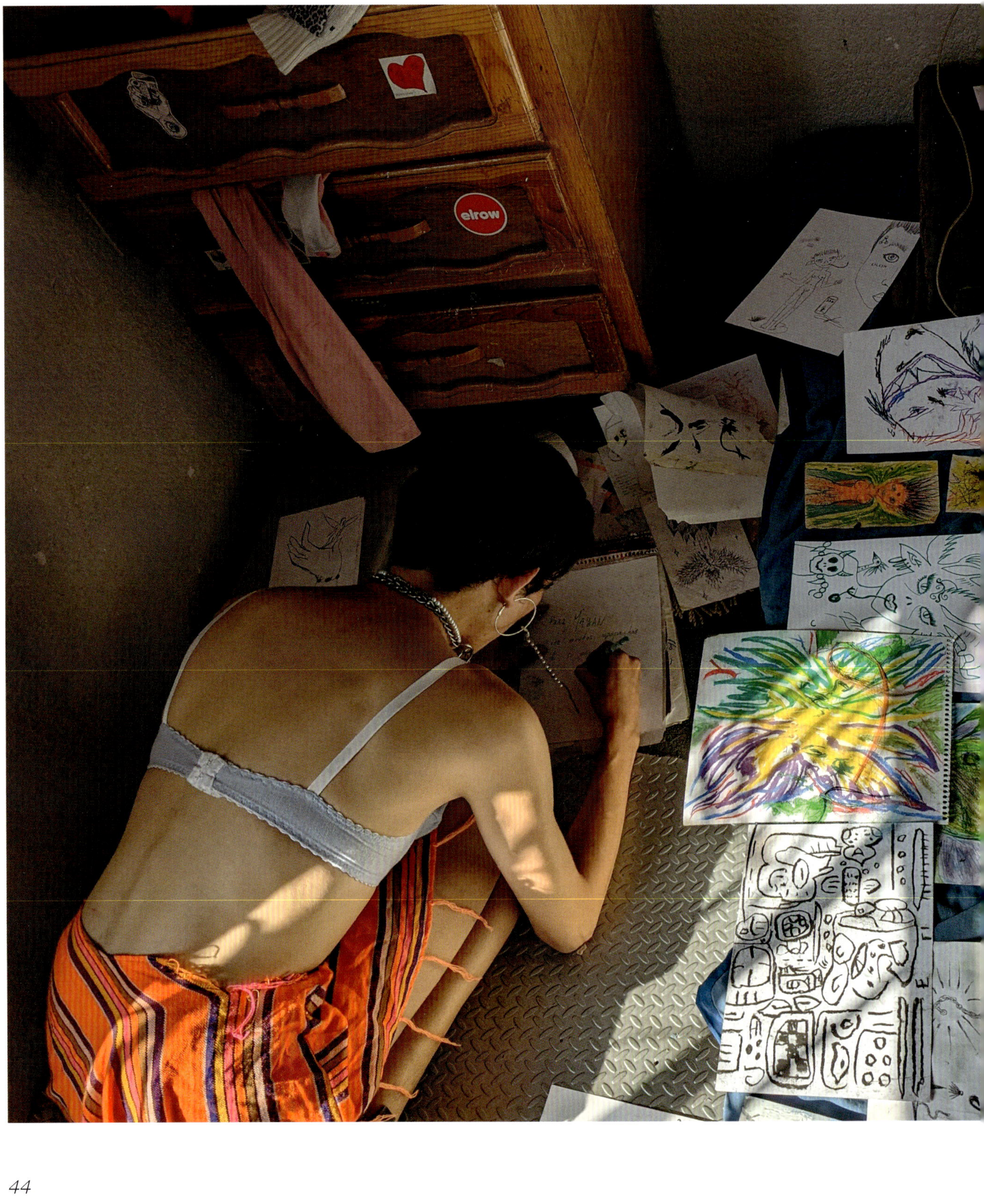
elrow

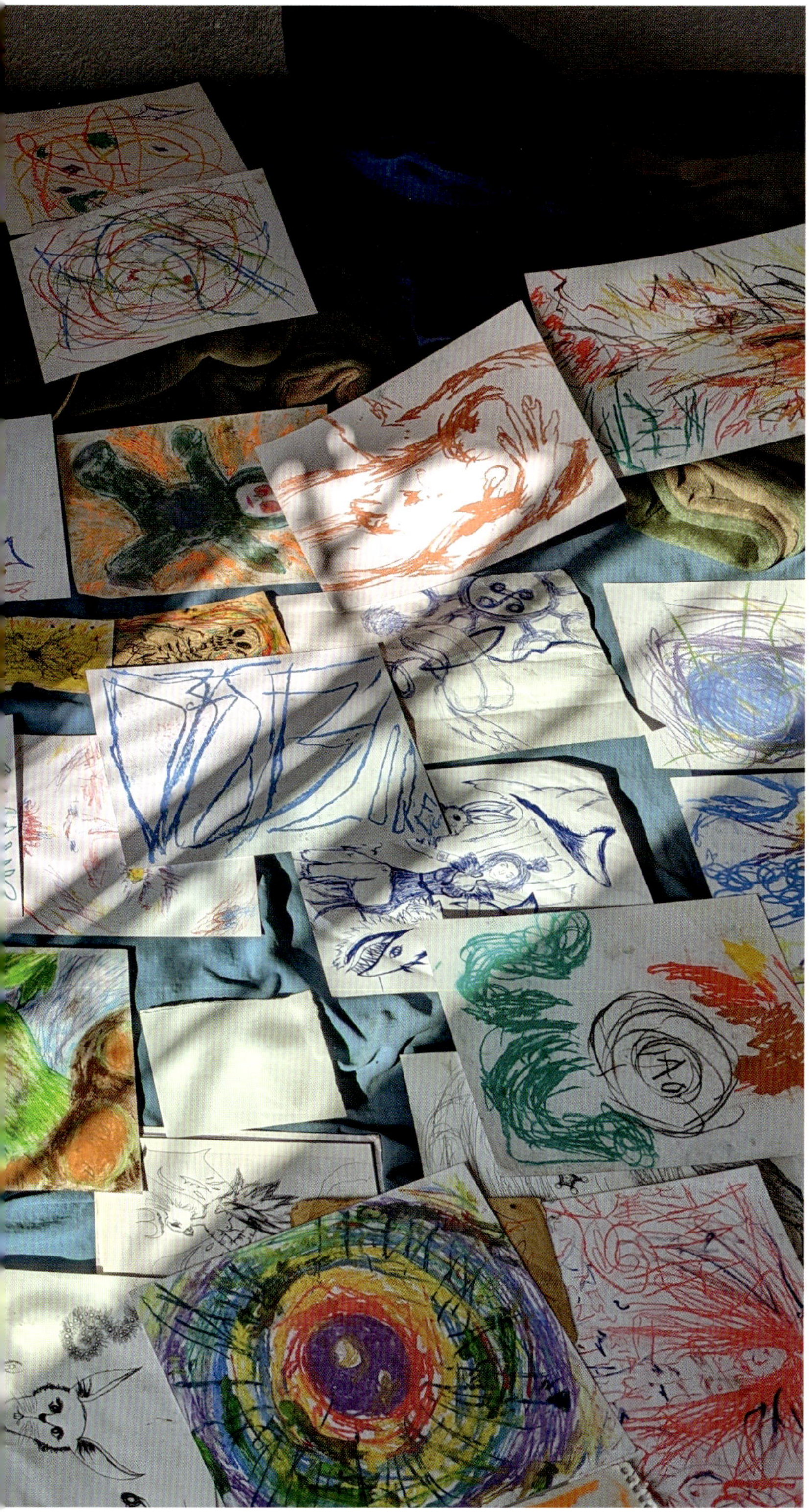

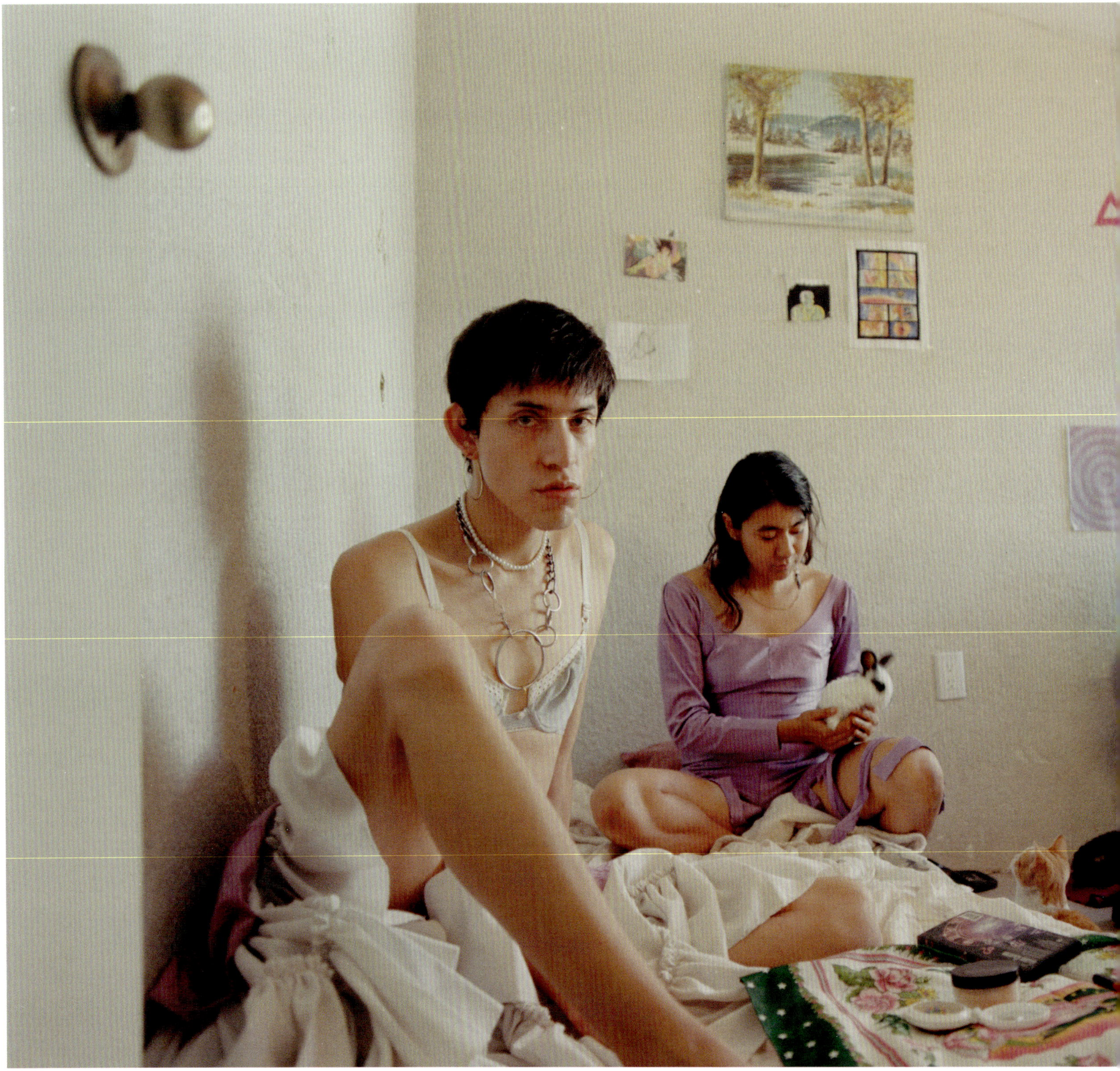

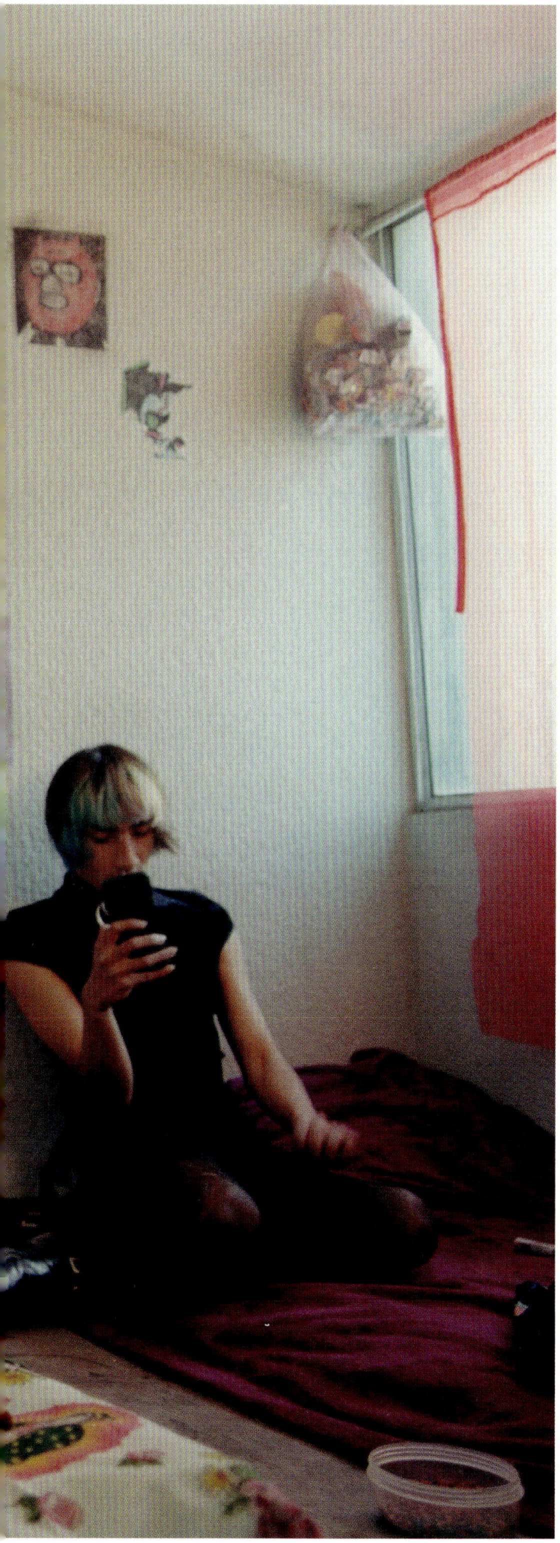

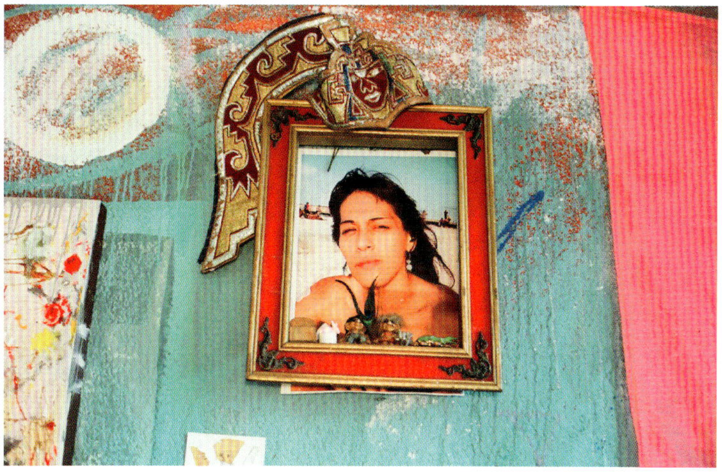

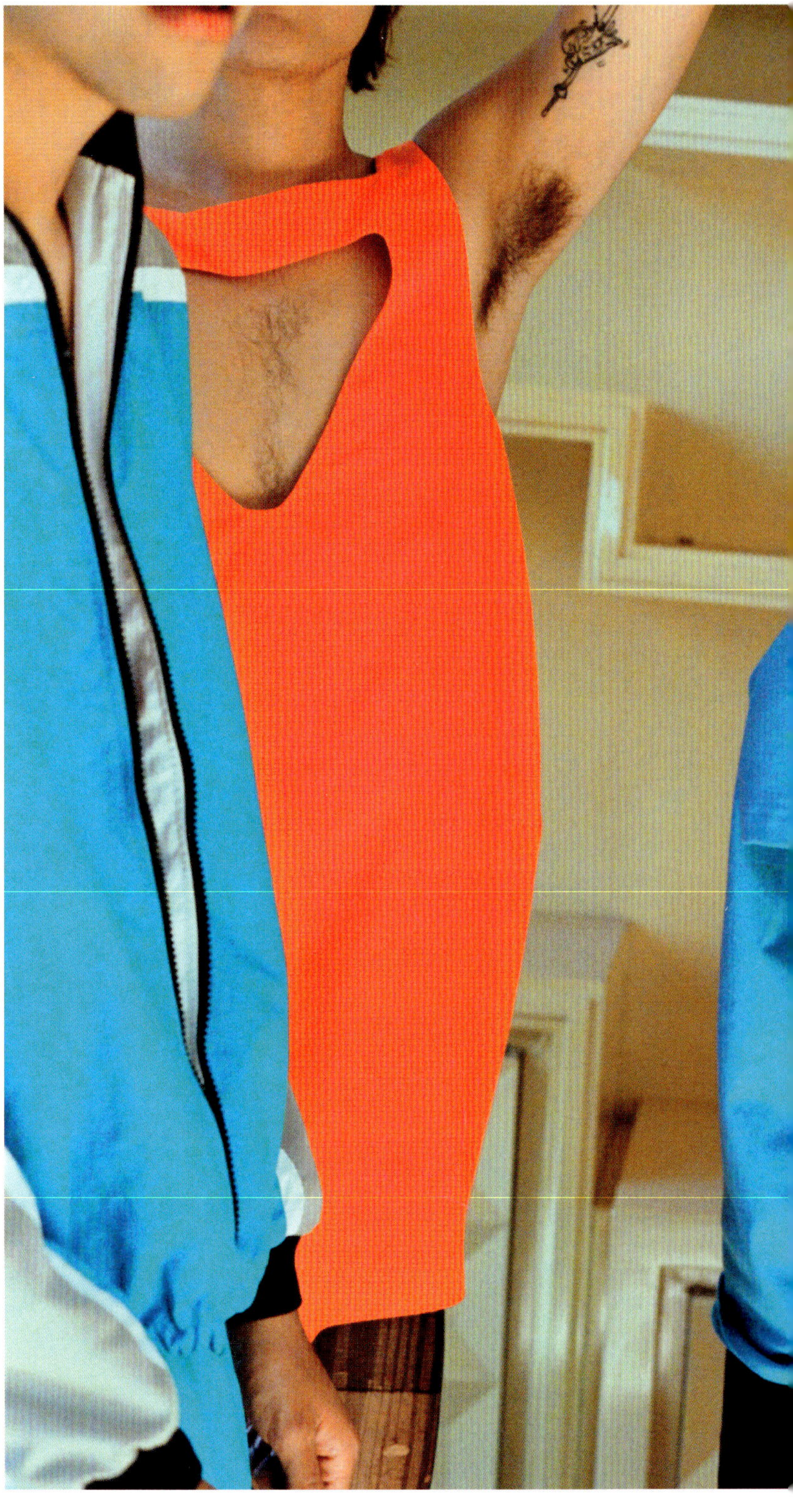

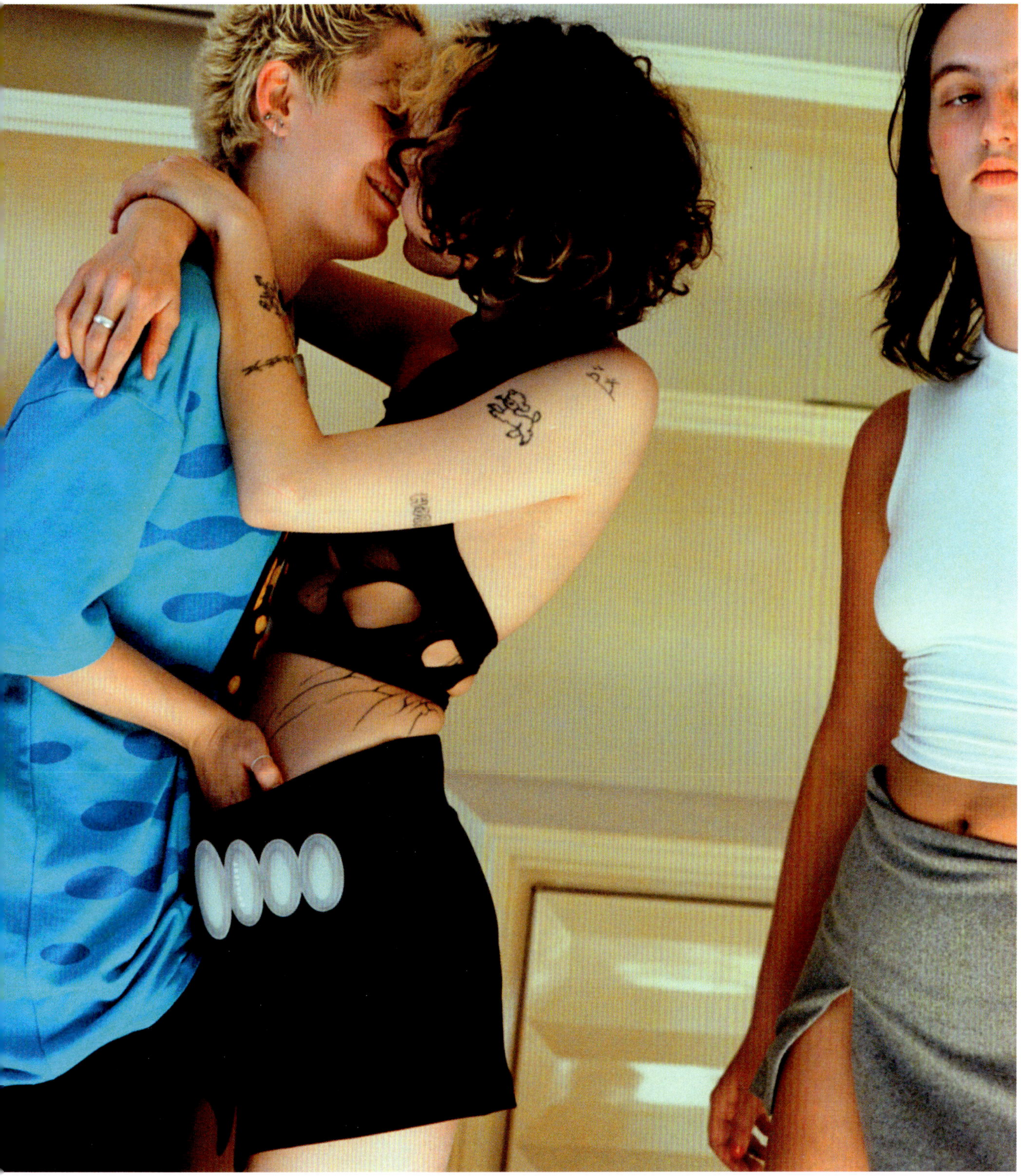

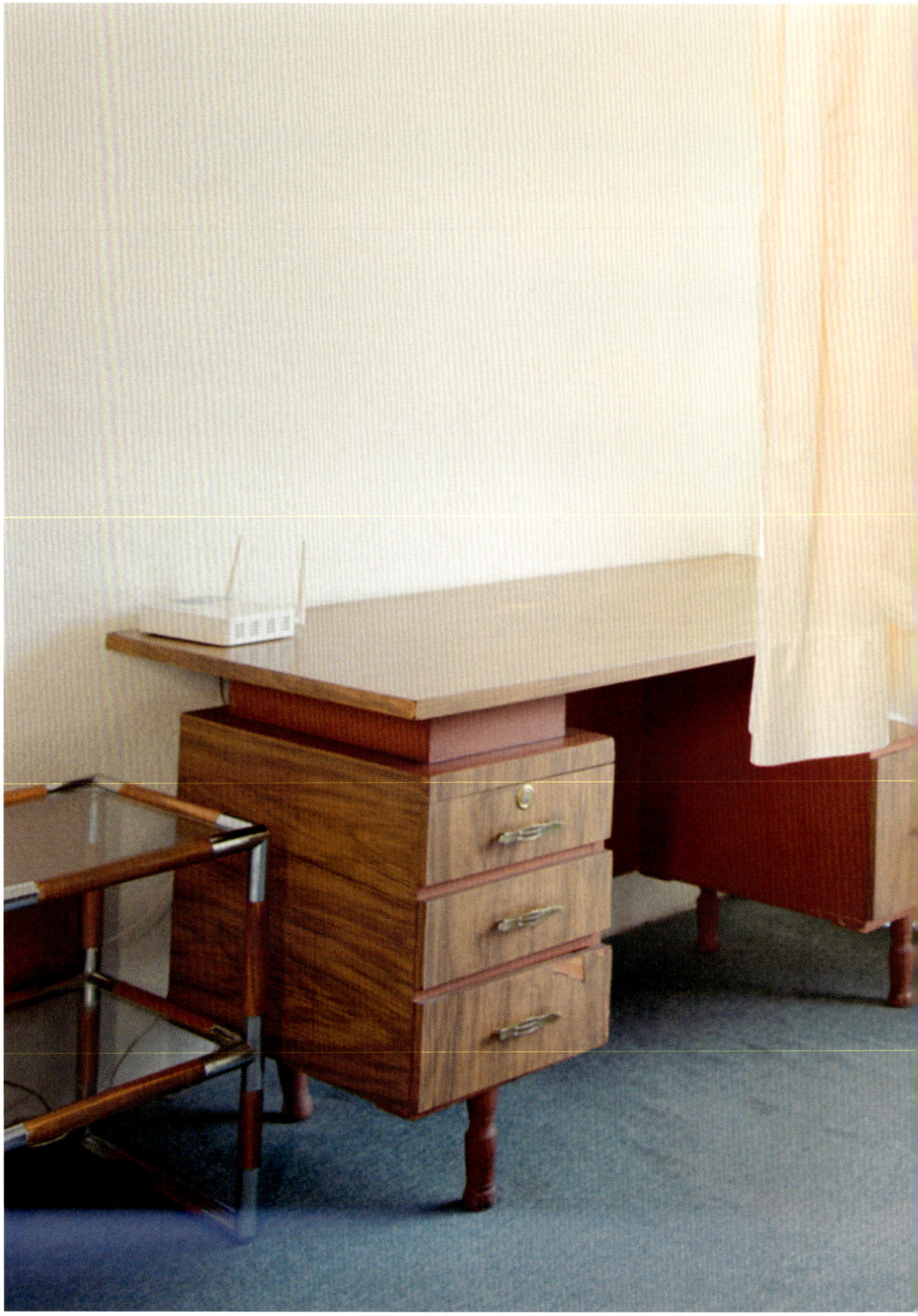

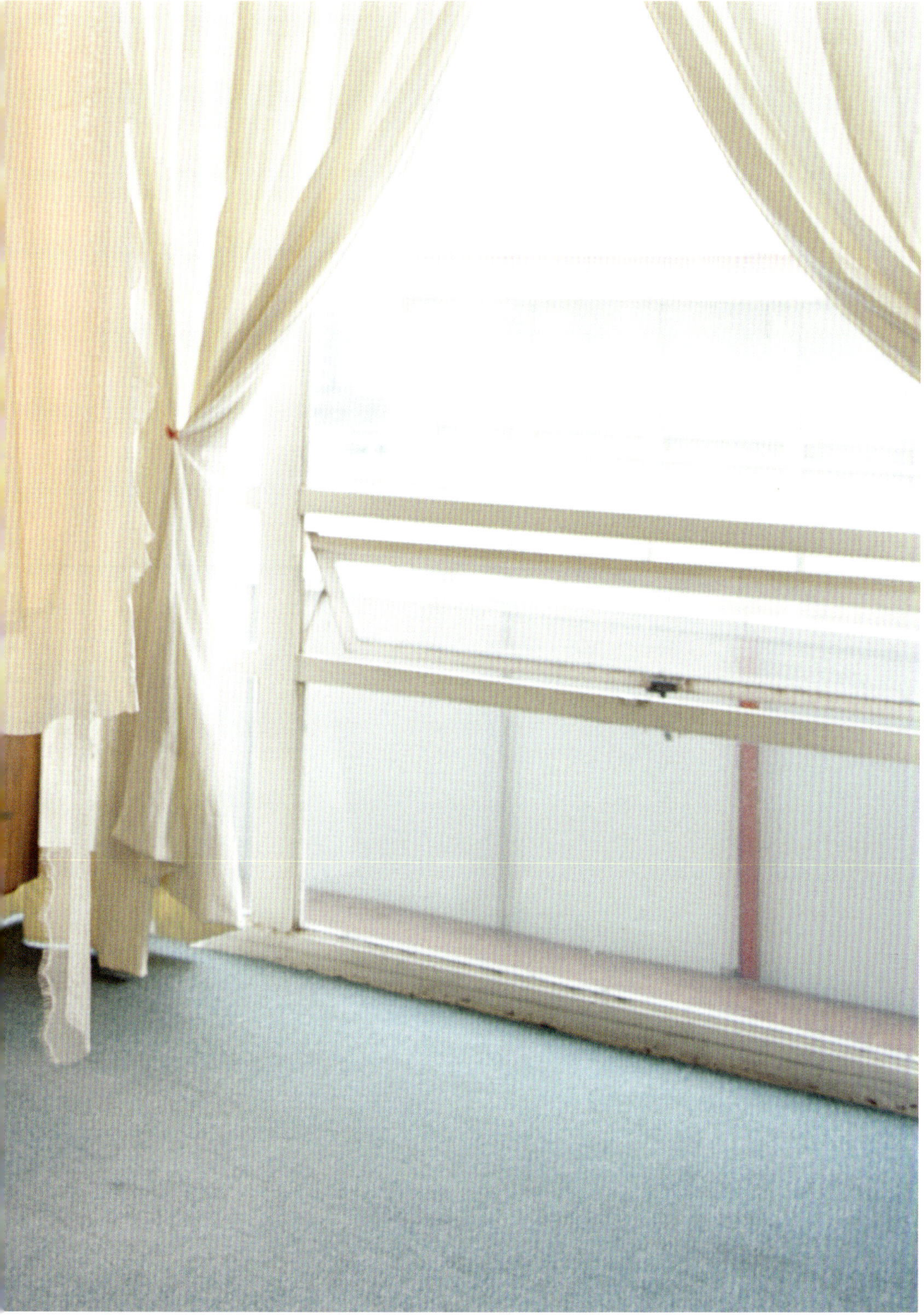

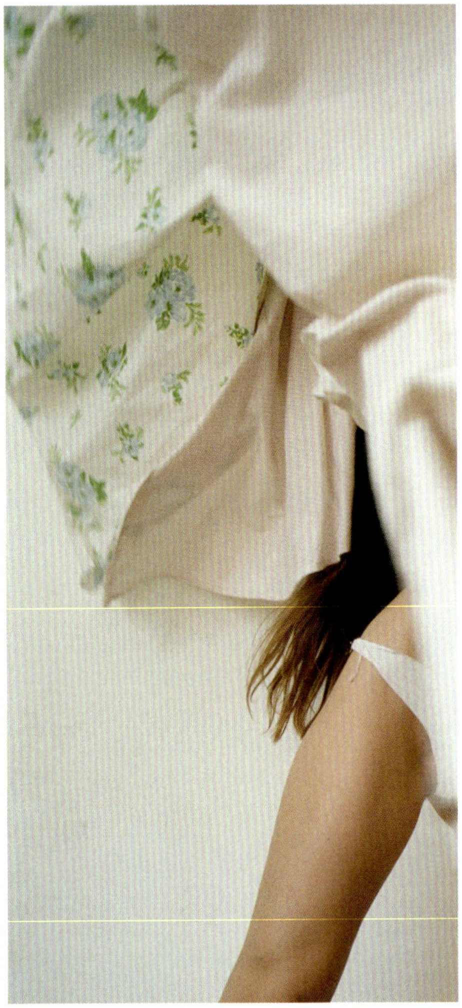
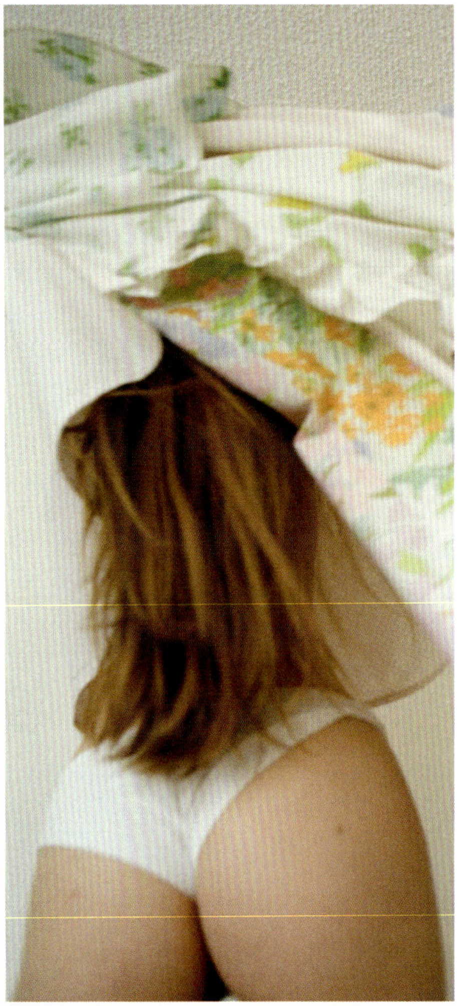
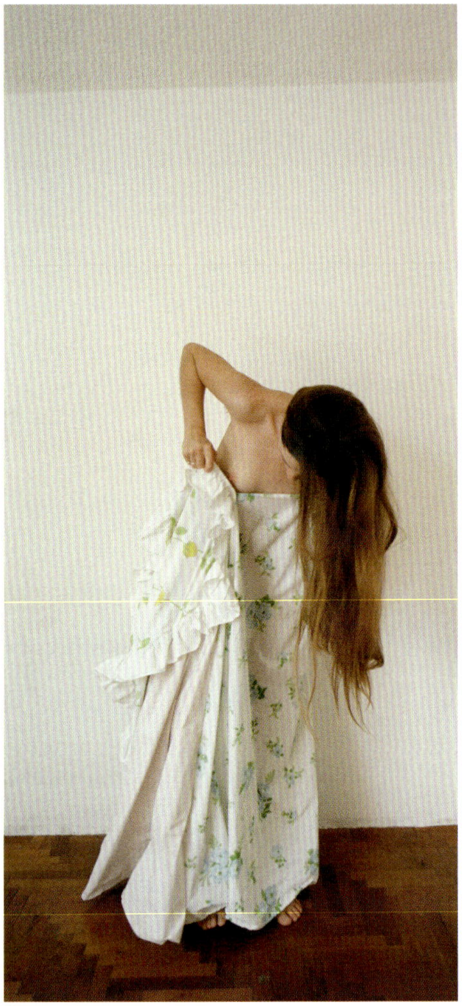

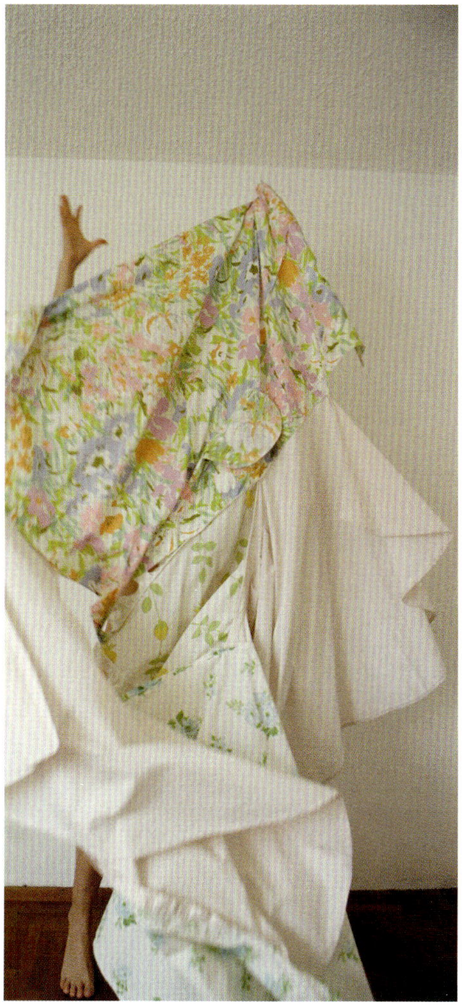

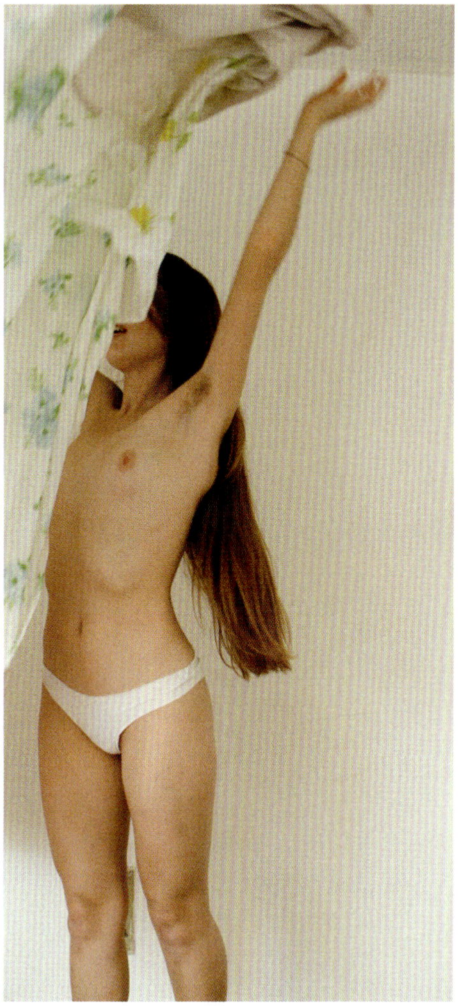

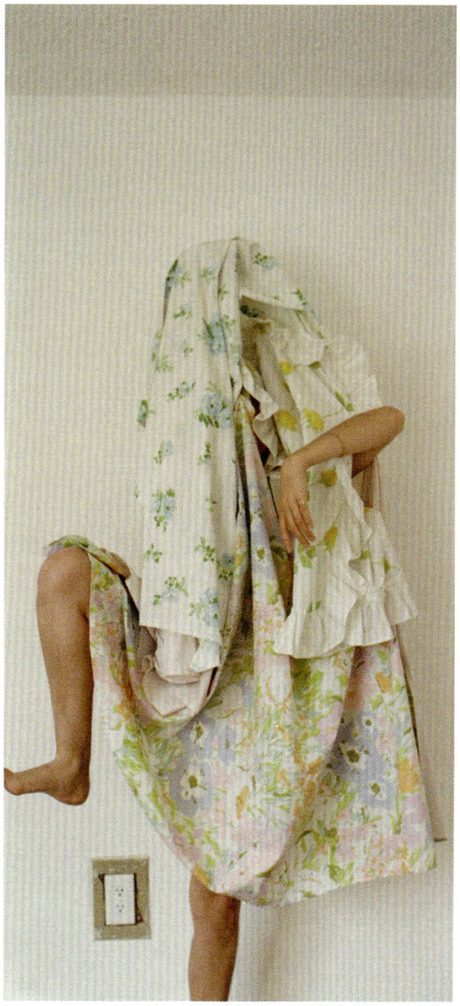

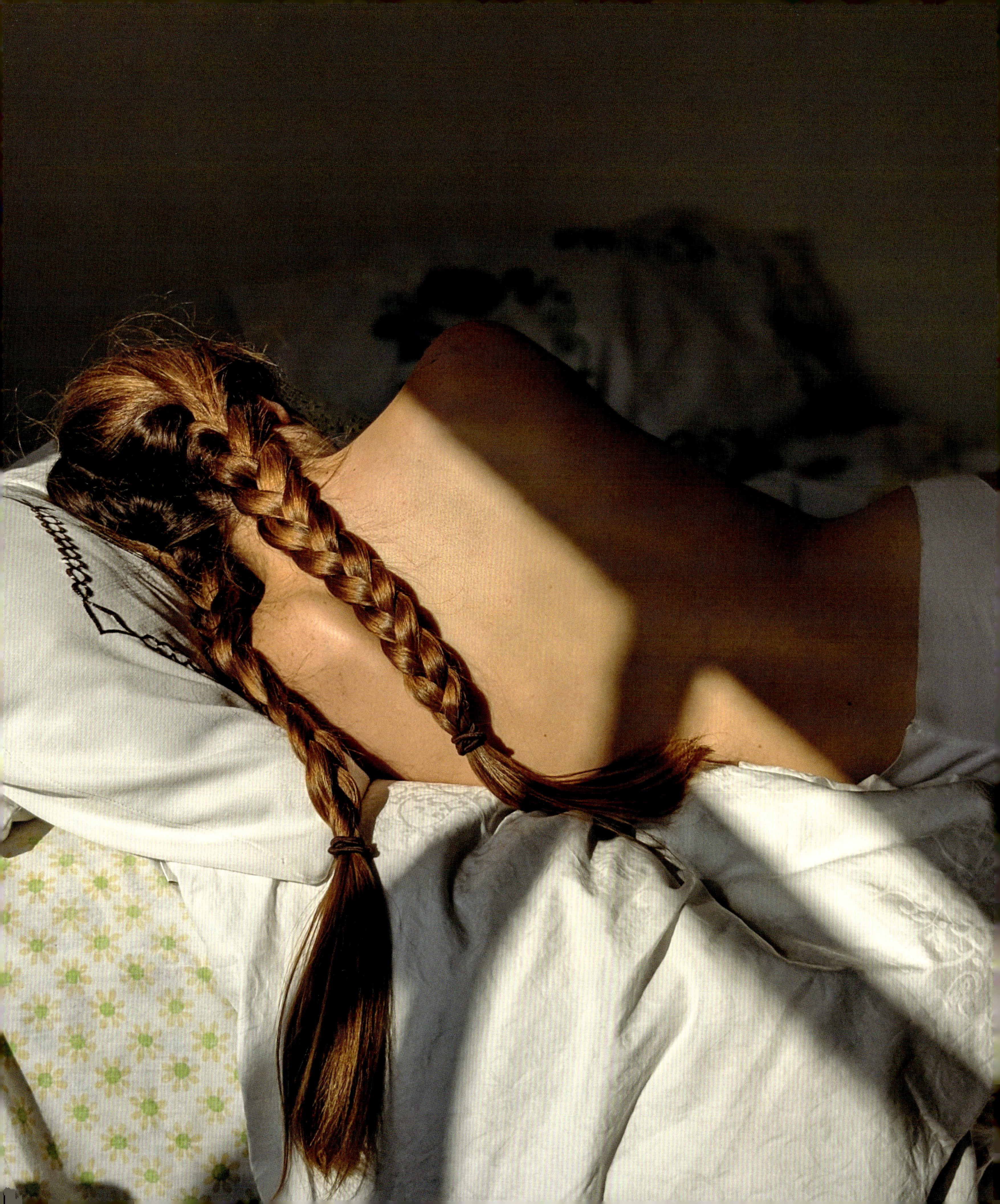

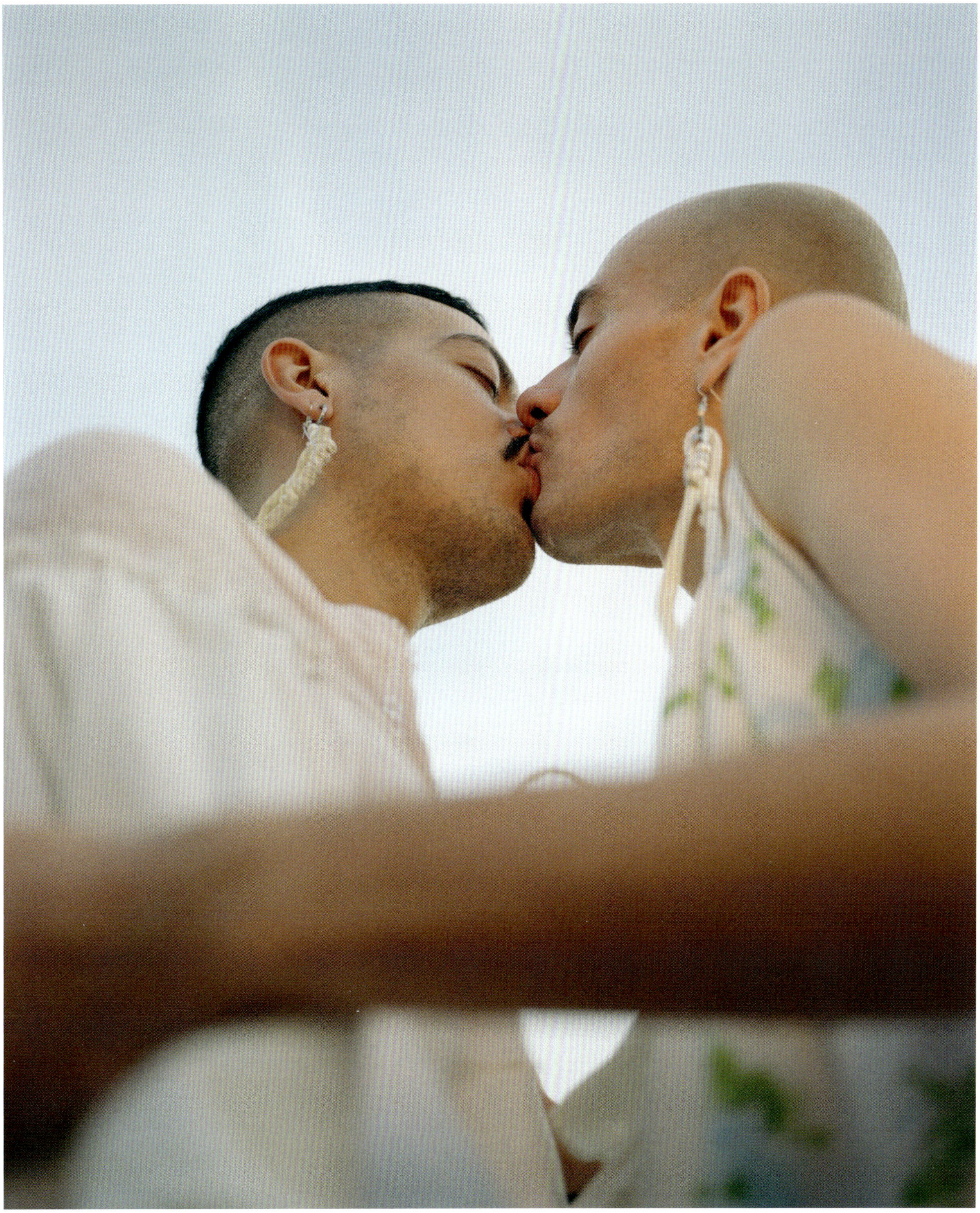

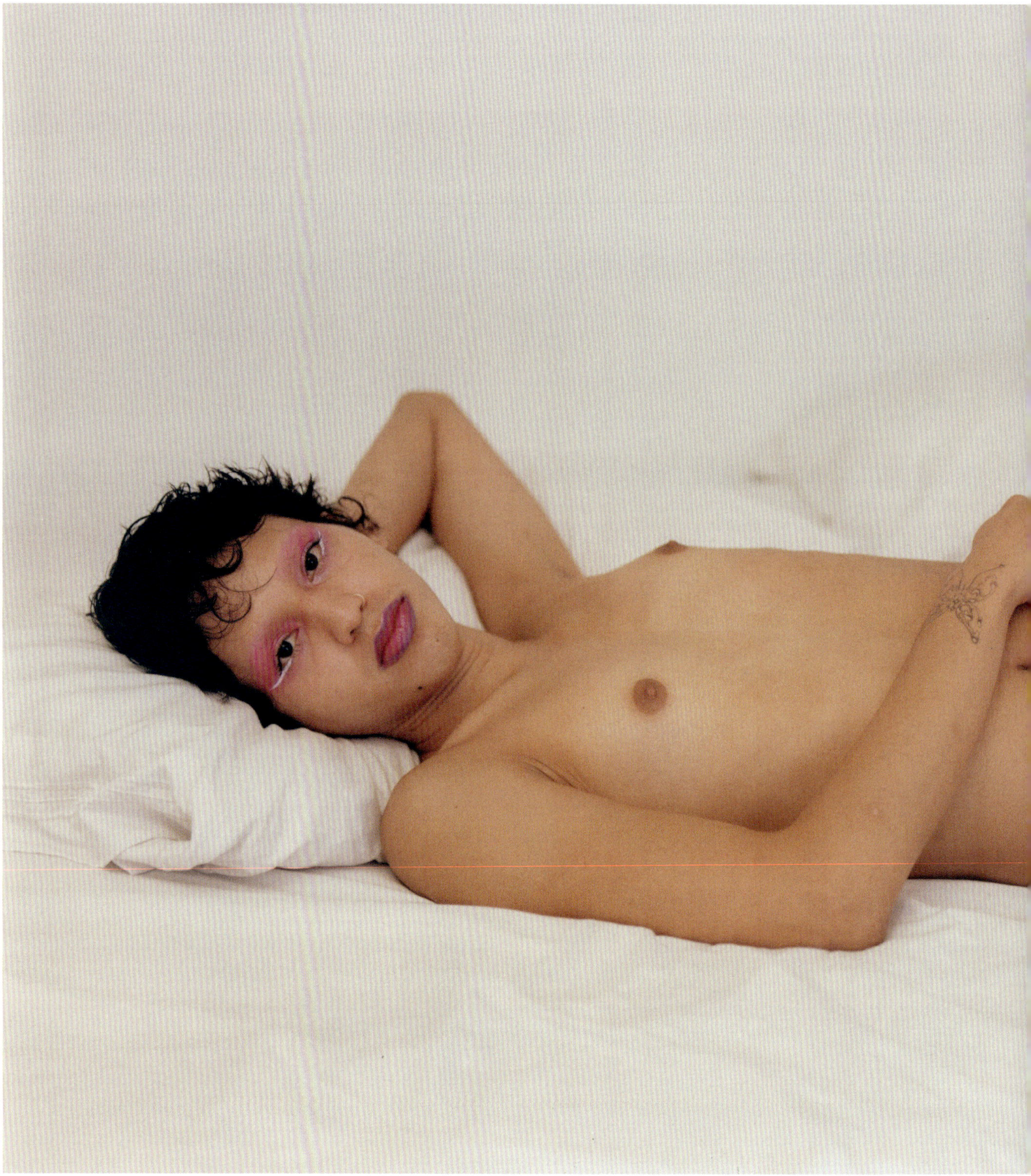

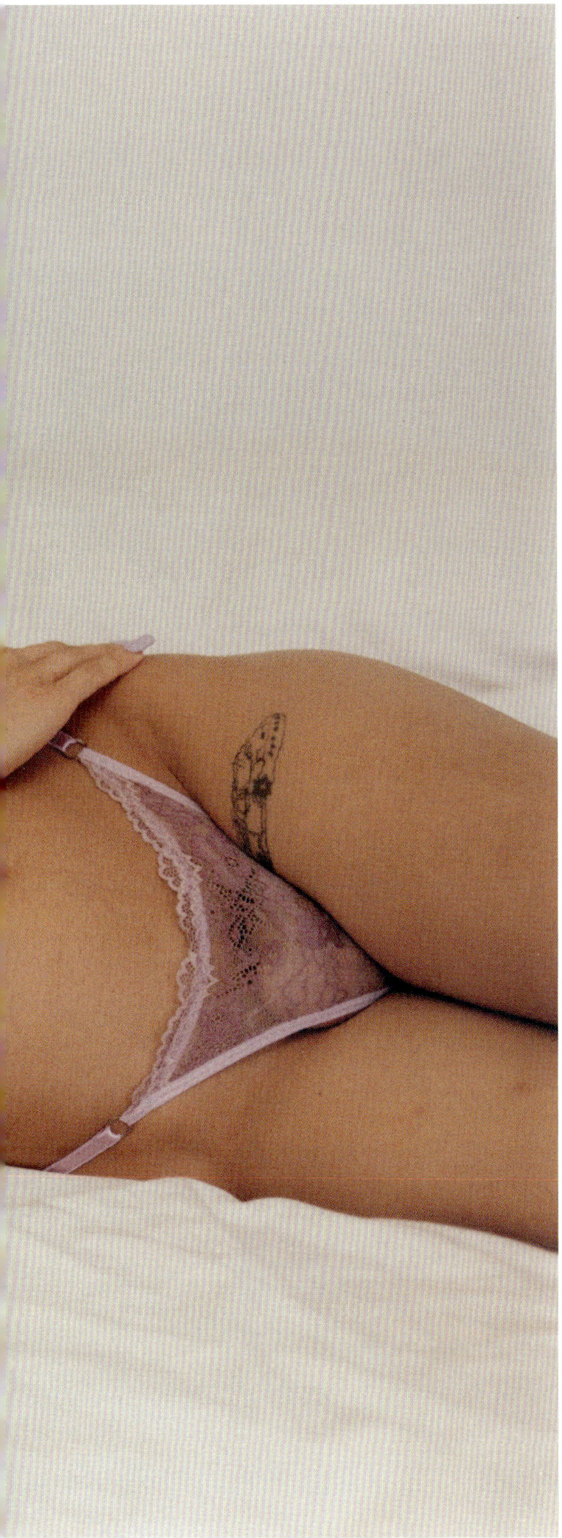

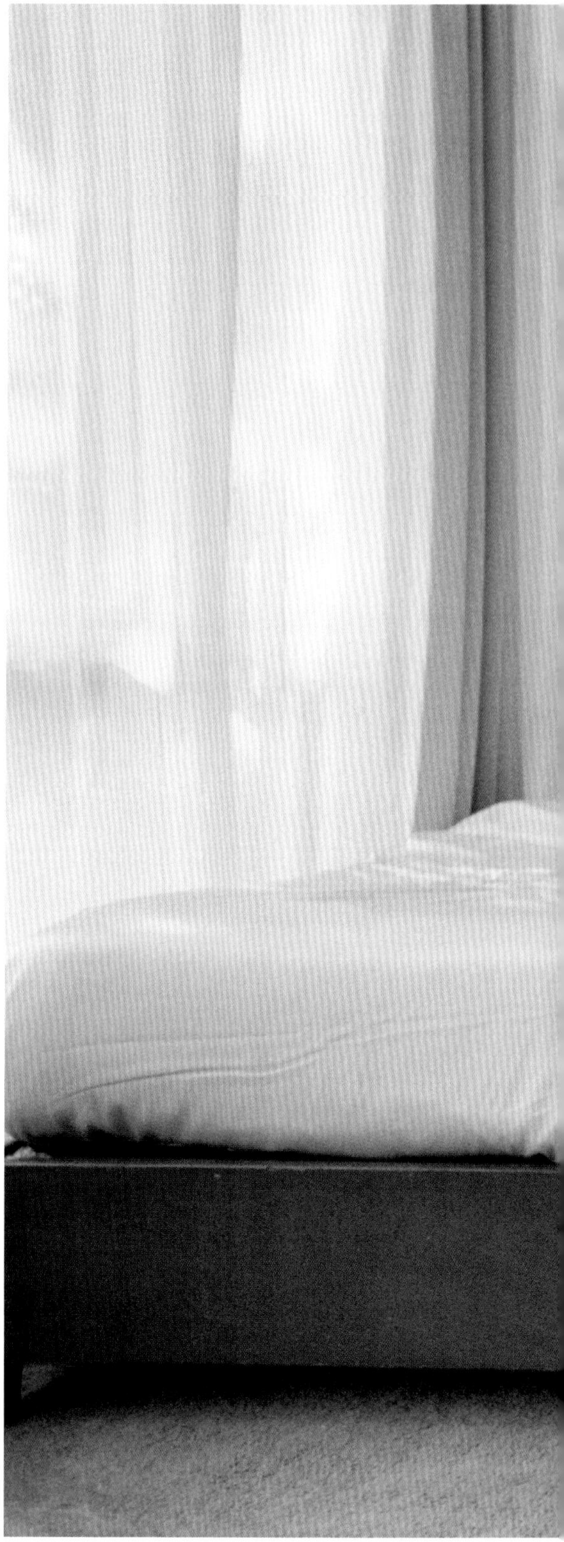

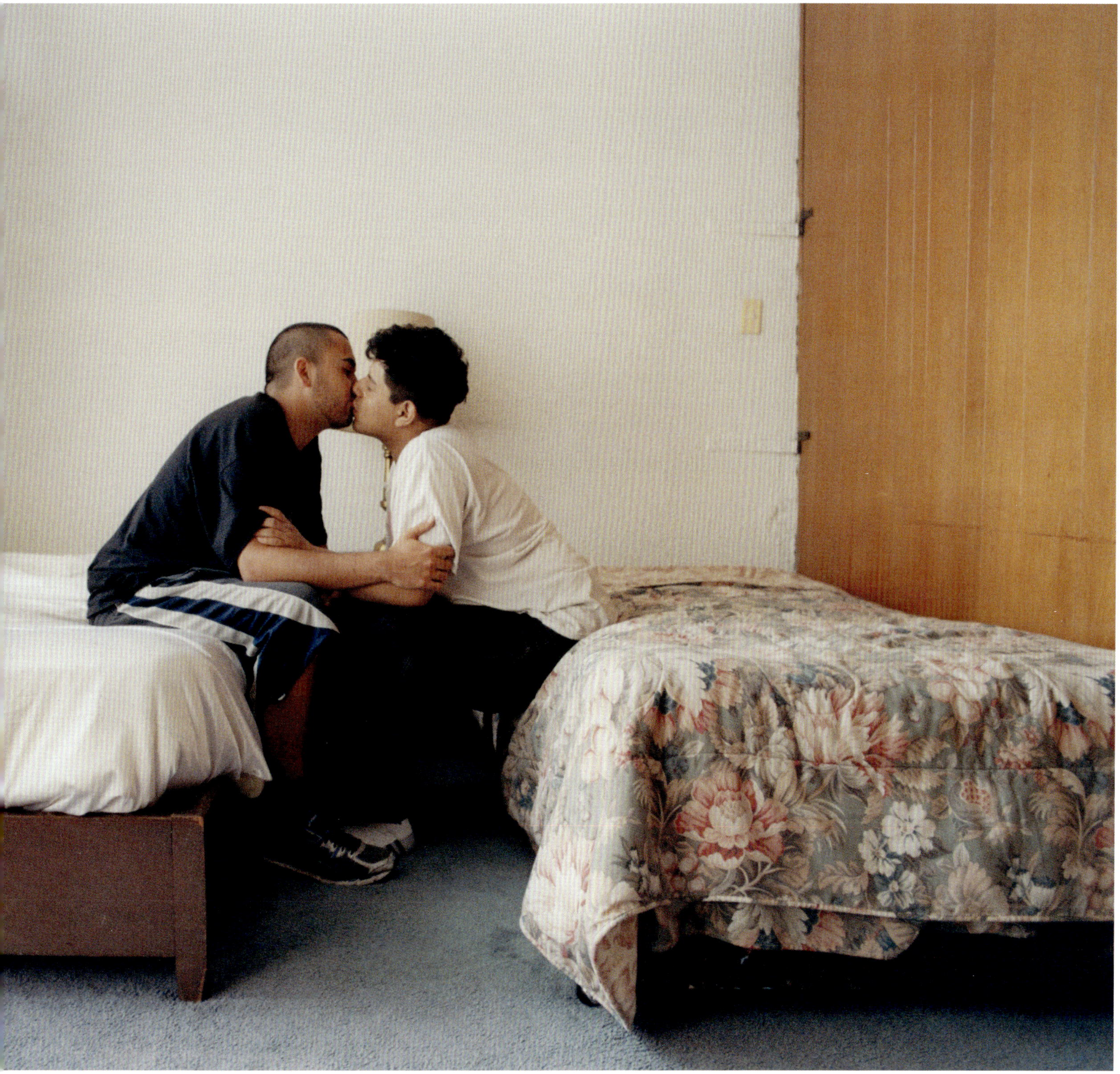

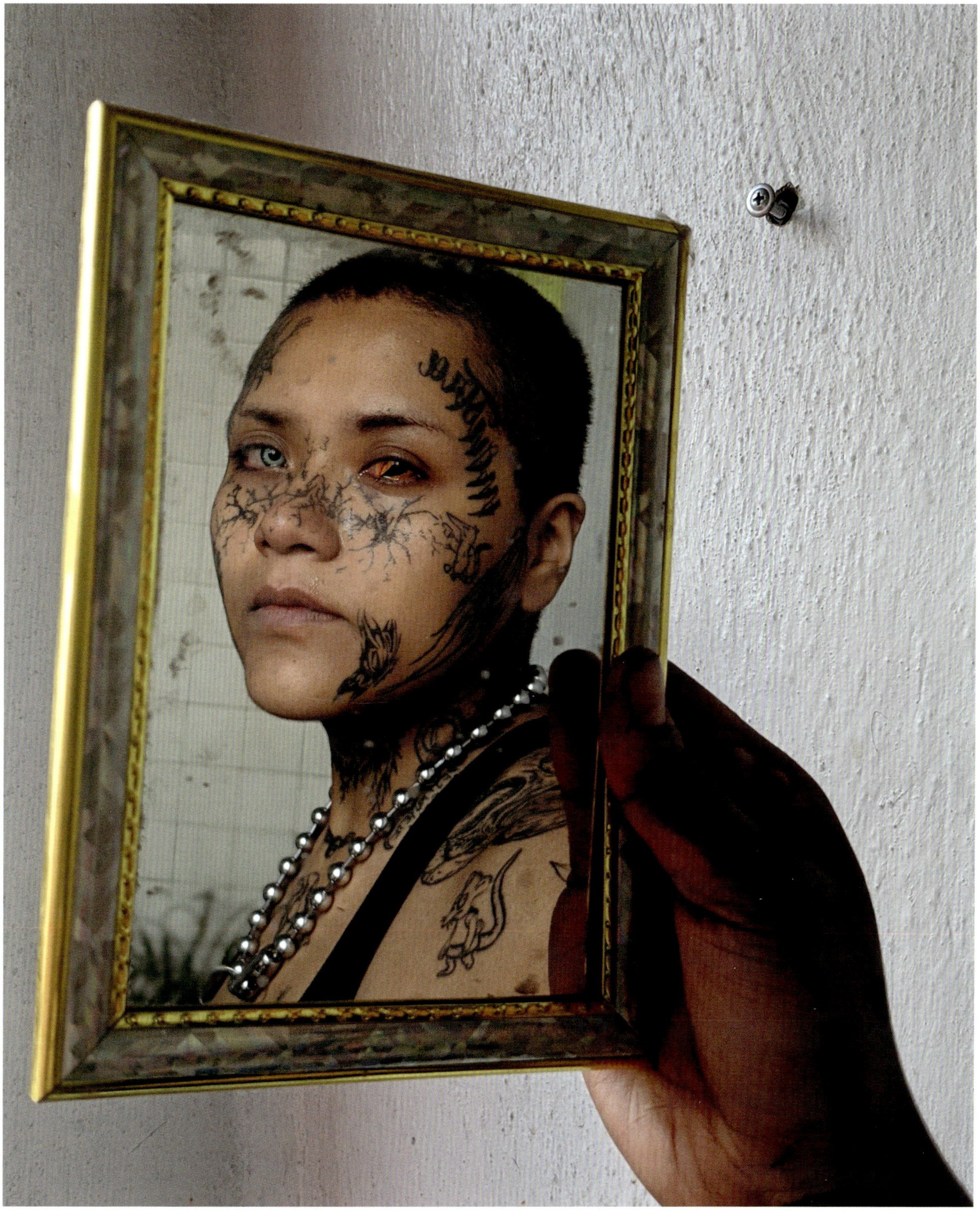

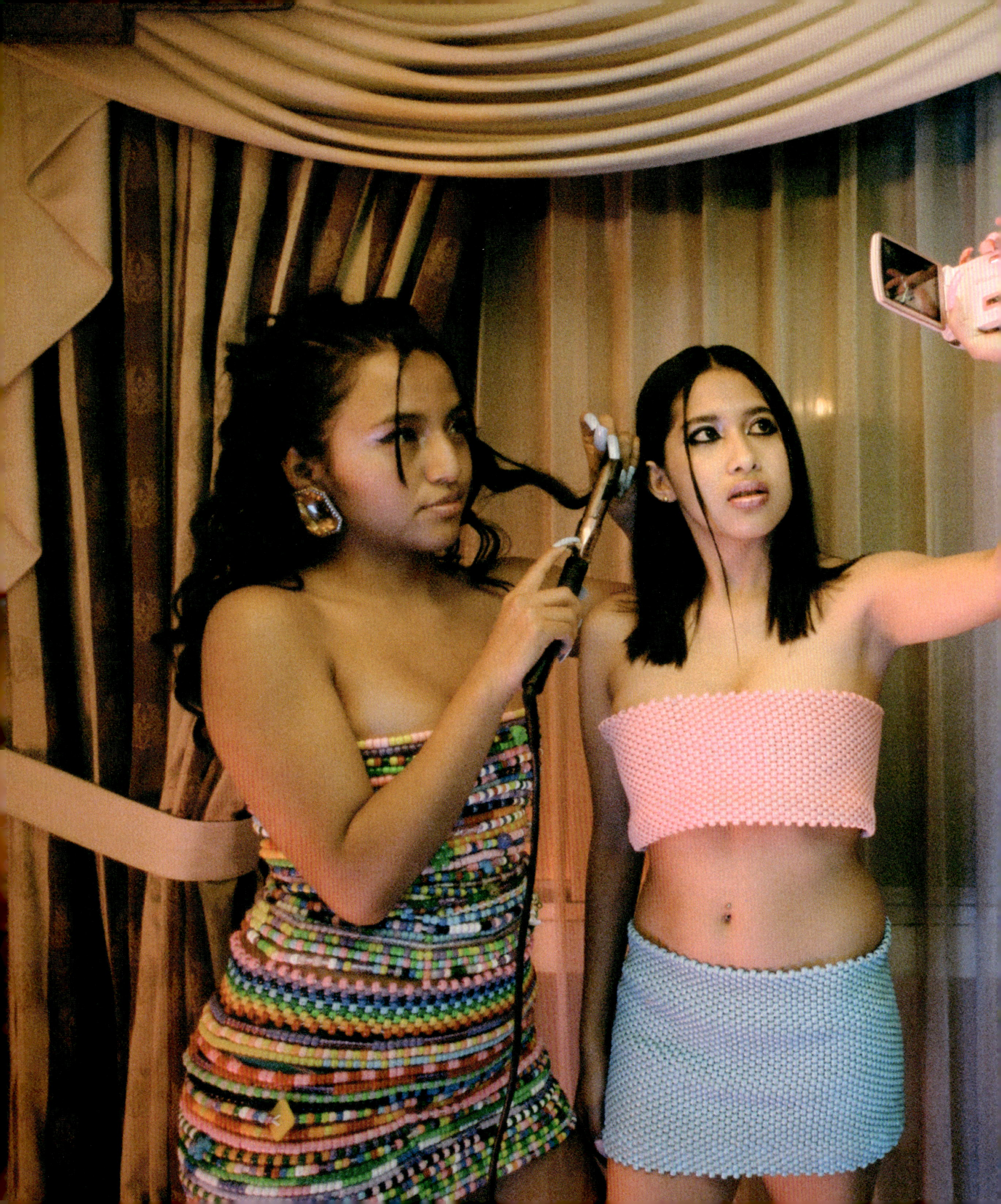

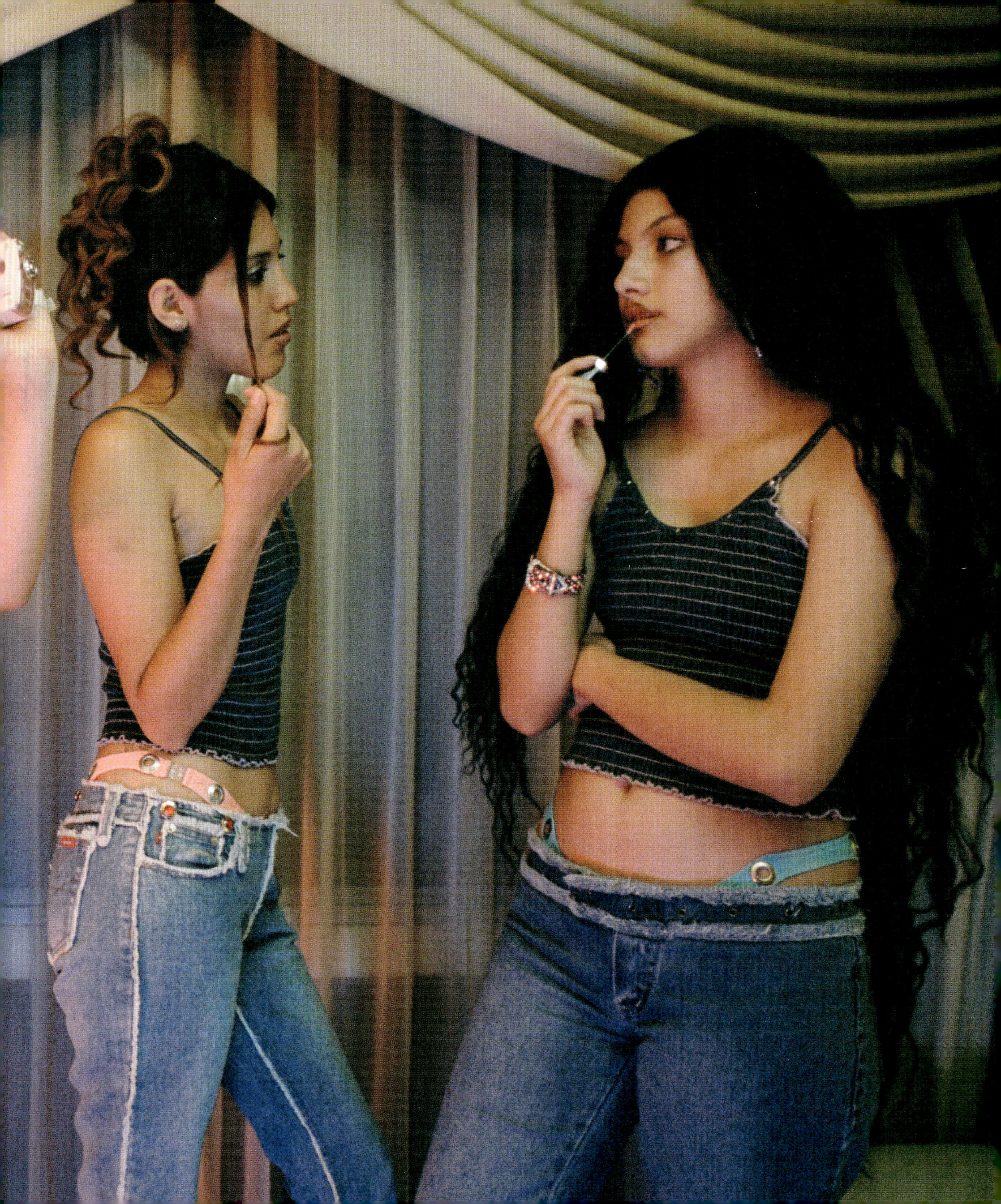

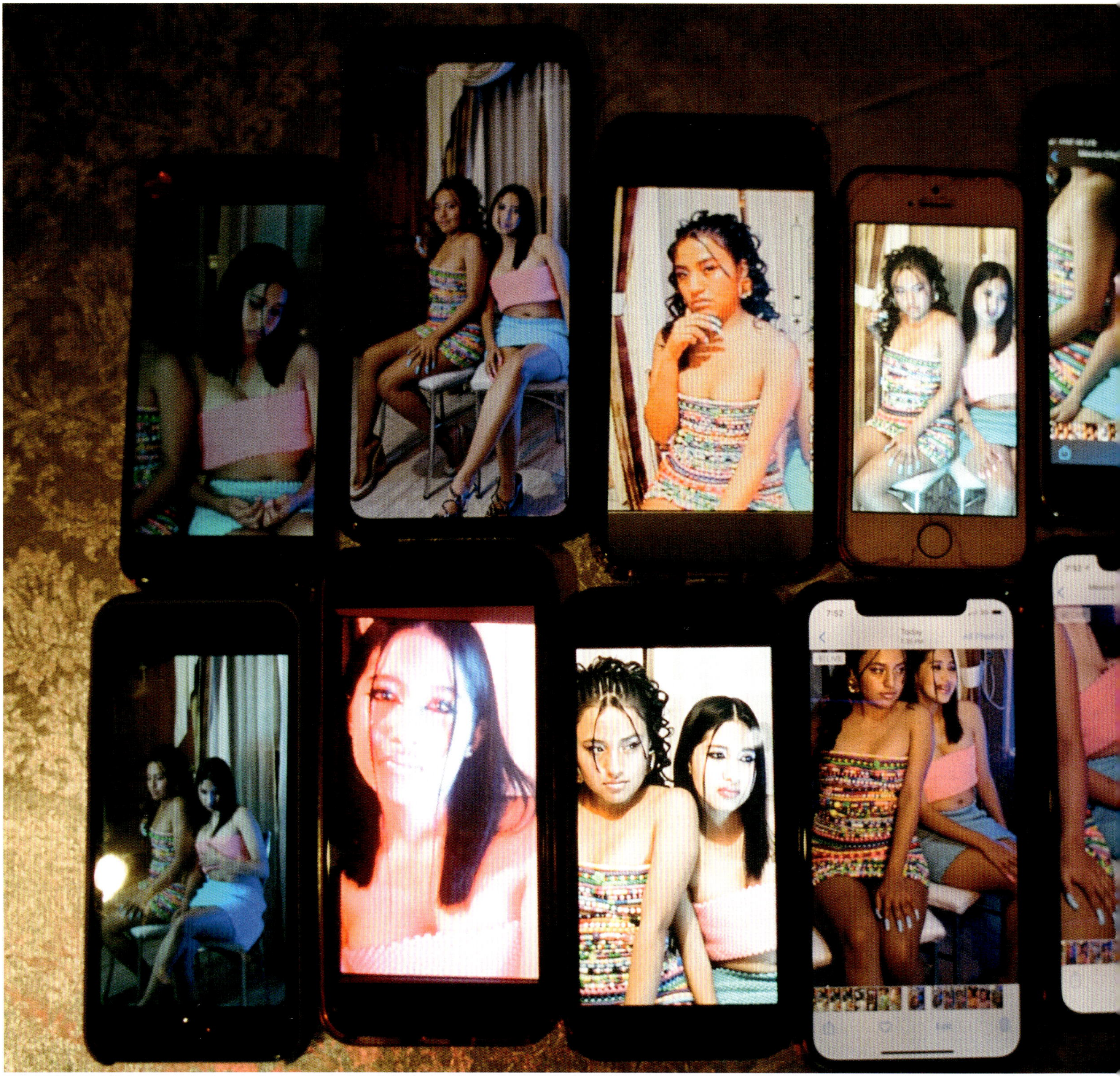

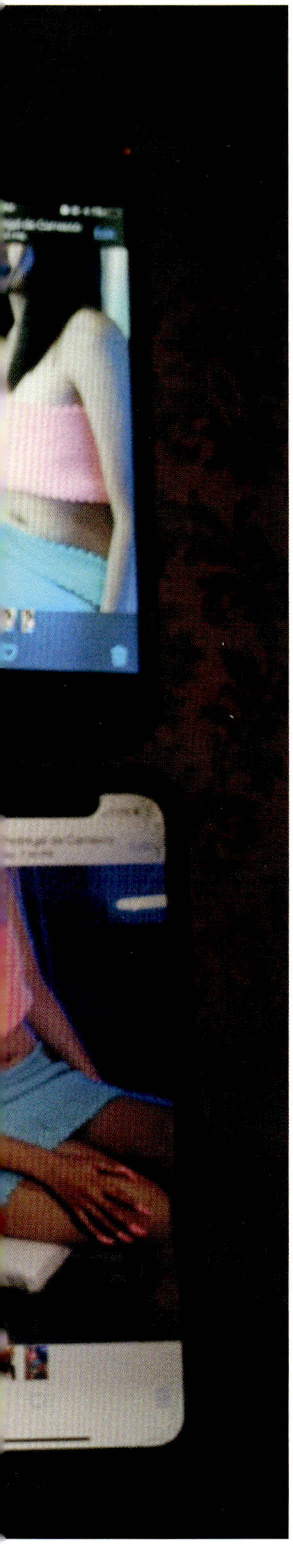

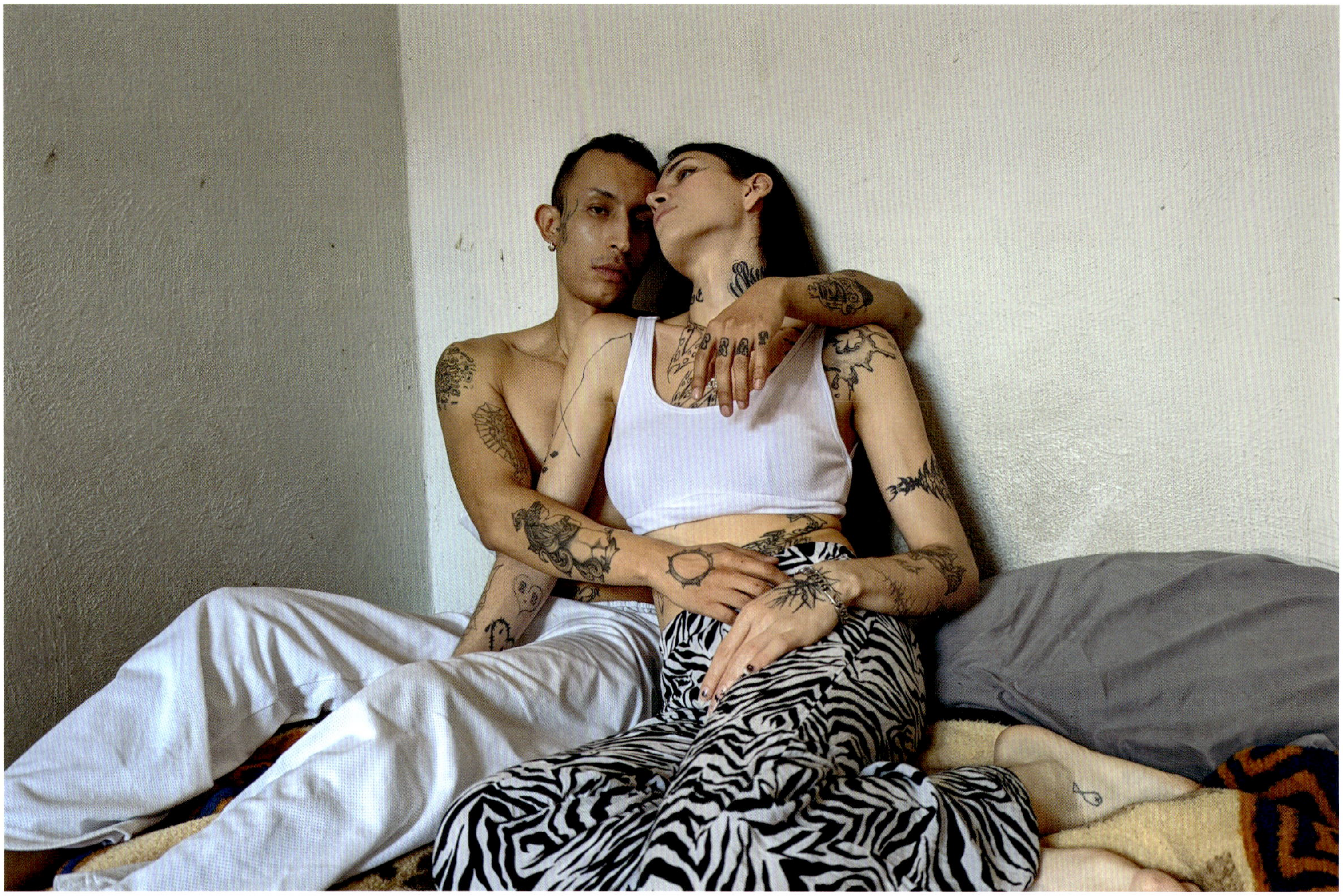

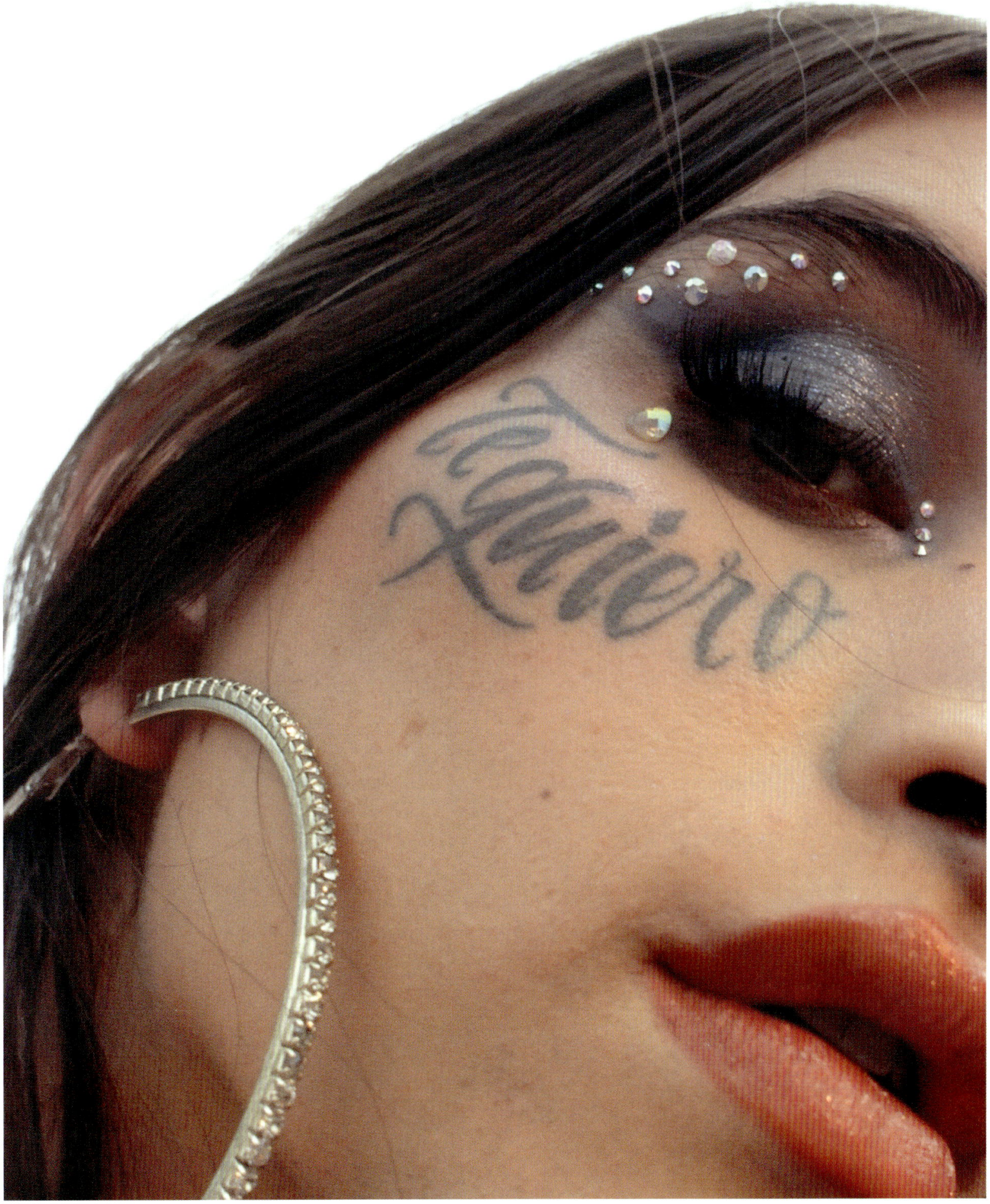
Te quiero

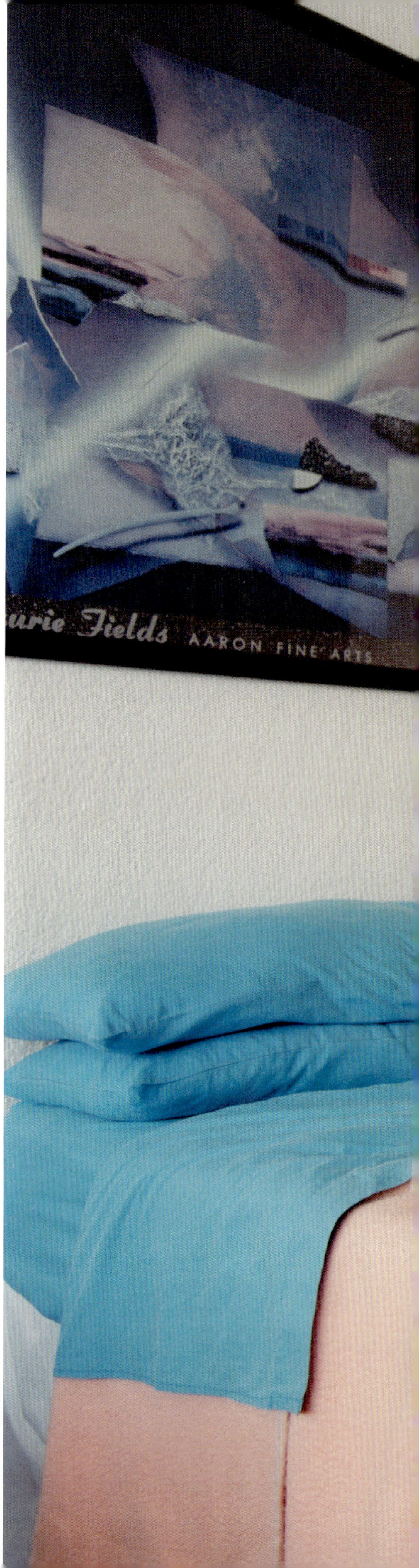
Fields
AARON FINE ARTS

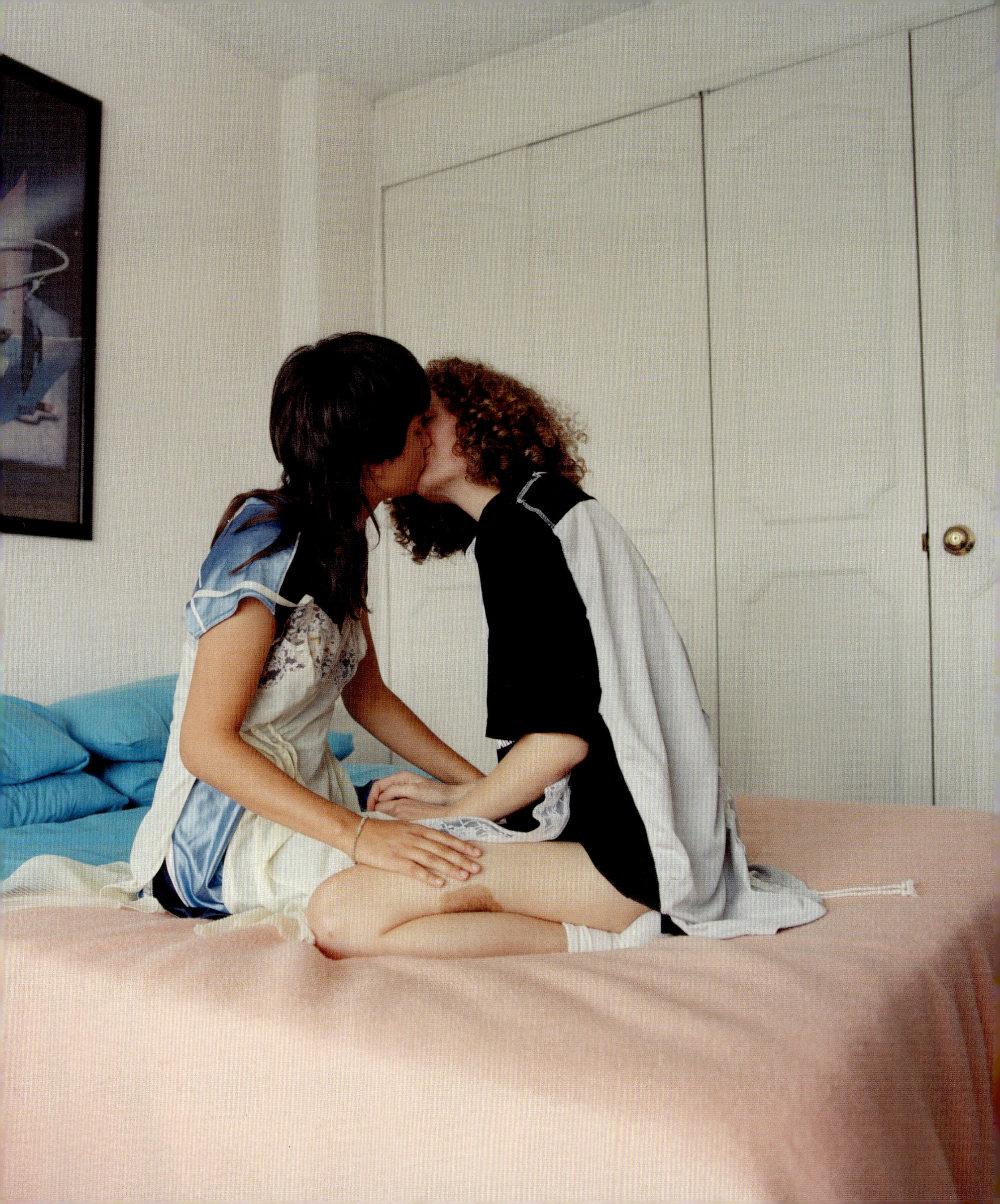

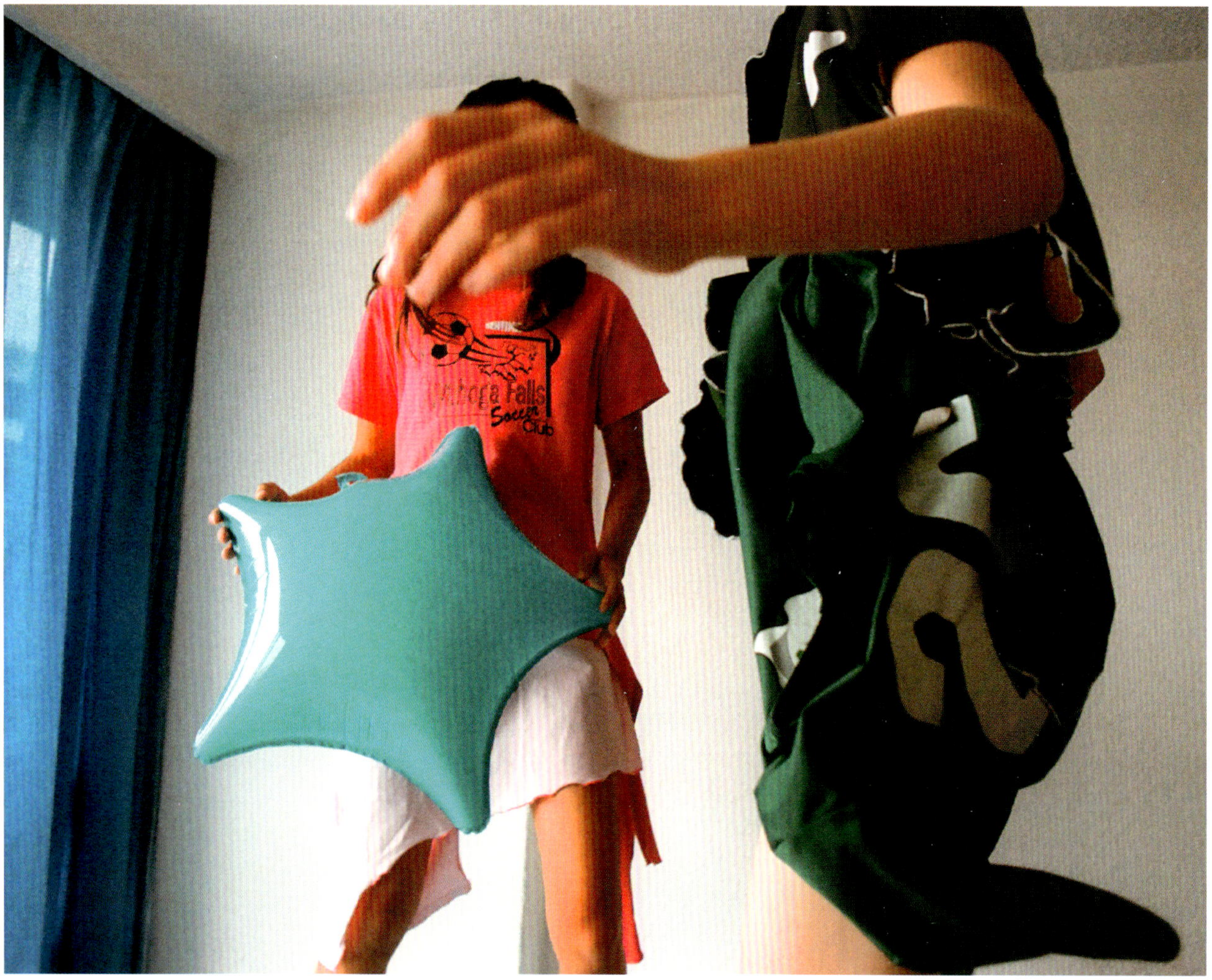
Falls
Club

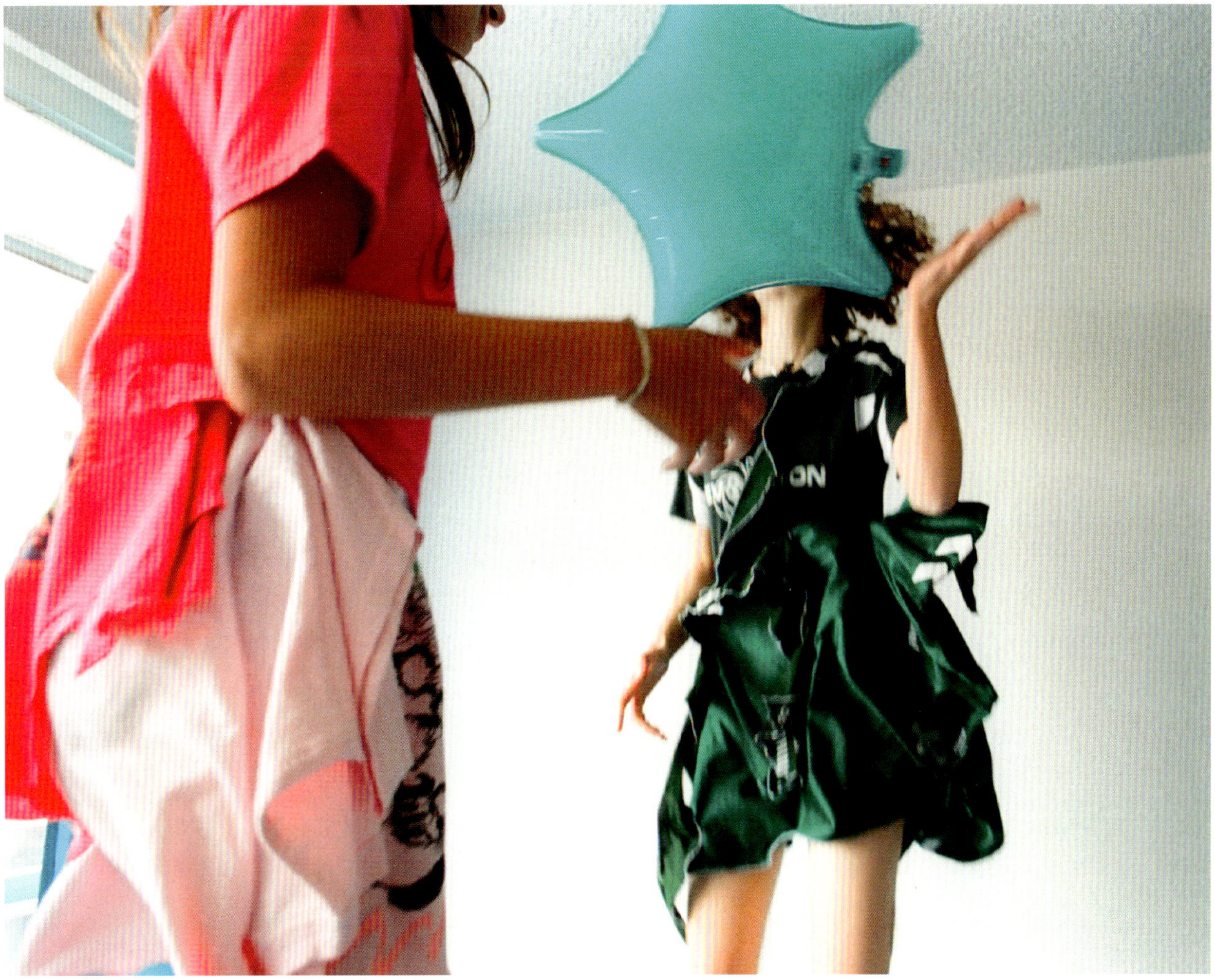

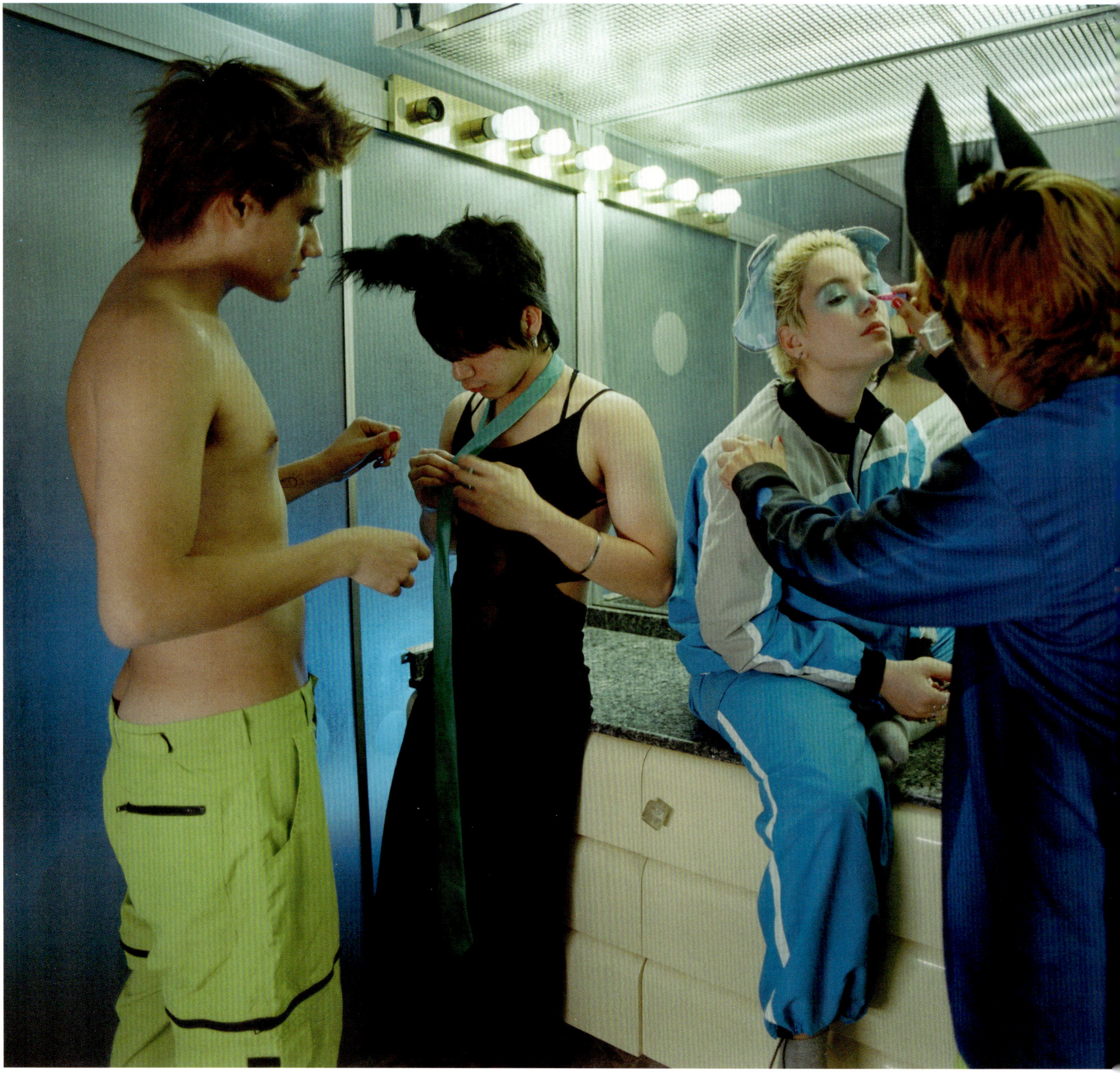

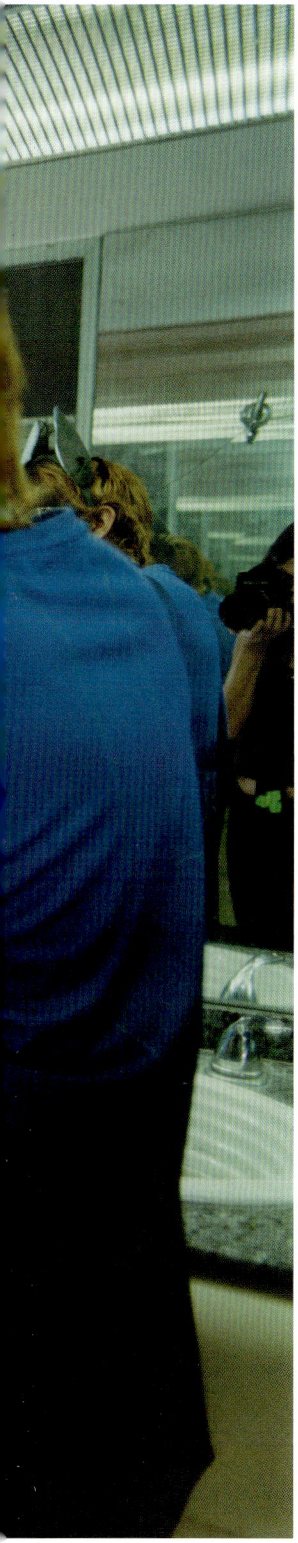

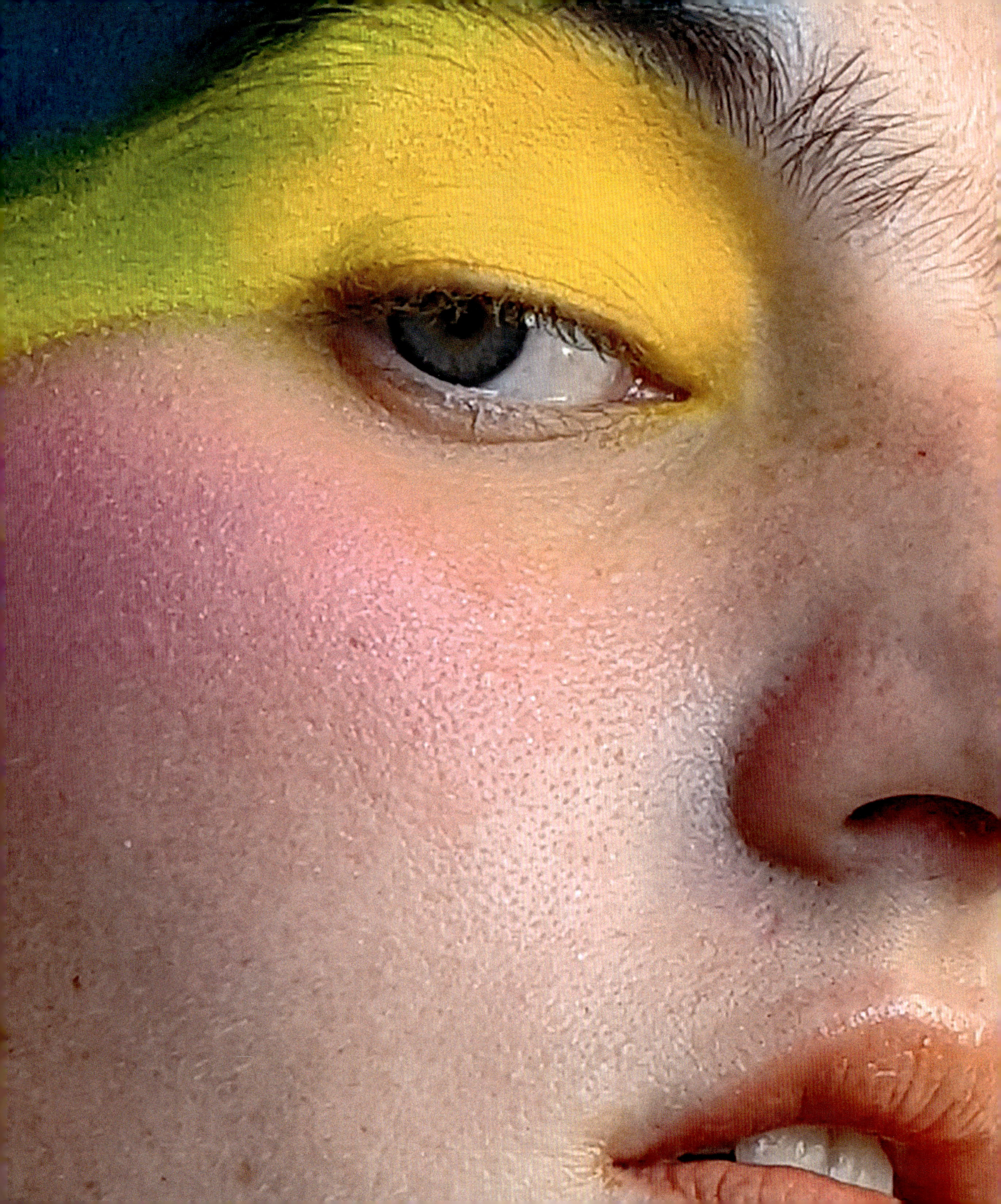

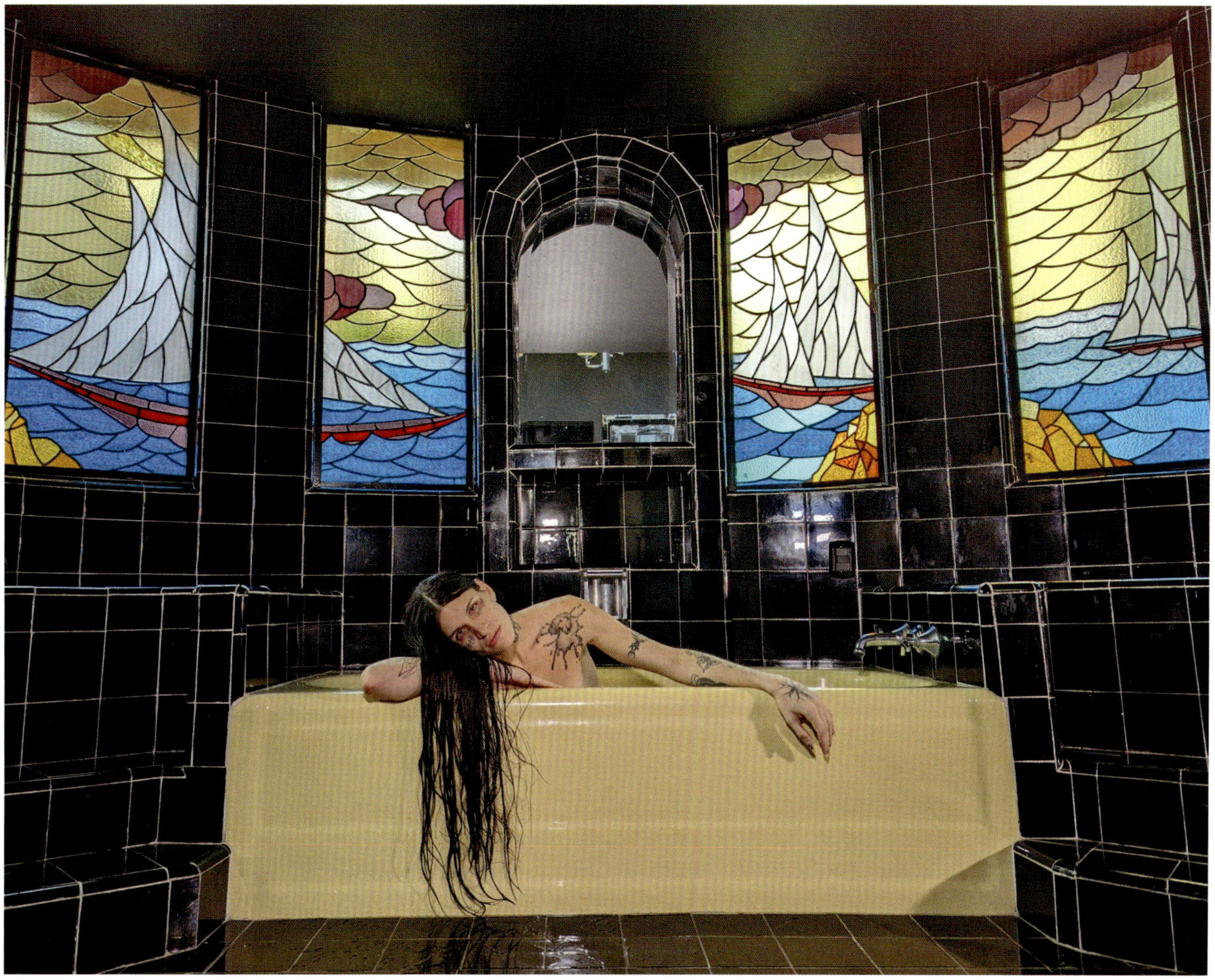

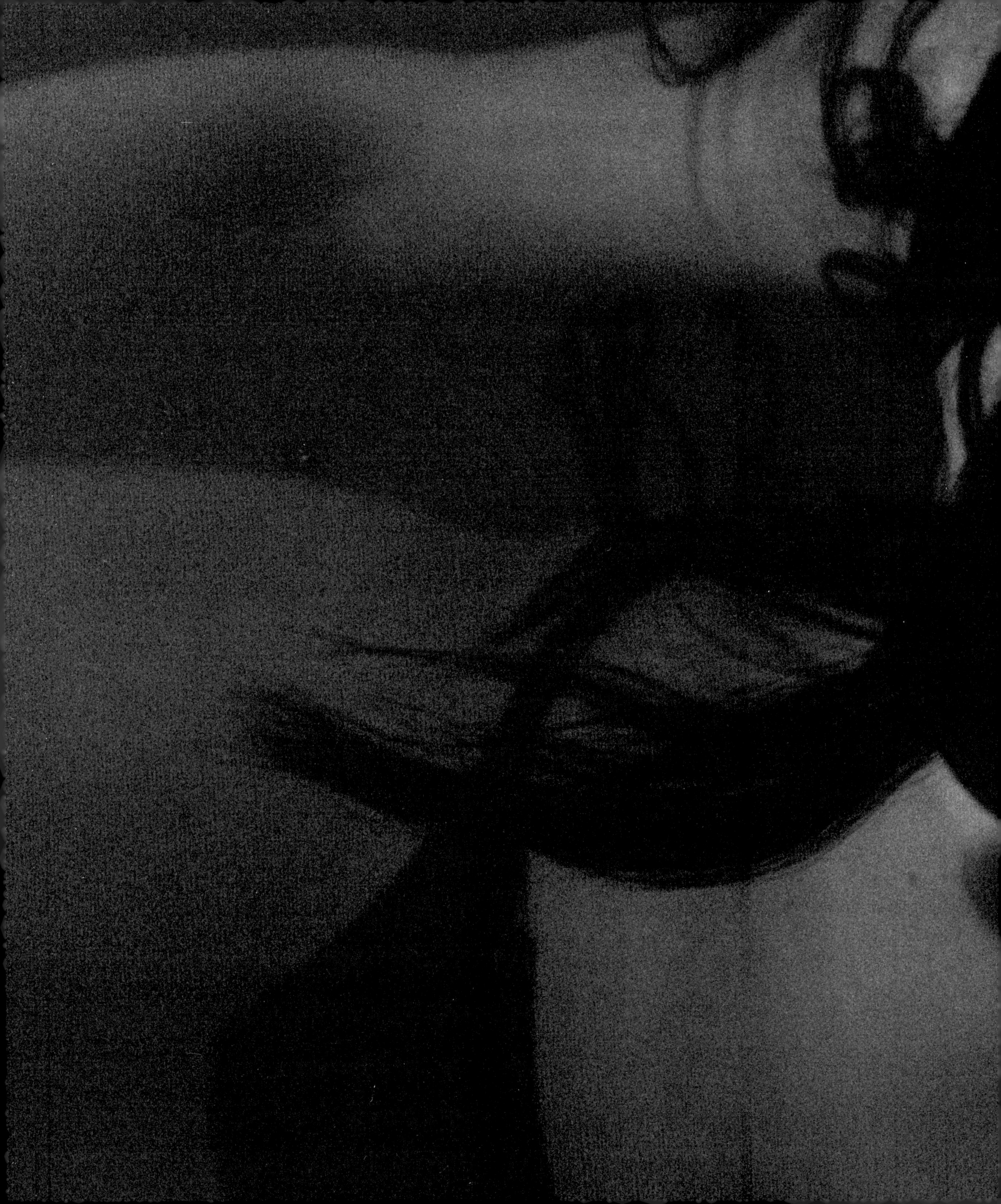

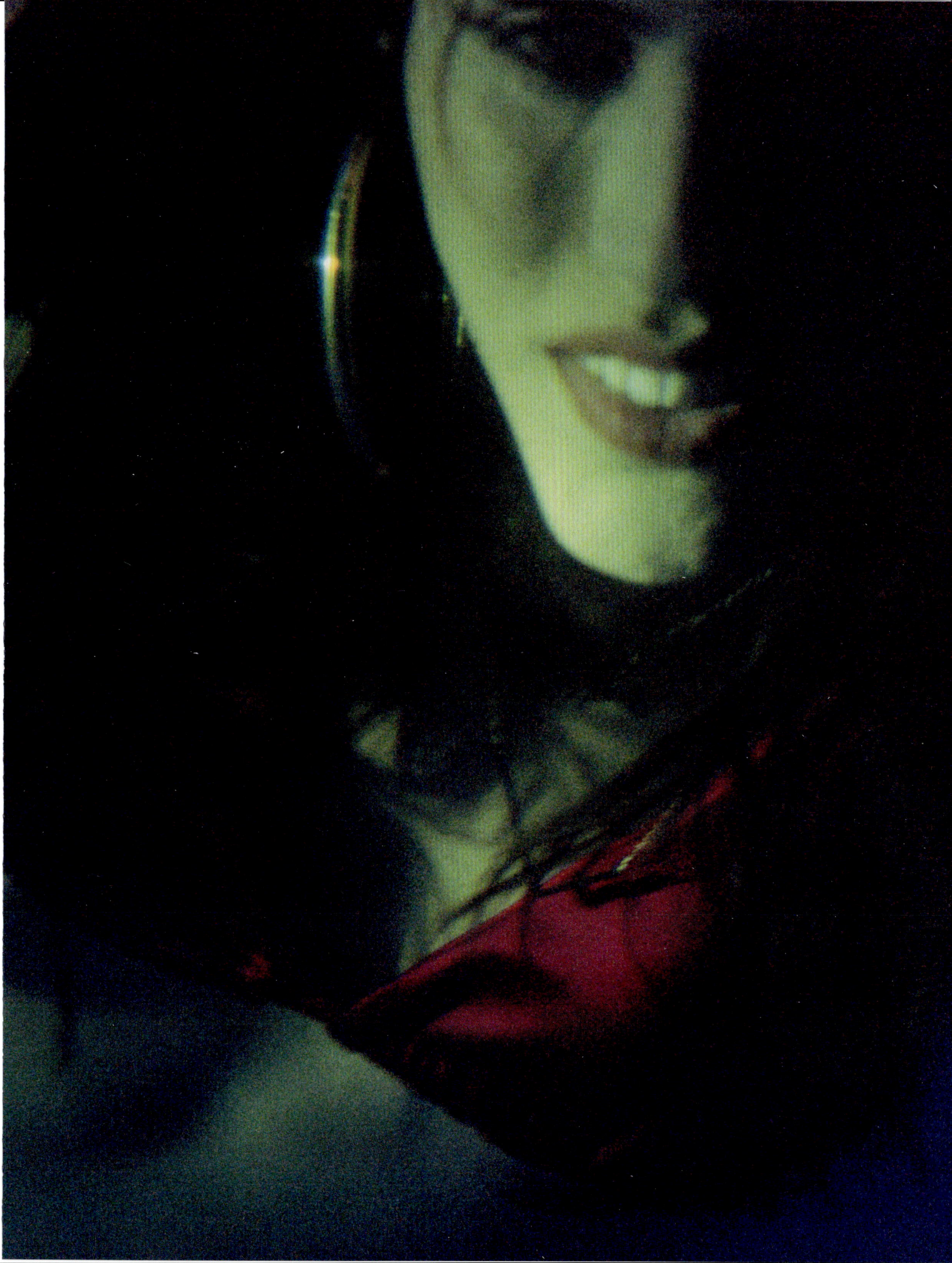

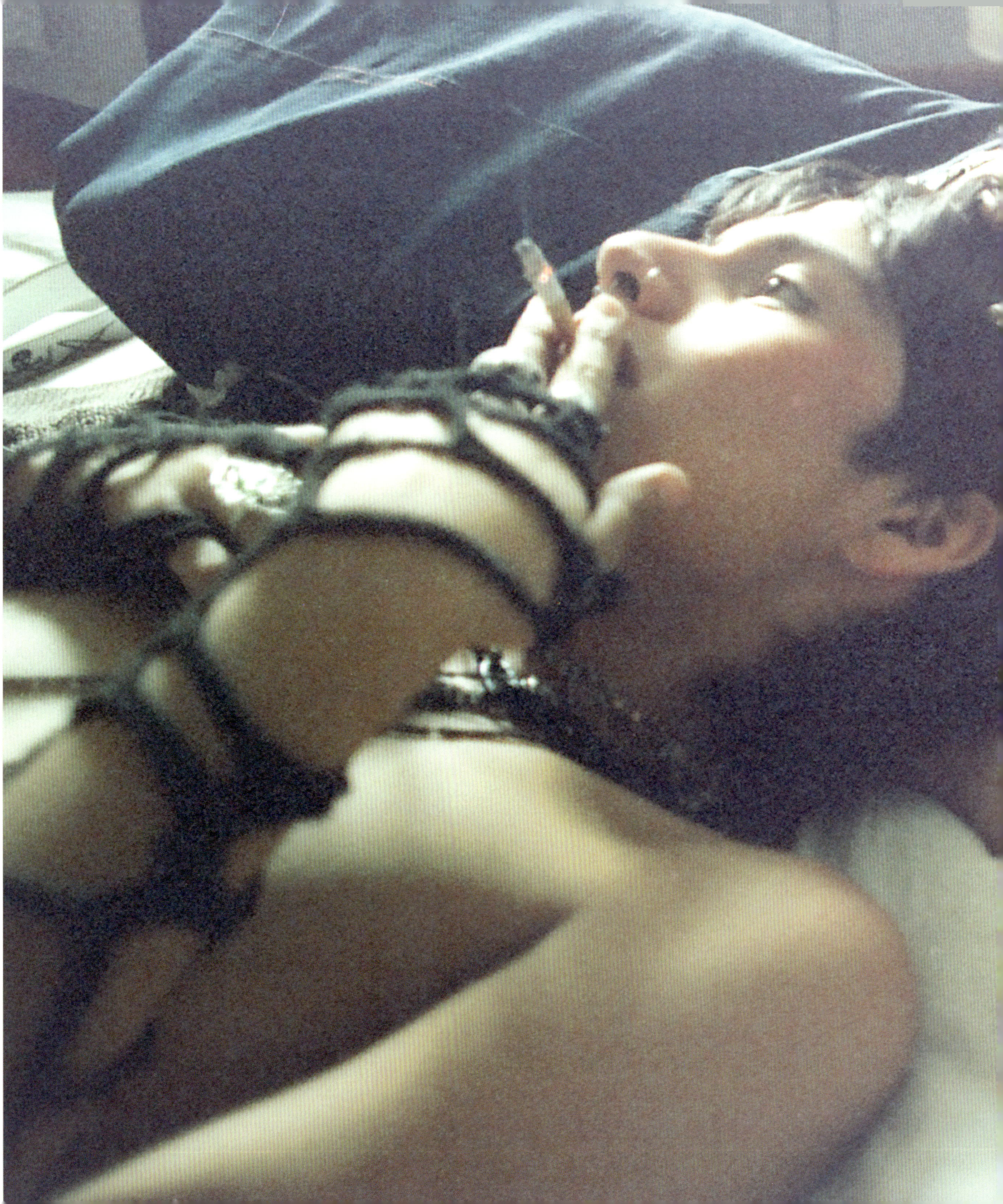

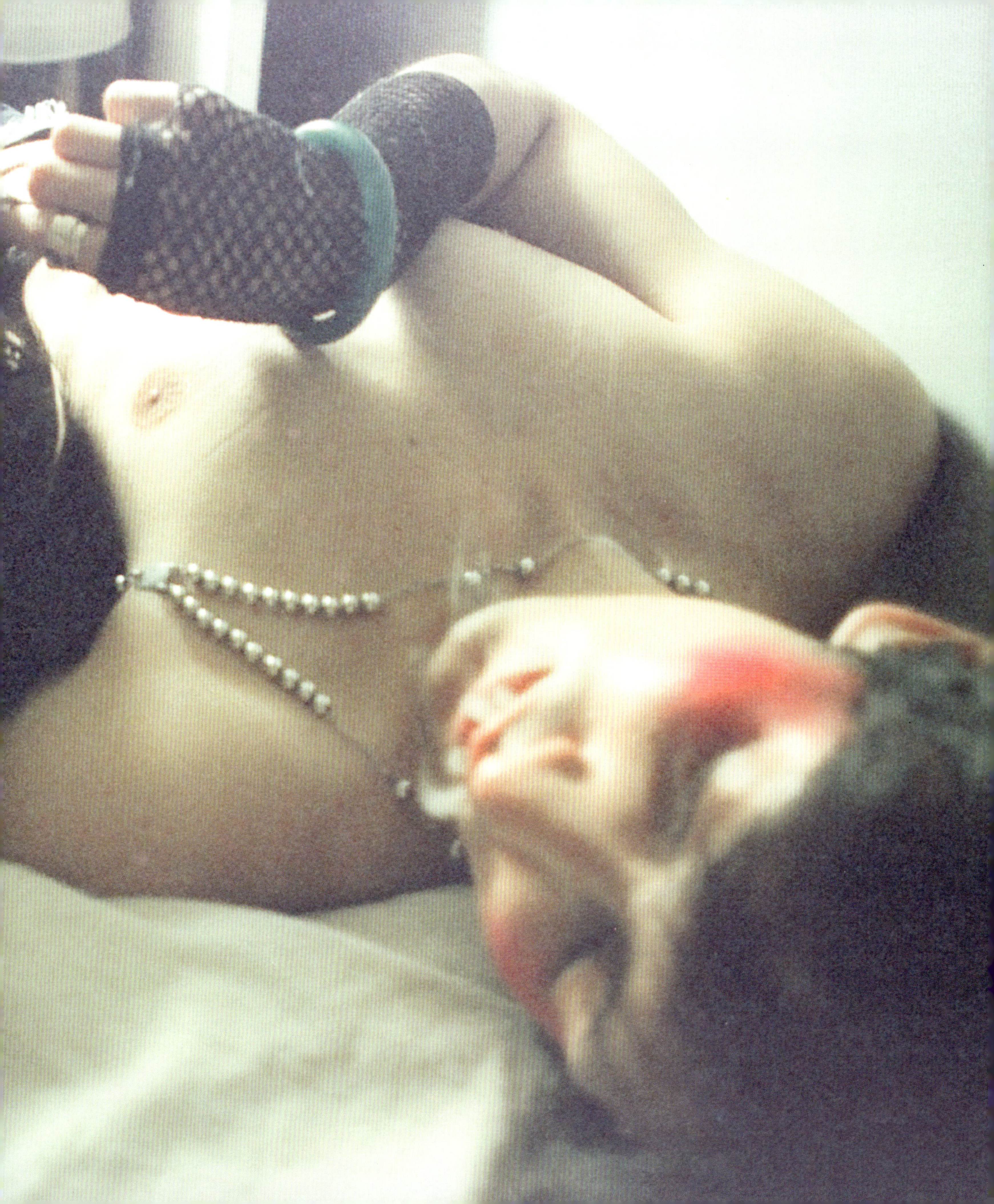

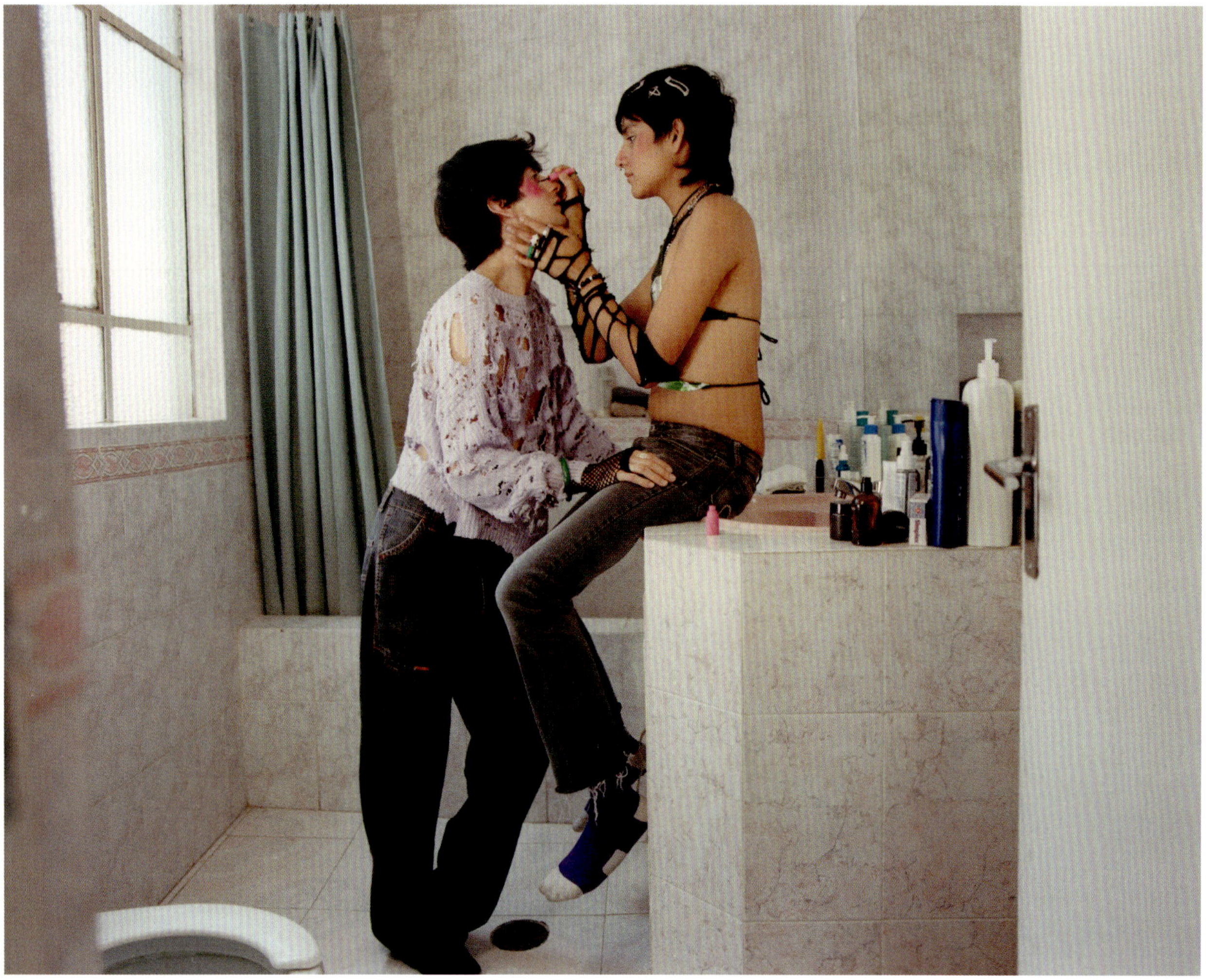

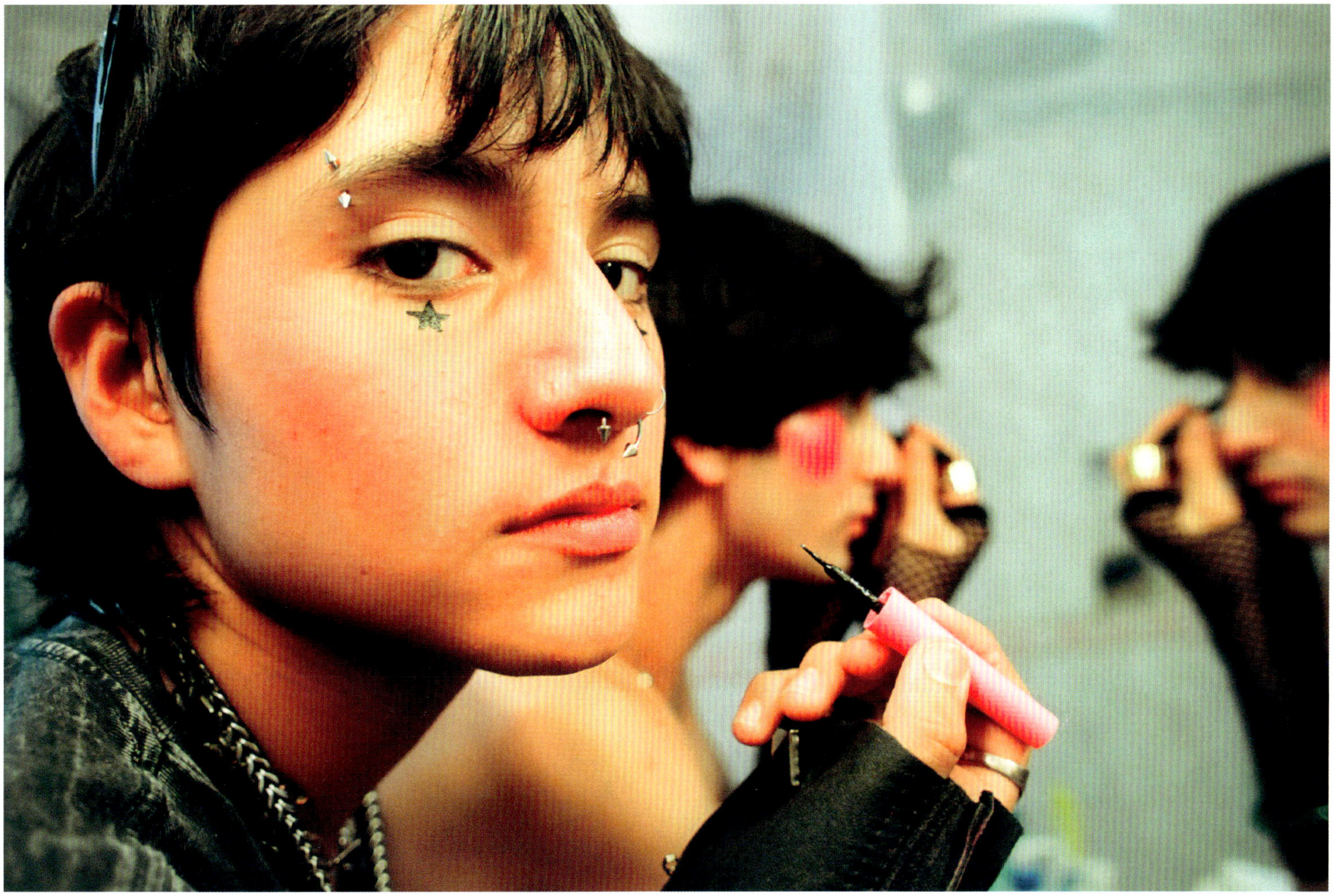

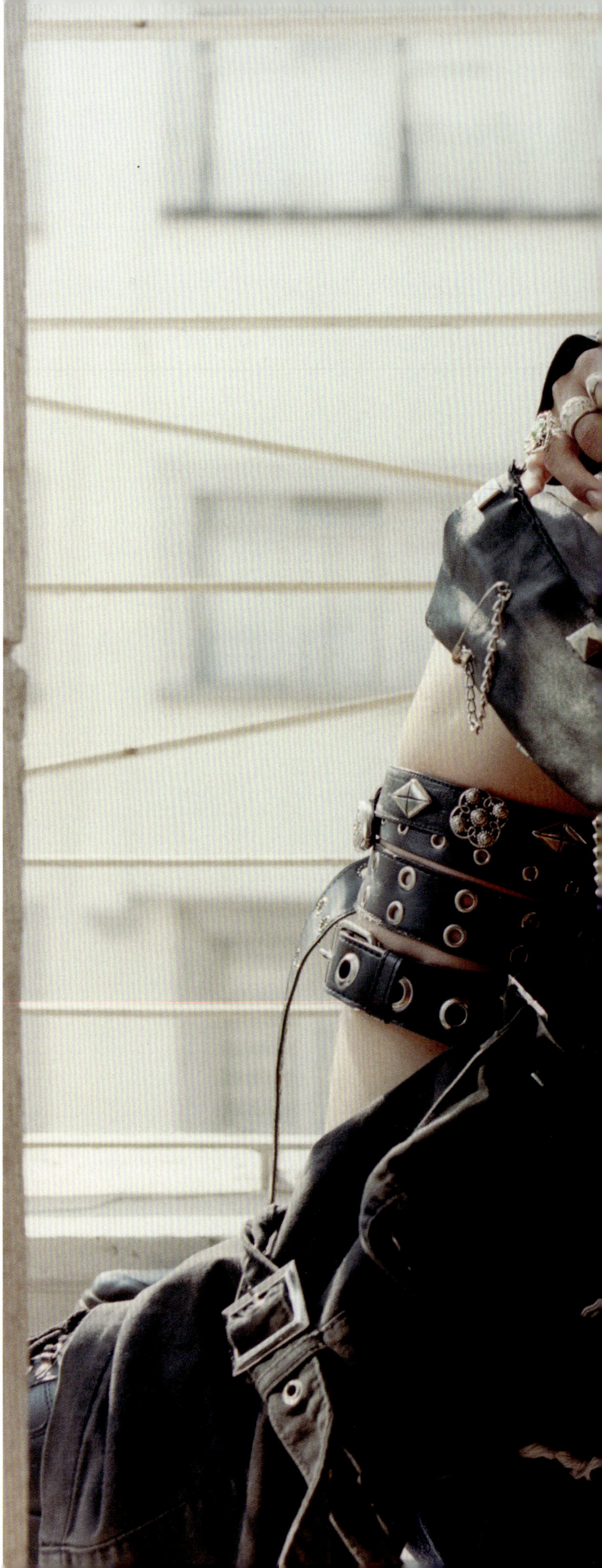

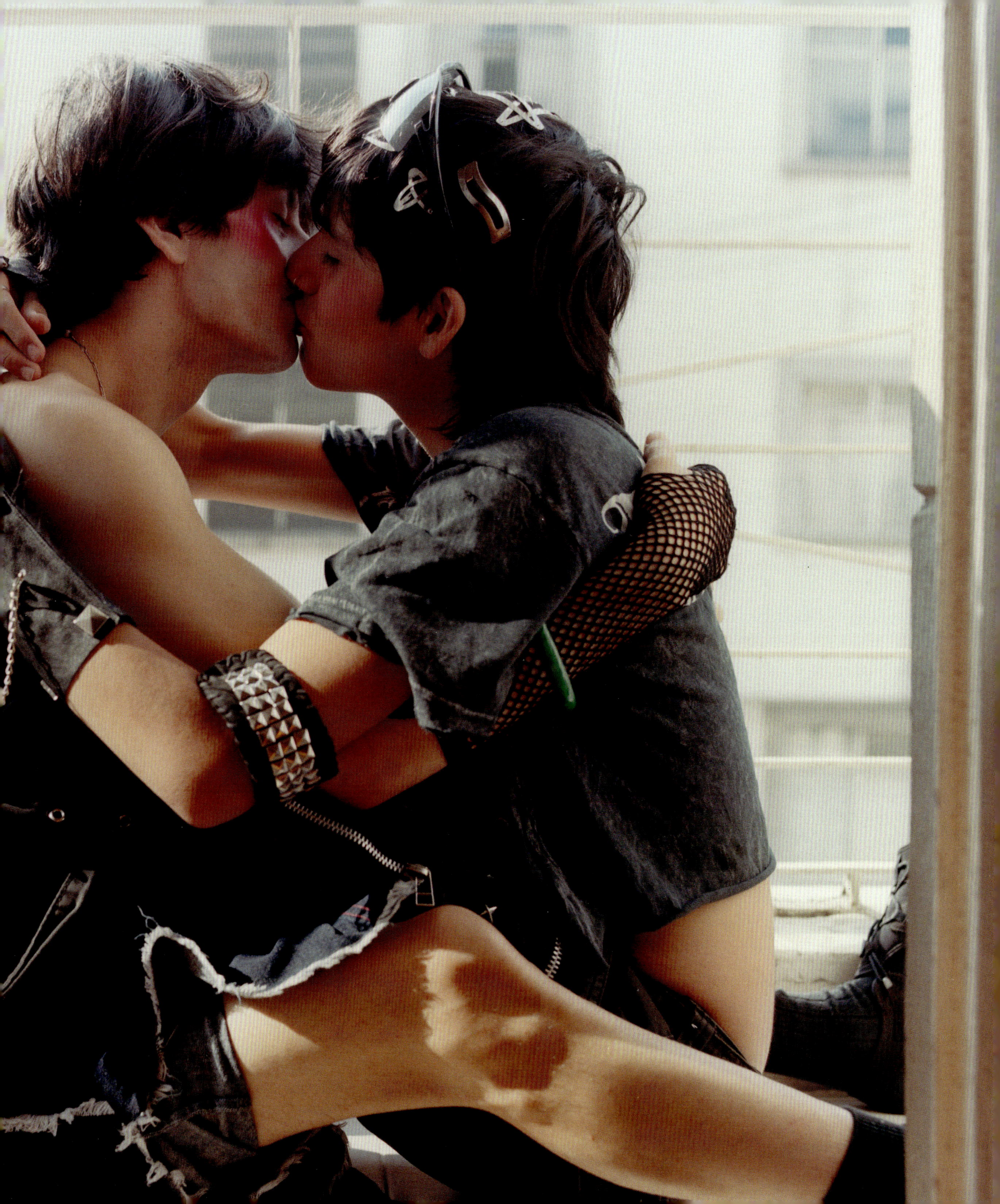

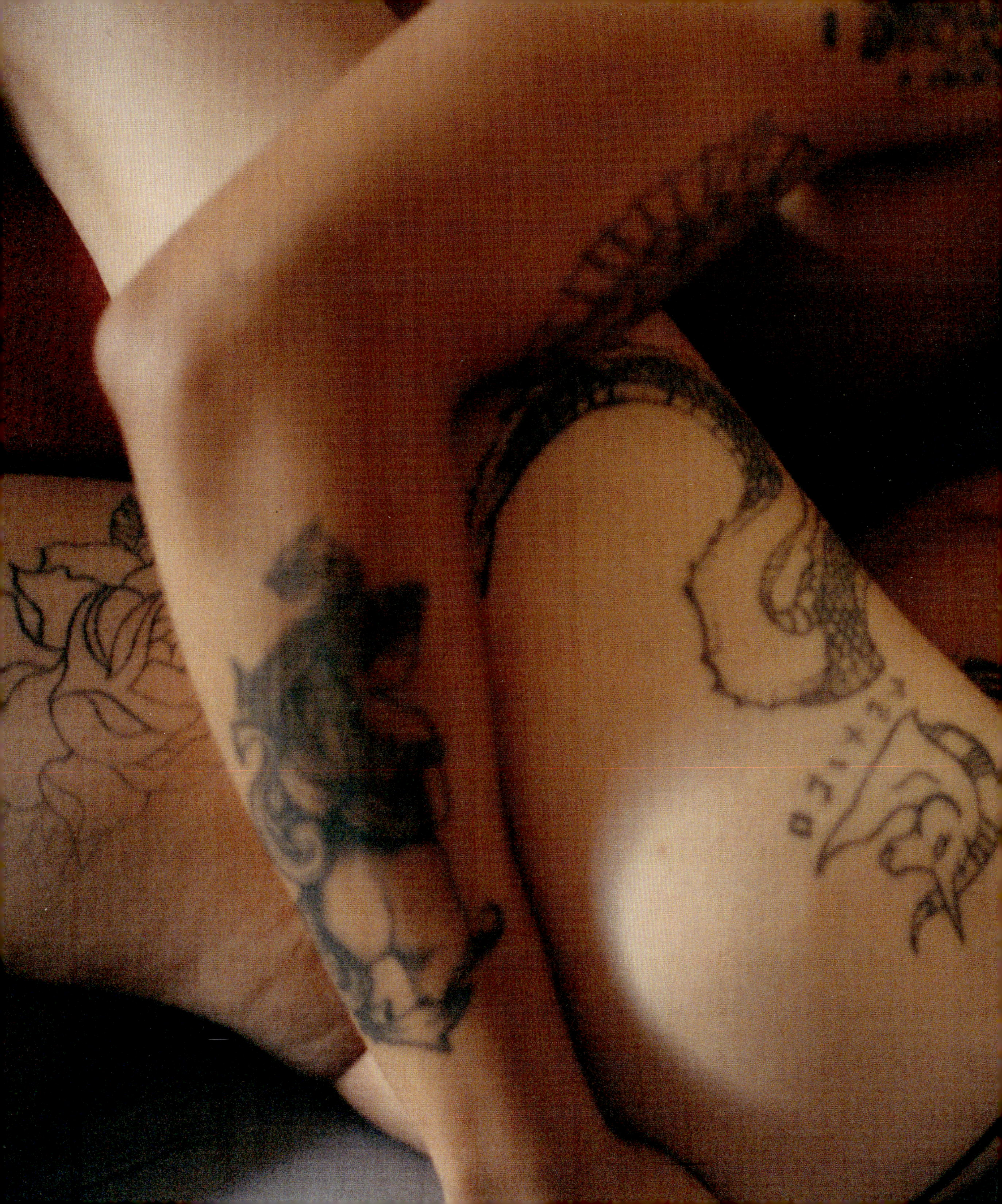

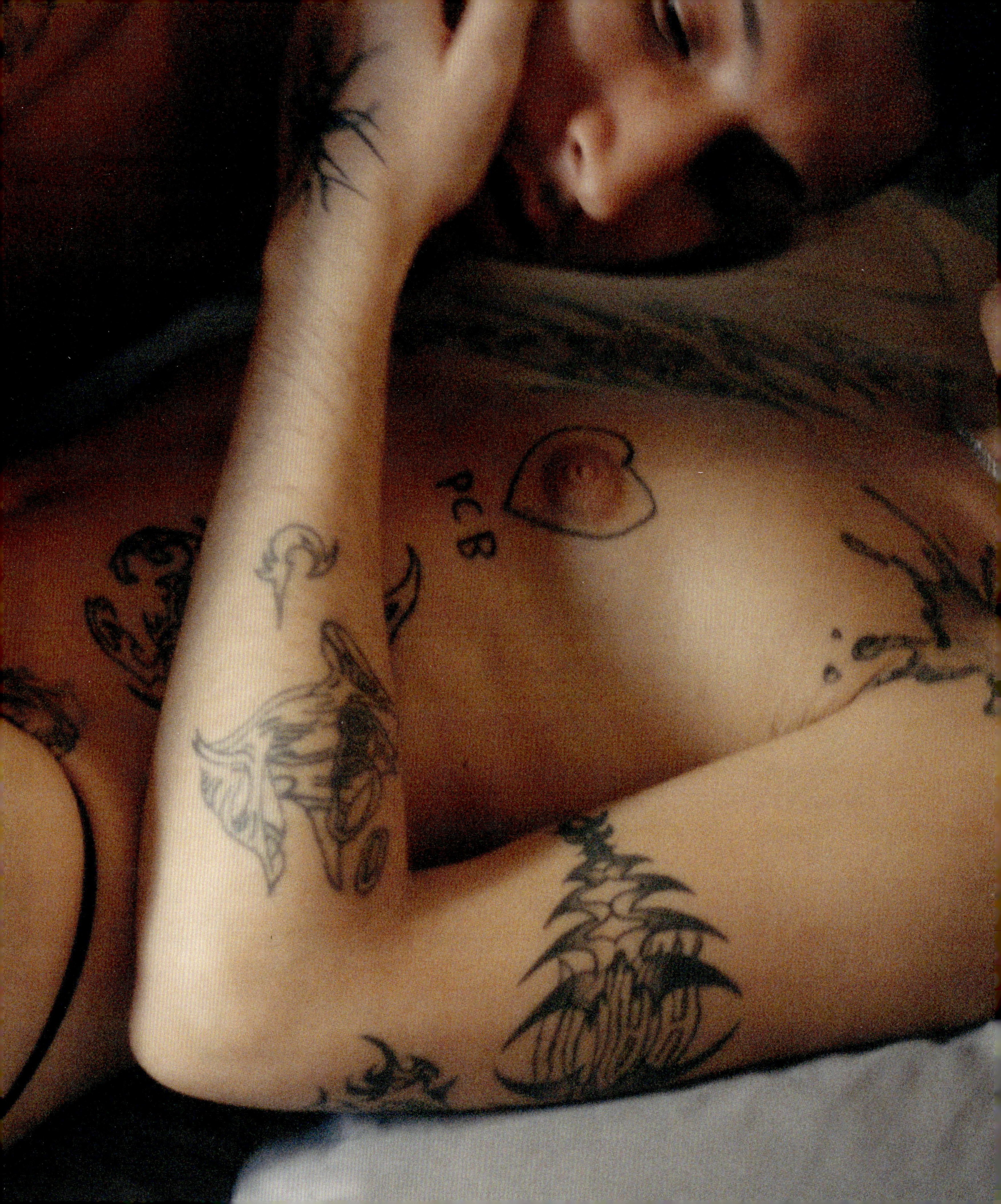
PCB

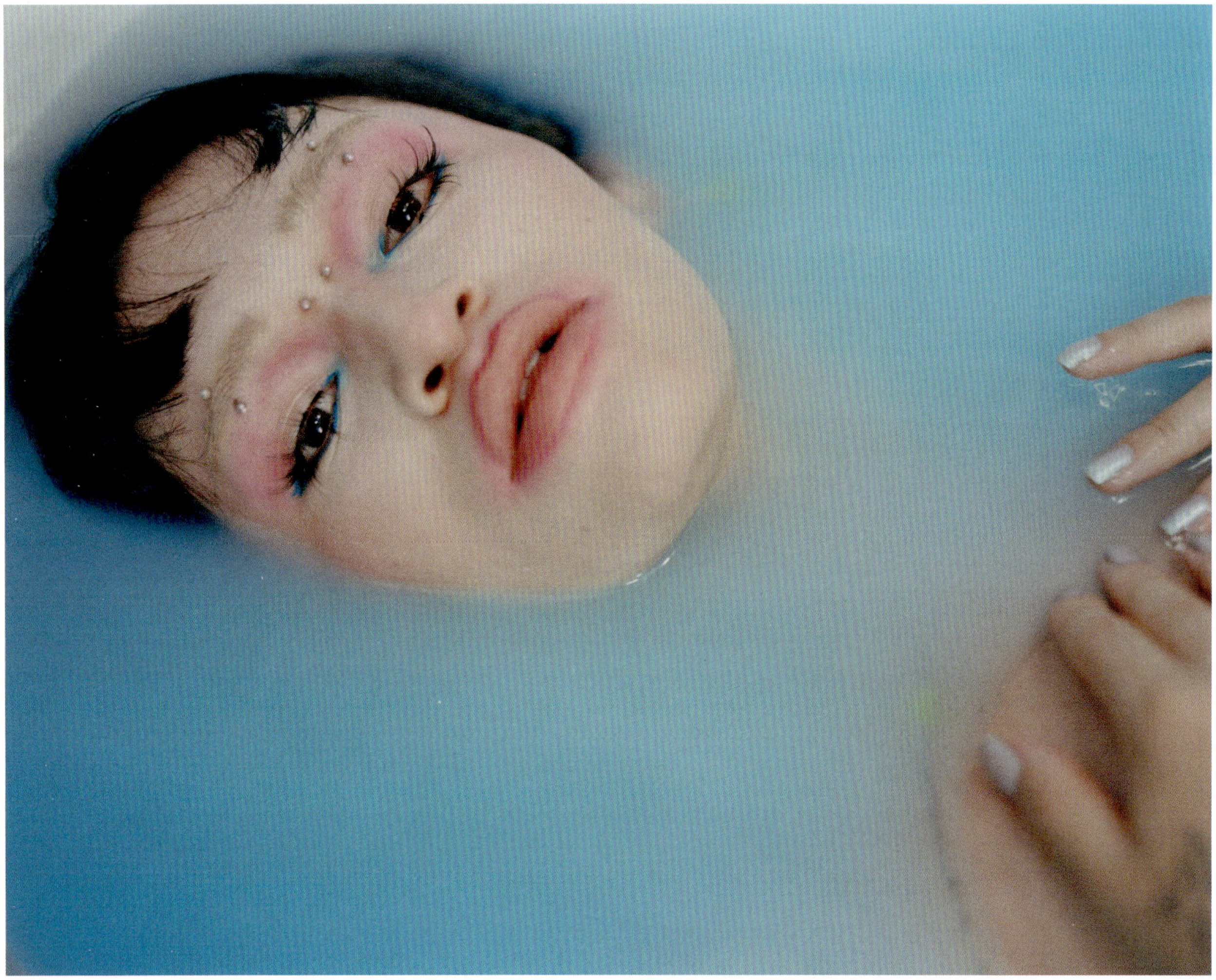

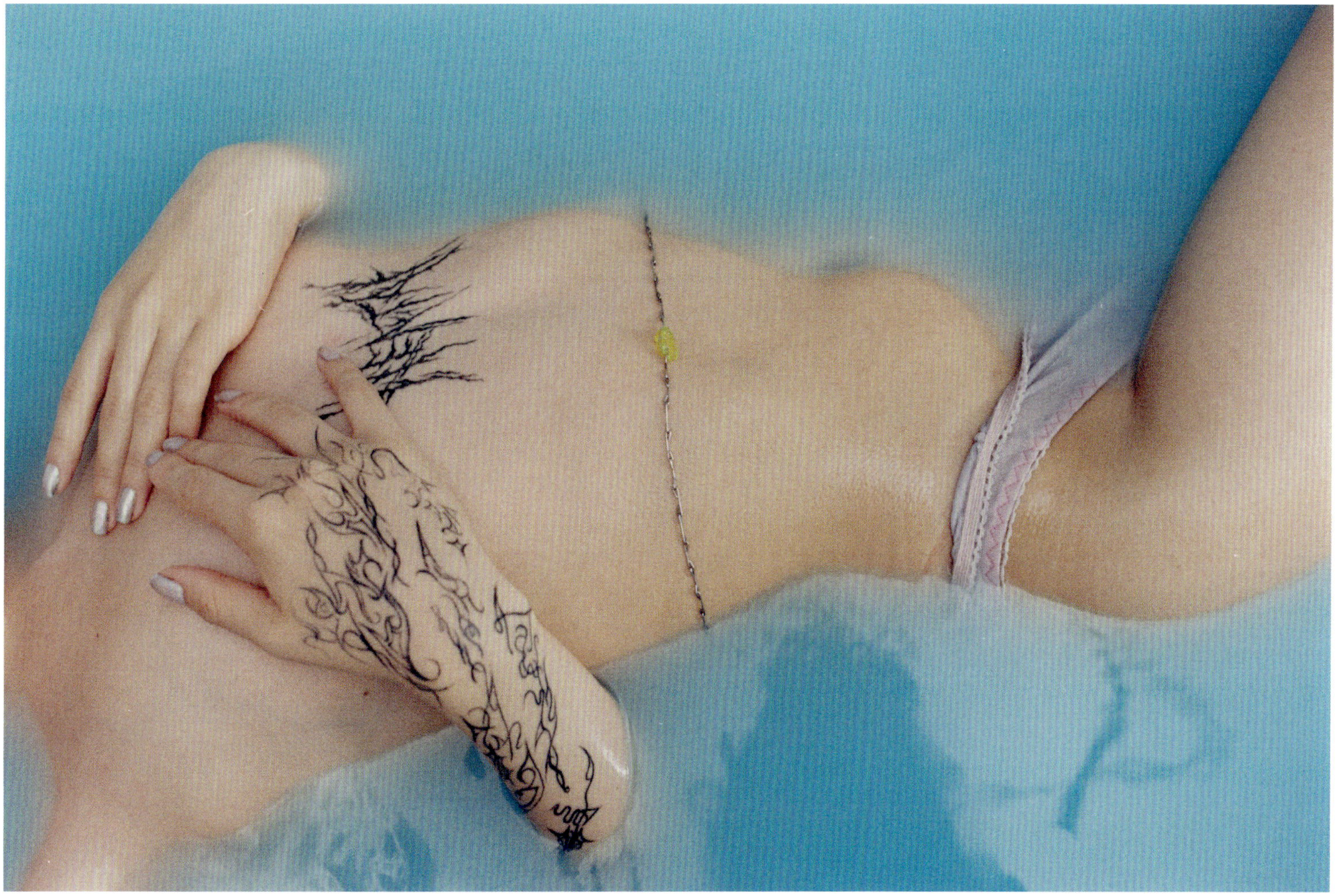

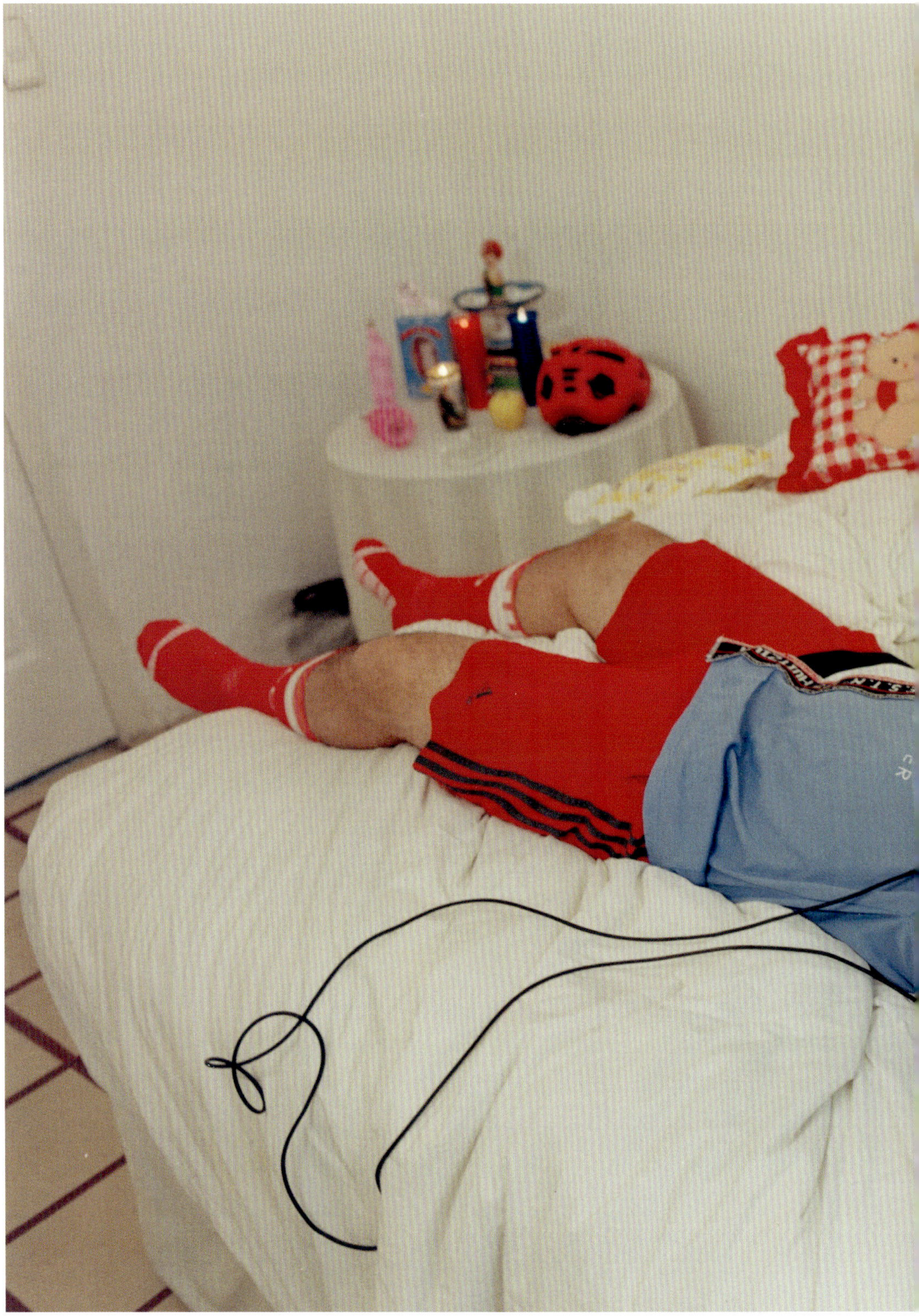

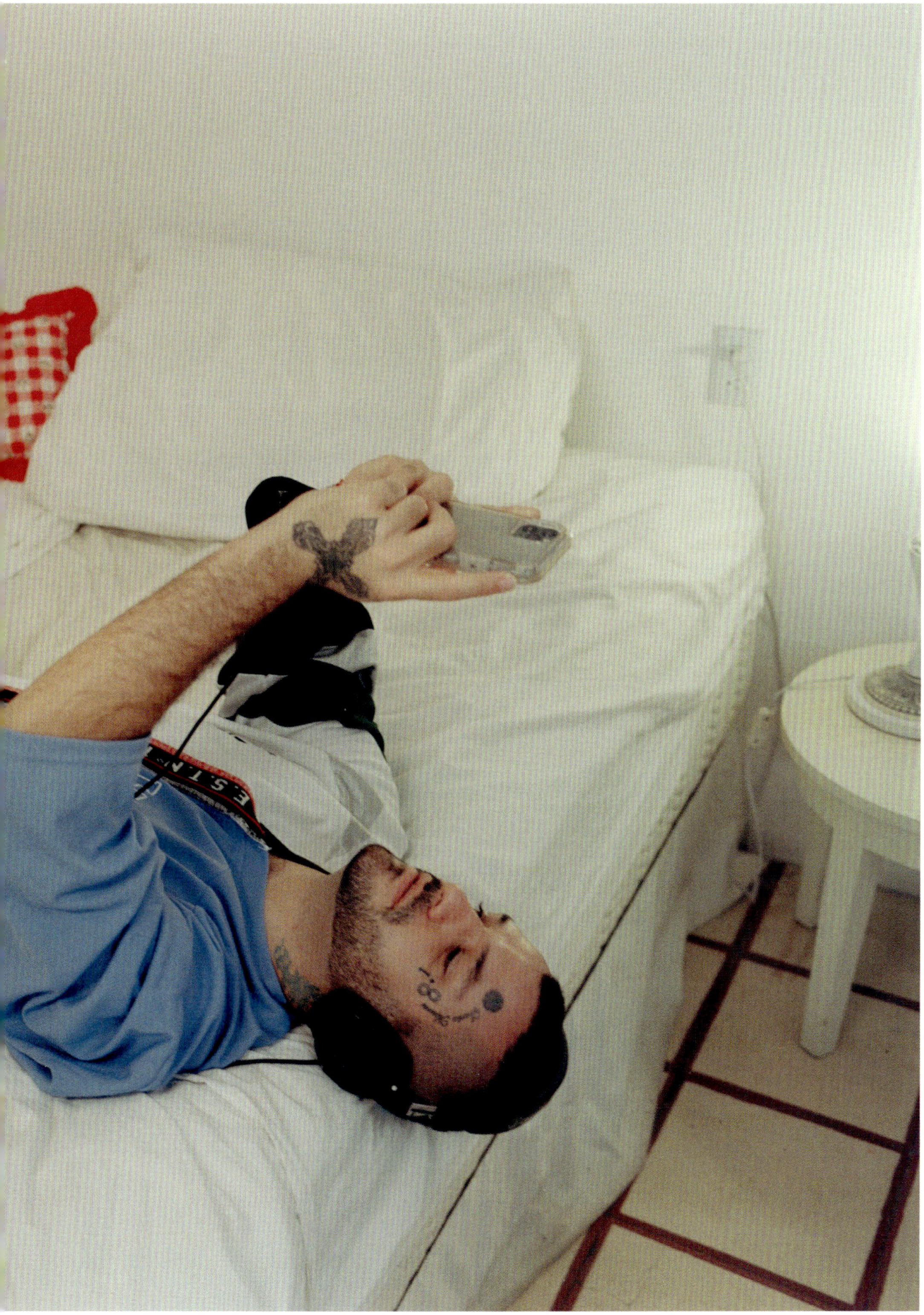

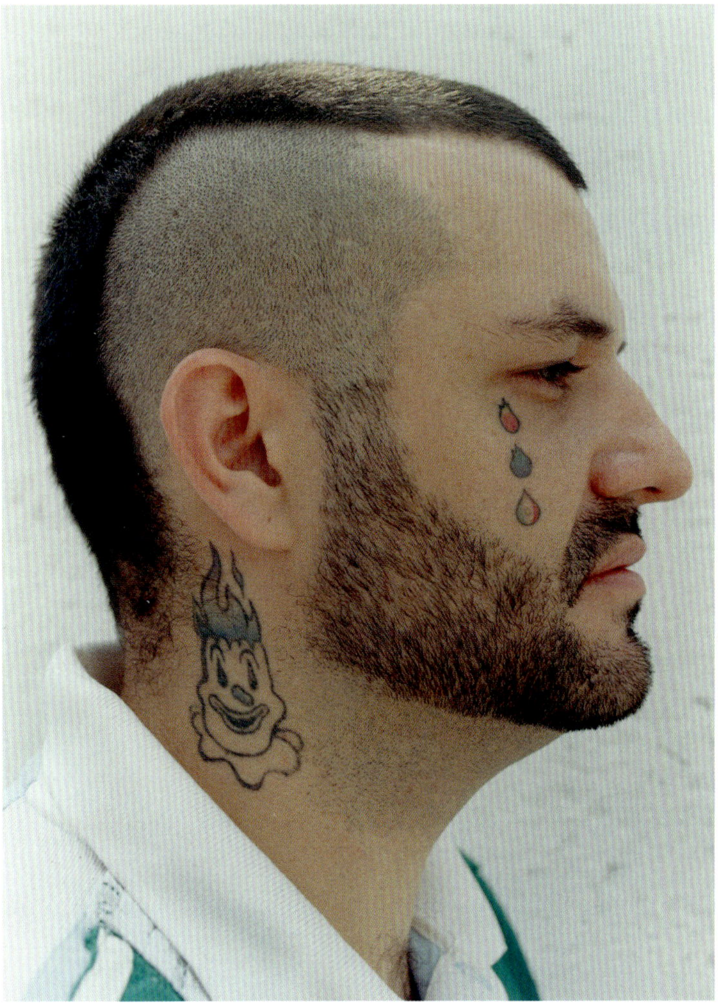

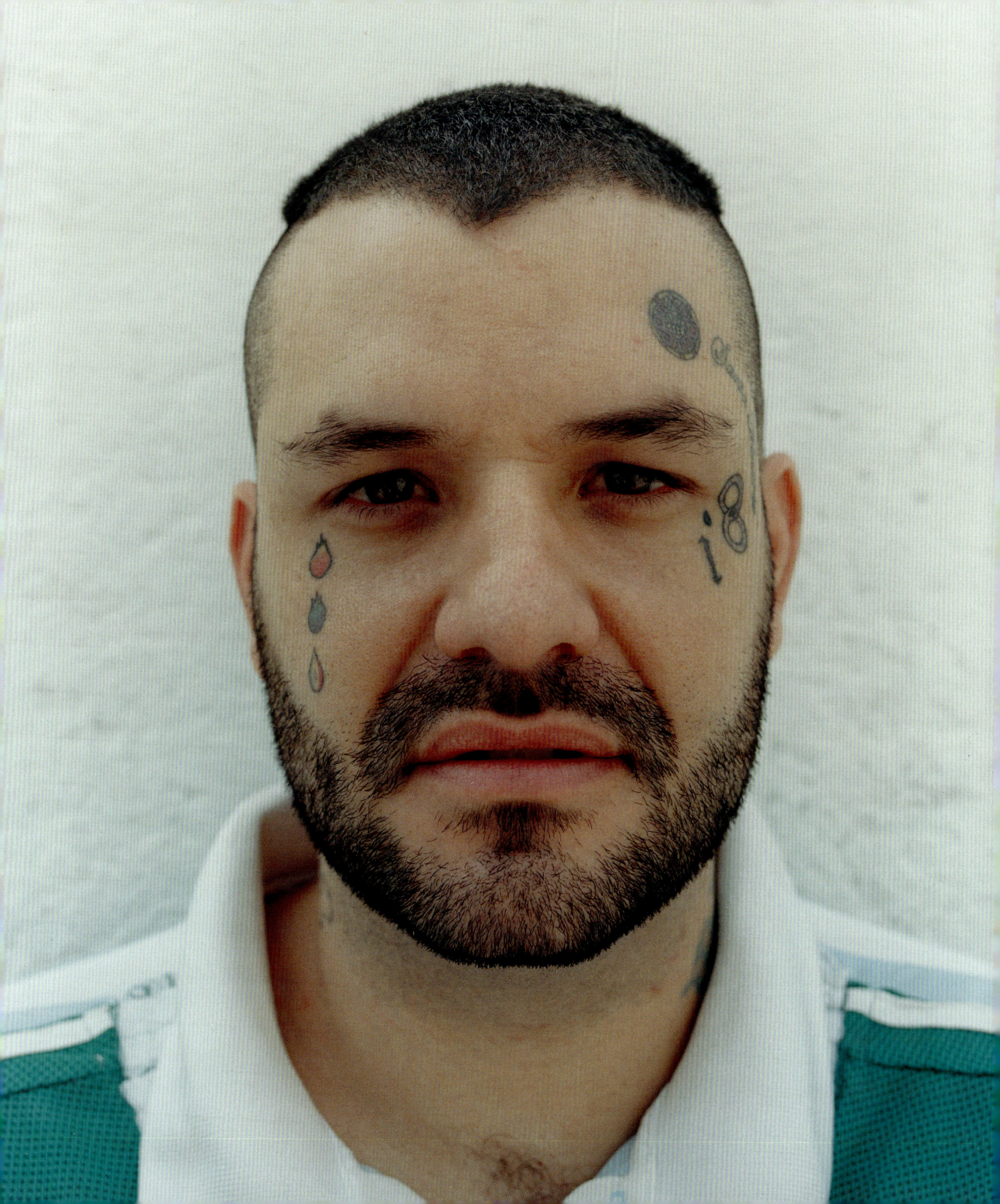

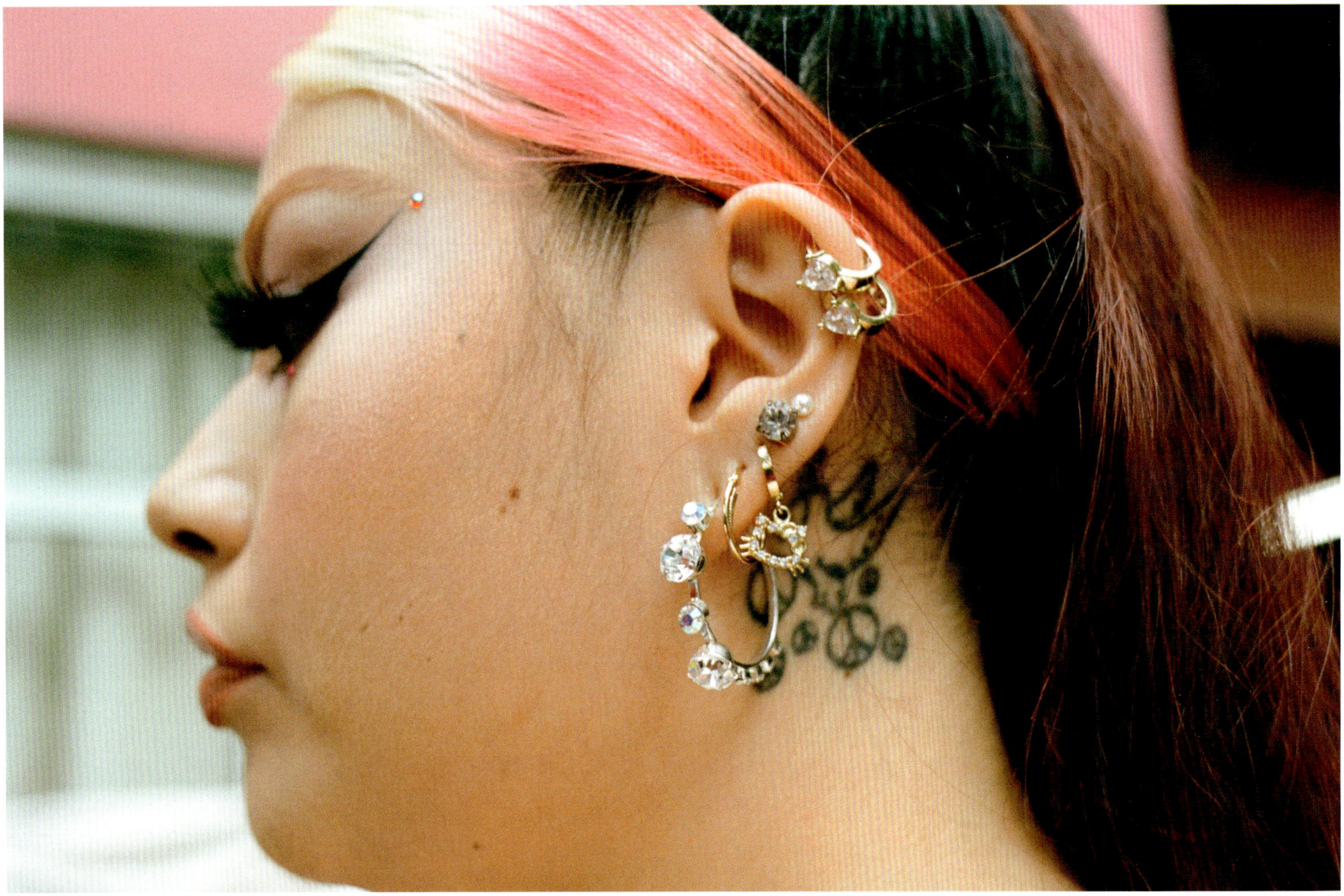

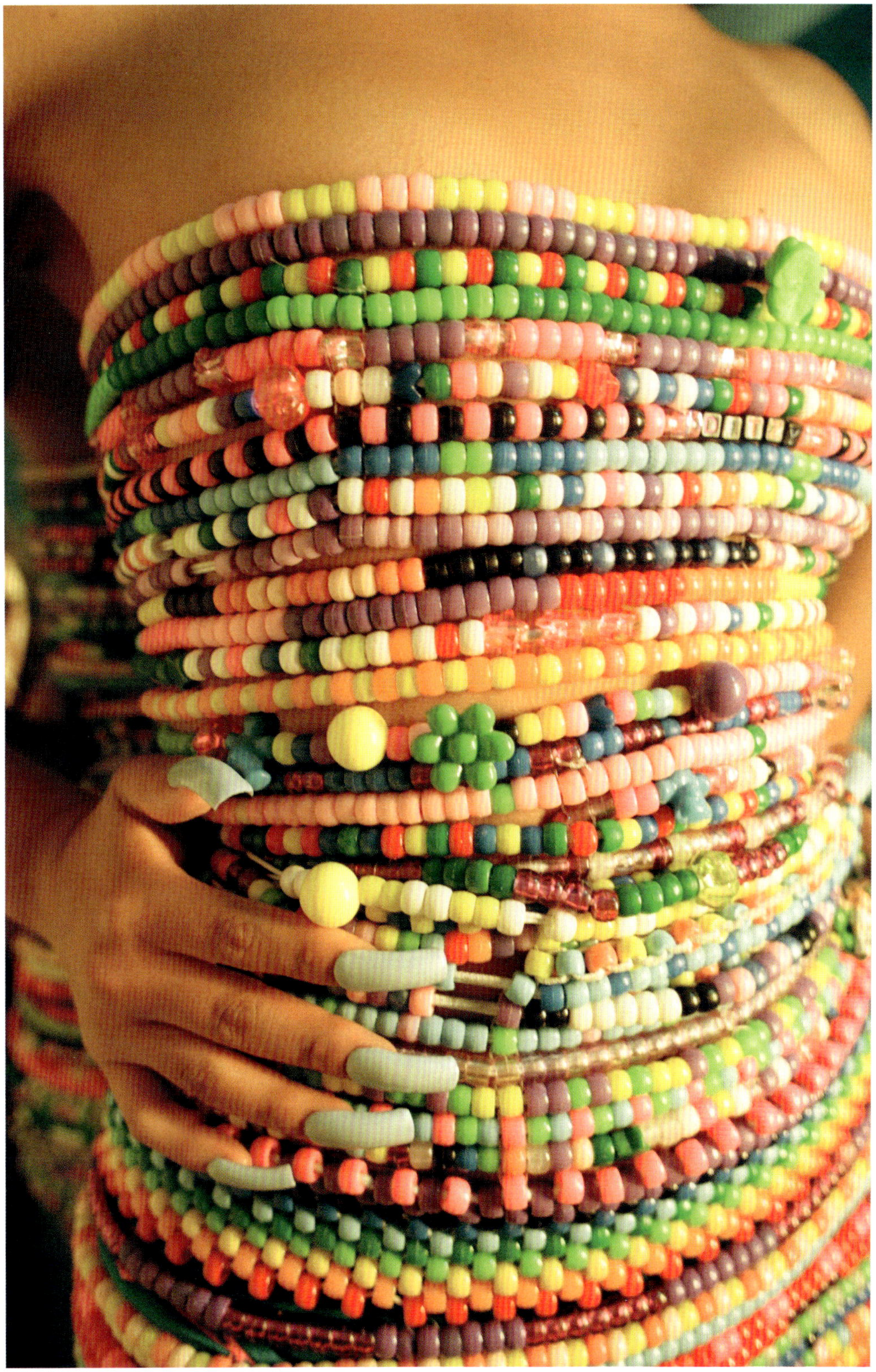

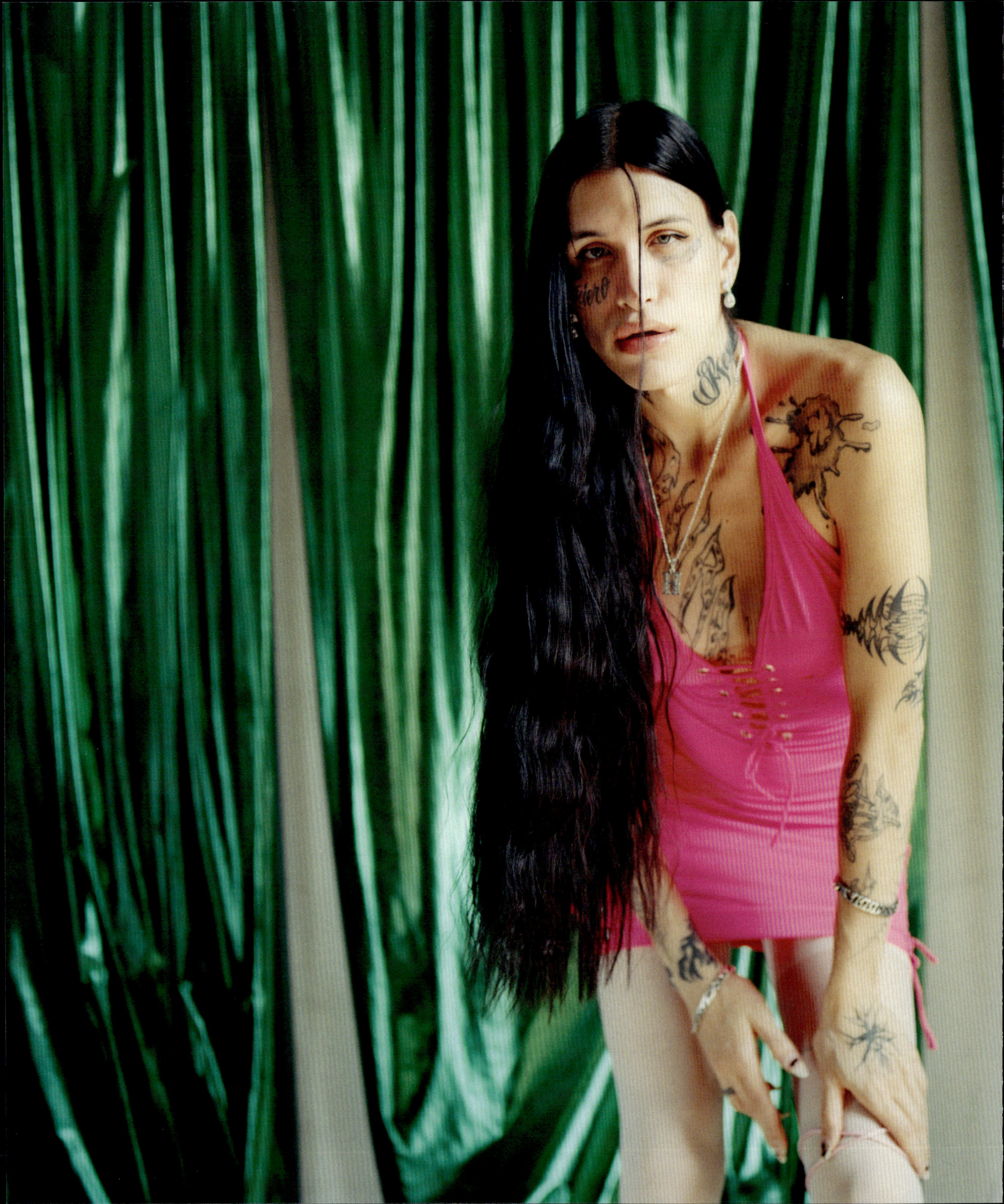

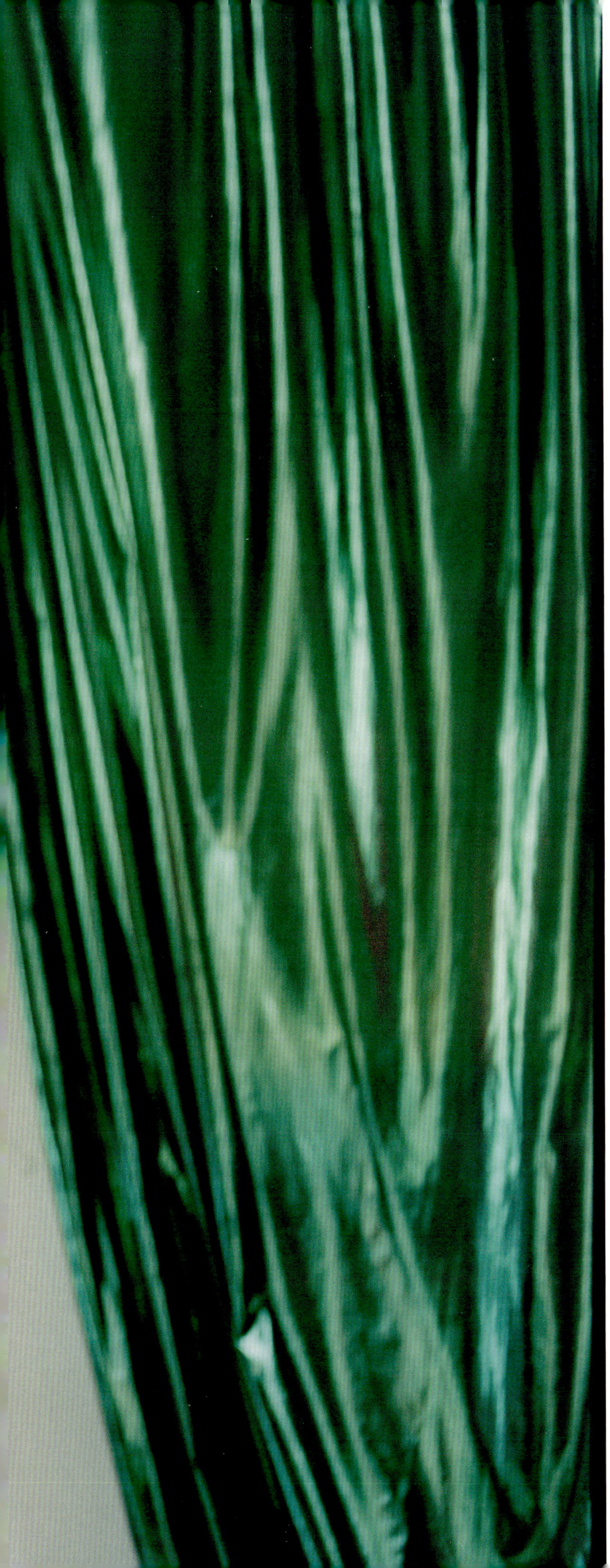

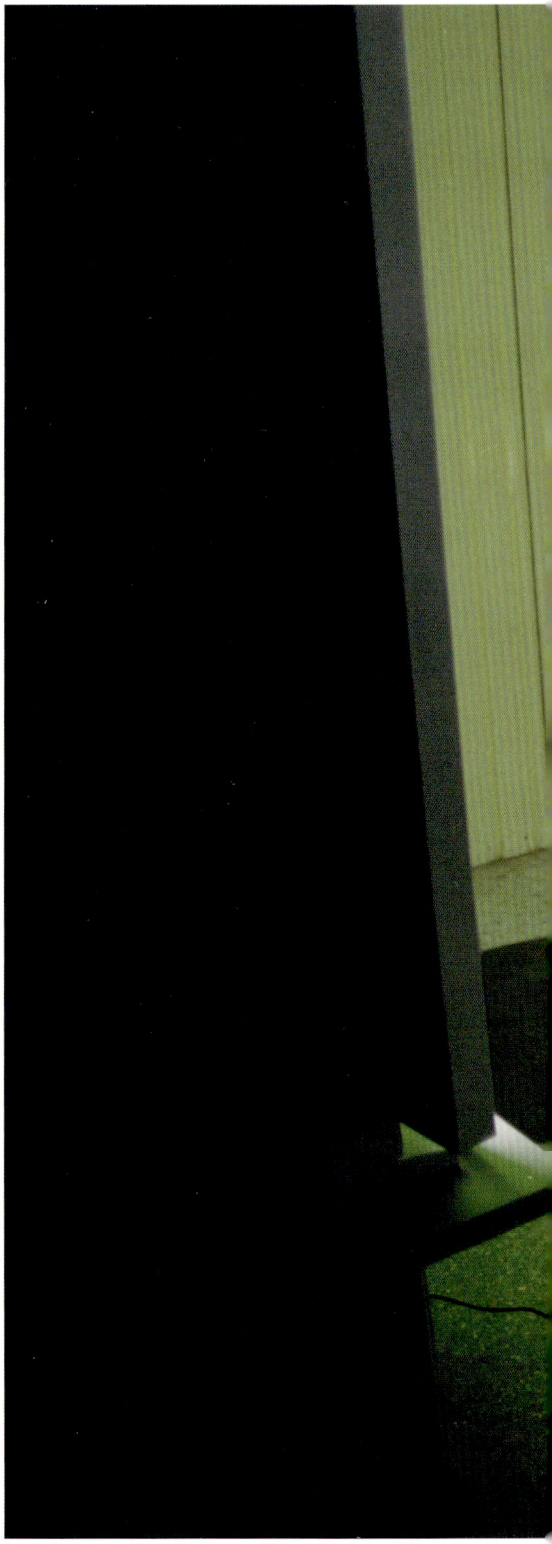

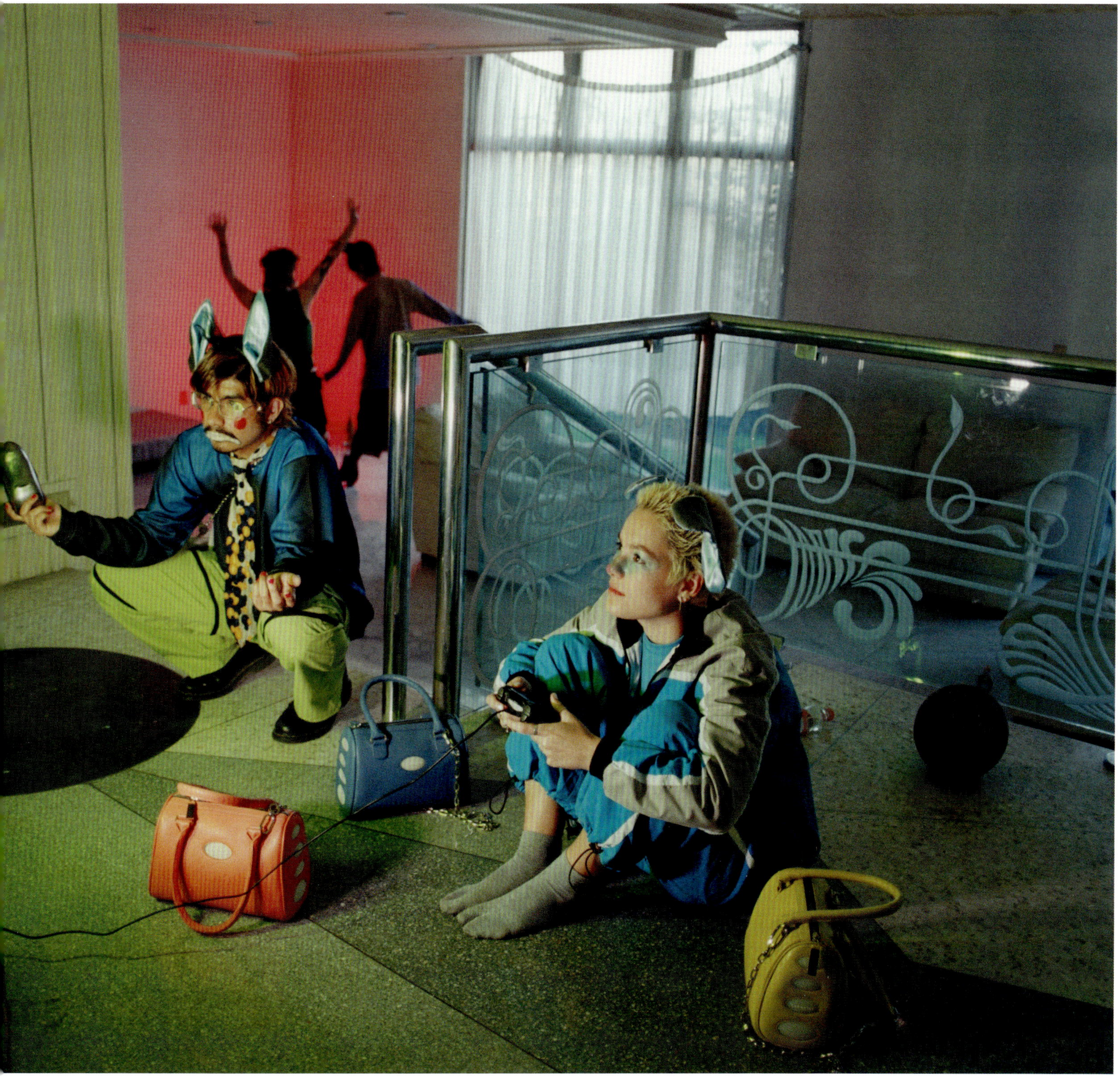

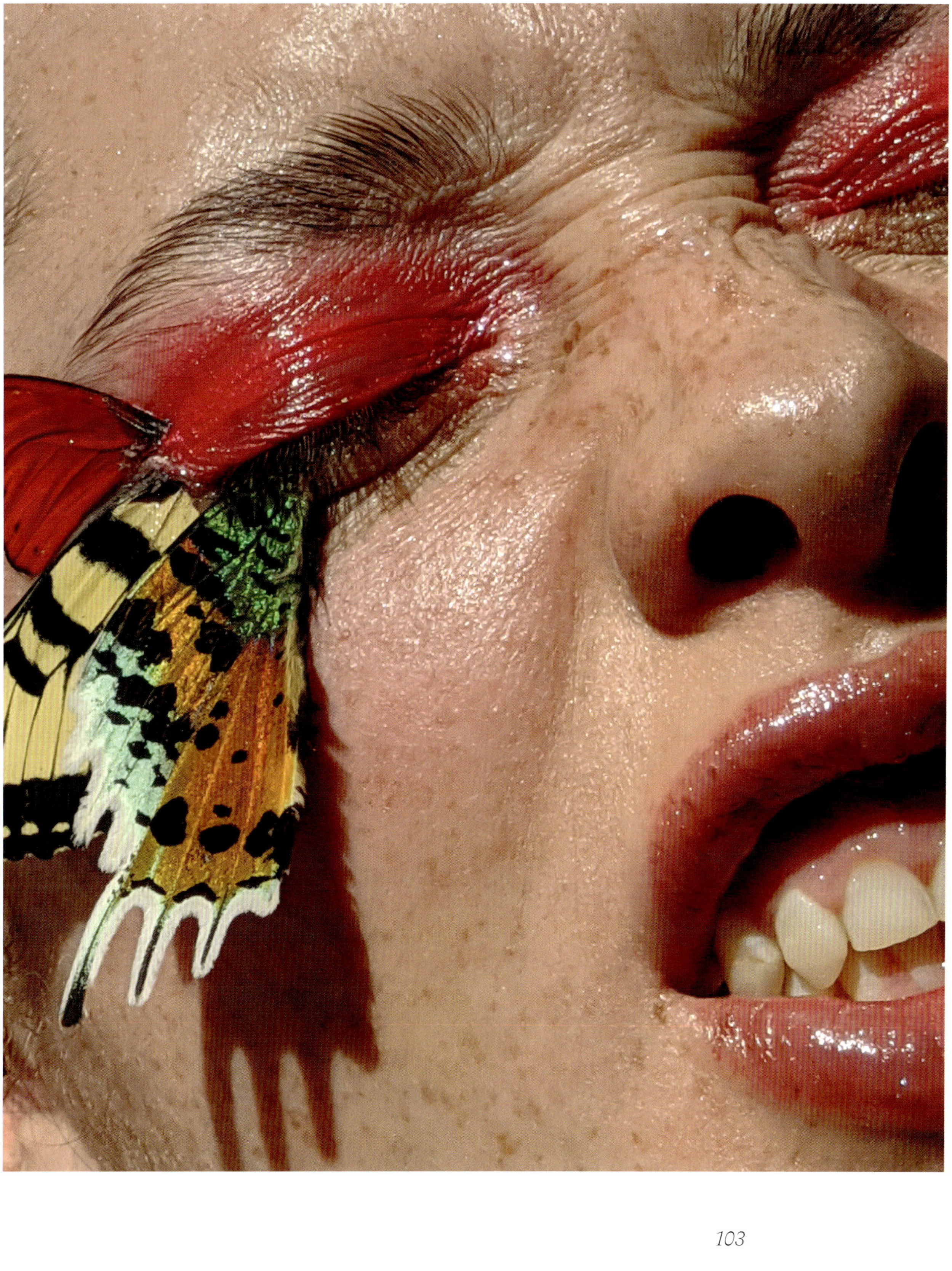

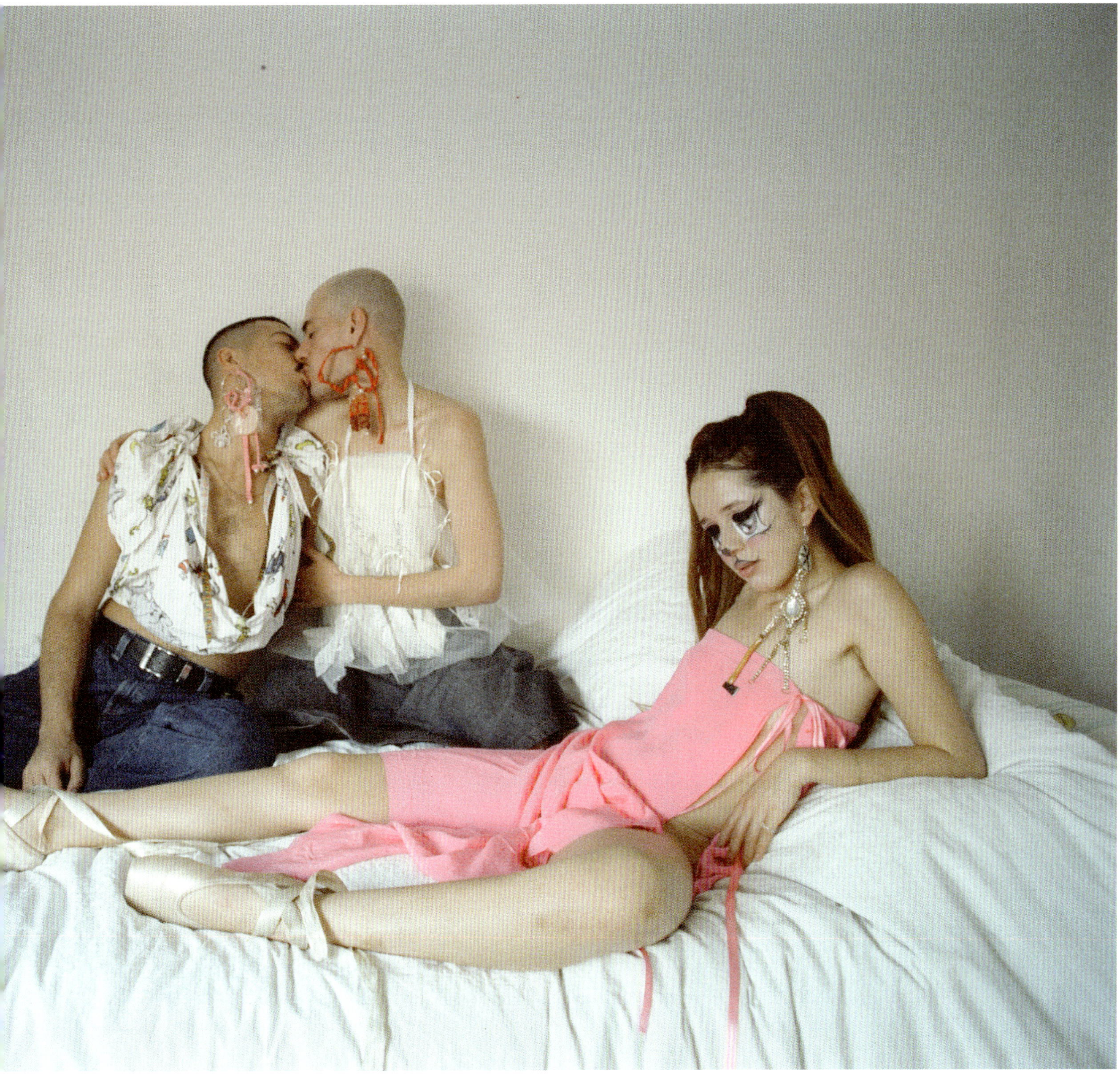

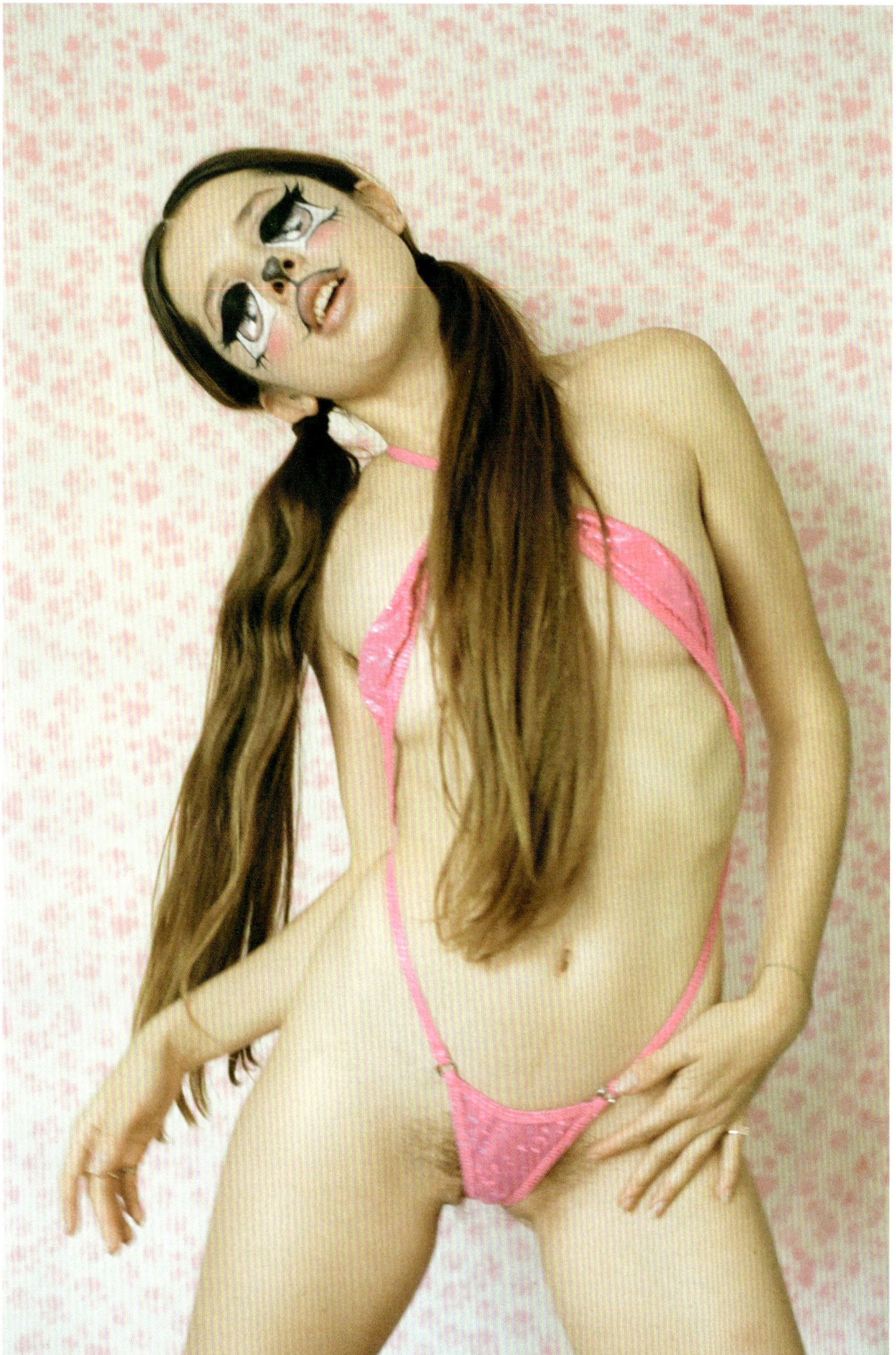

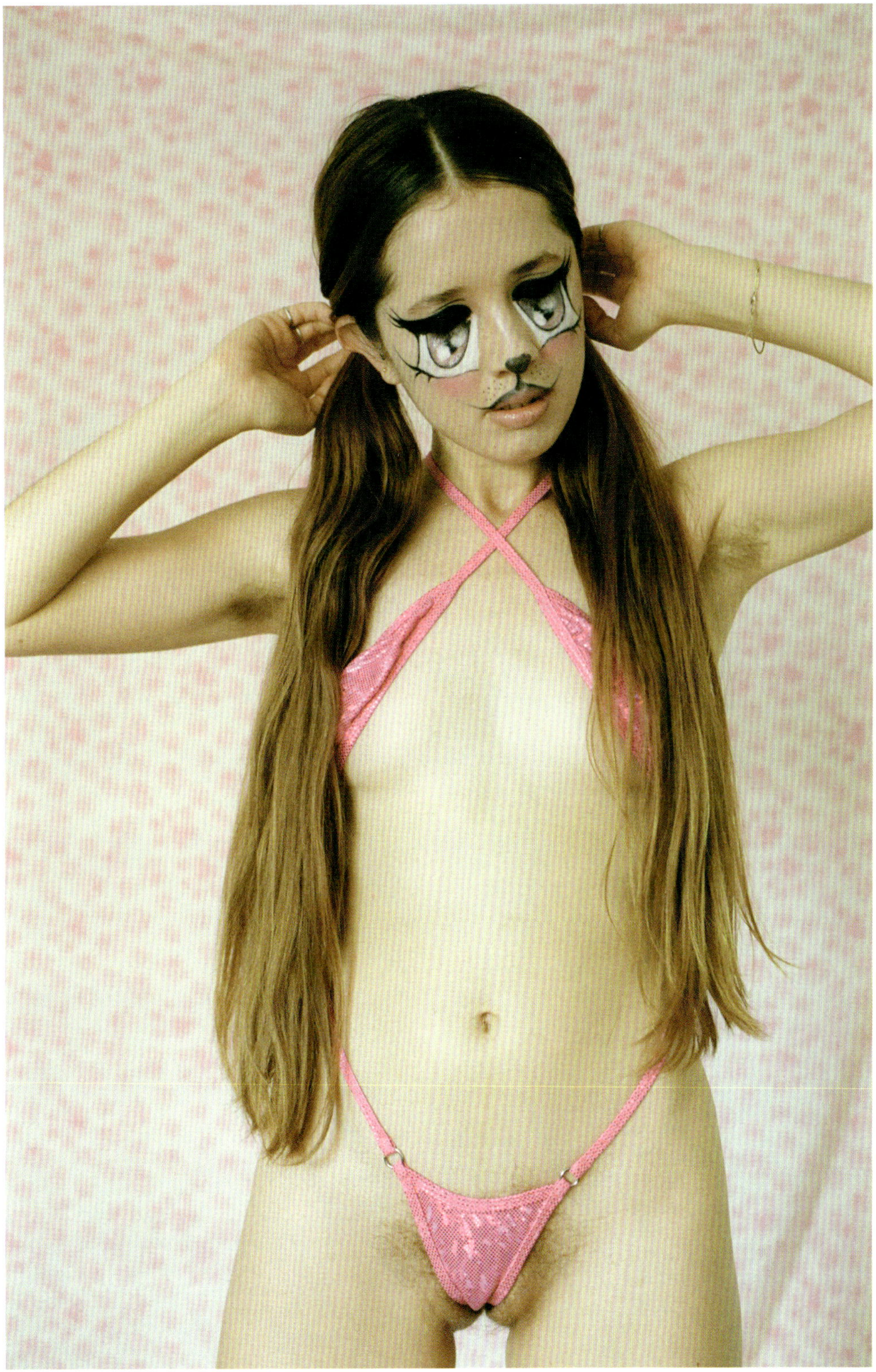

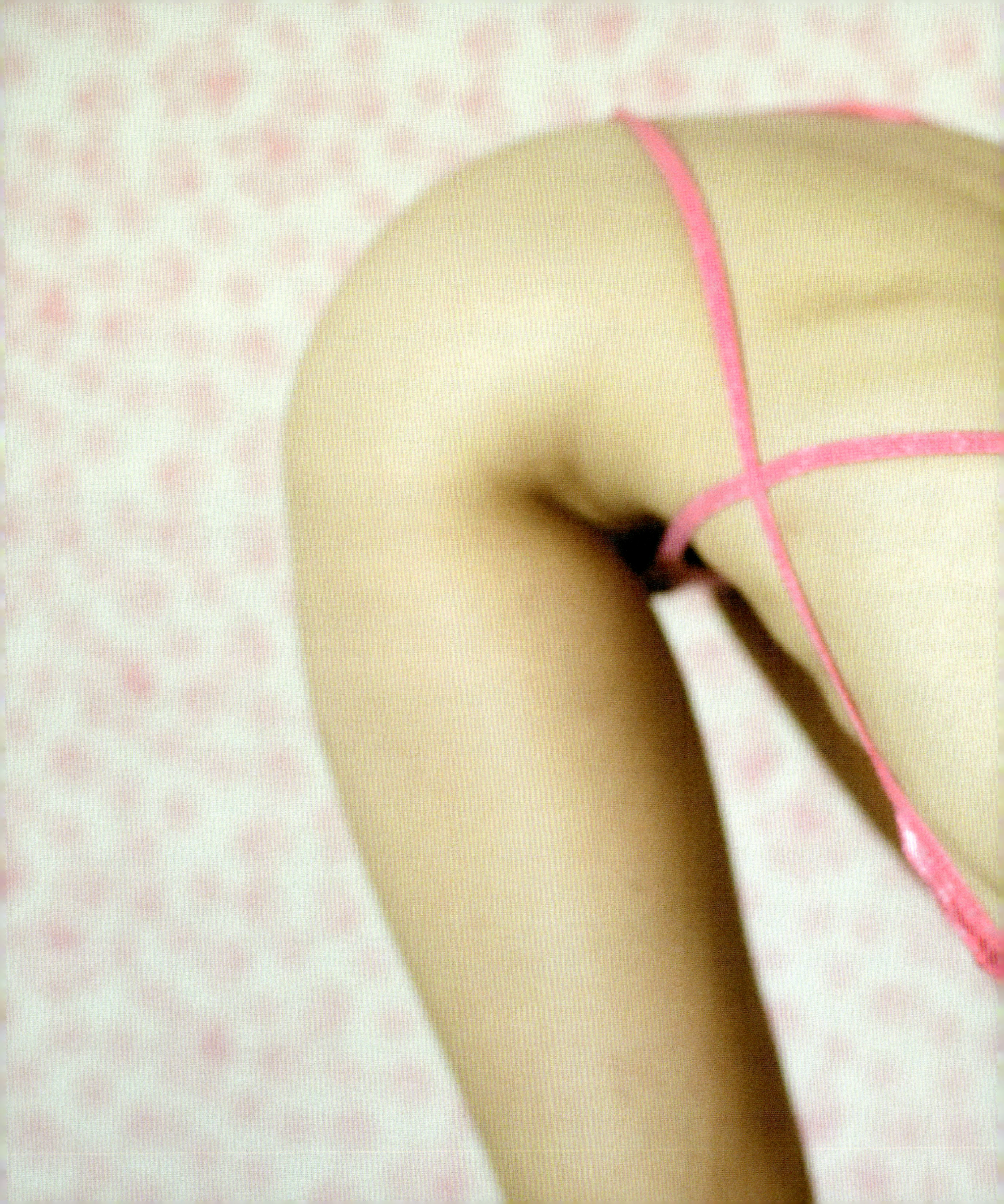

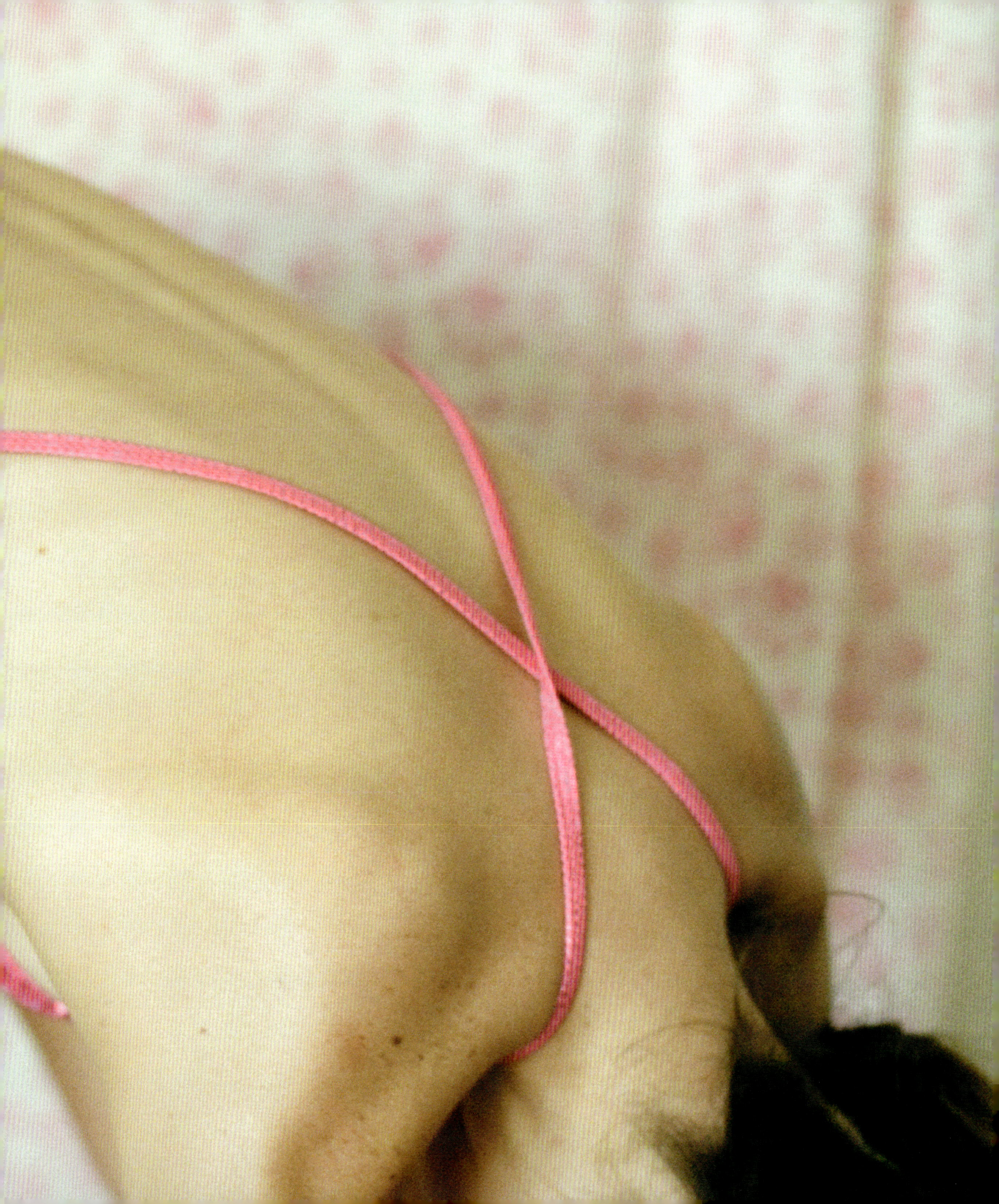

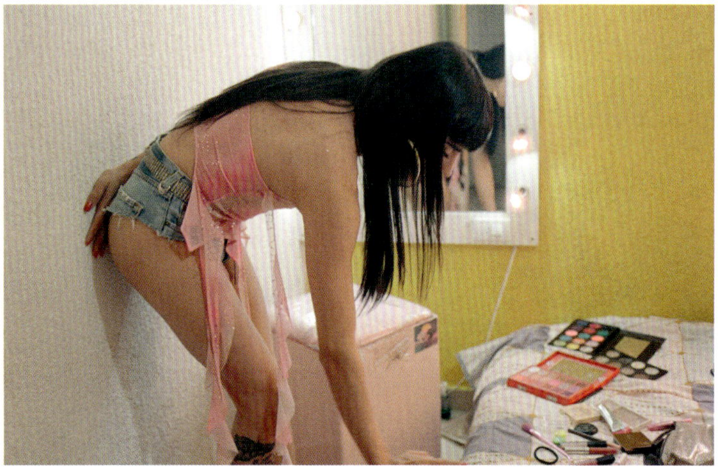

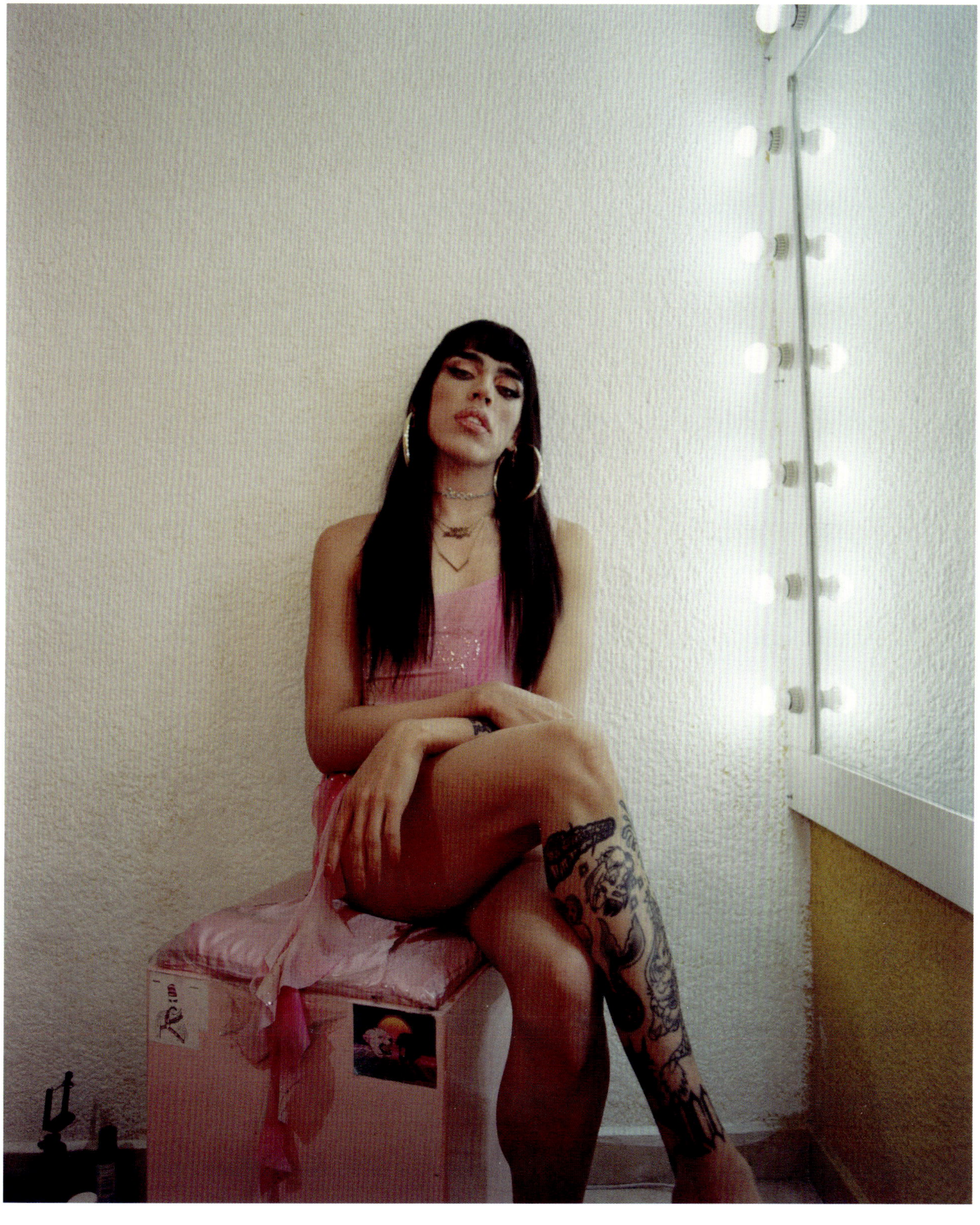

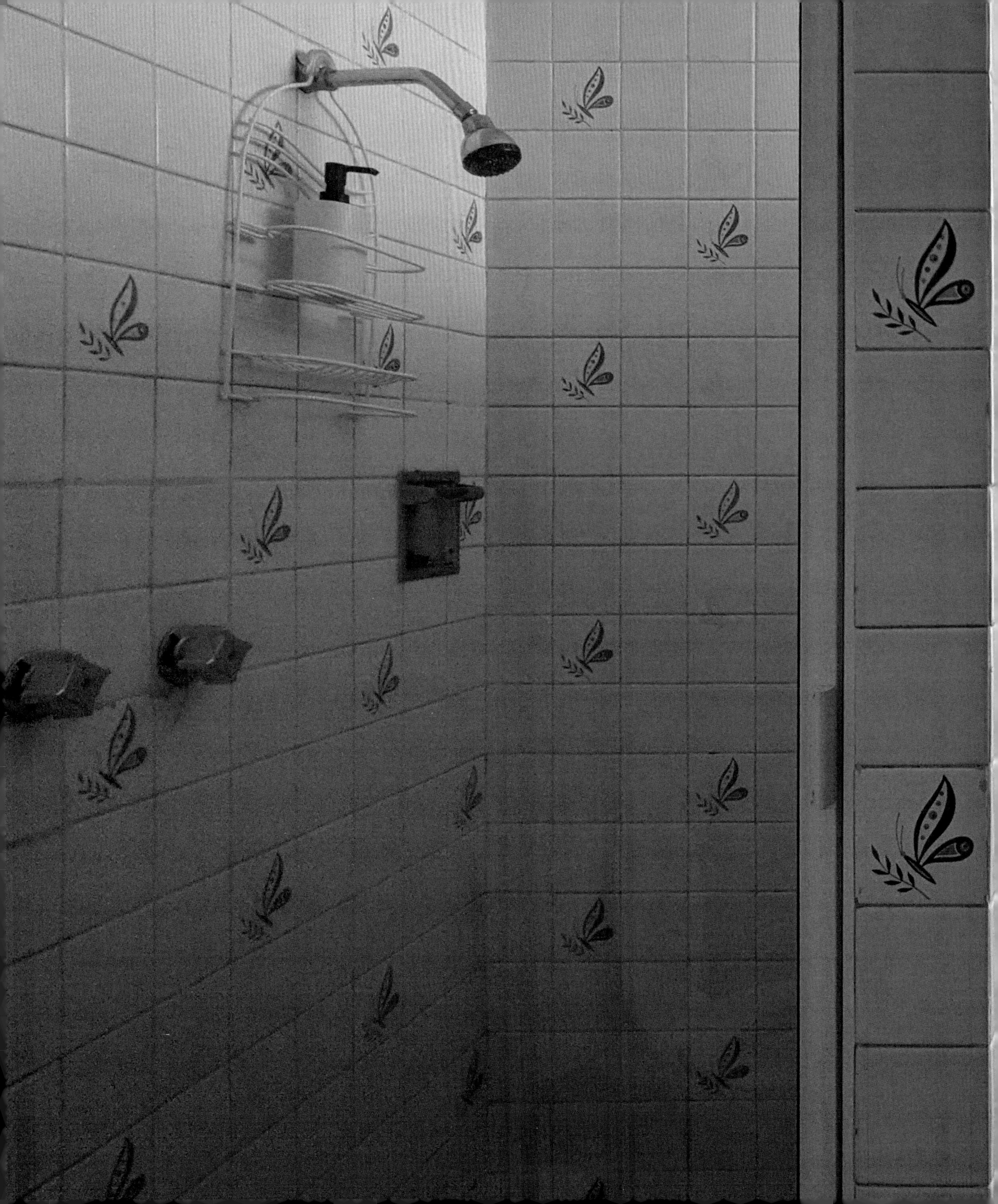

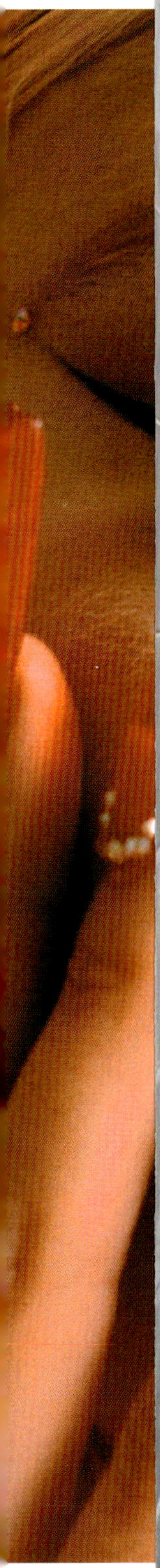
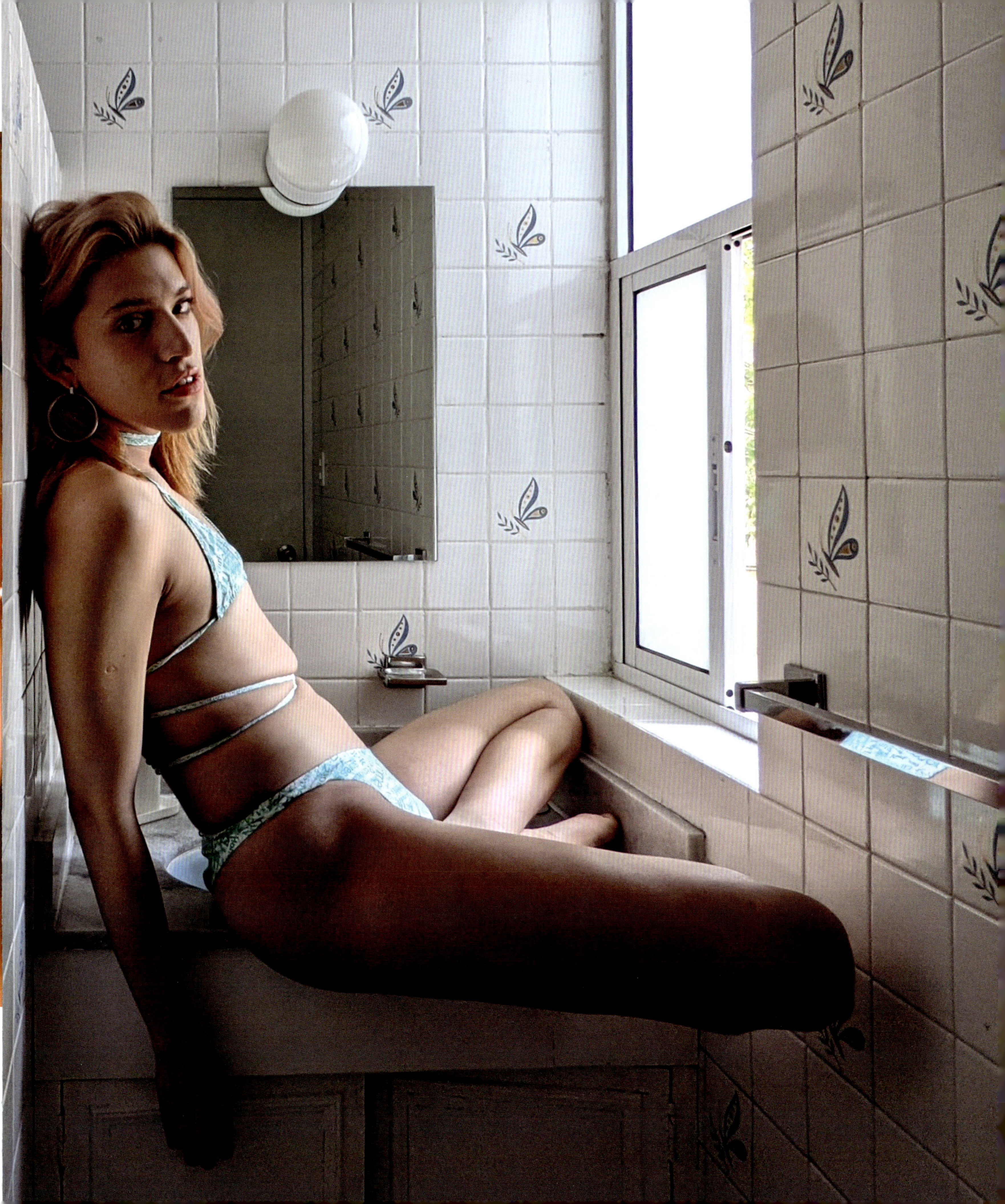

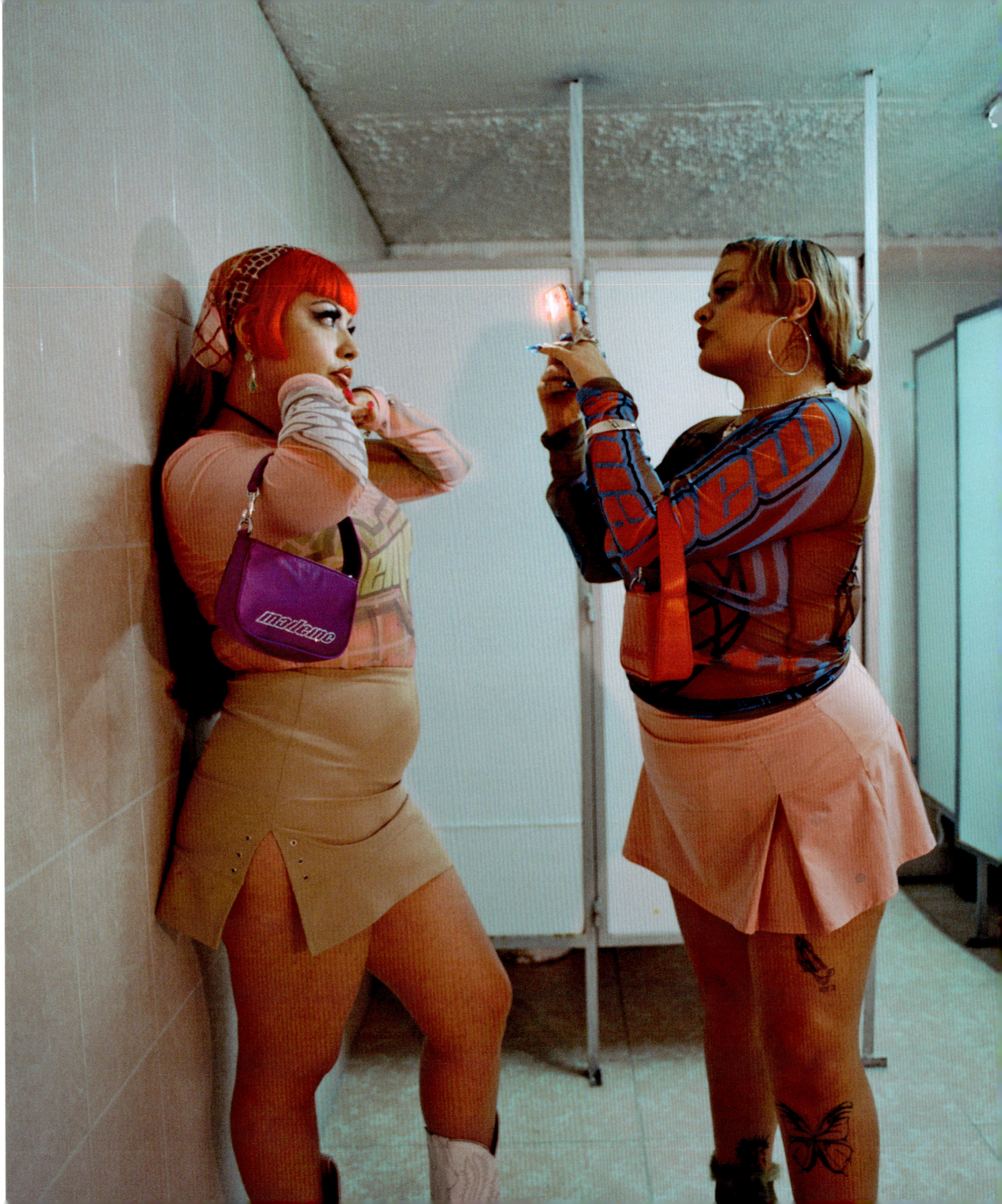

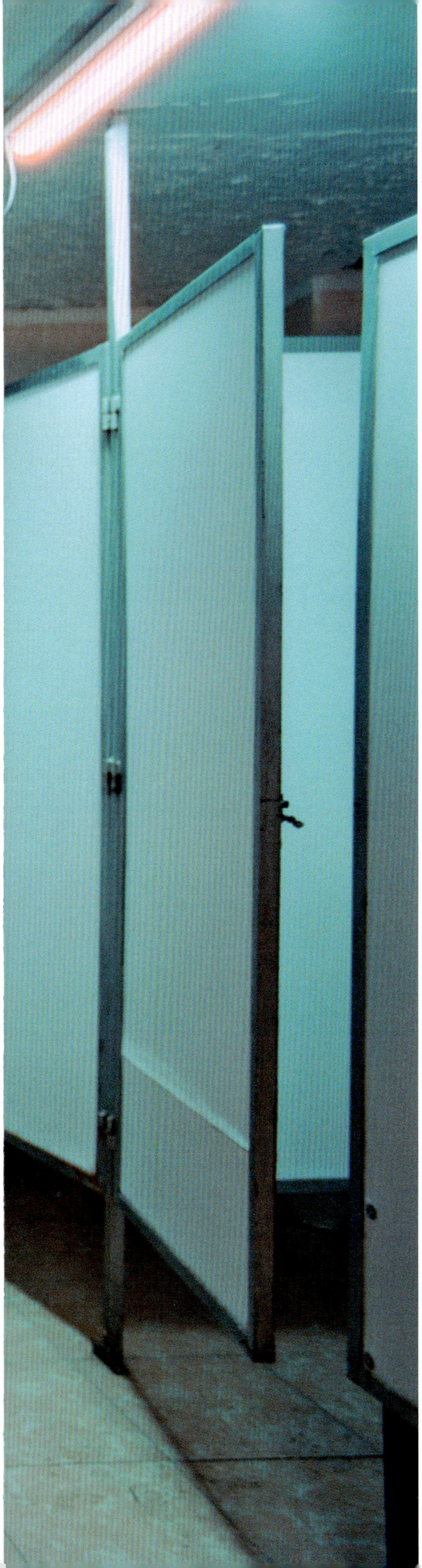

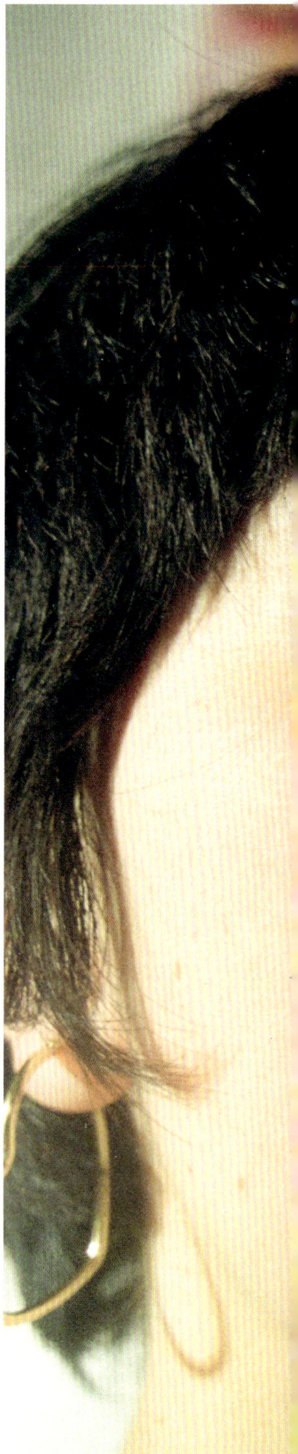

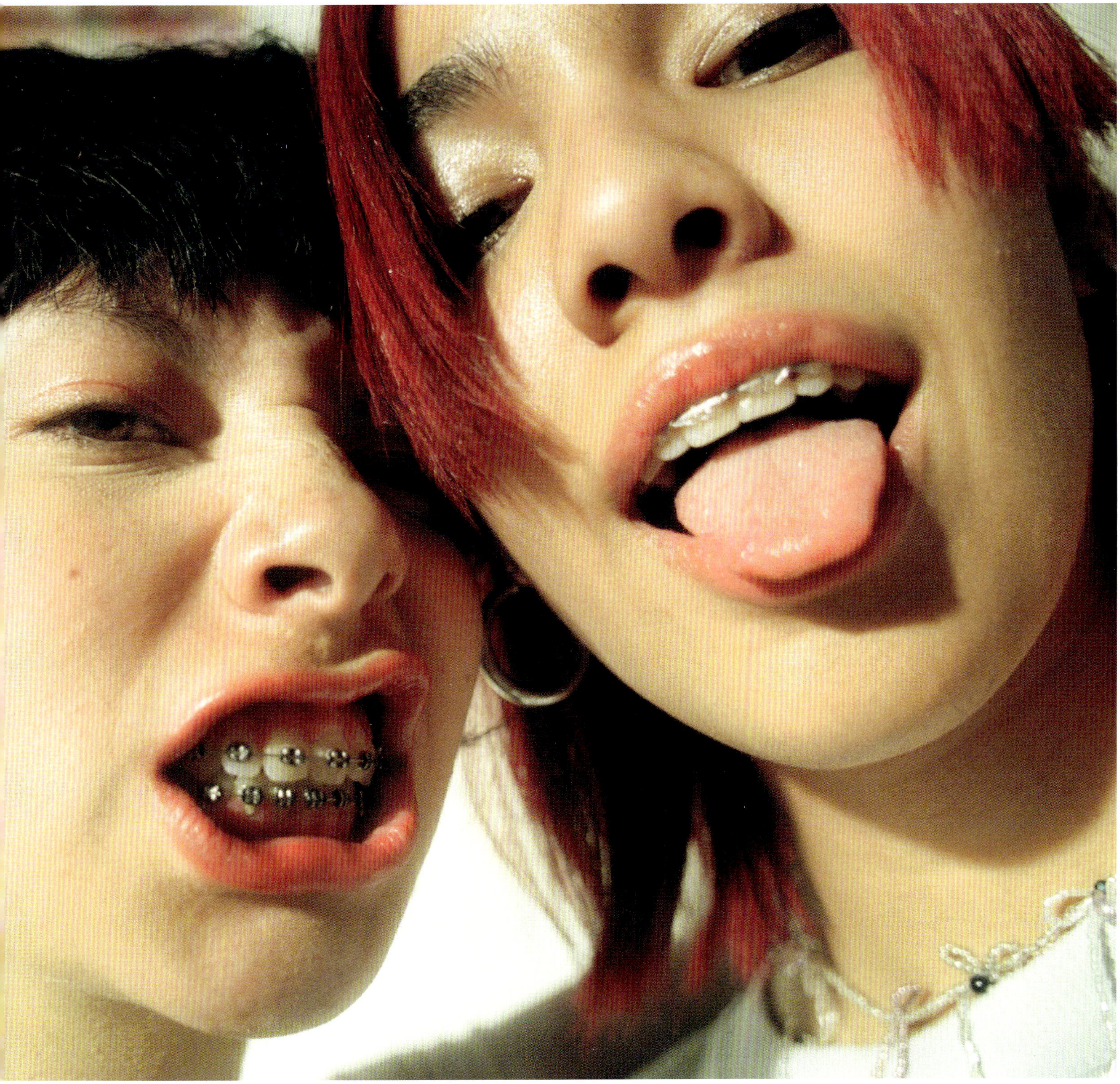

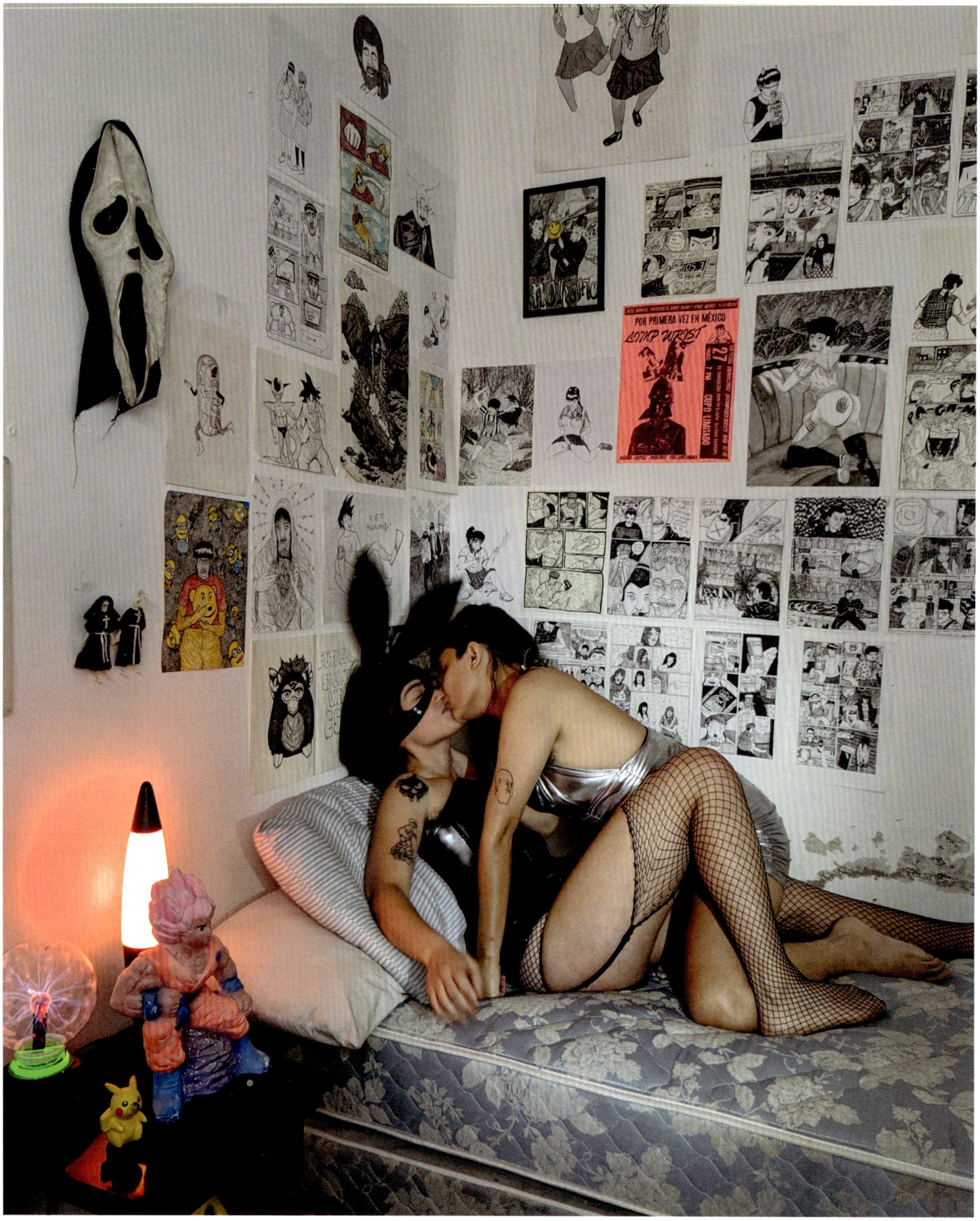

POR PRIMERA VEZ EN MÉXICO
LIMP WRIST
27
7 PM
CUPO LIMITADO

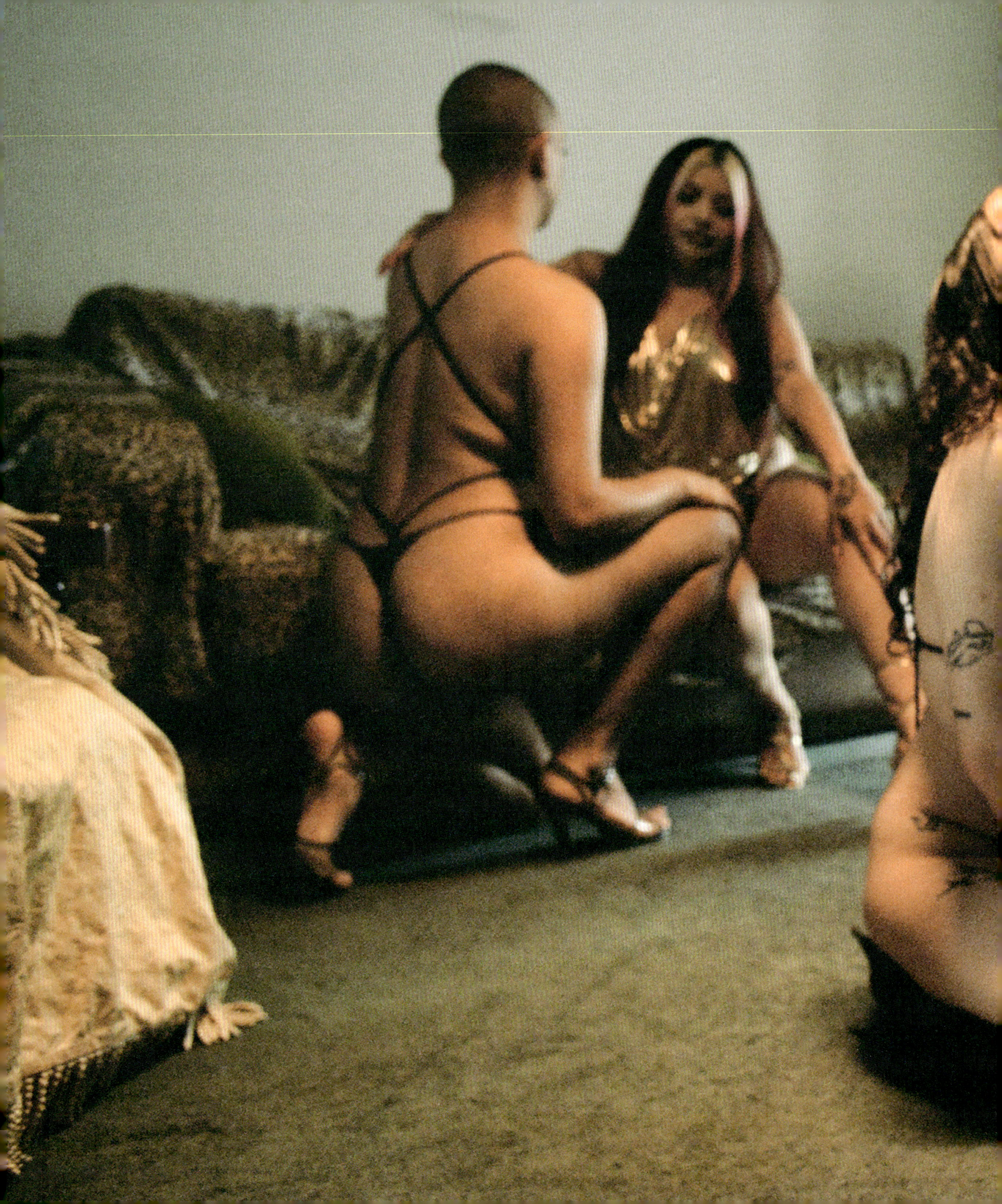

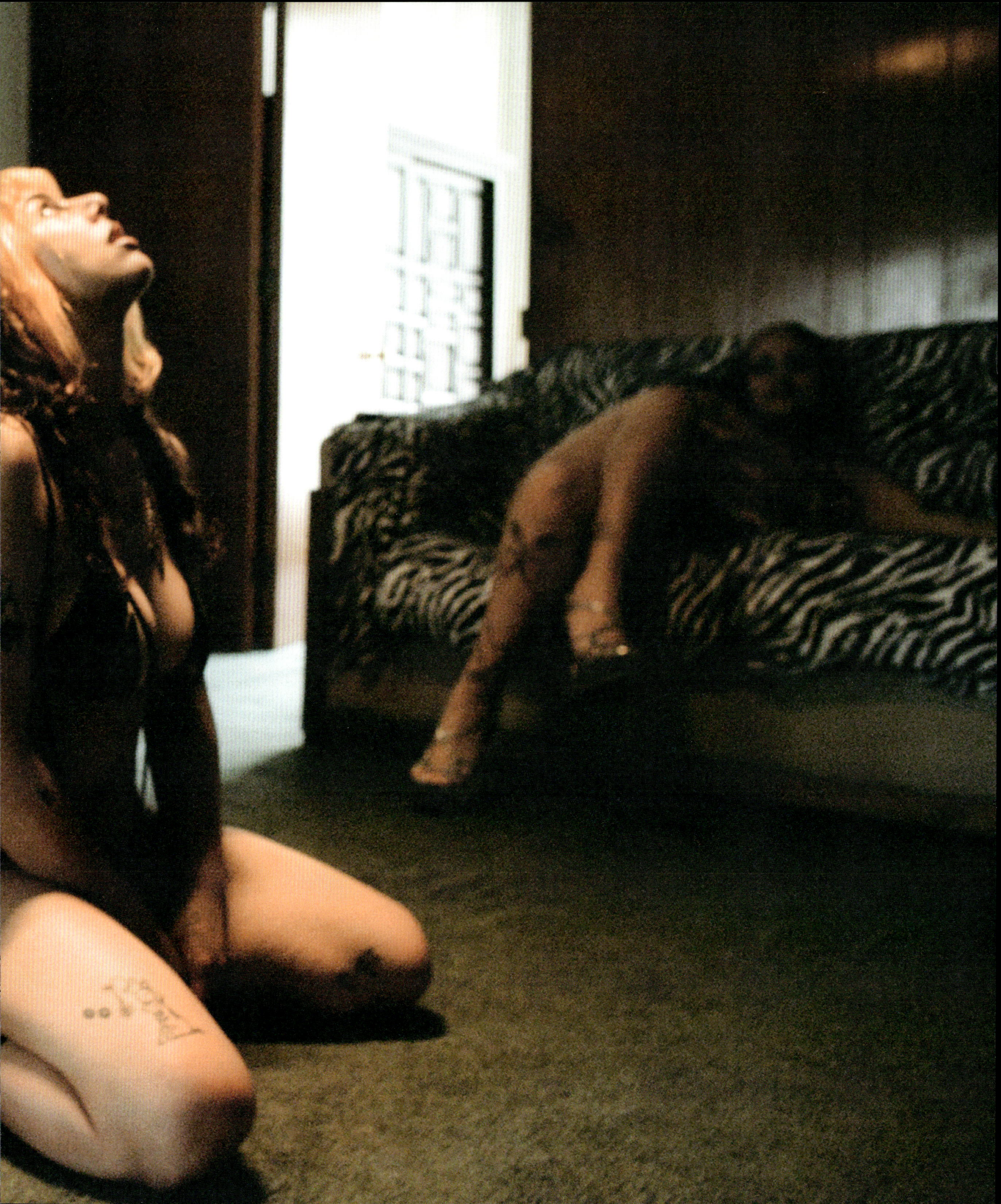

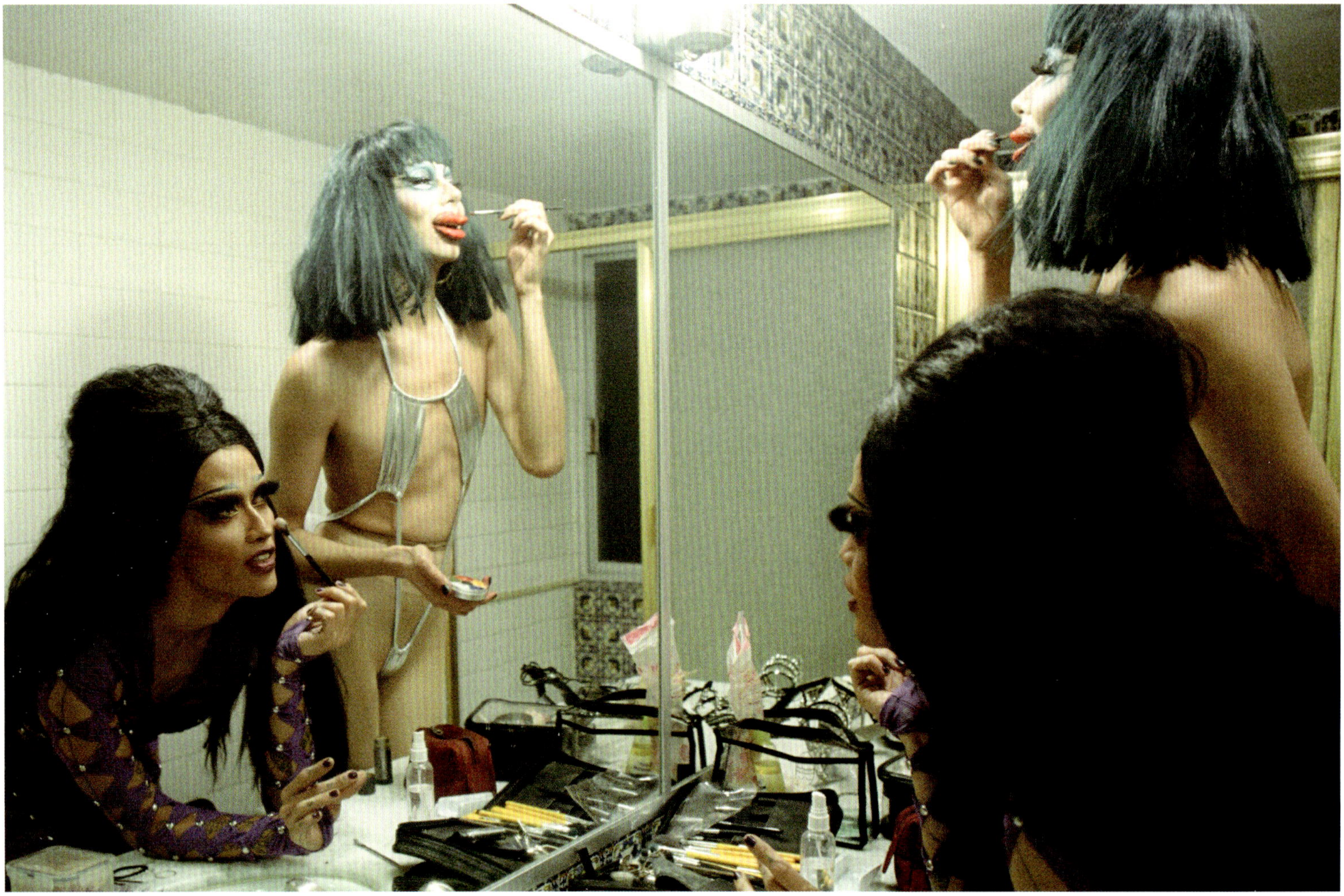

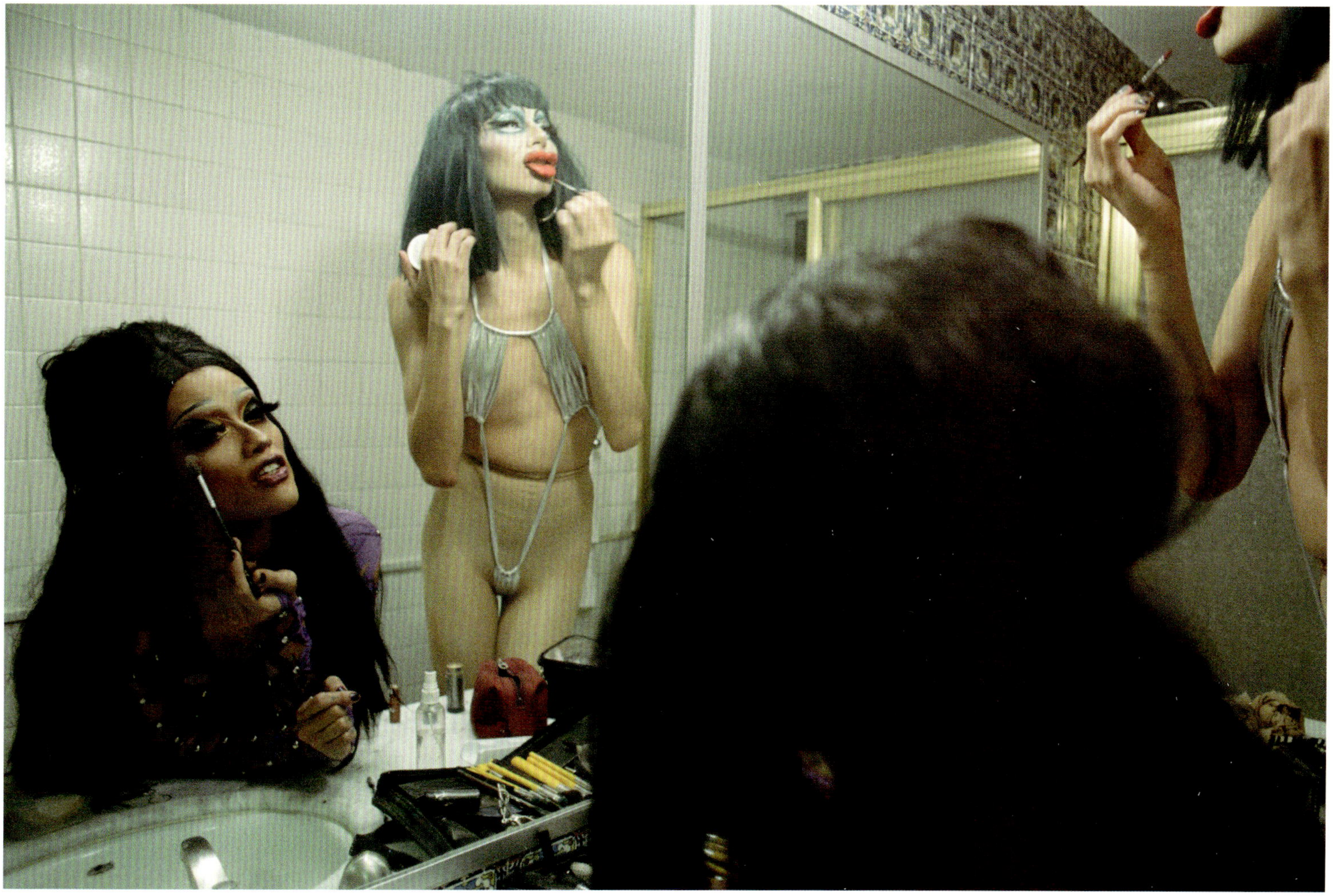

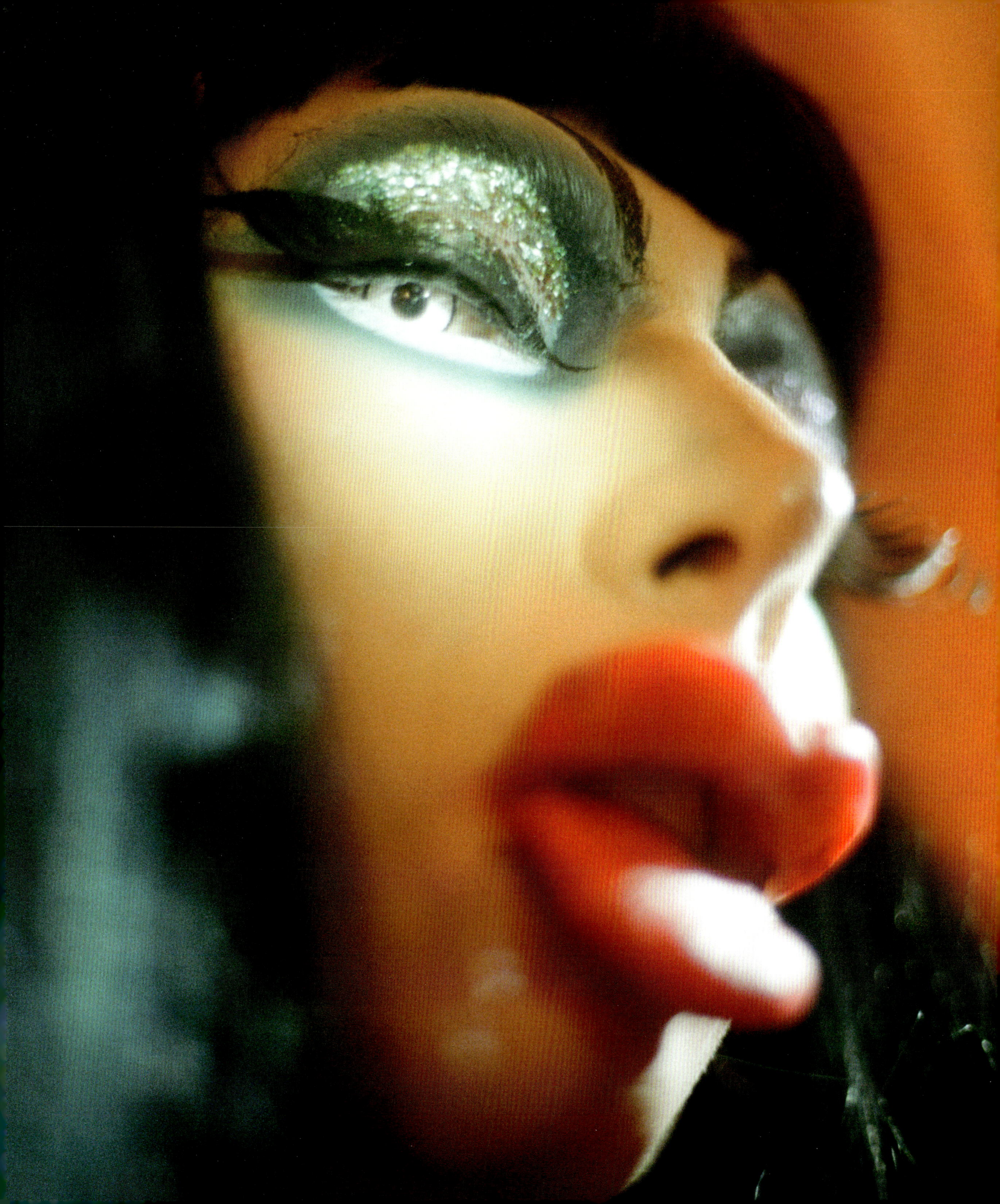

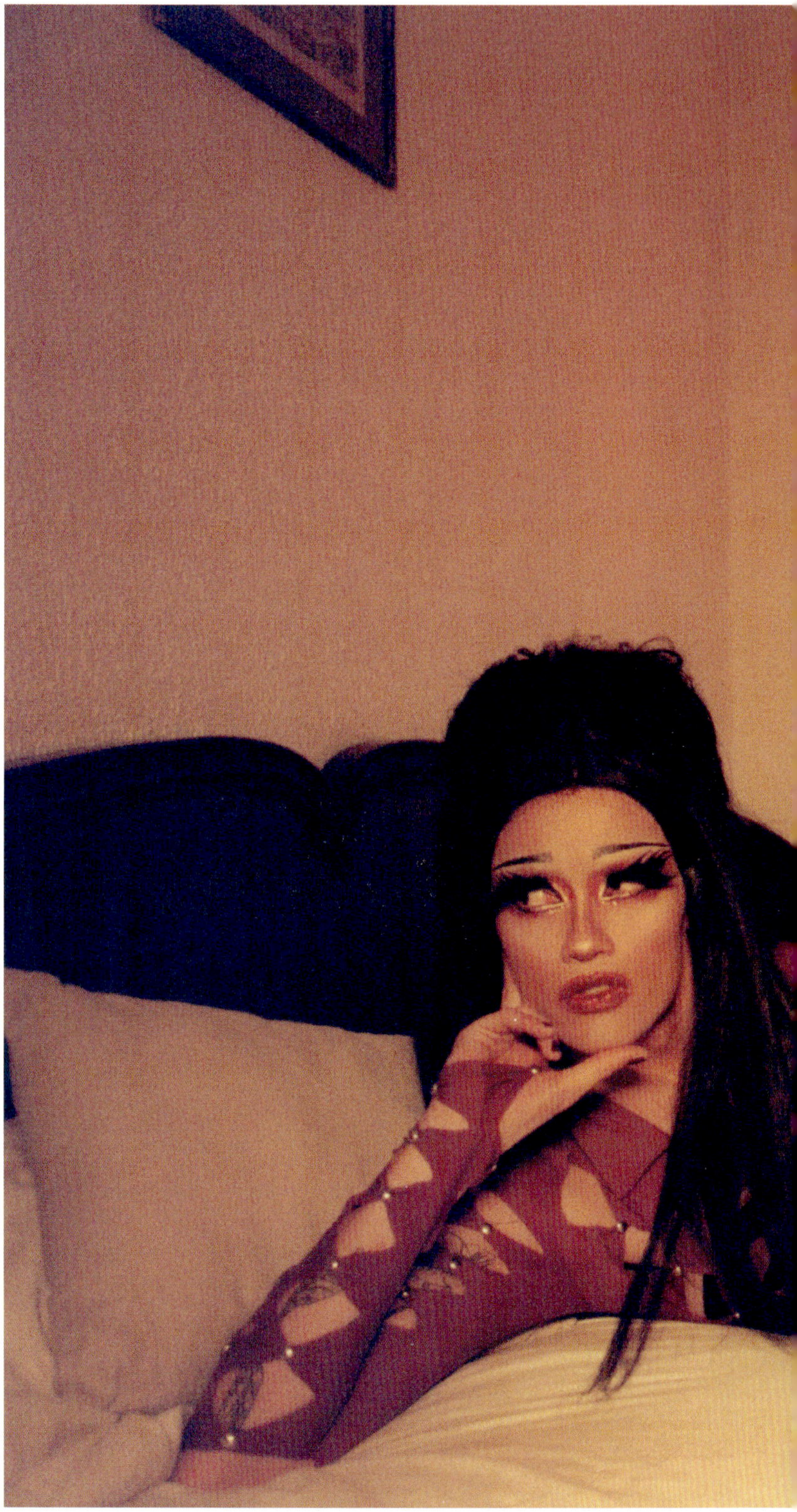

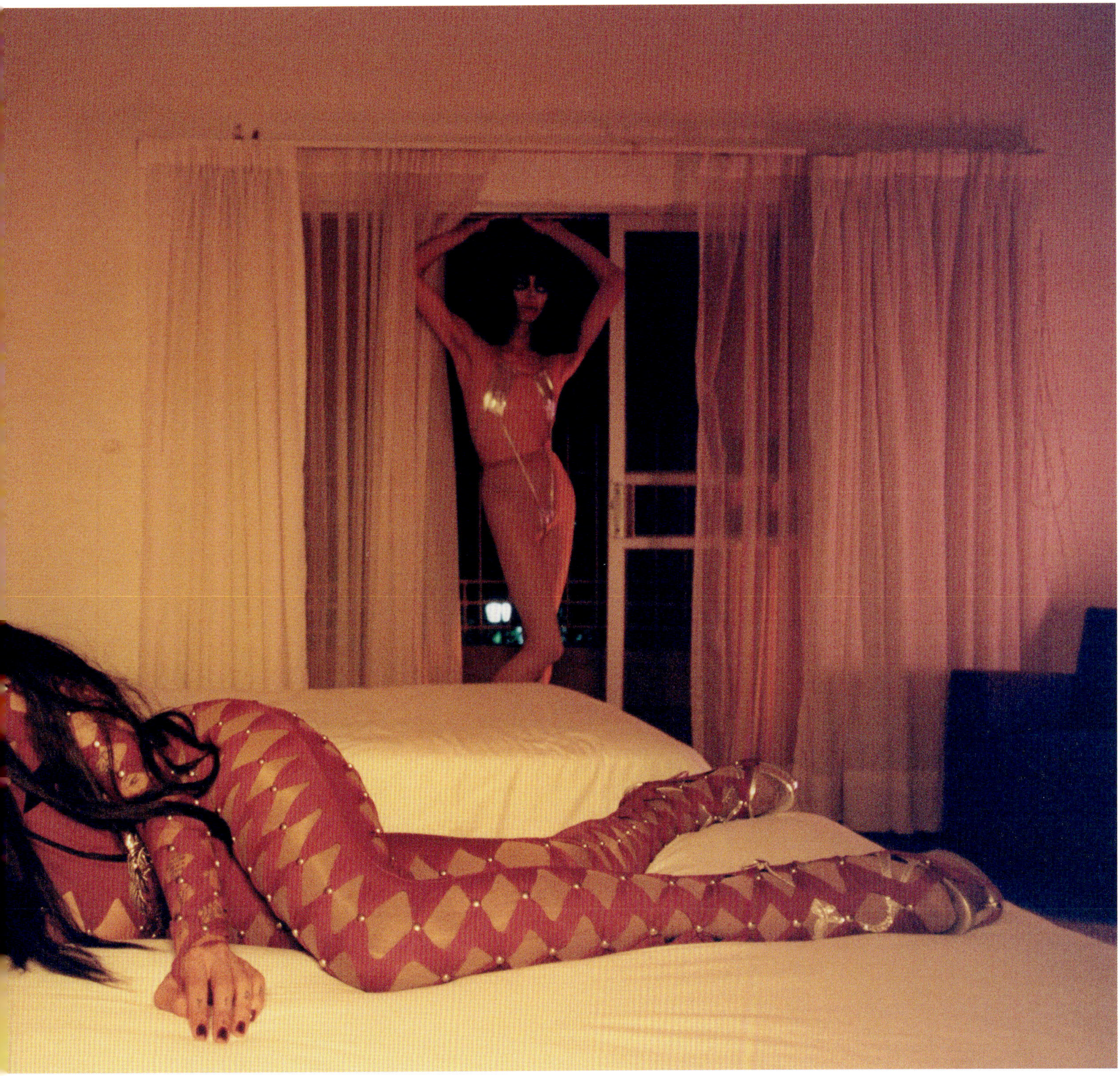

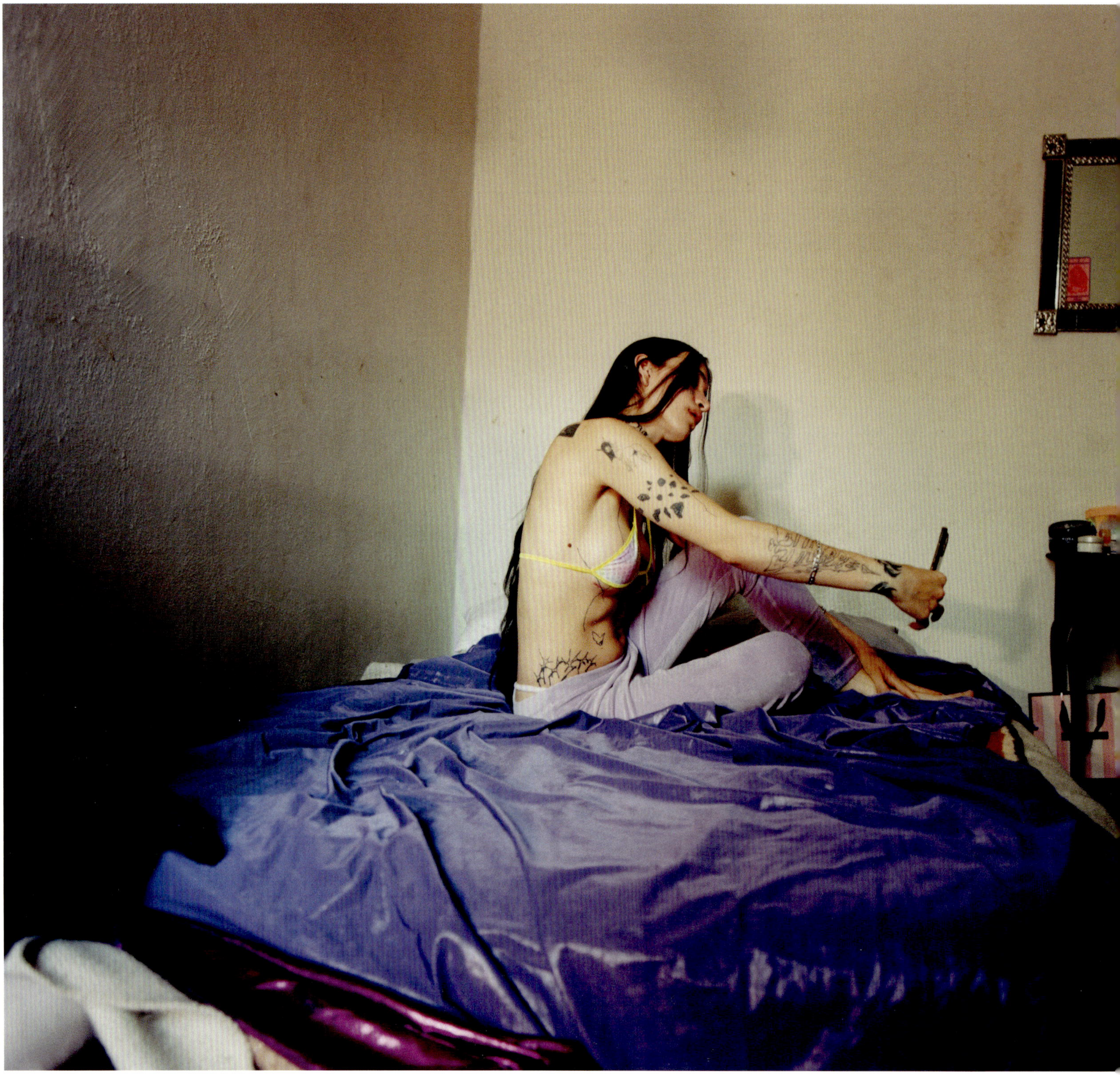

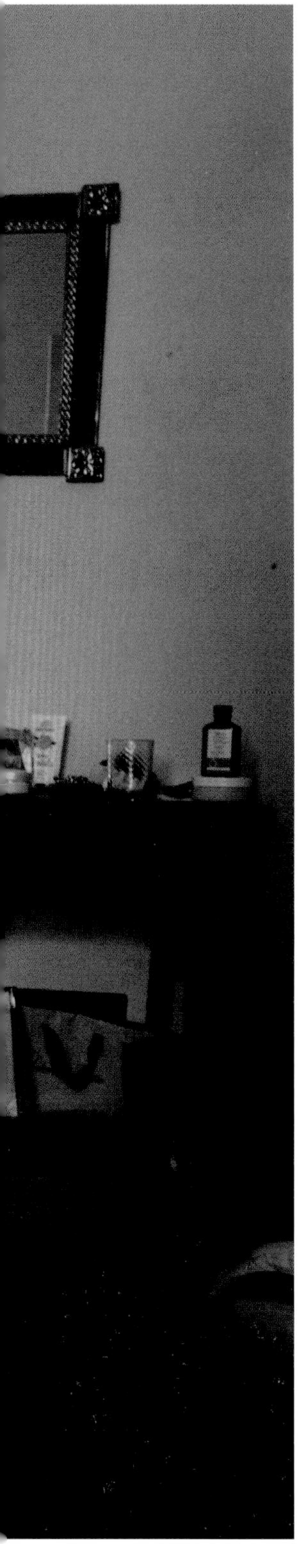

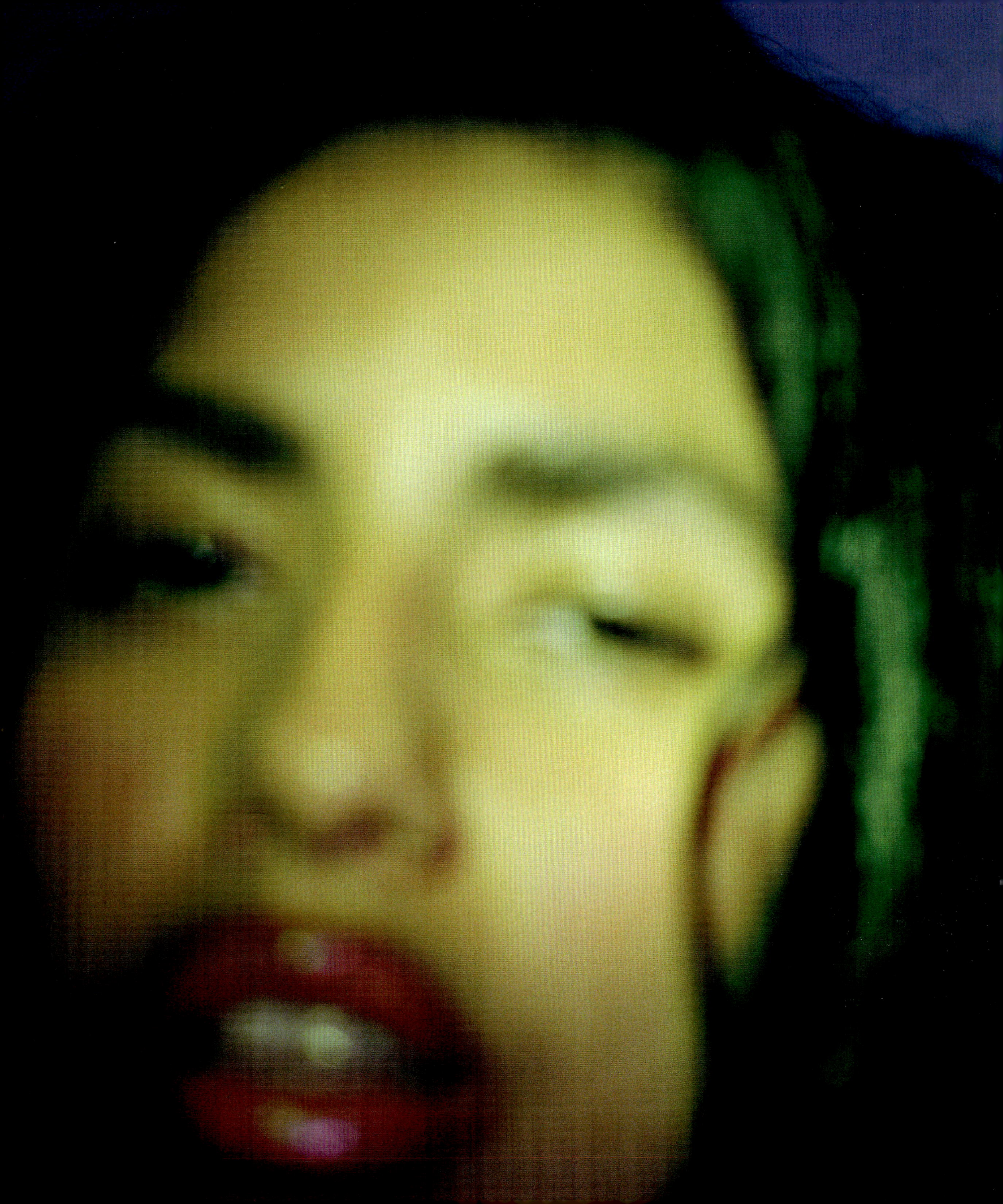

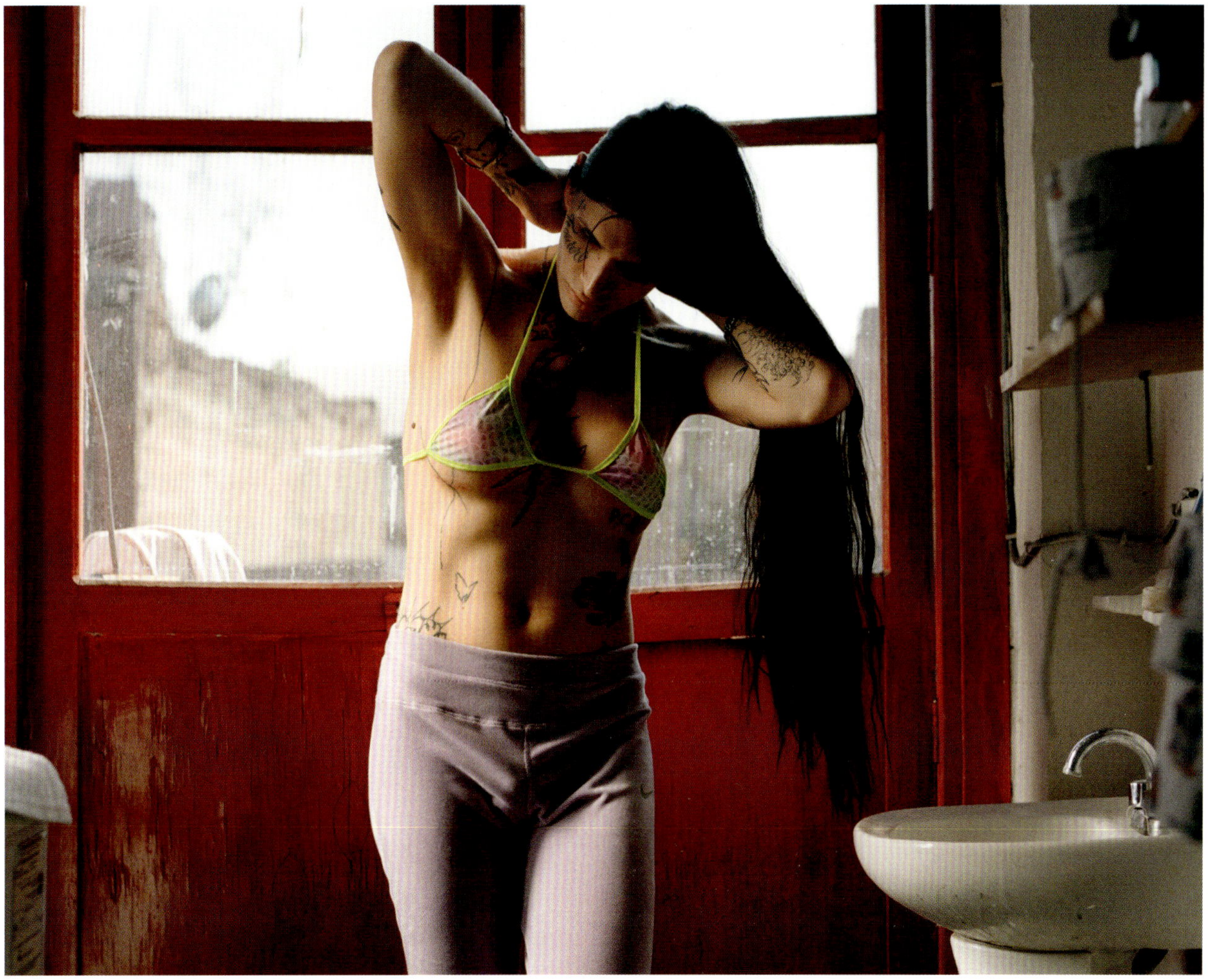

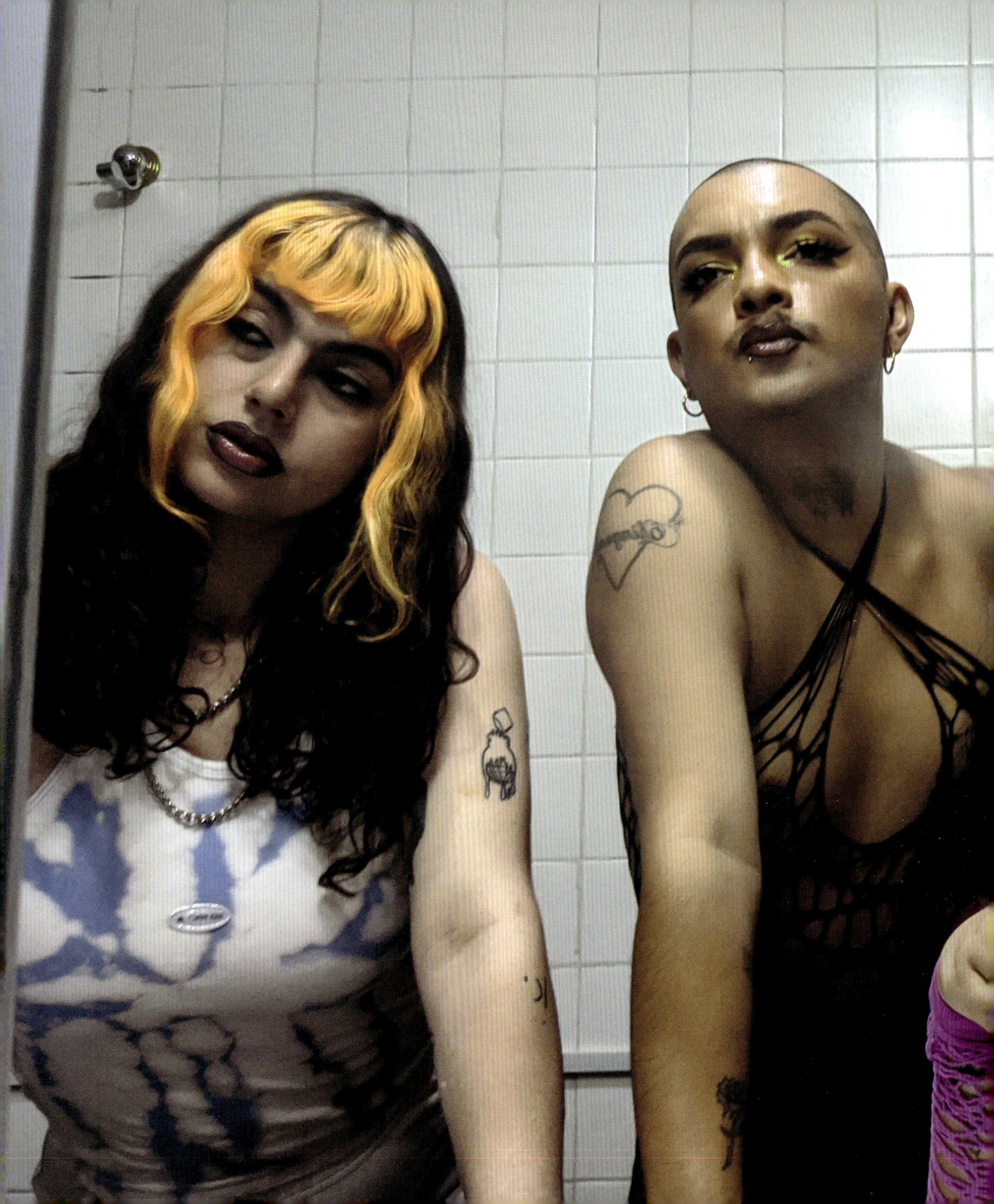

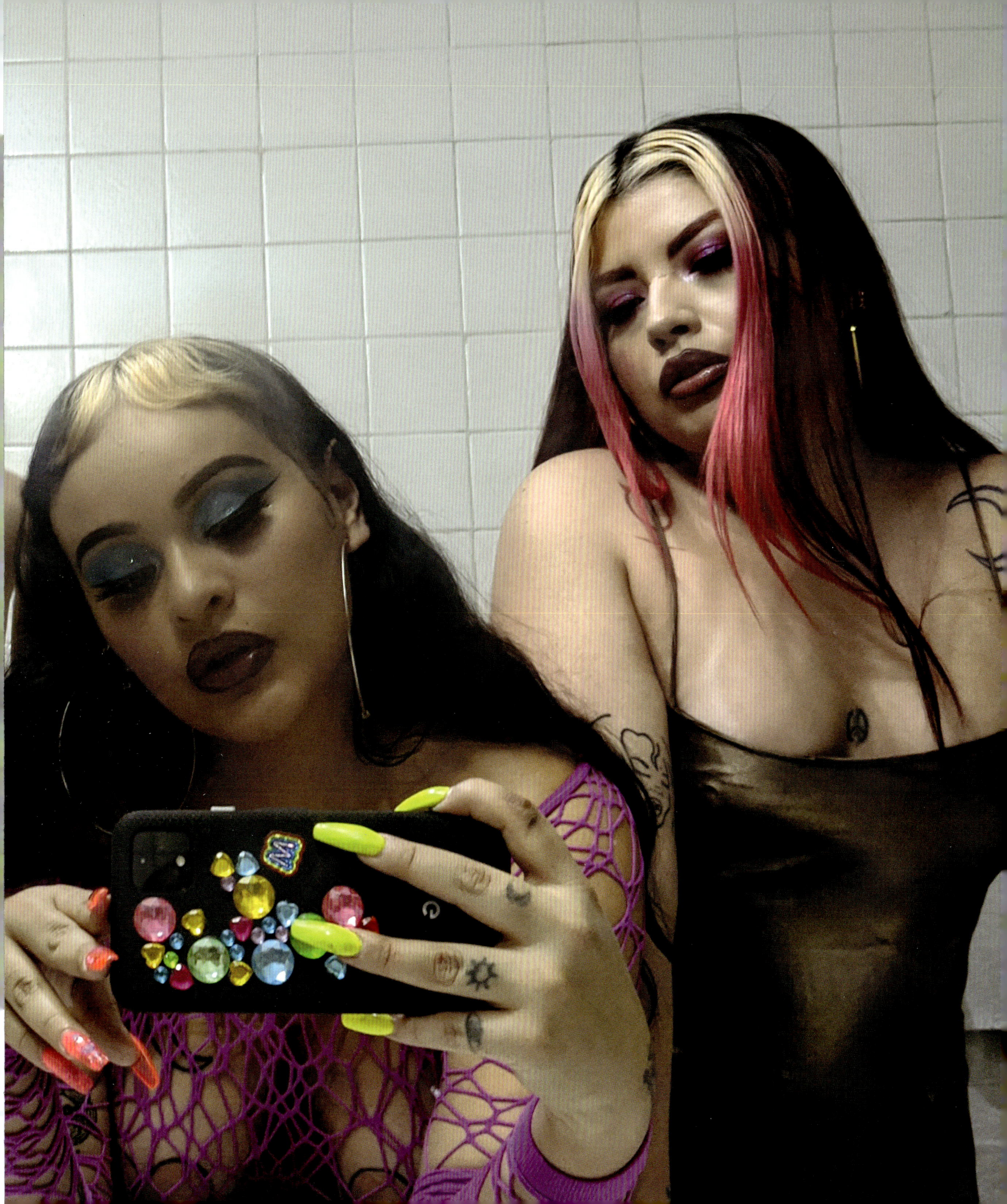

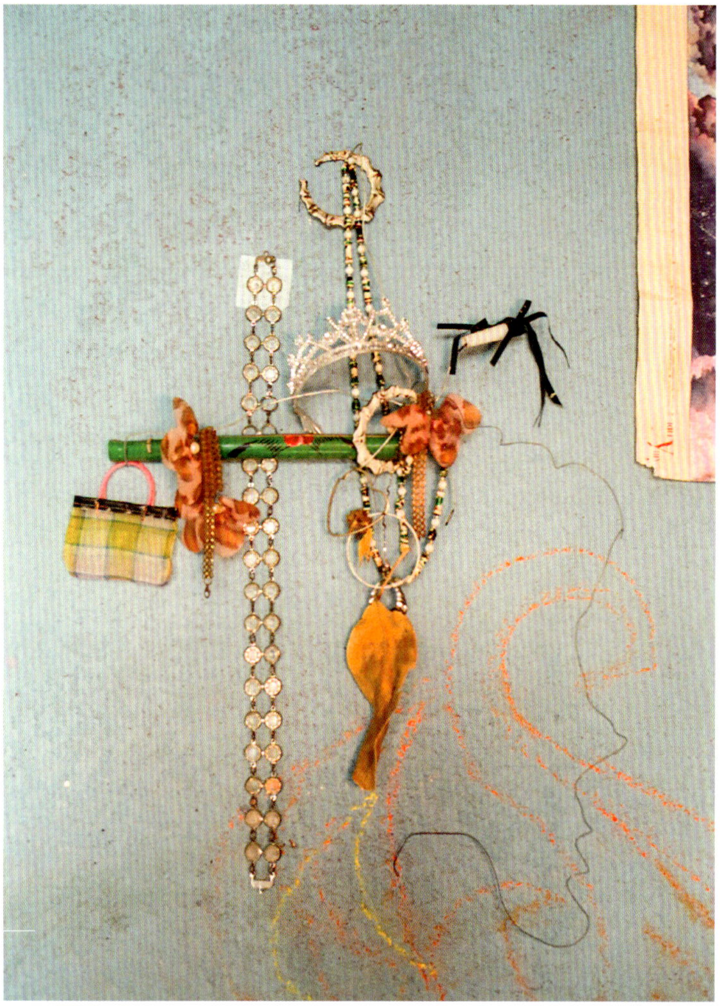

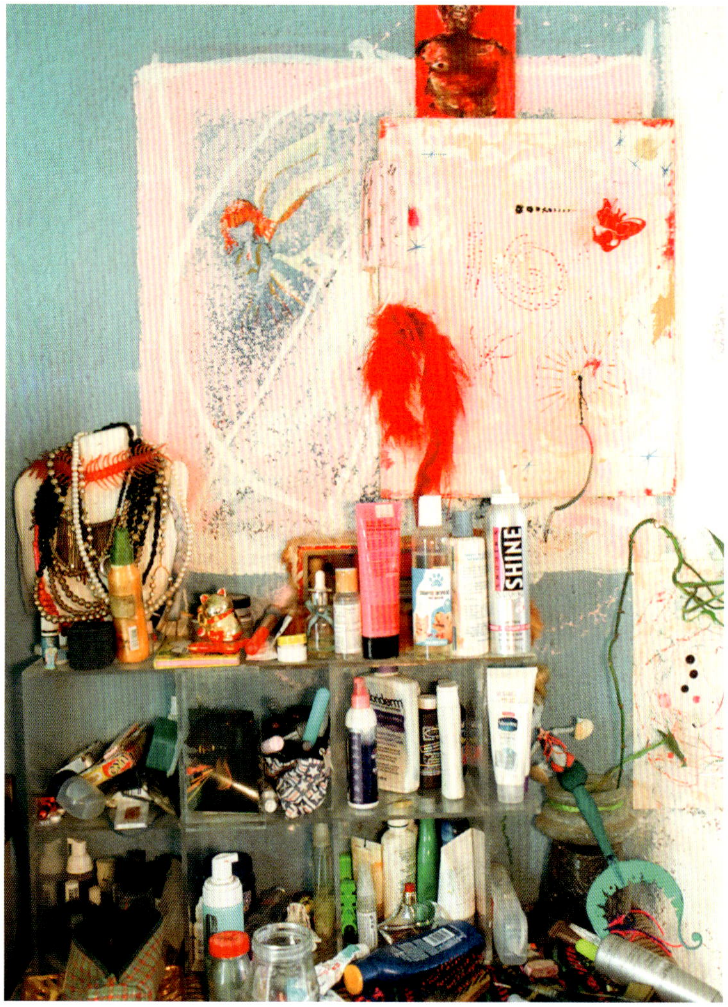
SHINE

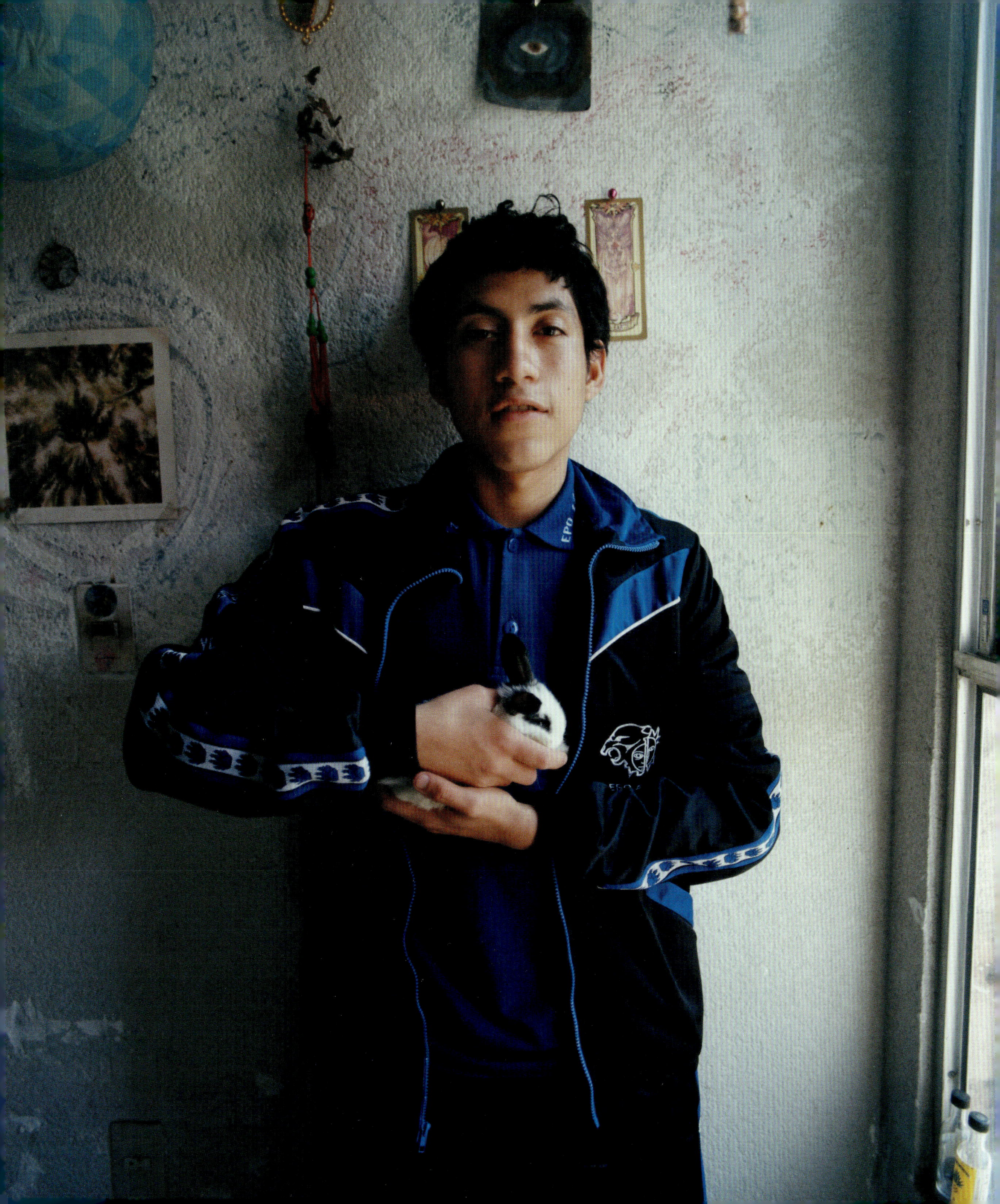

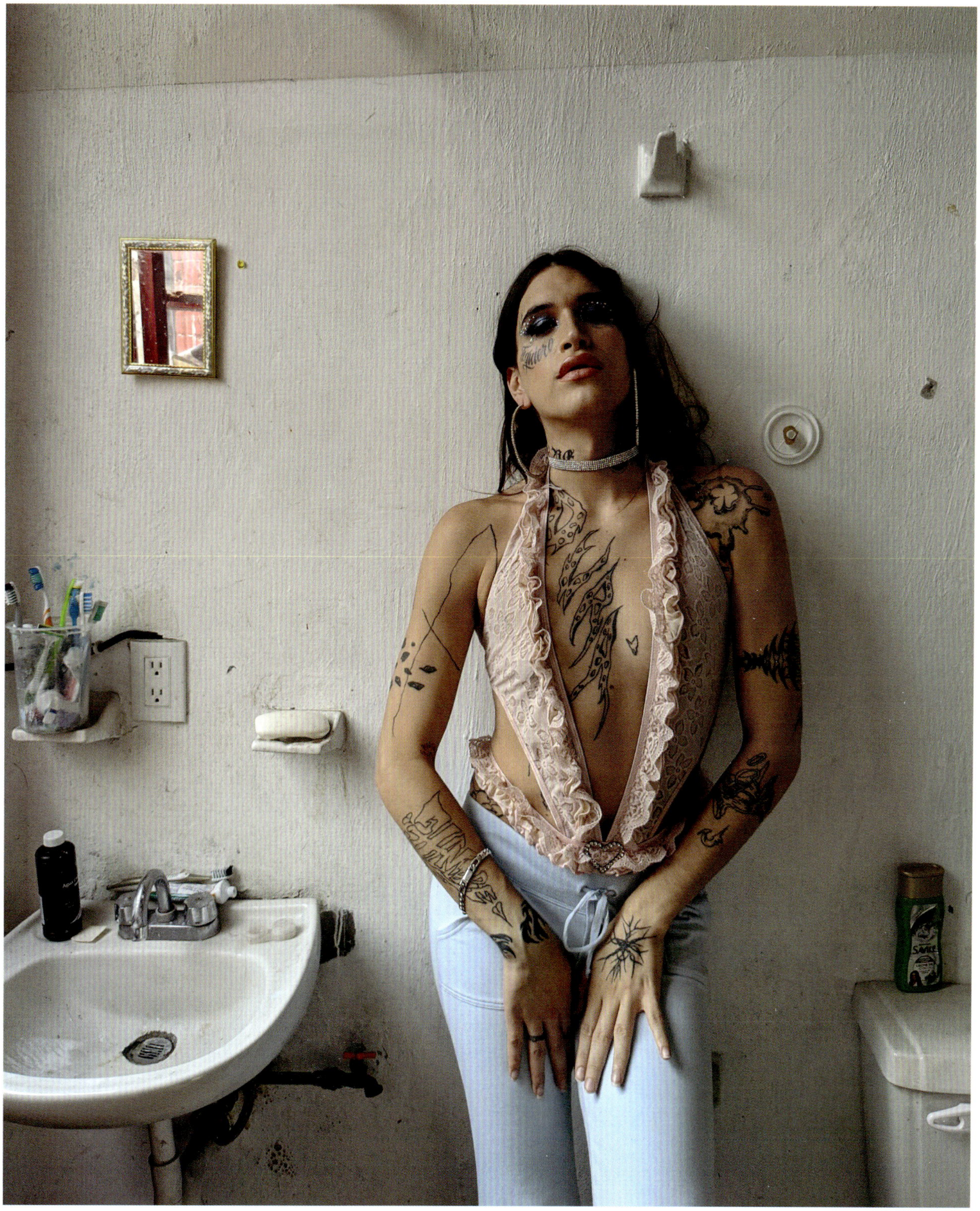

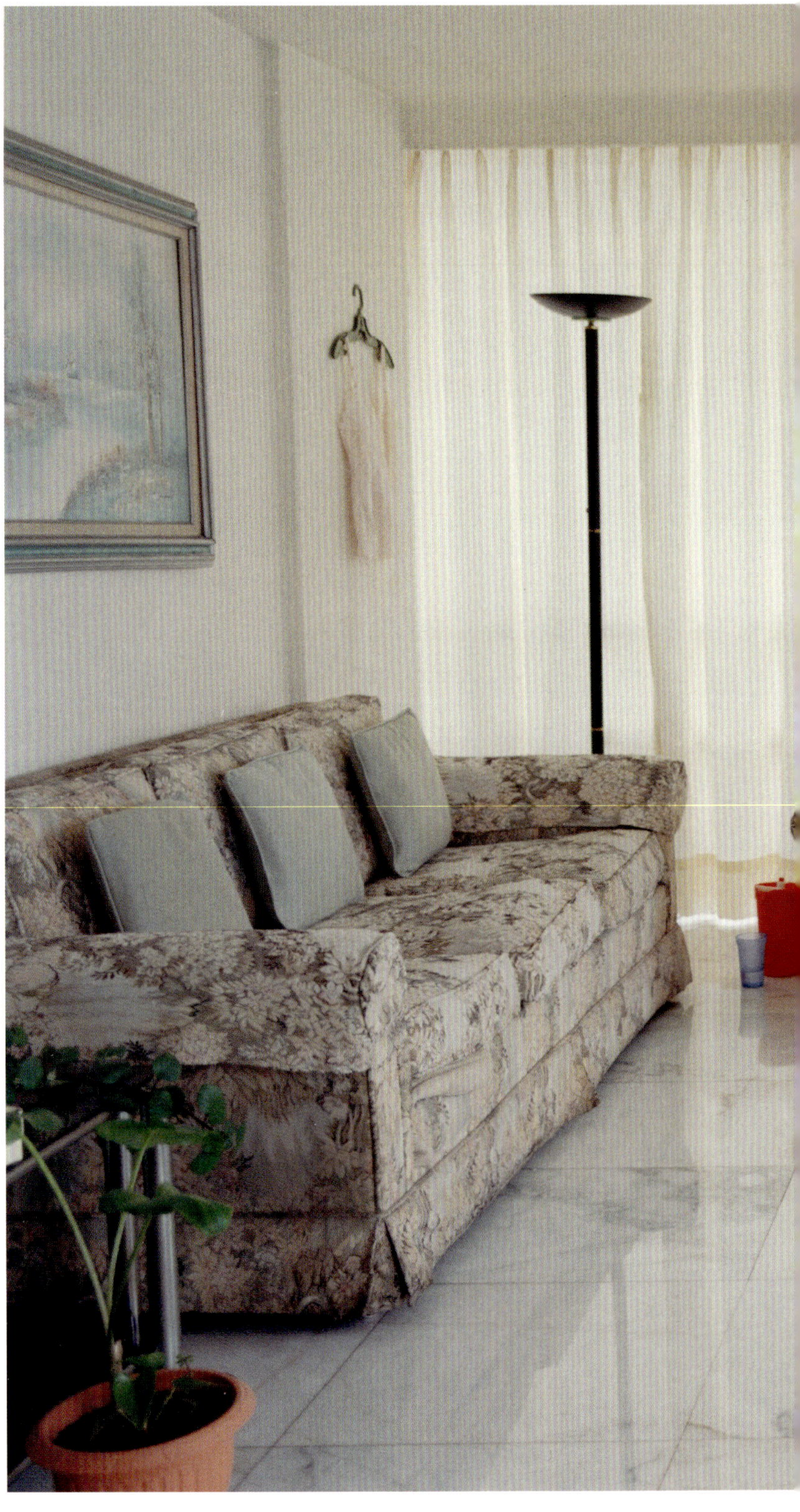

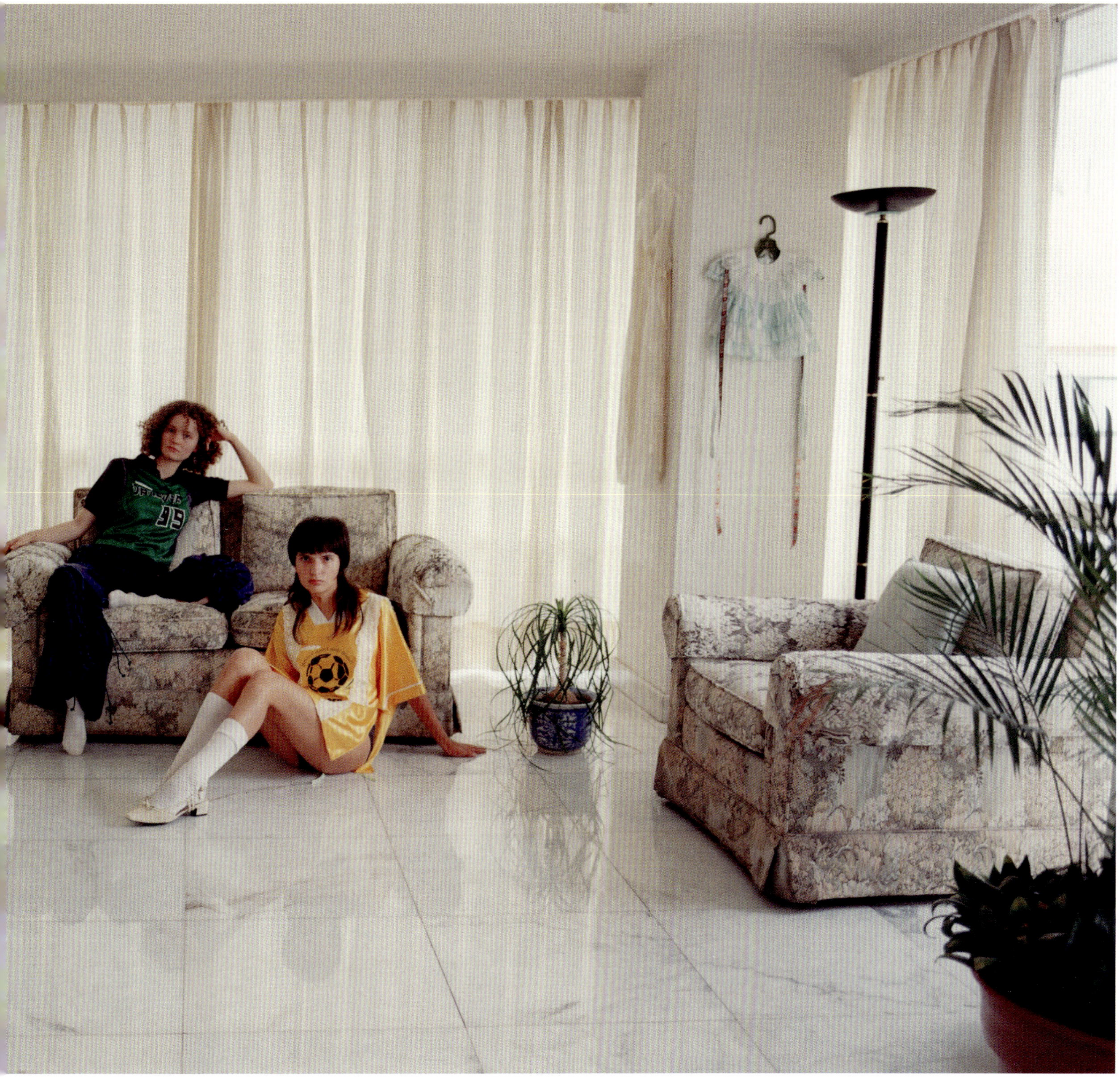

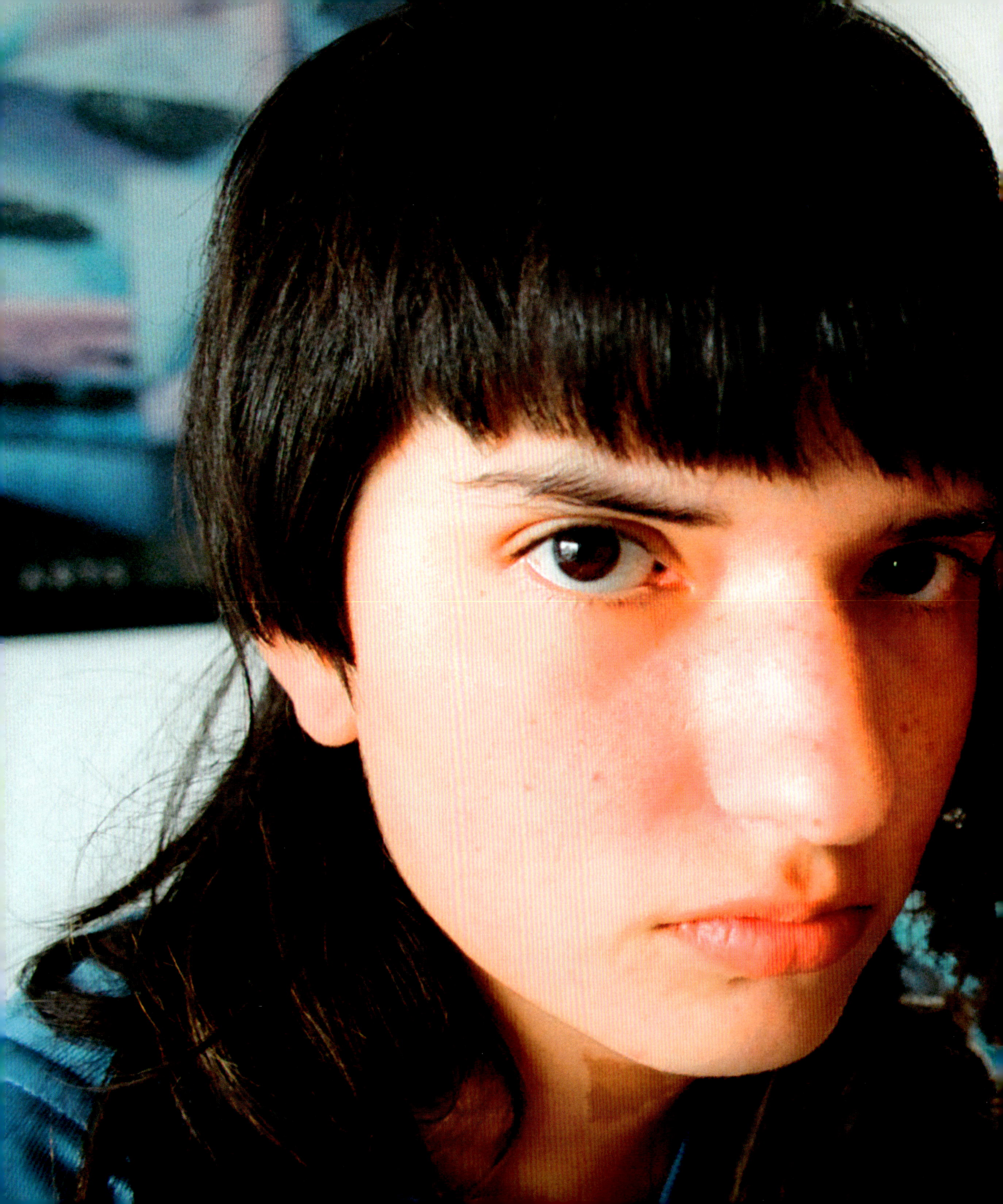

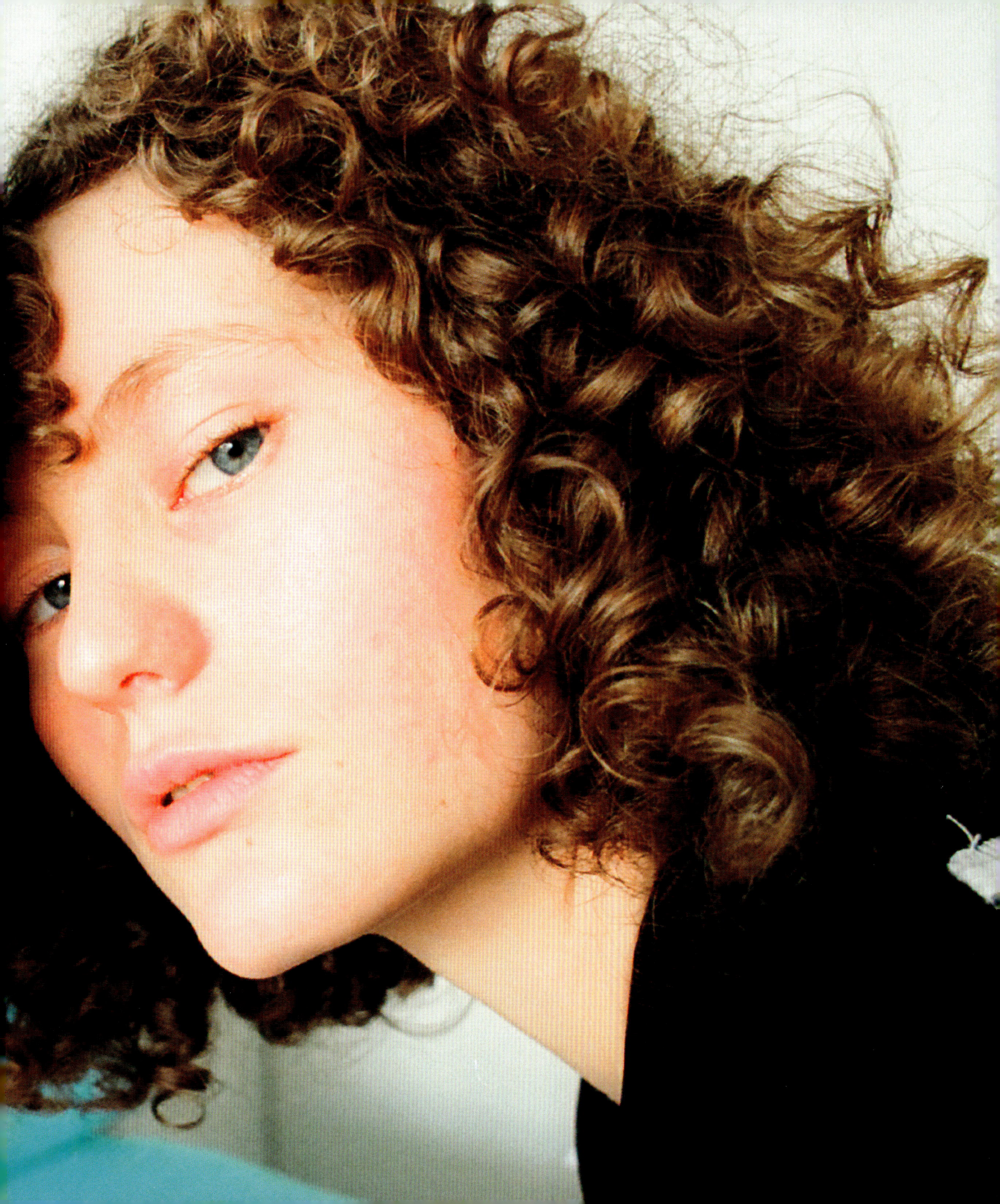

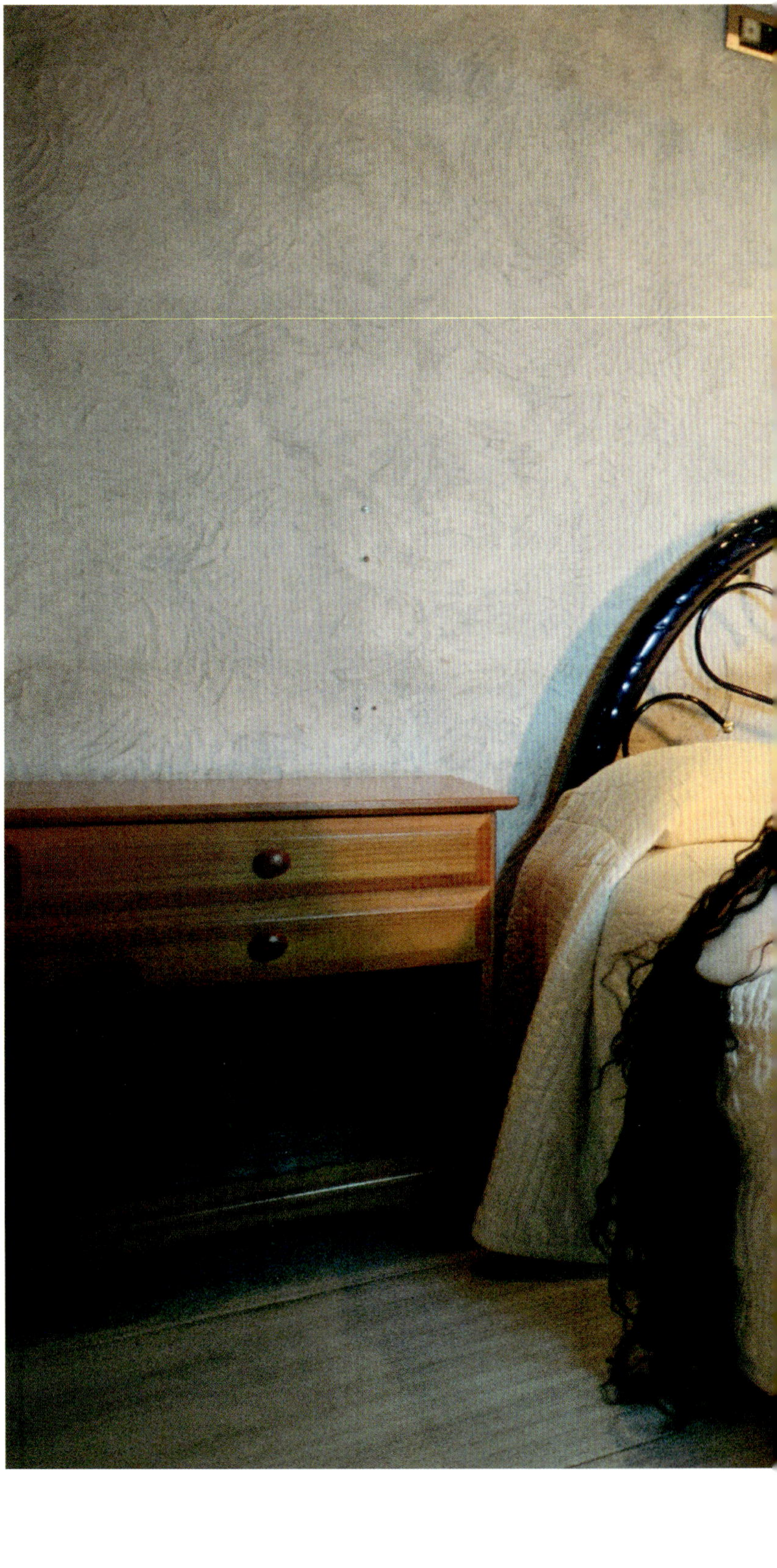

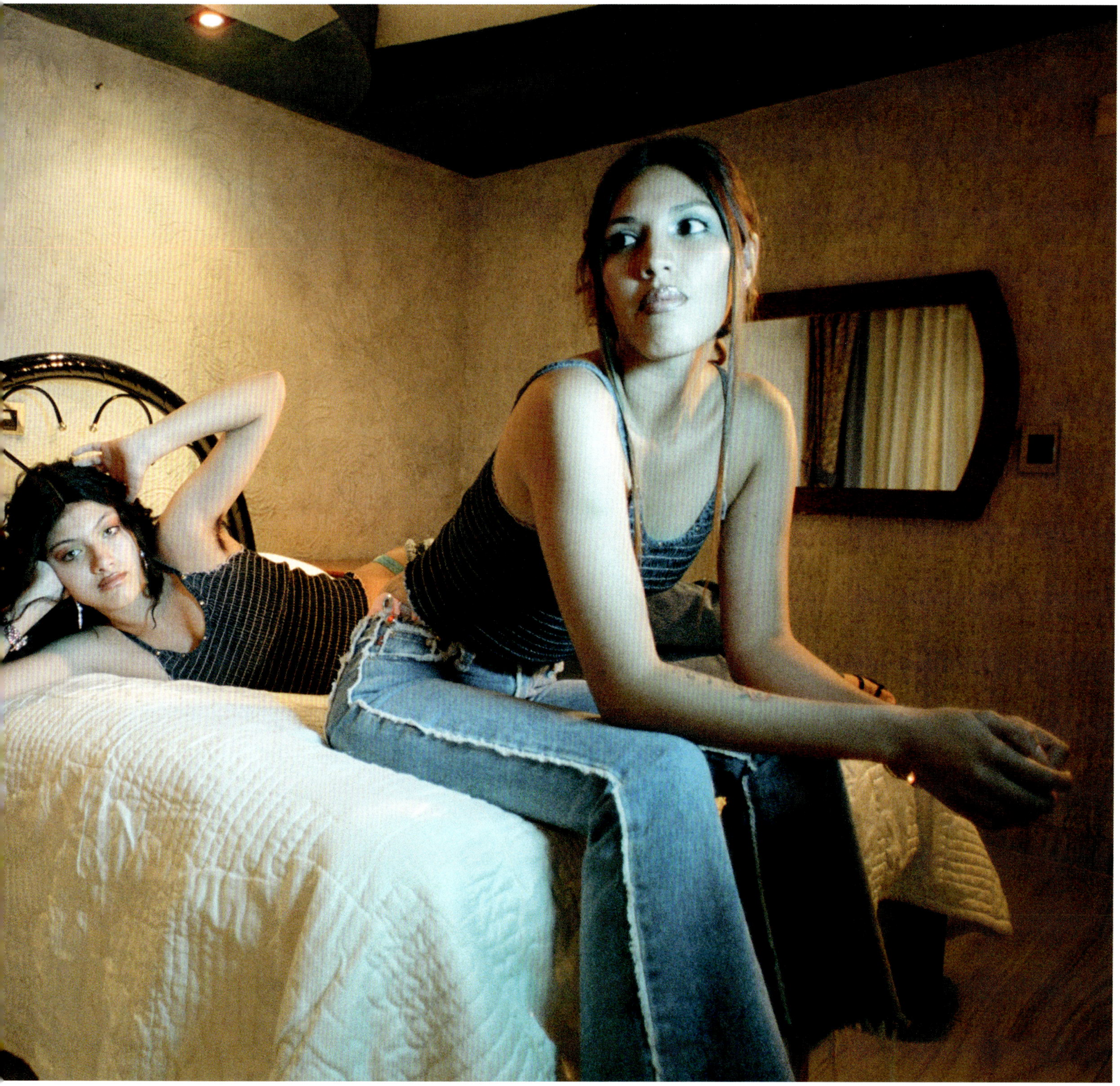

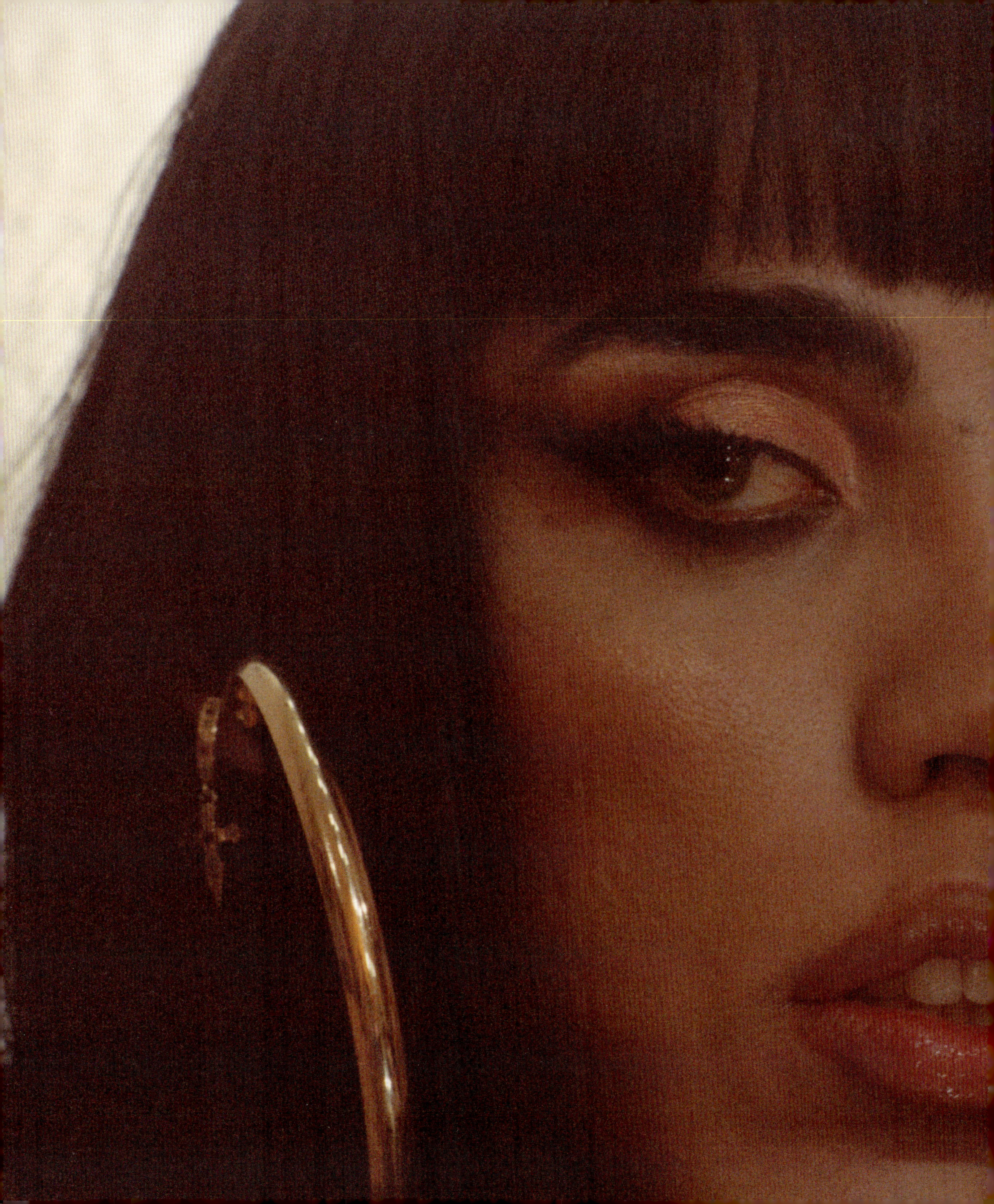

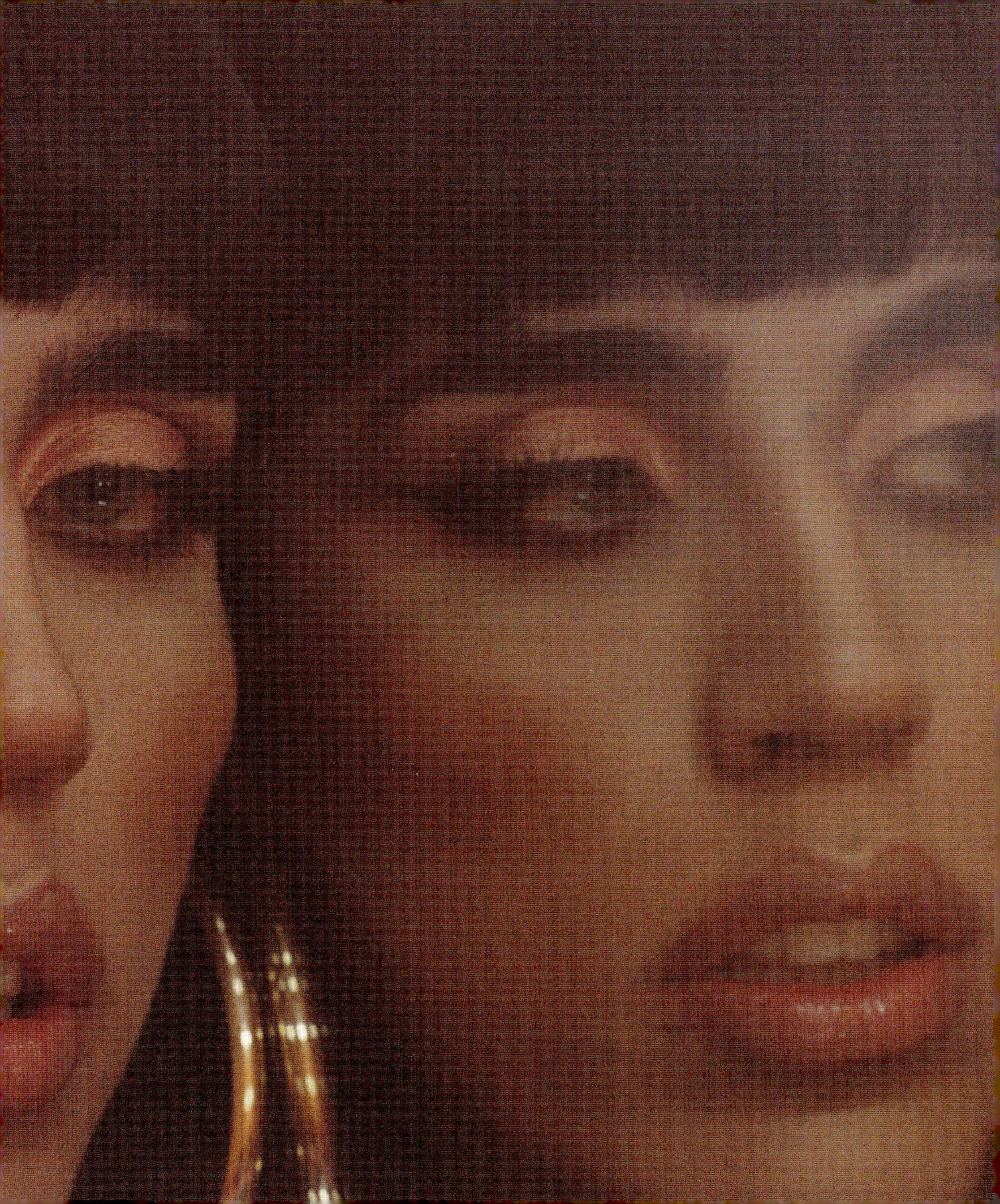

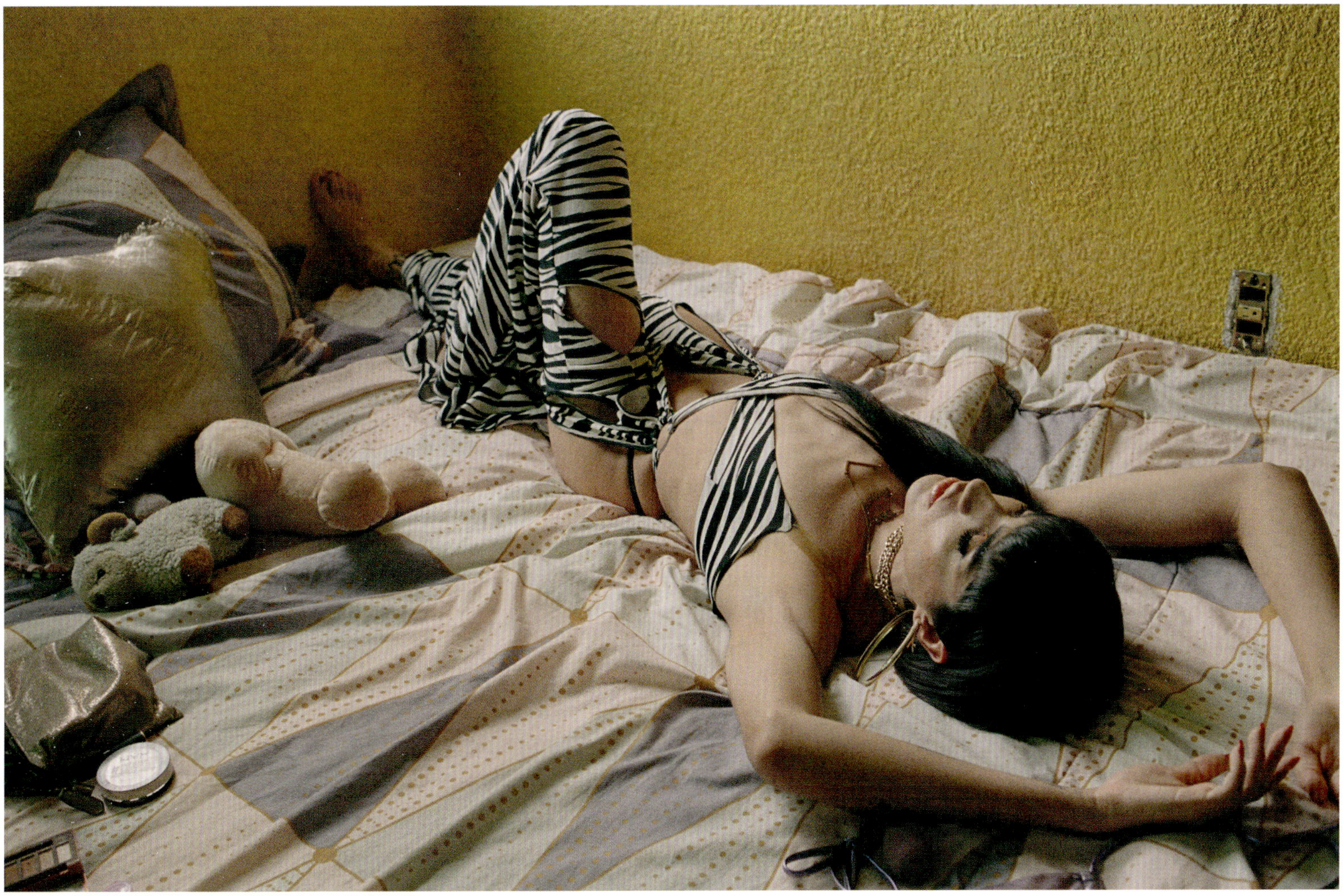

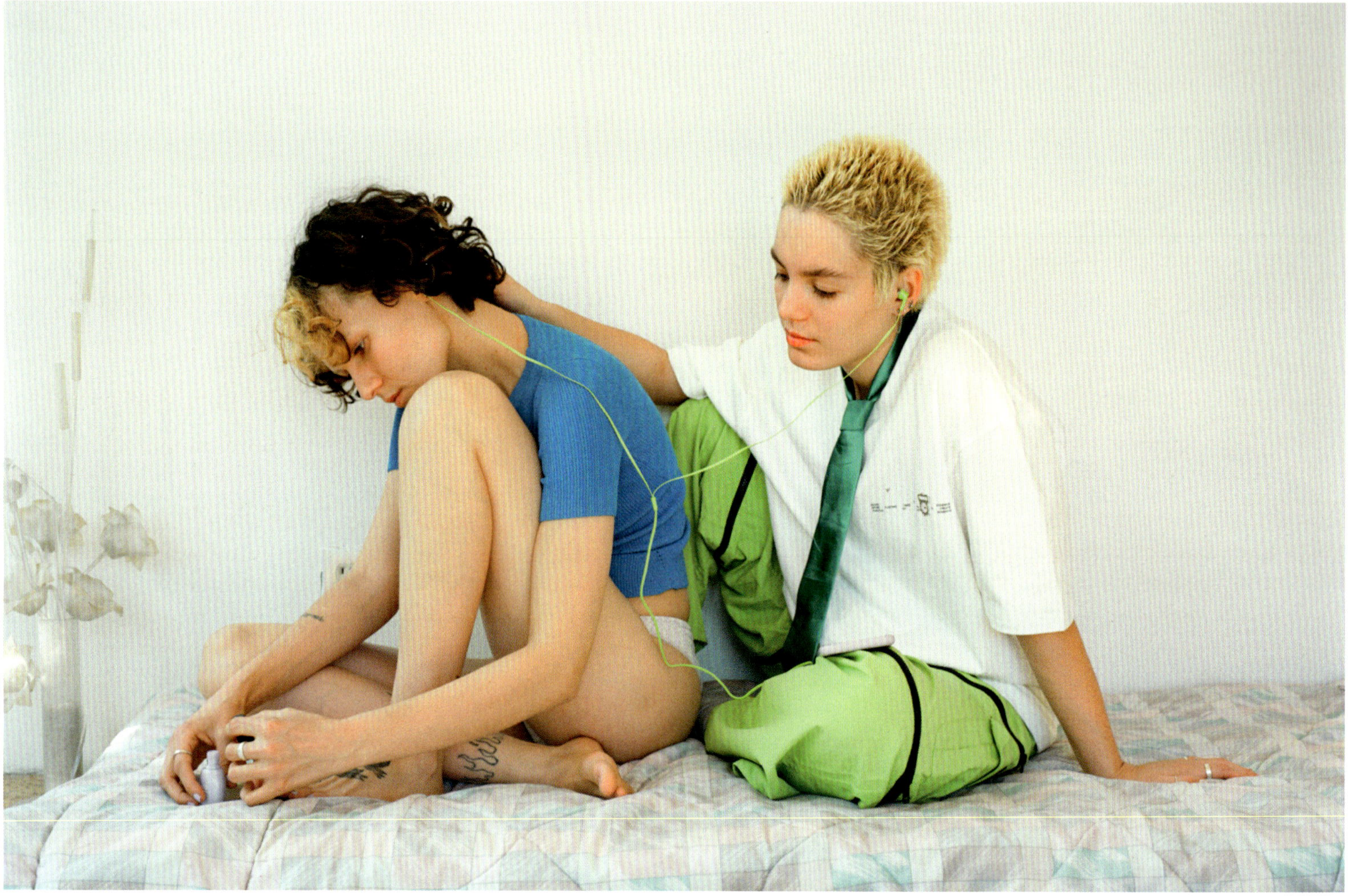

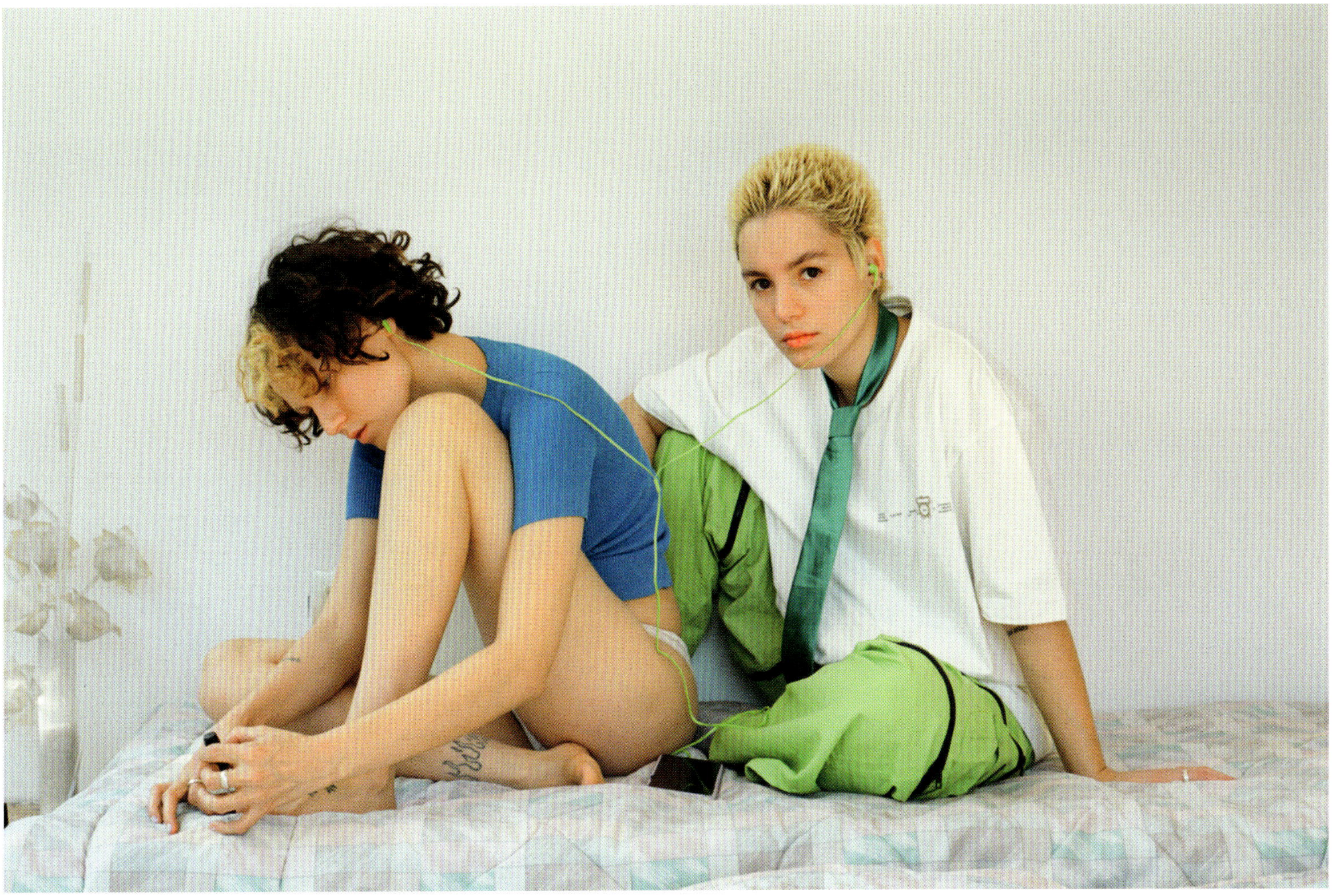

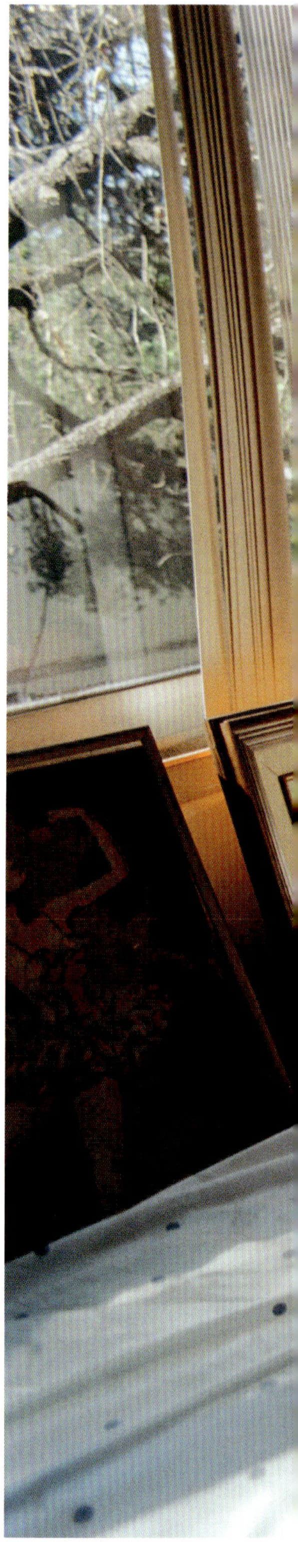

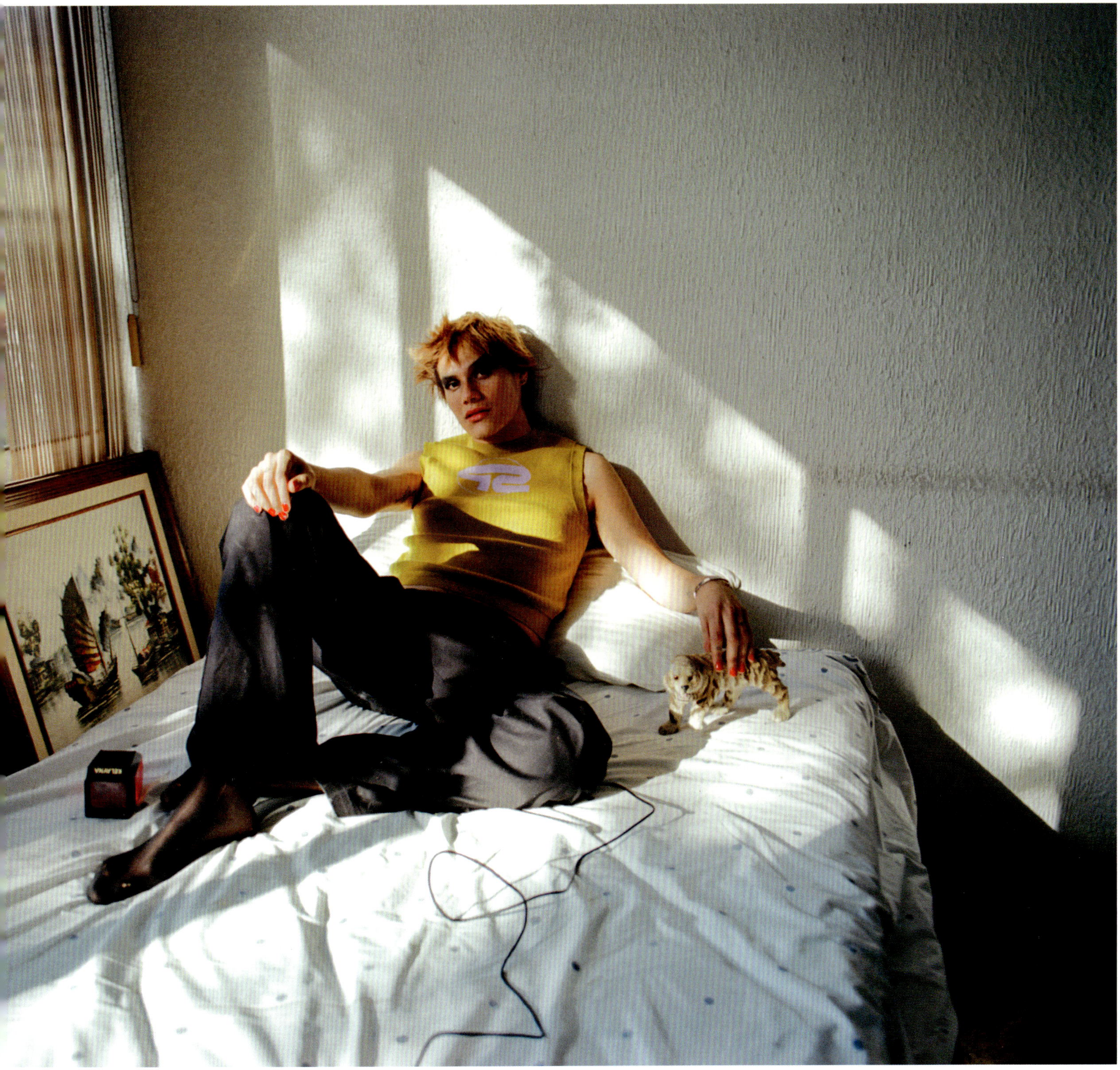

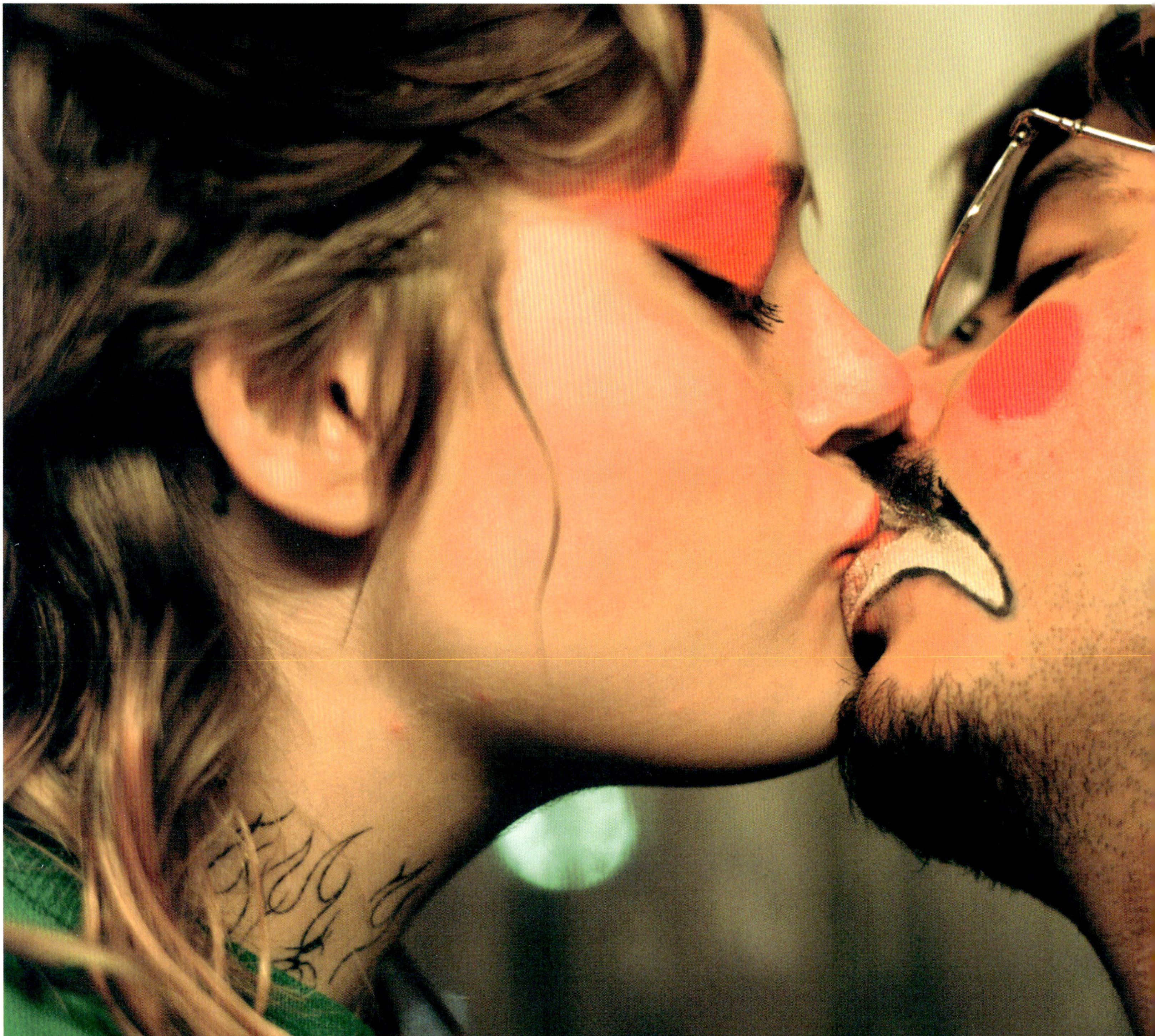

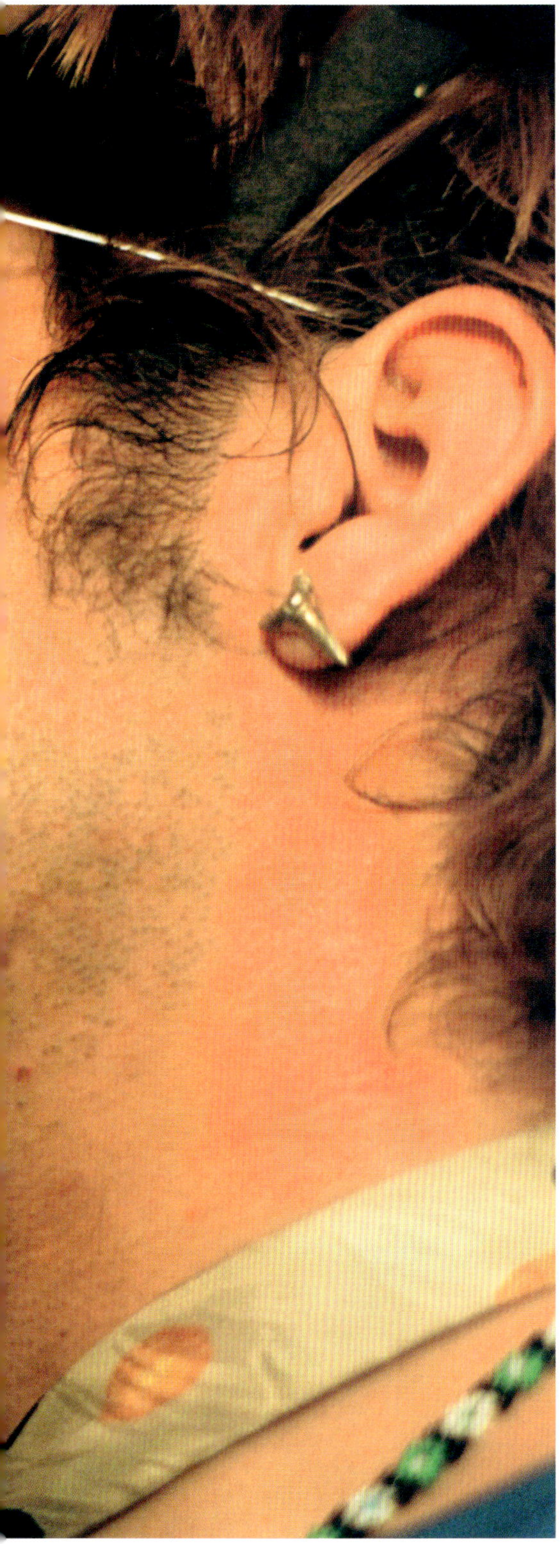

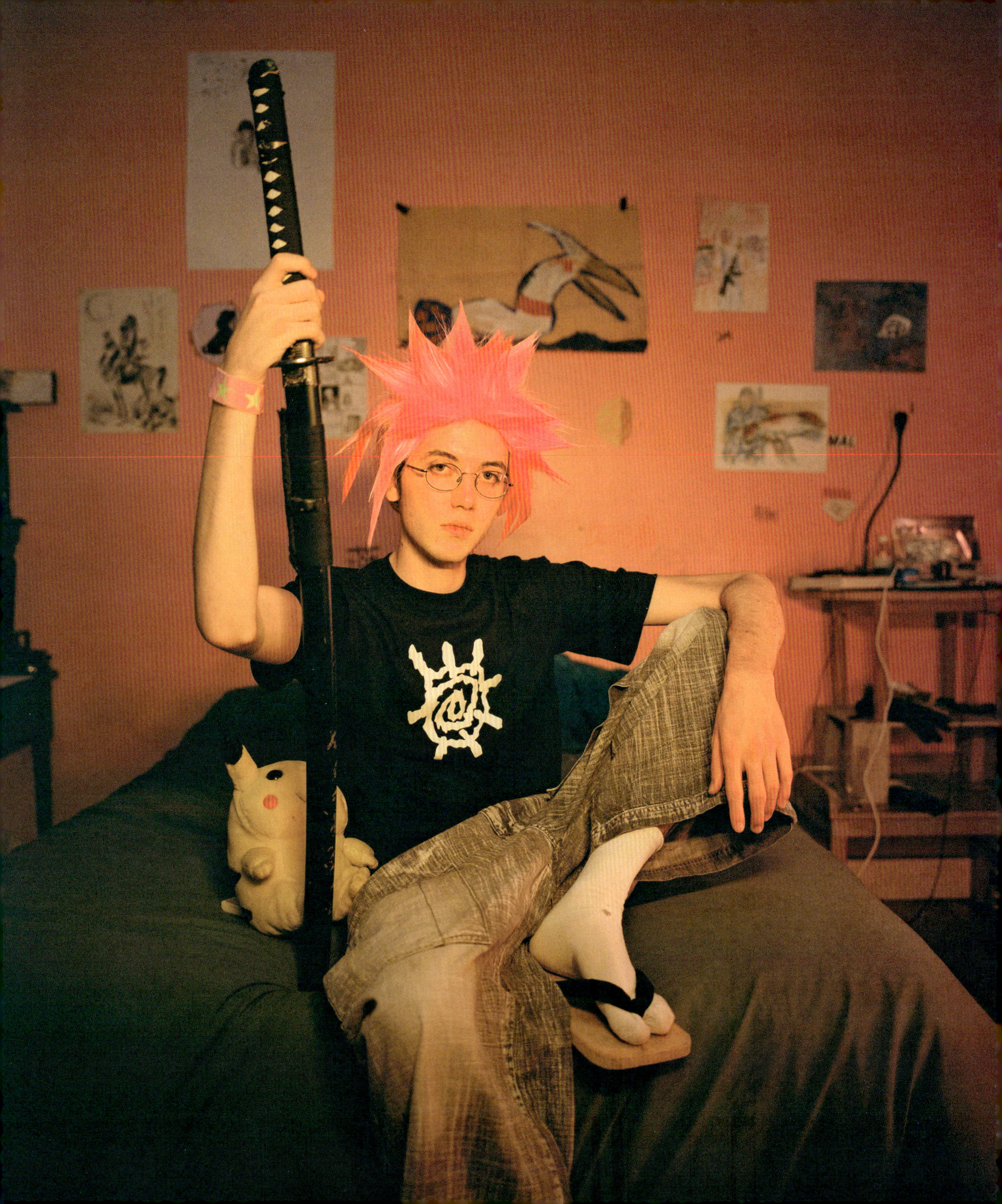

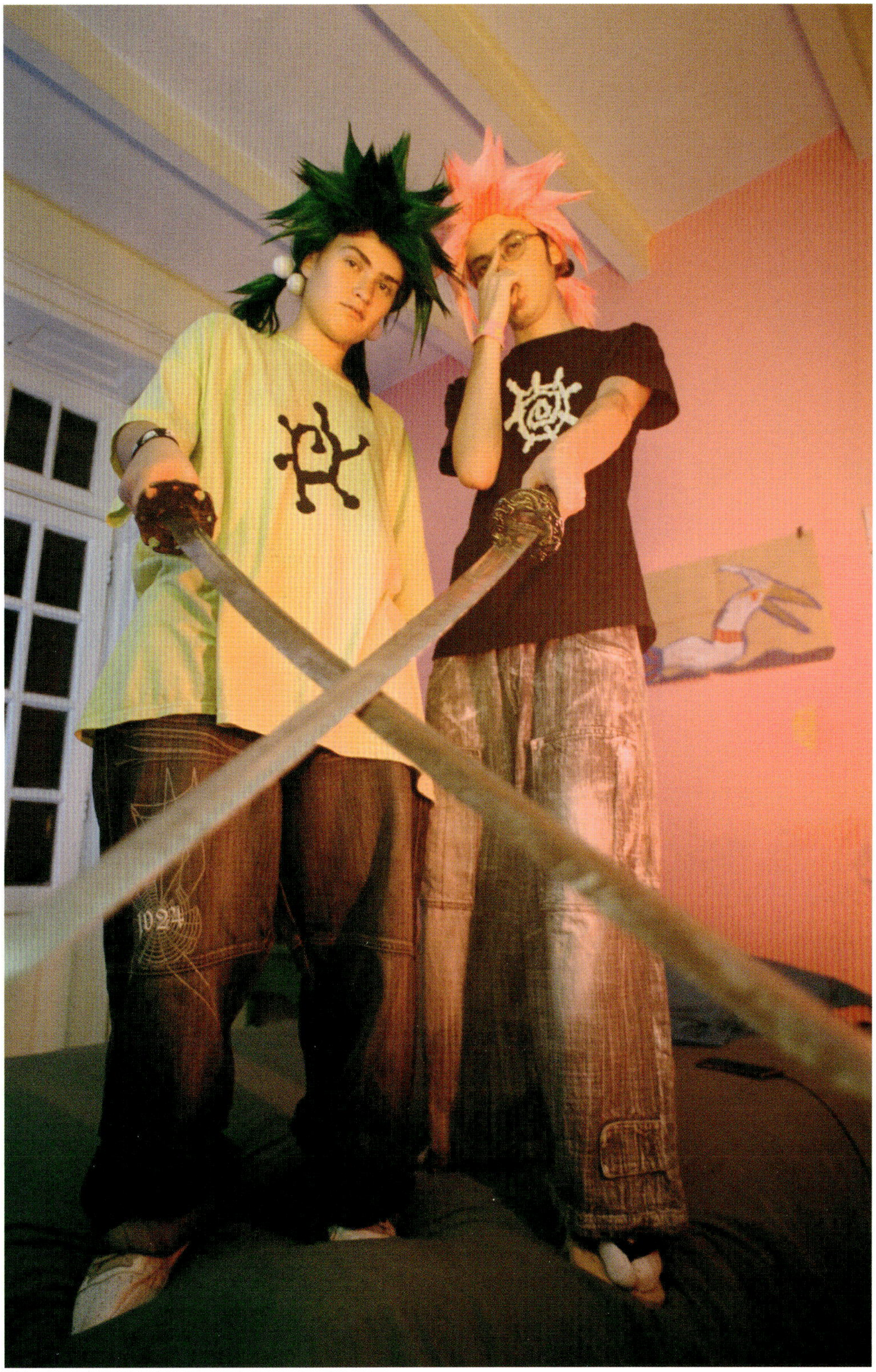
1024

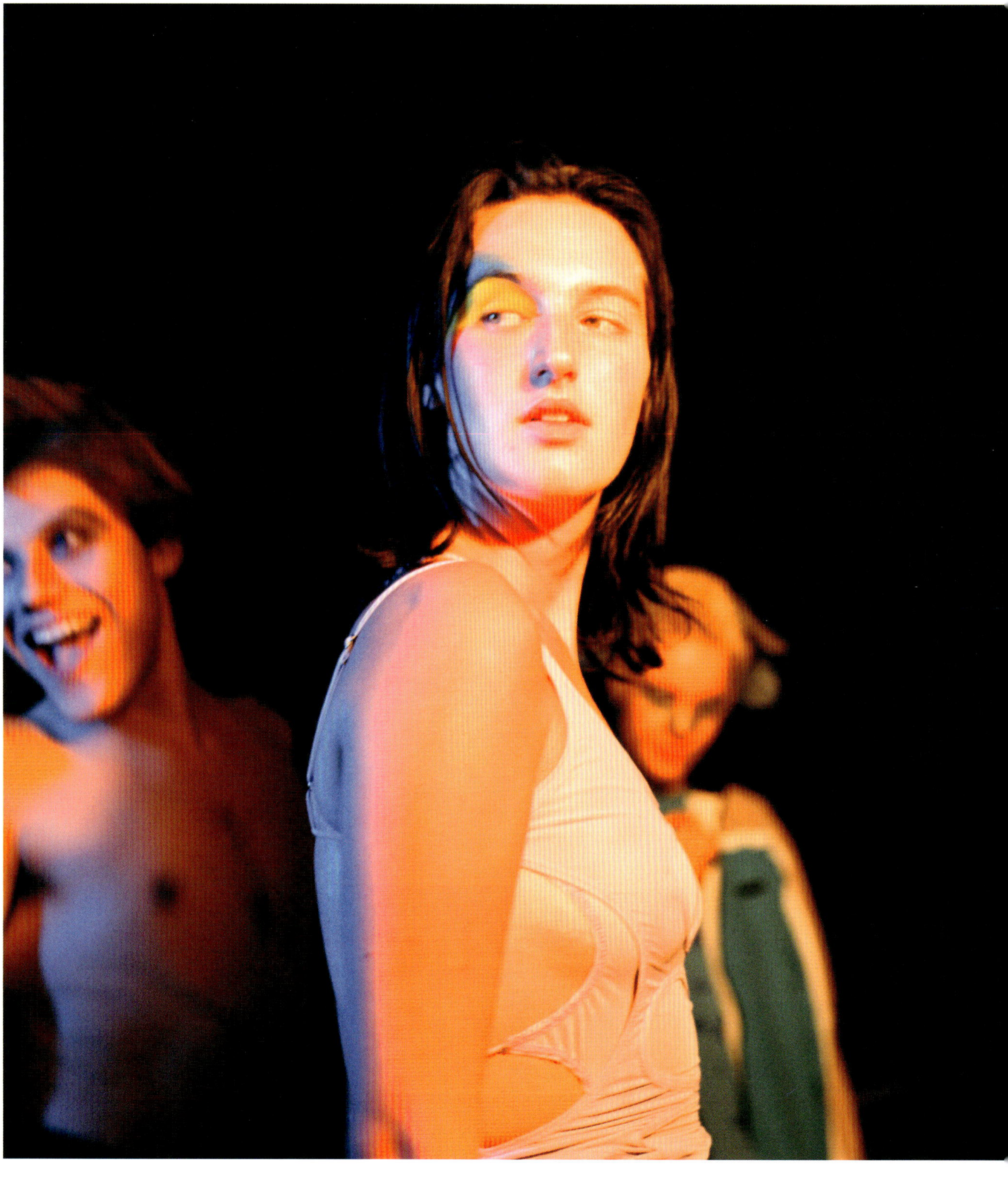

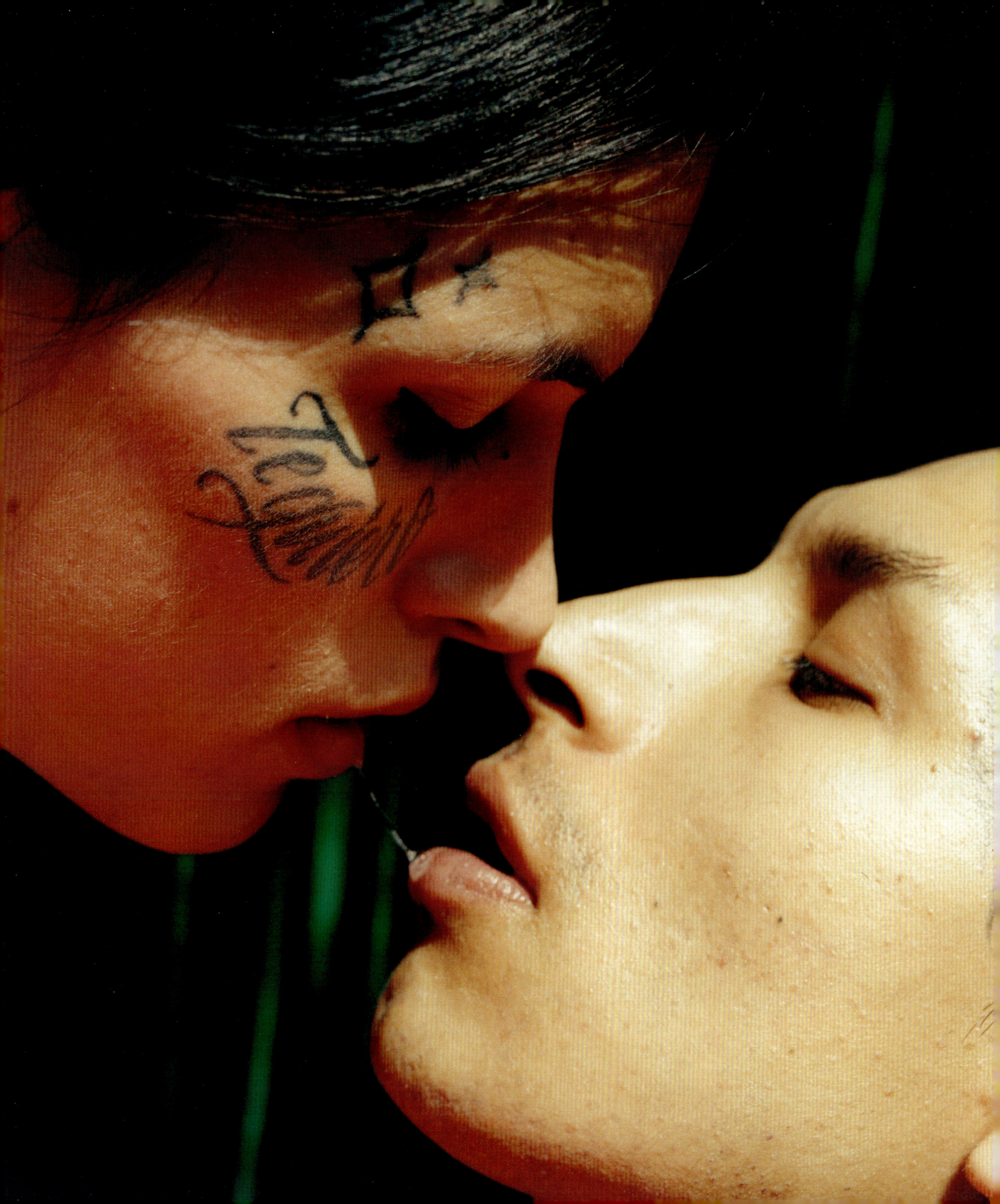

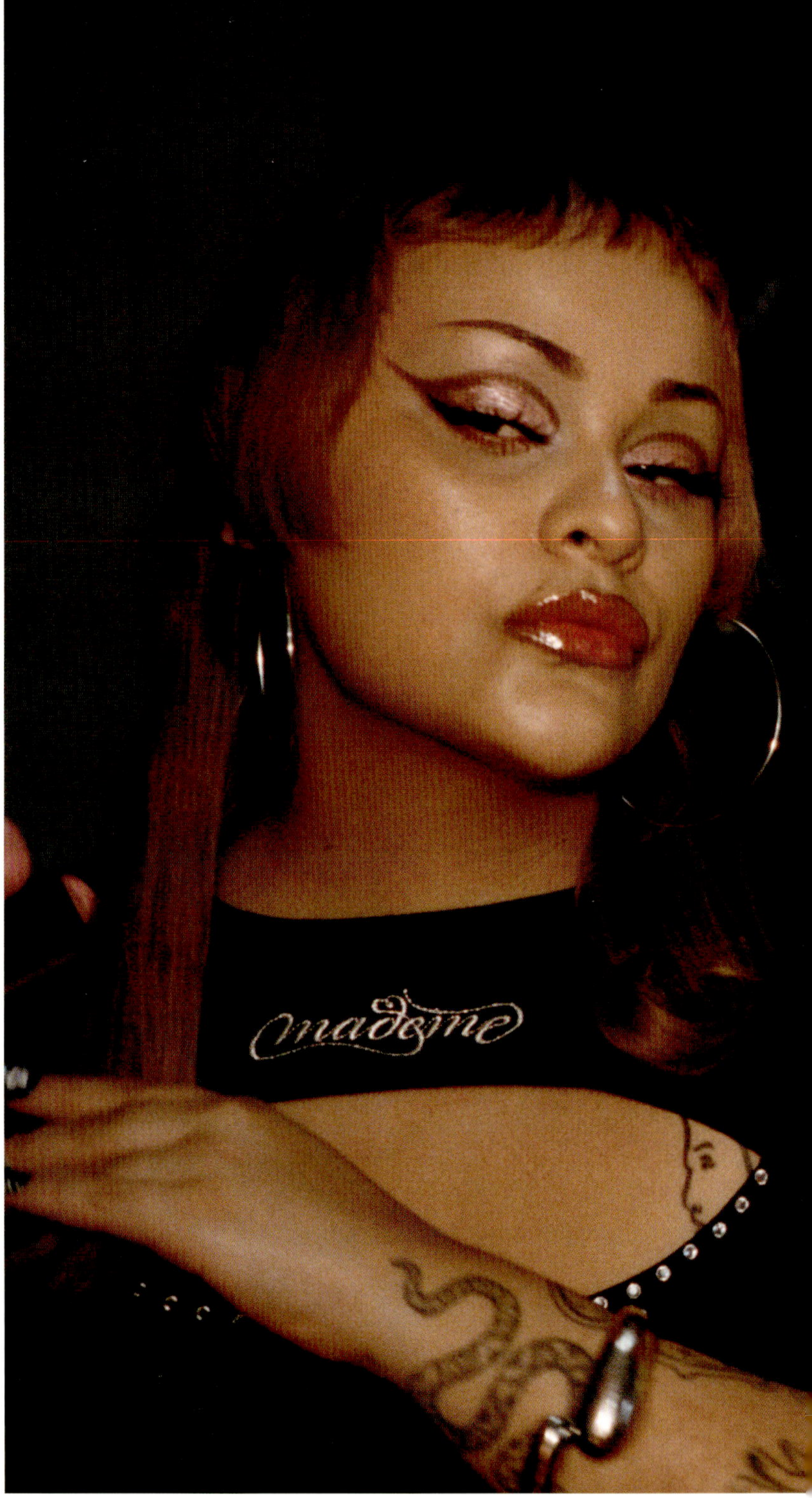
mademe

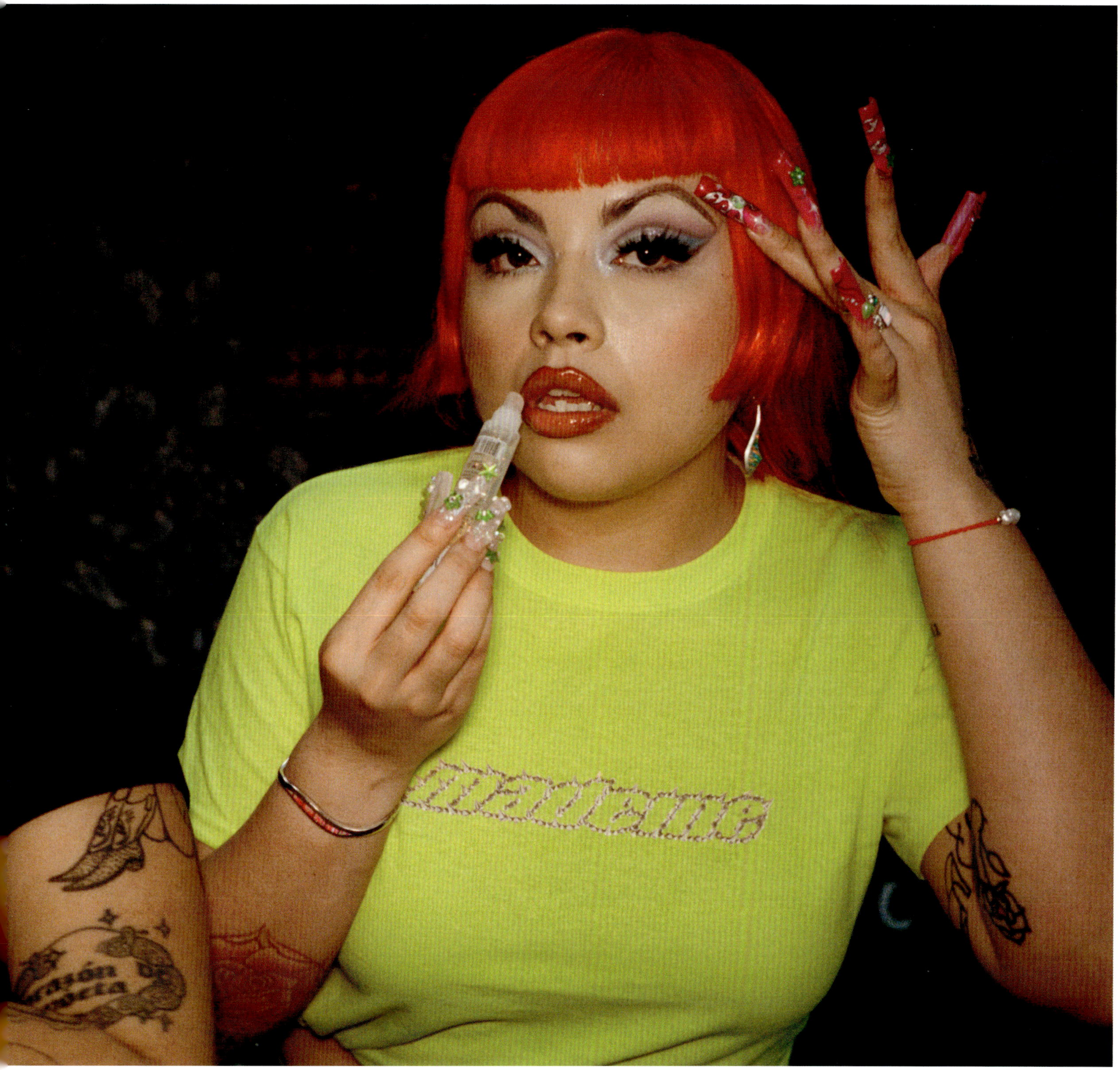

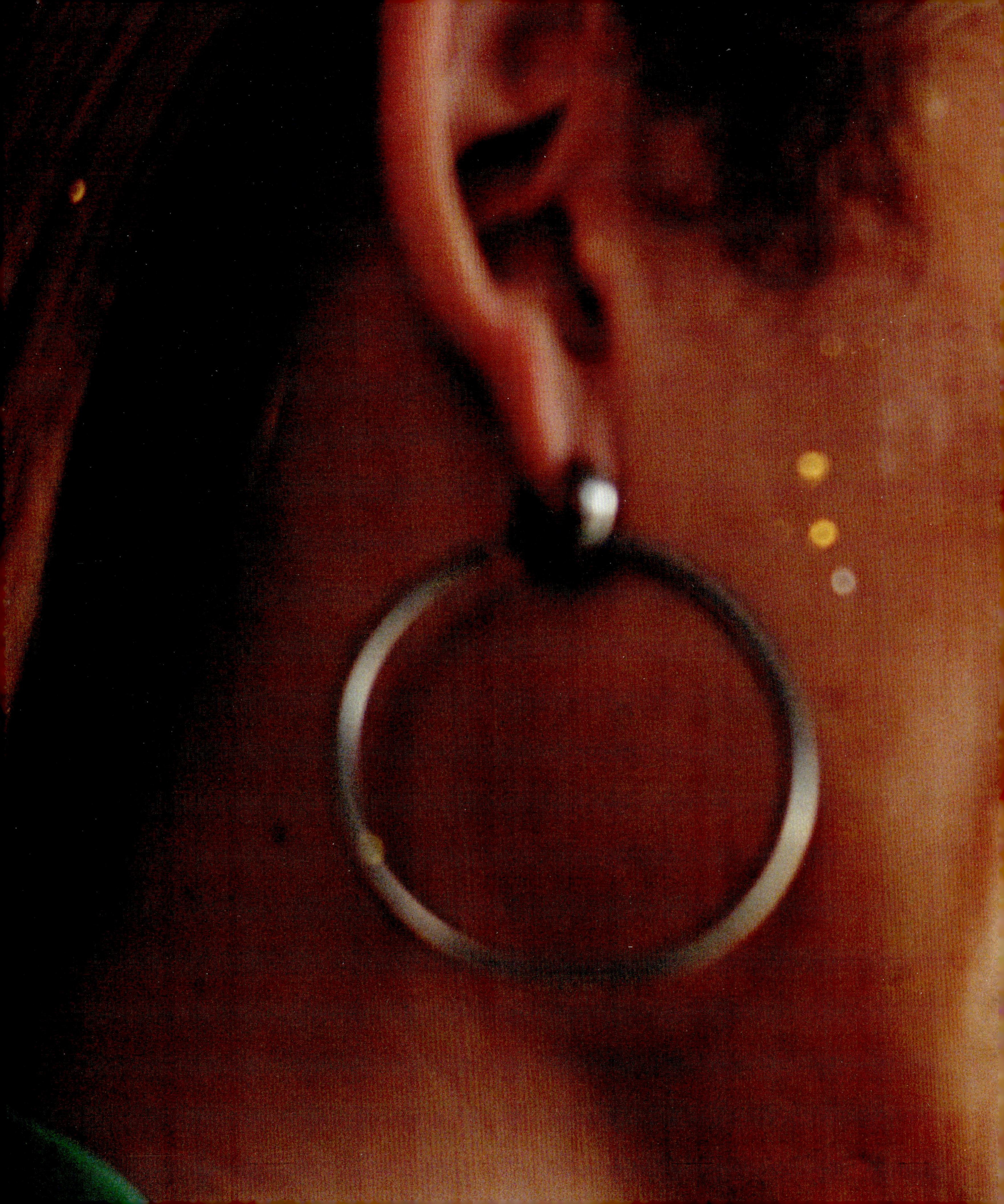

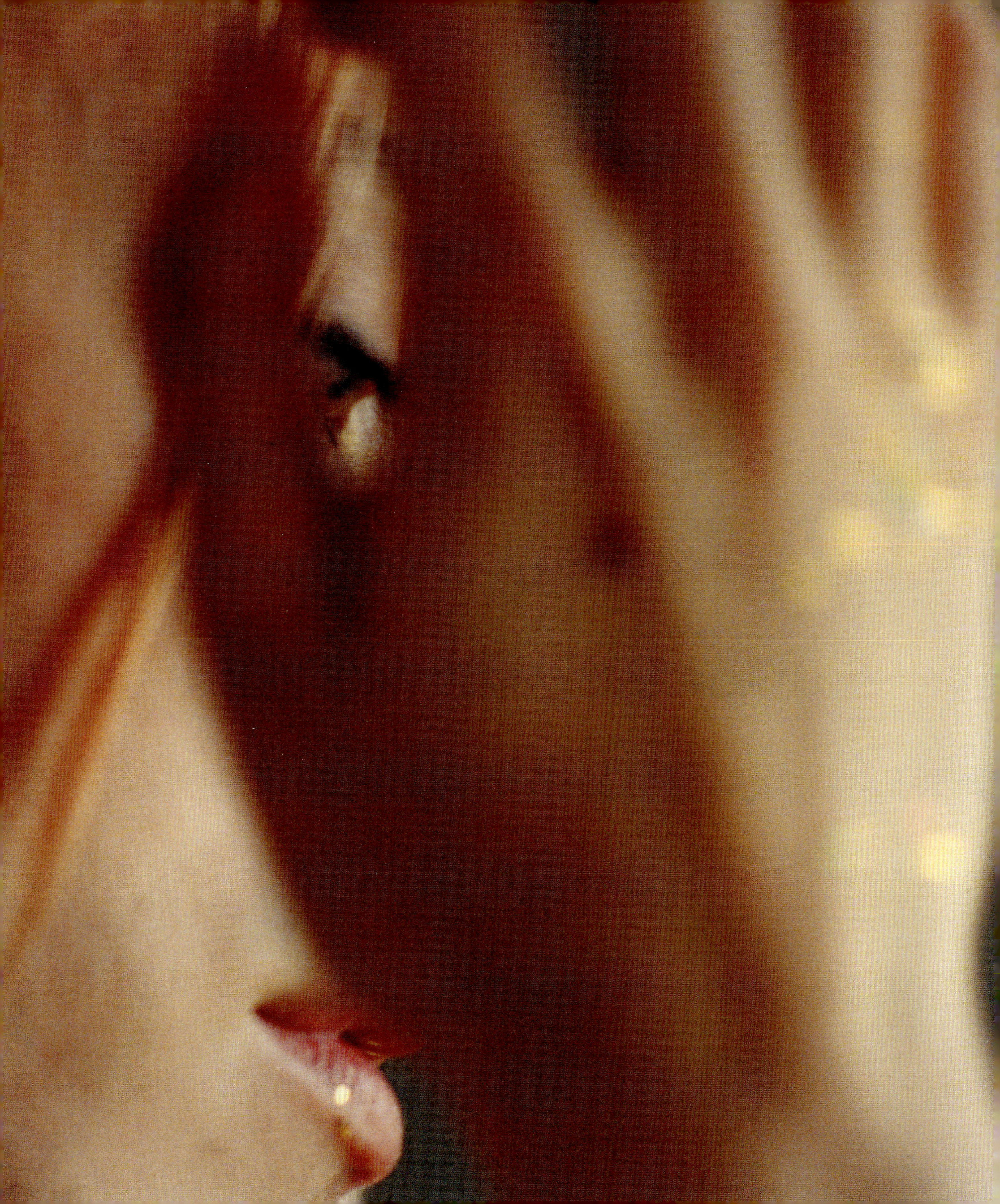

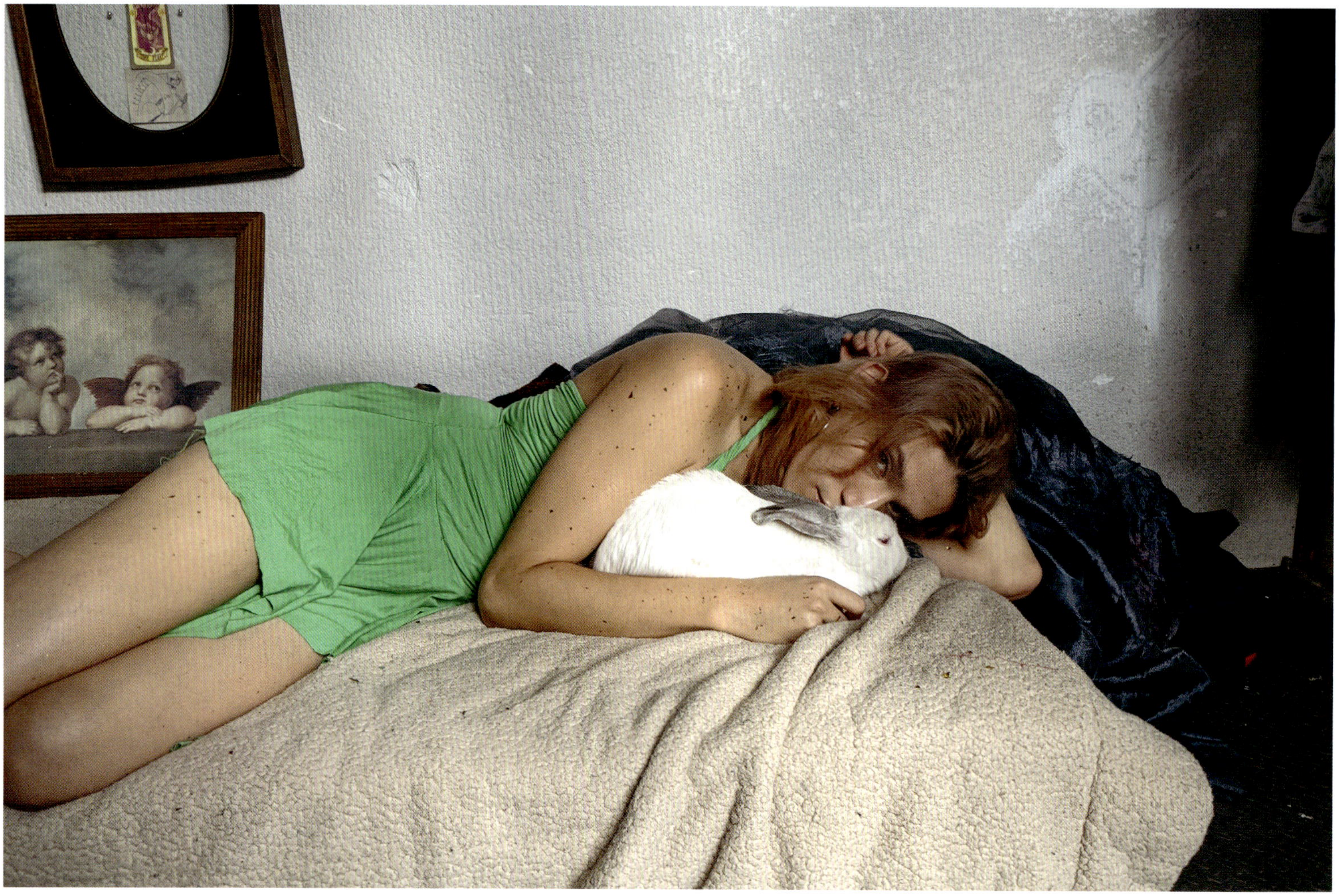

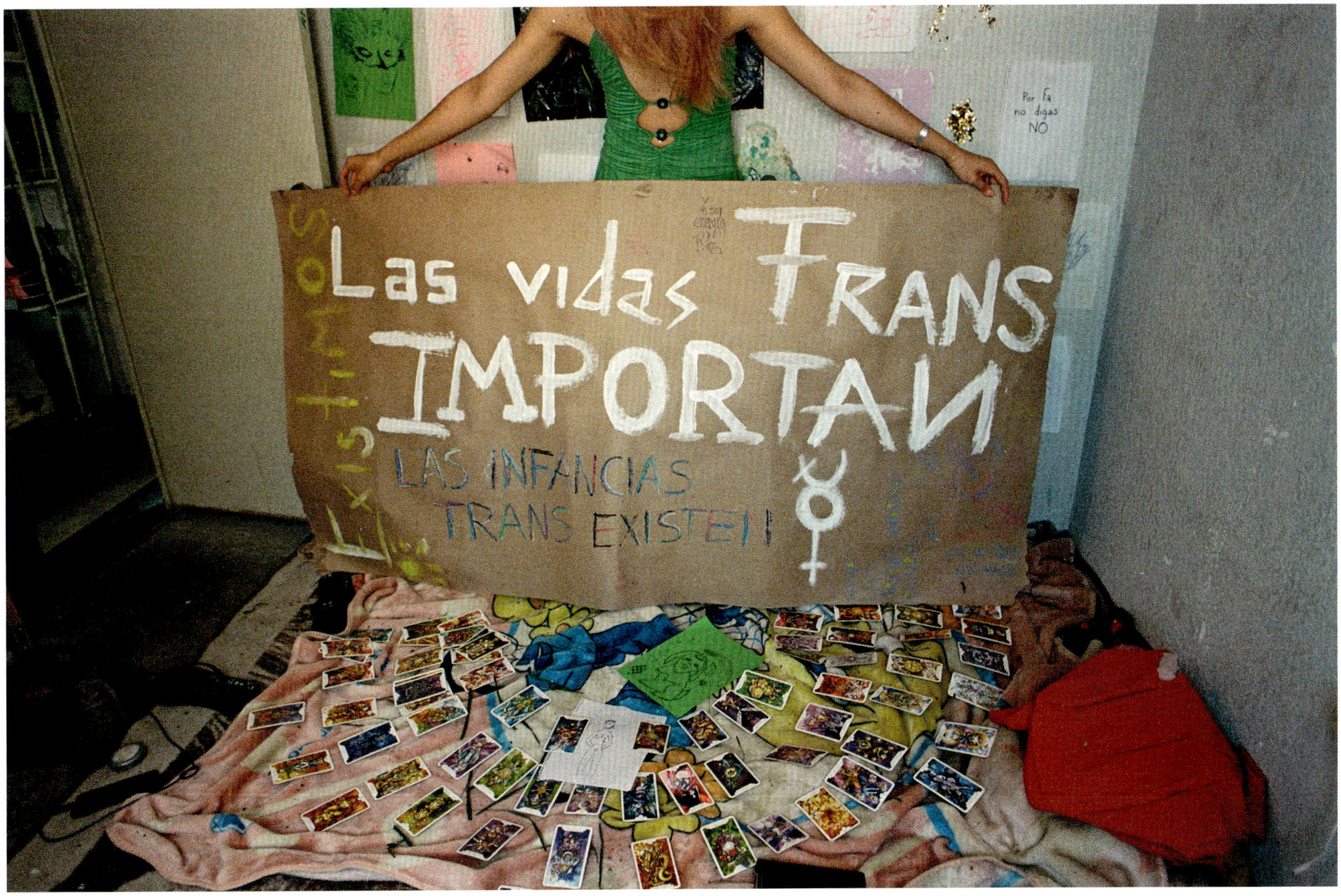
Por Fa
no digas
NO
Las vidas FRANS
IMPORTAN
LAS INFANCIAS
TRANS EXISTEN
EXISTIMOS

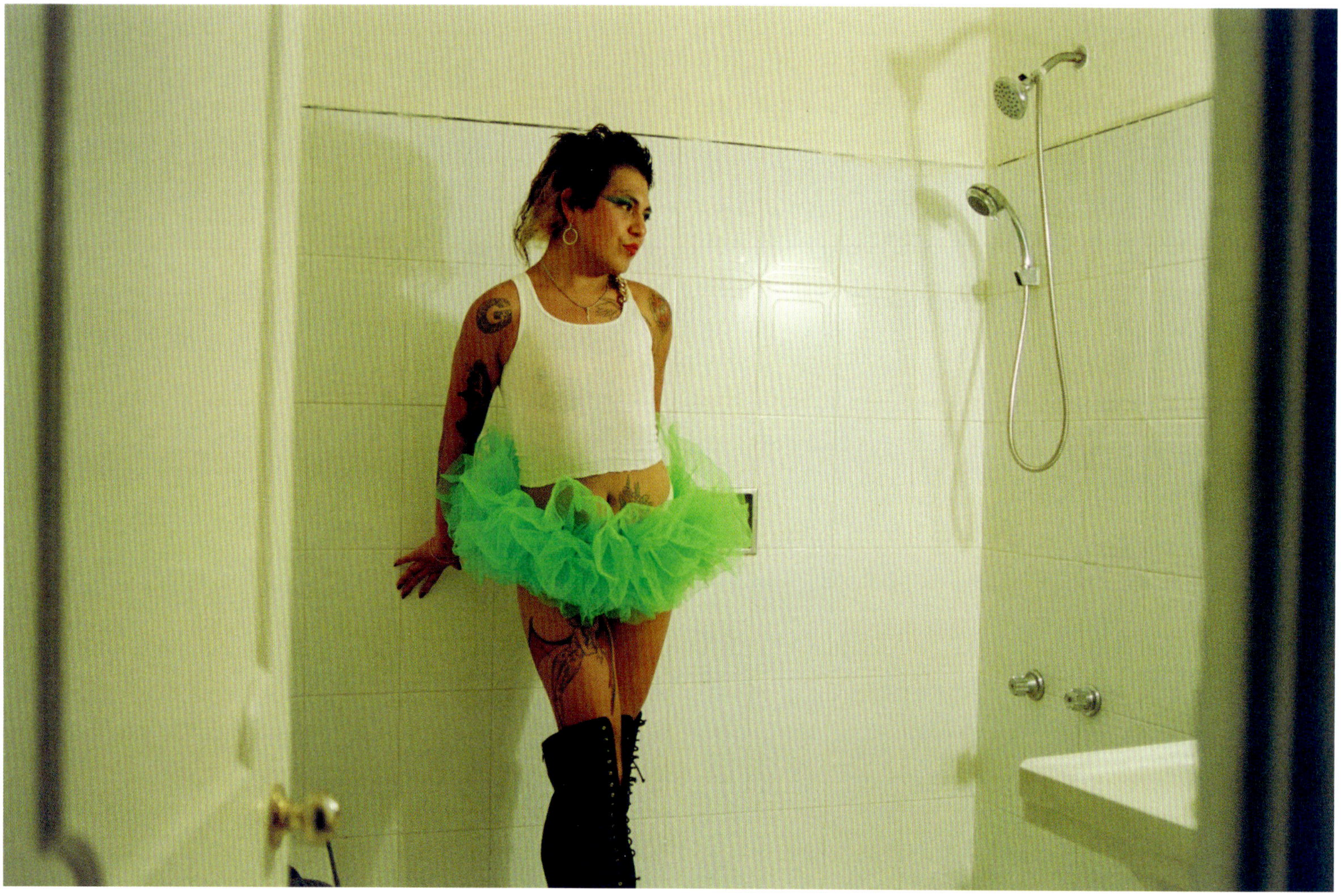

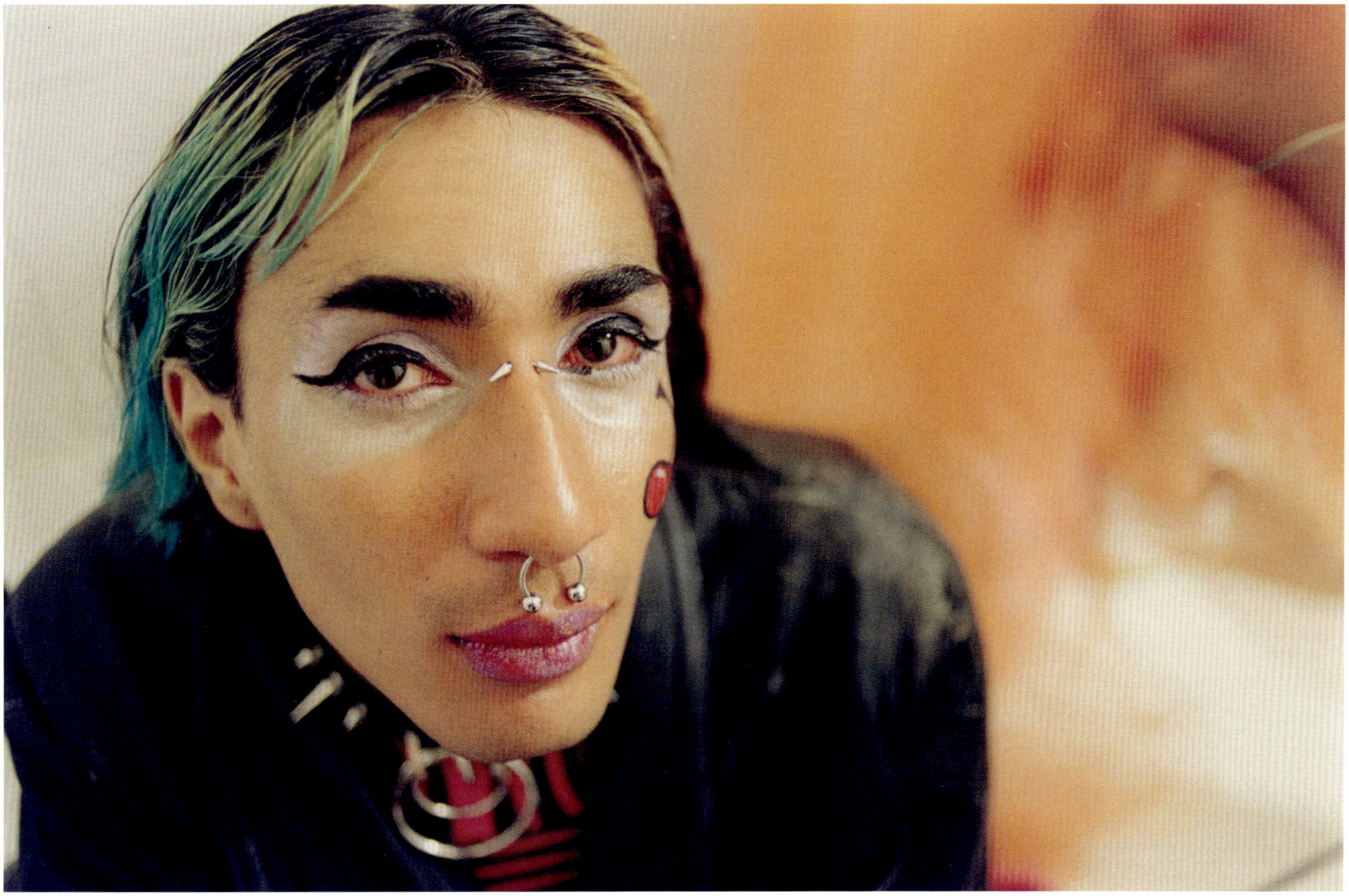

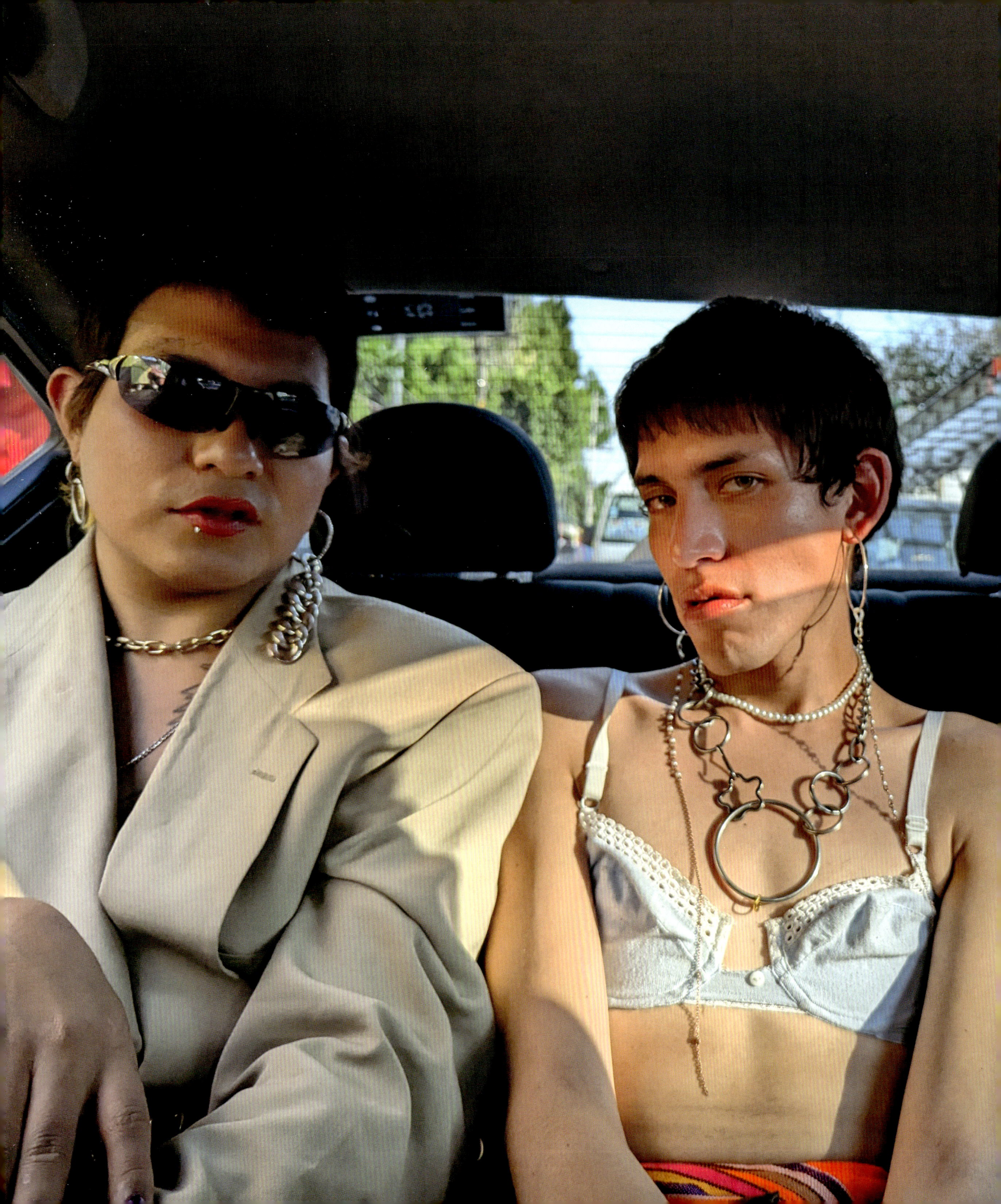

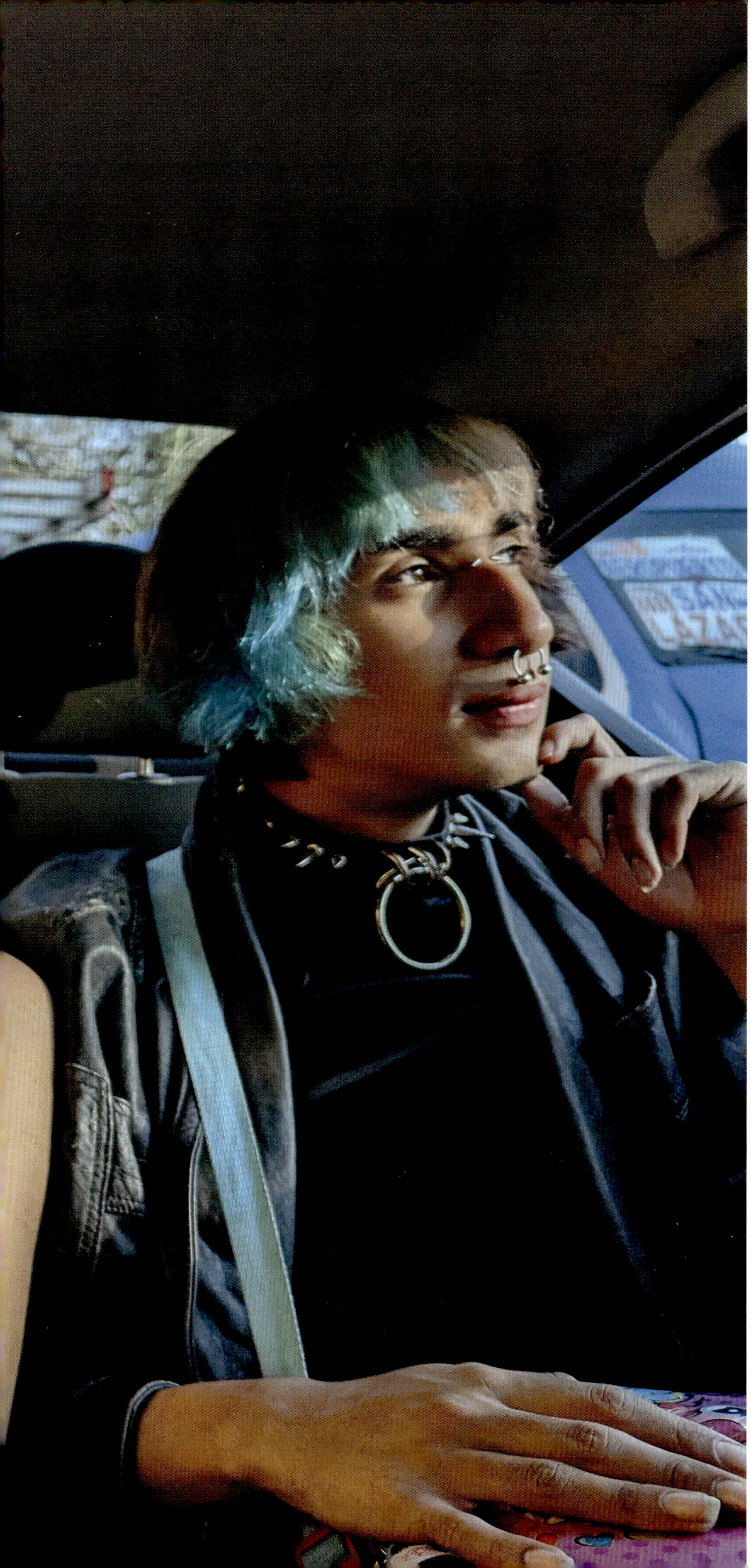

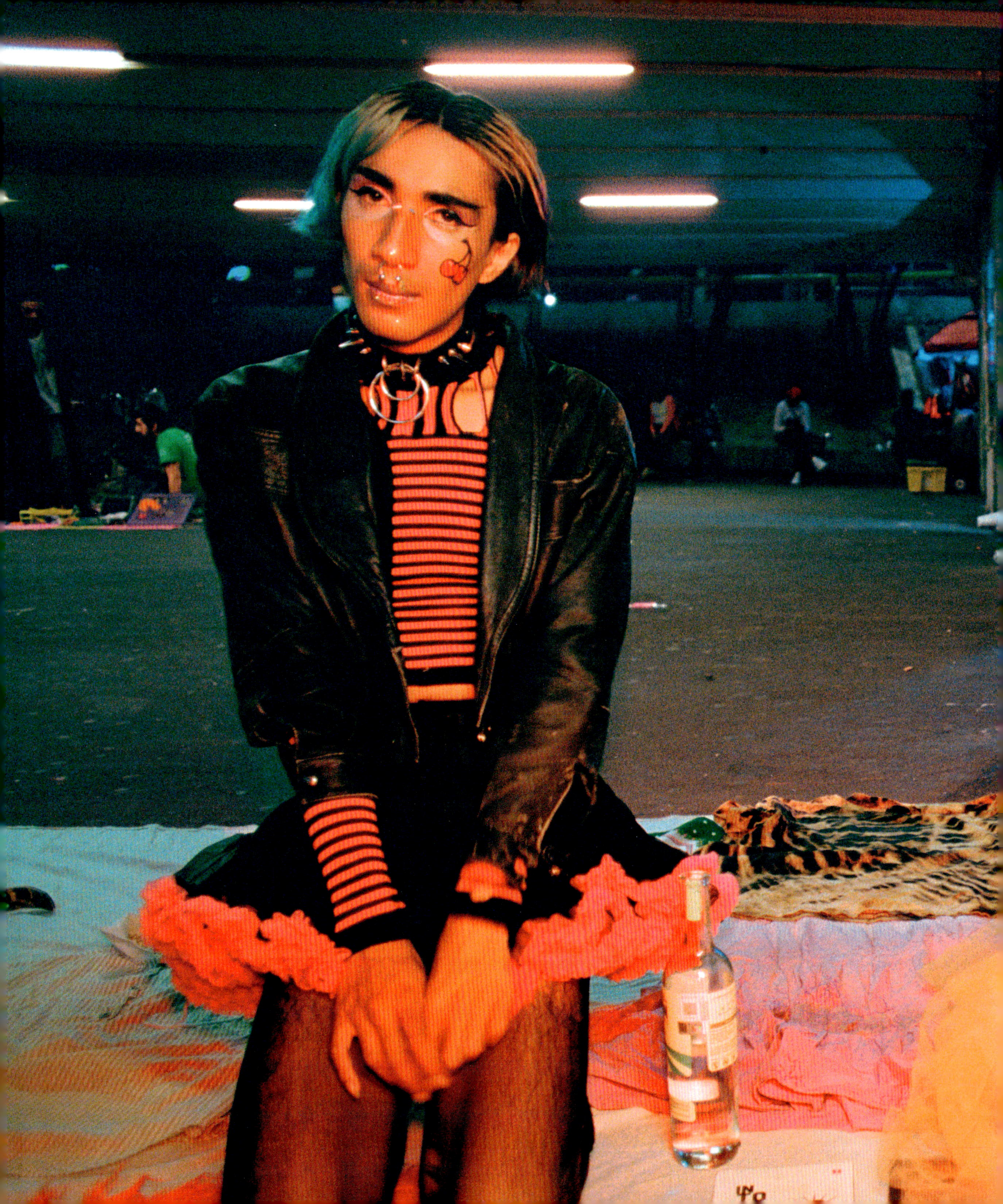

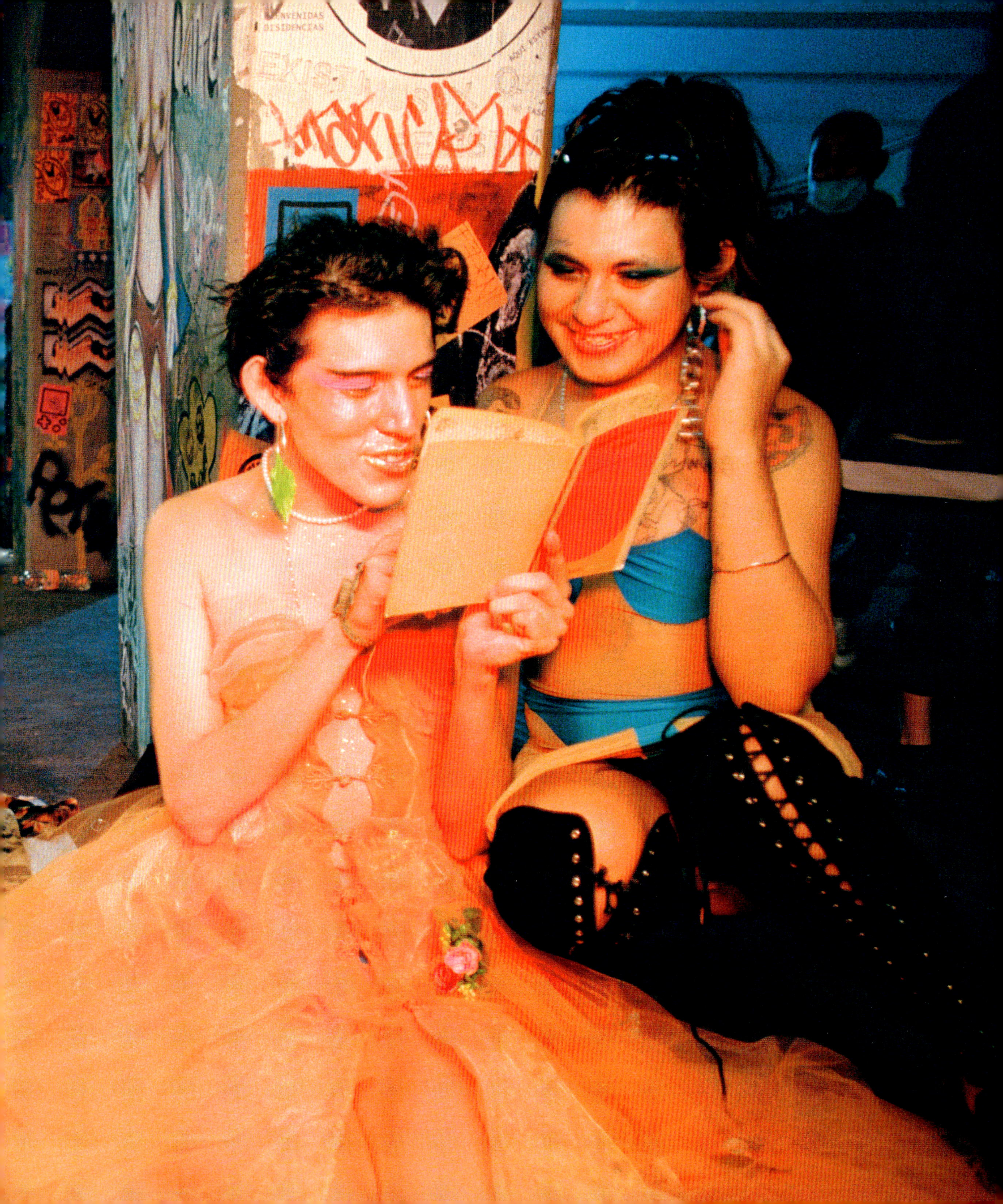

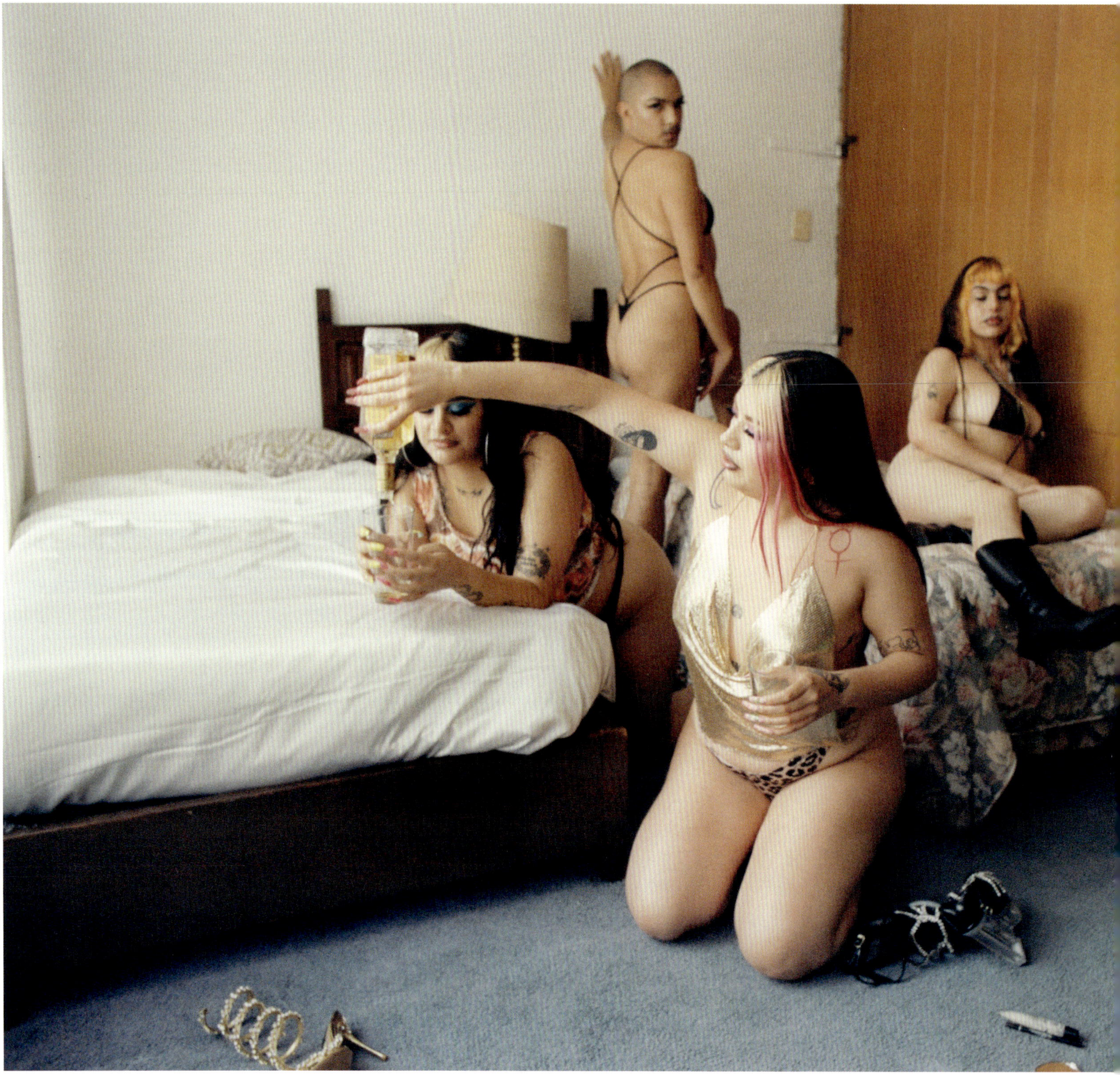

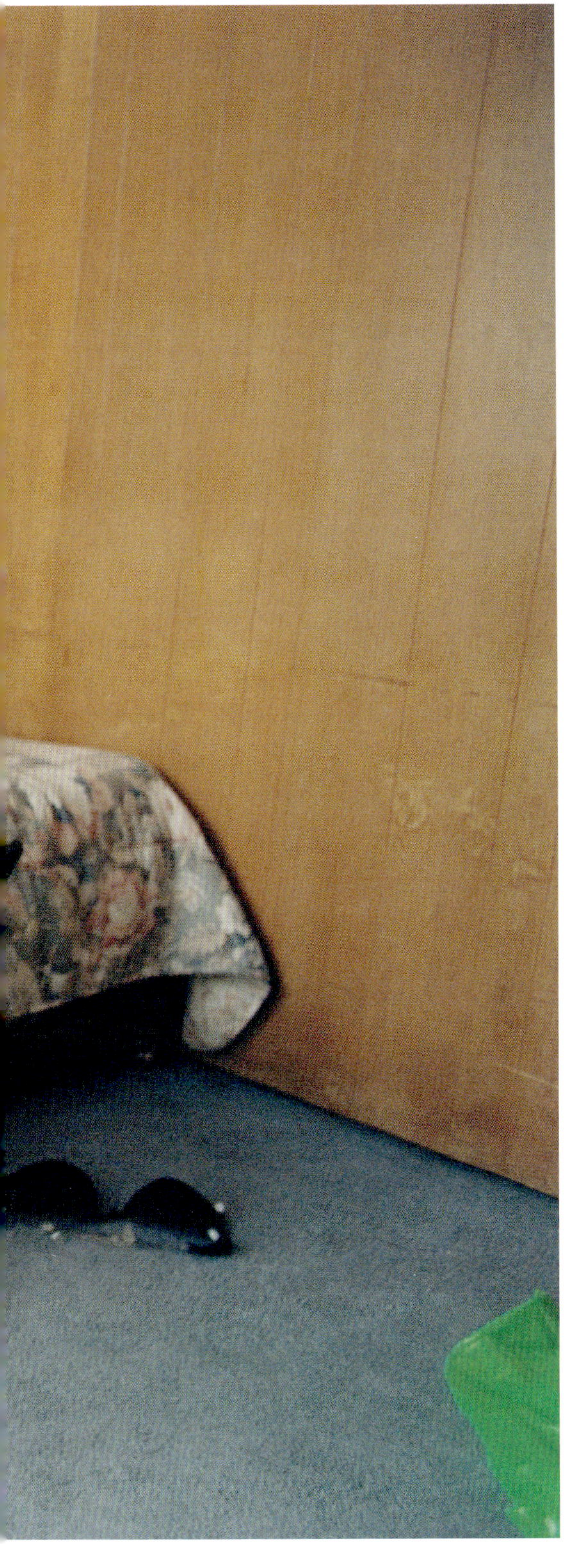

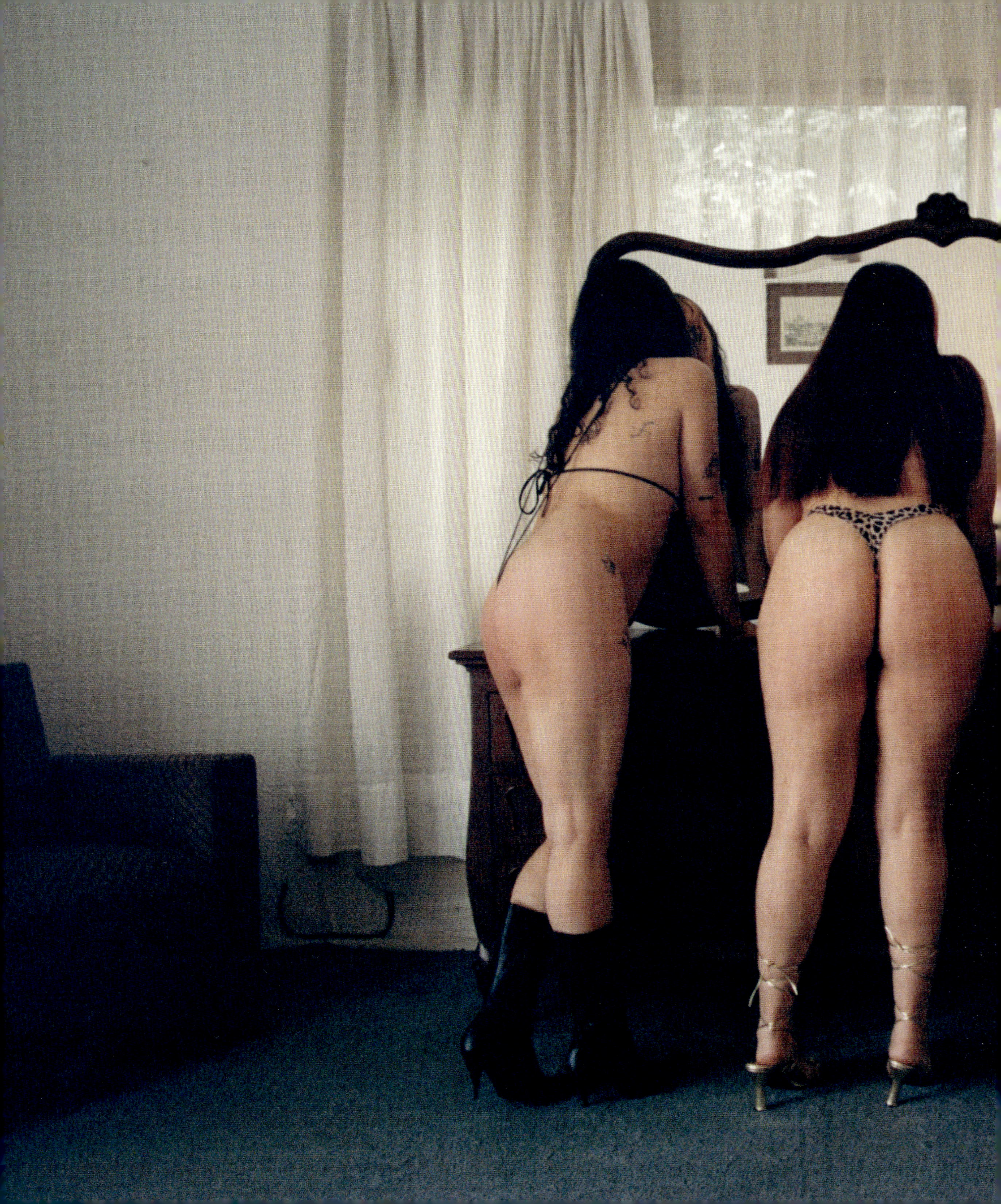

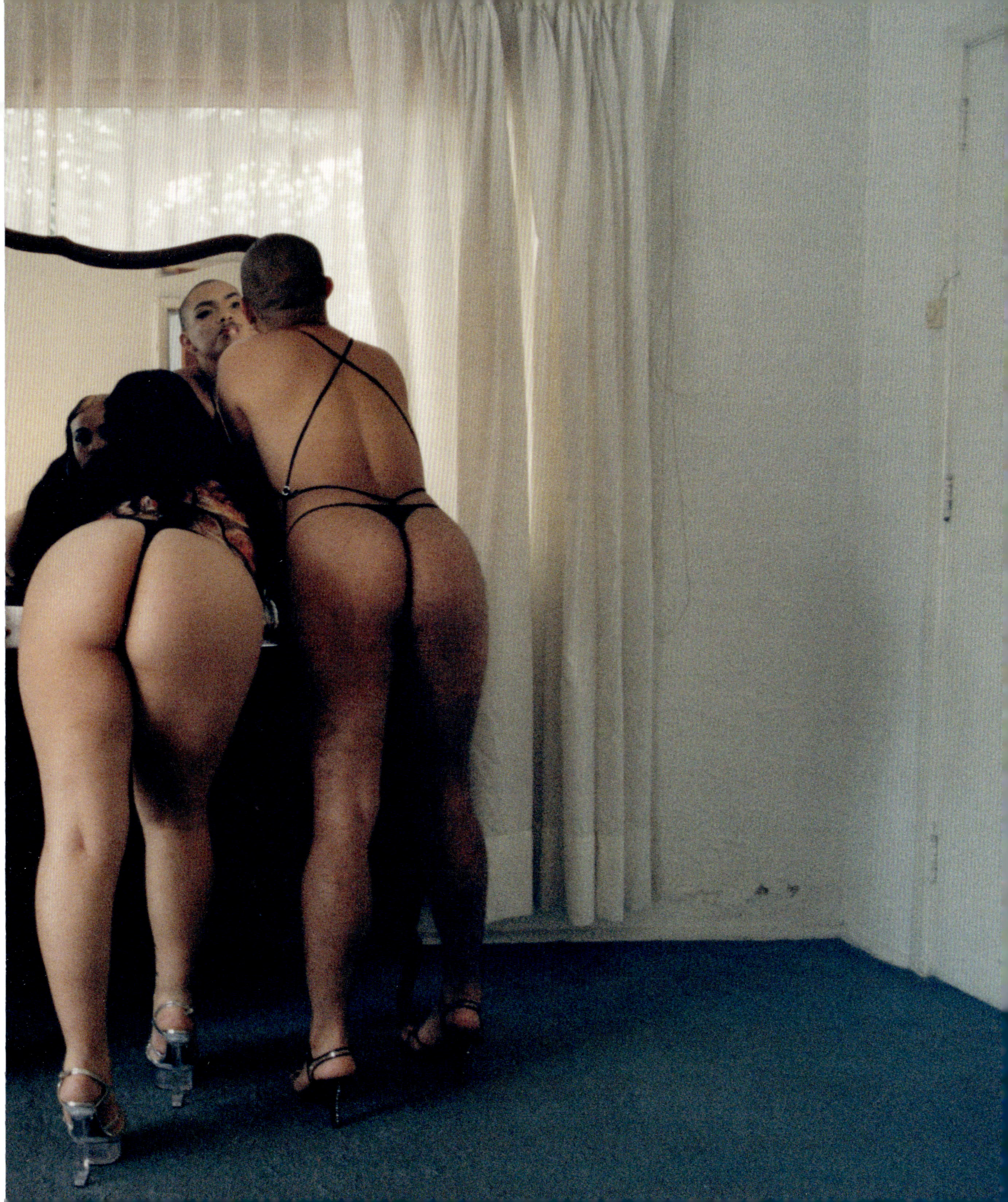

Magia Ilegal

Crecí en un país sangriento, en el estado que menos museos tiene en todo el país, exponer y encontrar lugar para la creatividad a veces parecía sólo una fantasía. Tenochtitlan y Magia ilegal se convirtieron en mi plataforma para seguir creando y dejar abiertas las puertas para las que vienen de mas lejos con otras historias pero mismos obstáculos siempre sean bienvenidas.

Me di cuenta que oculto mi activismo por la salud mental porque valoro más el hecho de ser artista que cualquier condición mental para que no me defina. Al mismo tiempo sé que conexión es permanente. Realmente creo que el arte puede salvarnos y la ternura. Parece repetitivo todo esto desde mi propia mente, pero no voy a normalizar nunca la violencia que vivimos. Nuestra resistencia fue creada por y para personas en situación de disidencia, económica, neurodivergentes, racializadas trans con capacidades/incapacidades diferentes, infancias que quieren dedicar su vida al arte y la magia otra relación inigualable.

Por el momento contamos con una casa para resistir siempre de forma gratuita con la única condición de que nos sigamos preparando cómo agentes de cambio en lo espiritual y la cultura. Por las del pasado y por las del futuro. Hemos sido incubadora de grandes procesos artísticos como lo son colectivas de activismo culturas madres y música. Magia Ilegal no se limita a ningún concepto, medio o disiplina posible de expresión, siempre buscando nuevas propuestas. Puede ser un oasis, un laboratorio, el templo se transforma como nosotras. Creemos en la comunidad y la fusión. Me siento agradecida de honrar otros saberes, estoy rodeada de talentos que su existencia construye la cultura de mi país, un territorio que a pesar de las fronteras impuestas, nos transforman para entendernos.

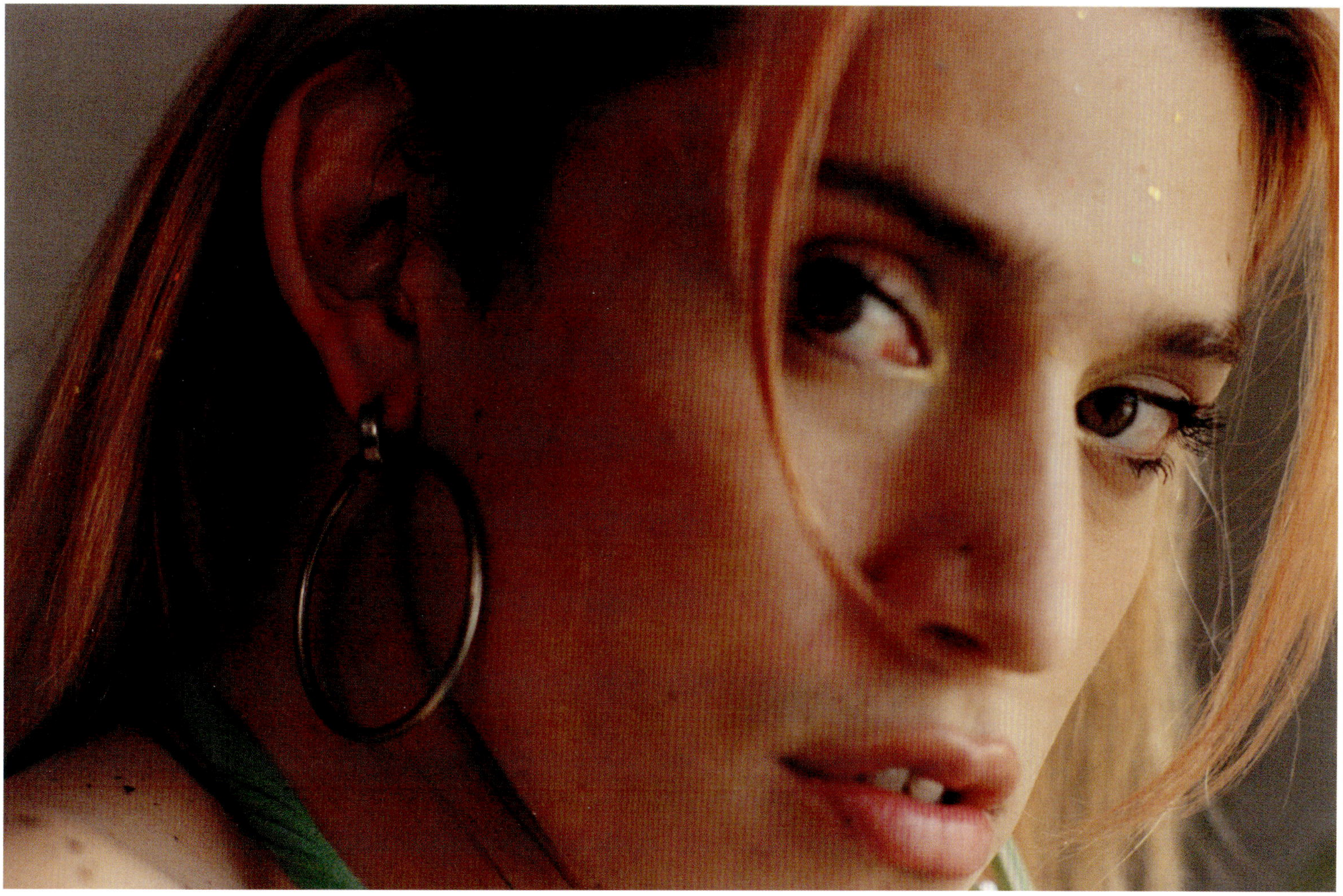

Fusion Strengthens

To all my sisters that died fighting for our rights, for our spirits to be free and for us to be able to inhabit our full selves. To my guardians. I'm writing to you here, knowing that, like me, there are others who since their youth have felt drawn to transition in spirit or in body.

Trans children exist, we challenge and transform established canons to reach those who want to understand their place in the cosmos through a new perspective. I am aware of both the scientific method and the knowledge that Western civilizations have produced on a wide range of matters, but I also know that academia is only one of many ways to transmit ideas; the wisdom that is passed down from generation to generation, practical know-how, and the understanding that comes from the process of adapting to our surroundings are just some of the other available forms of learning. I propose opening our minds without ceasing to question ourselves; with the intention to break down the barriers that hegemonic ideas have imposed upon our collective subconscious. Tirelessly, I stress the cultural debt we owe our ancestors for the knowledge that they have imbued us with. Their struggle and resistance has gifted us more than one way to perceive the complexity of life.

The internet, a true ally, has made things once obscured visible through only a click. But that unearths a new obstacle: Within a sea of information, how do you select what is useful to your reality? I understand that every person contains a universe of particular needs, chaos, and harmony.

Resignifying Family

The people I love most are victims of violence, though perhaps so is everyone else. Some hide their wounds and others get tattoos to camouflage their scars. The women speak of healing while the men defend themselves, but I believe it is those who exist without gender who will save us. To those who feel defeated already and want to surrender, I say, do not be afraid of abandonment from those with no intentions to support you, who want to manage you, tame you, use you to later cast you aside. For centuries, trans, lesbian, gay, and queer+ people have been murdered and stripped of a dignified life. Spaces to enjoy our lives are vital to our community because memories of love and joy are necessary refuges from the Latin American reality we inhabit and in which we risk our lives being our trans selves. To celebrate and come together in this resistance is a matter of life or death, and to heal from all the blood spilled throughout our history is our birthright. We deserve a nucleus that can function as a sanctuary.

A family should walk lovingly and tenderly beside you as you grow, but that is sadly not always the case. This is why the term "chosen family" is increasingly used; as identities become more diverse, the possibility of paternal rejection also grows. Choosing your family can be a challenging process of trial and error, but if one thing is certain, it is that when we succeed we find ourselves sheltered by a sense of true support and safety. Family may be too brief a term to describe the energetic force of what we are accomplishing by resisting together.

Magia Ilegal

I grew up in a violent nation, within the state that harbors the least museums in the country, and finding a creative outlet often seemed to me a futile daydream. Tenochtitlán and Magia Ilegal became my platforms for creation, where the doors were always open to women who came from further away, carrying different stories but having faced the same obstacles.

I noticed that I hide my mental health activism because I value myself as an artist more than any psychological condition that I refuse to be defined by. At the same time, I know they are inherently connected. I truly believe that art and tenderness can save us. These thoughts of mine may seem repetitive, but I will never normalize the violence we experience. Our resistance was created by and for people enacting dissidence: anyone facing financial precarity, anyone neurodivergent, racialized, trans, or disabled, who wants to dedicate their lives to art and magic.

At this time, we have a house where it is always free to stay, with the only condition that those there continue their development as agents of spiritual and cultural change. For those in our past and those in our future. We have served as an incubator for the great artistic processes of collectives dedicated to activism, ancient cultures, and music. Magia Ilegal is not limited to any one expressive concept, medium, or discipline; we are always open to new proposals. It can be an oasis, a laboratory, or a temple that transforms as we do. We believe in community and connection. I feel grateful to honor other consciousnesses and find myself surrounded by talents that shape the culture of my country through their existence, in a landscape that, despite imposed barriers, transforms the ways in which we understand ourselves.

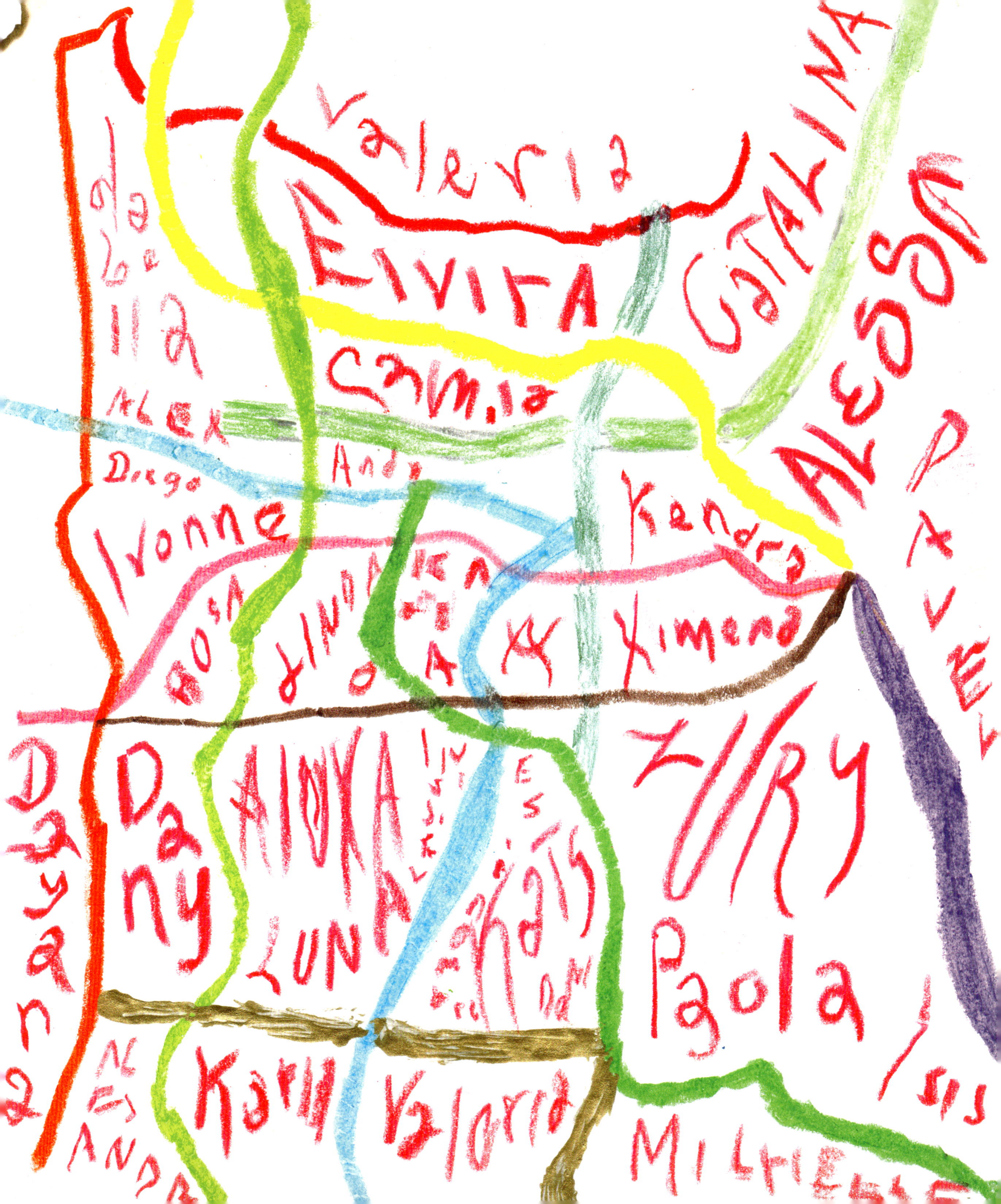
Valeria
ELVIRA
CATALINA
Camila
ALEX
Diego
Andy
Ivonne
Kendra
ROSA
Ximena
Dany
LUNA
Paola

NO

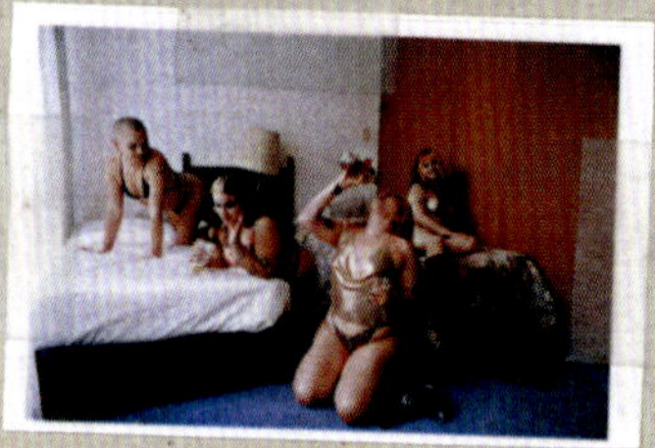

MAMES

~~OHAN~~
JOVANA, SHEILA,
KARLA AND ANDREA,
2019

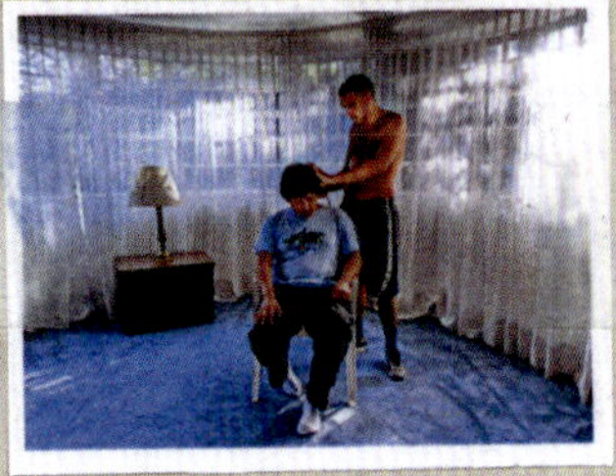

ADRIAN AND TE ARIKI,
2019

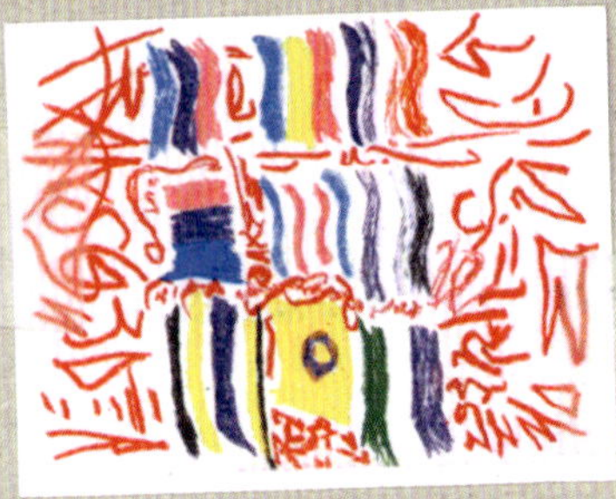

ARTWORK BY AINE MARIN, 2023
"FLAGS THAT REPRESENT ME,
REFLECTION ON THE MULTIPLE
CATEGORIES THAT EXIST
FOR ONE BODY AND IDENTITY"

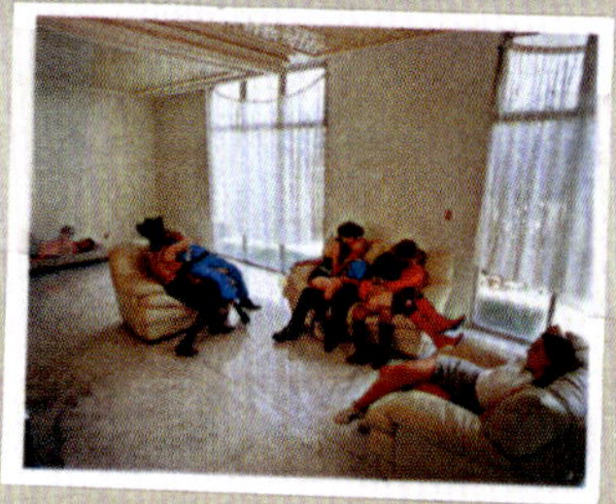

TIEMPOS KISSES,
LOMAS DE TECAMACHALCO,
2022

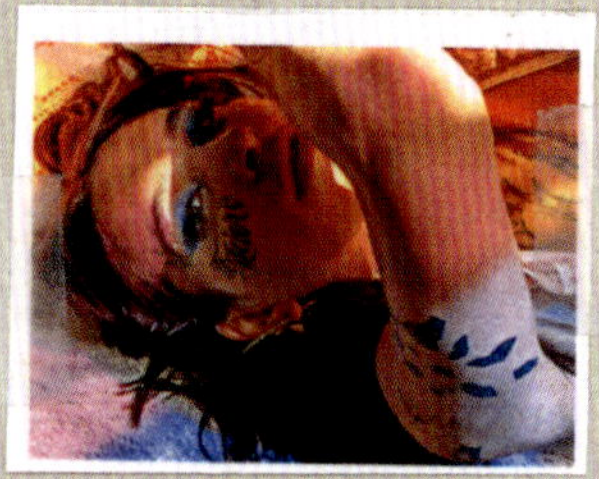

HAVI IN HER LIVING
ROOM,
CENTRO,
2019

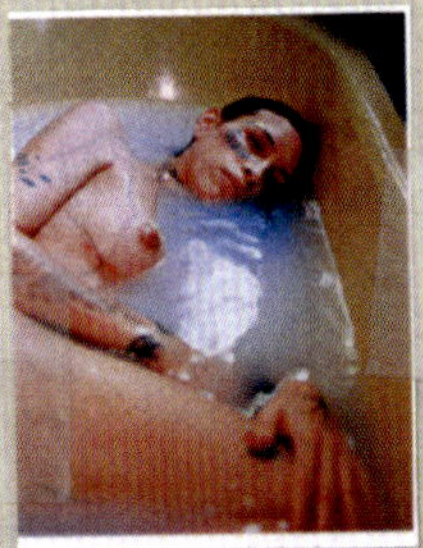

HAVI POST BREAST
AUGMENTATION SURGERY,
CONDESA,
2021

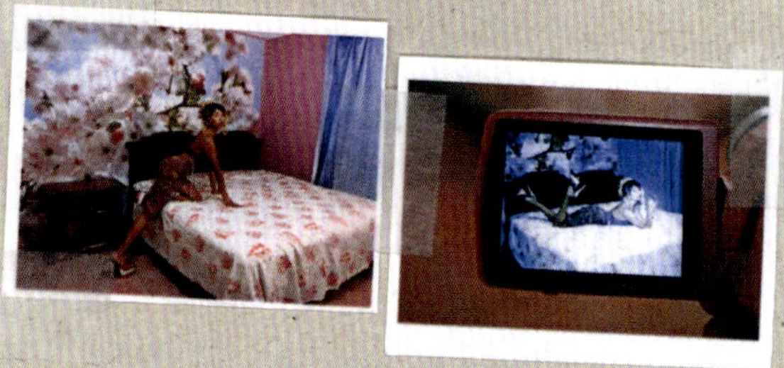

DITZY,
TEXCOCO,
2019

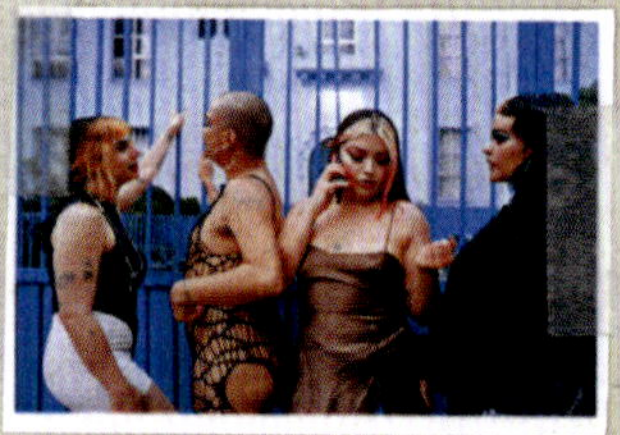

ANDREA, JOVANA, KARLA
AND SHEILA,
LOMAS DE CHAPULTEPEC,
2019

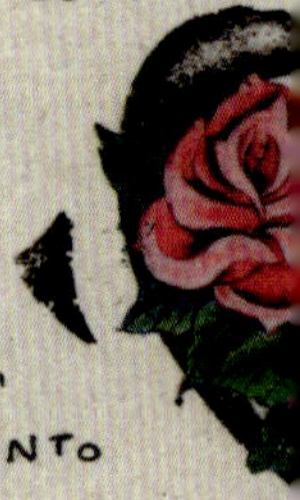

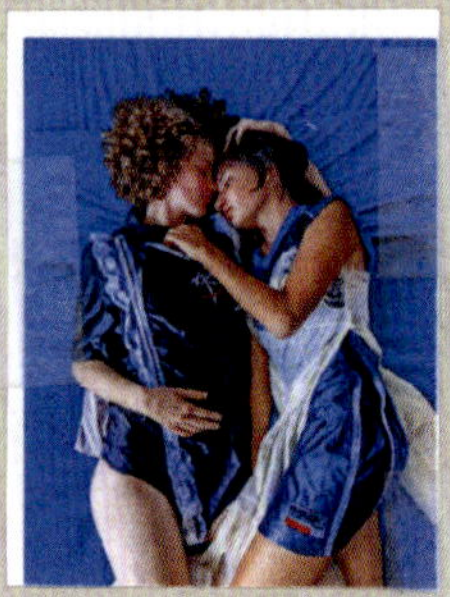

UMA AND ADA,
WEARING SENTIMIENTO
BY MARIA ISAS,
POLANCO,
2022

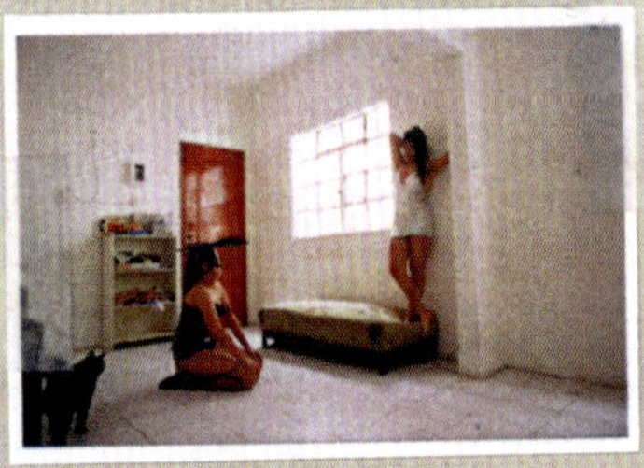

CUMI AND CYNTHIA
AT HOME,
ÁLAMOS,
2019

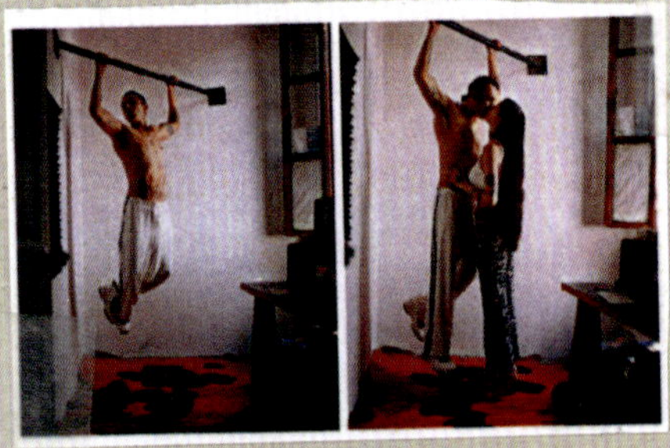

HAVI AND FER
AT HOME,
CENTRO,
2021

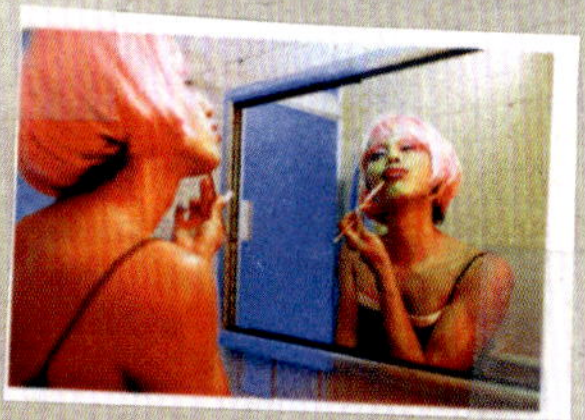

☆ TATSUMI ♡

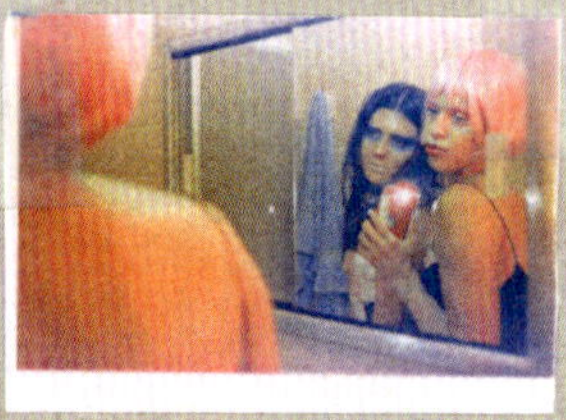

~~TAS~~
CALIAN
~~AA~~ AND
TATSUMI,
NÁPOLES,
2022

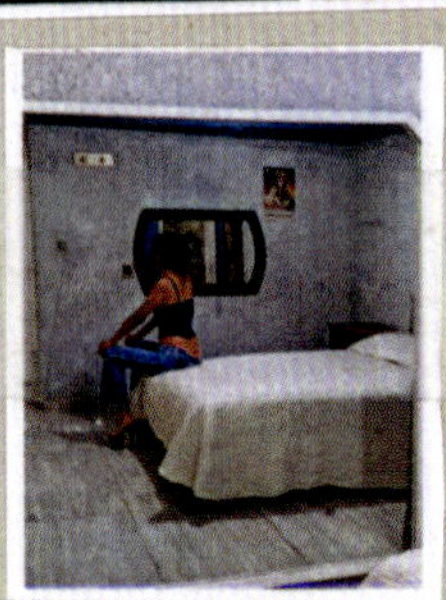

DITZY GIRL,
TEXCOCO,
2019
STYLING: ZARA MIRKIN

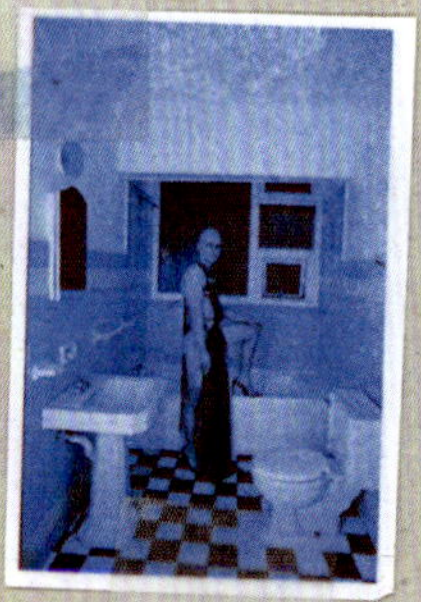

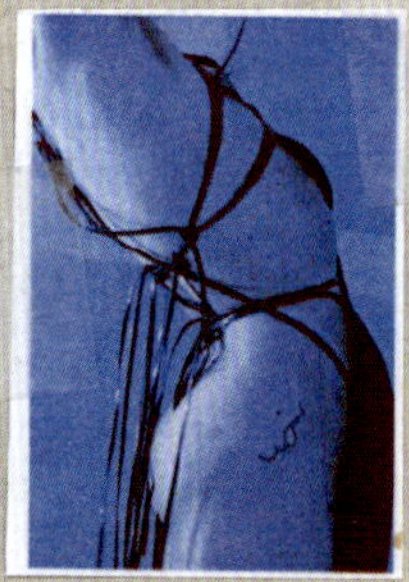

~~AZZMA~~
AZZMMA IN THE STUDIO,
CONDESA, 2019

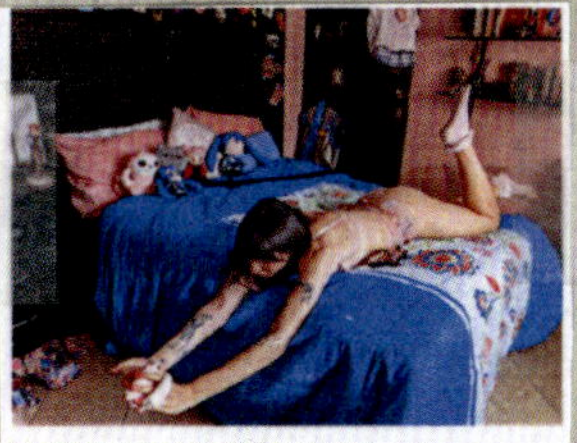

LULA IN HER ROOM,
LINDAVISTA,
2020

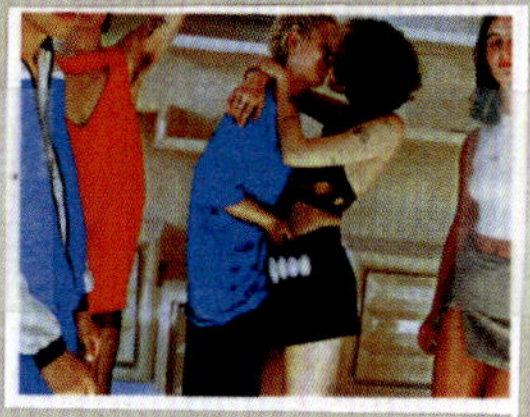

TIEMPOS PARTY
2022
LOMAS DE TECAMACHALCO

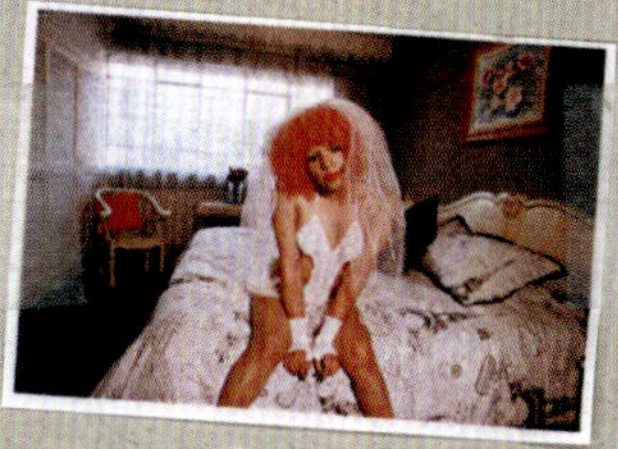

ALEXANDRA,
LETRAN VALLE, 2019
STYLED BY SAMANTHA
~~SAMANTH~~ RODRIGUEZ

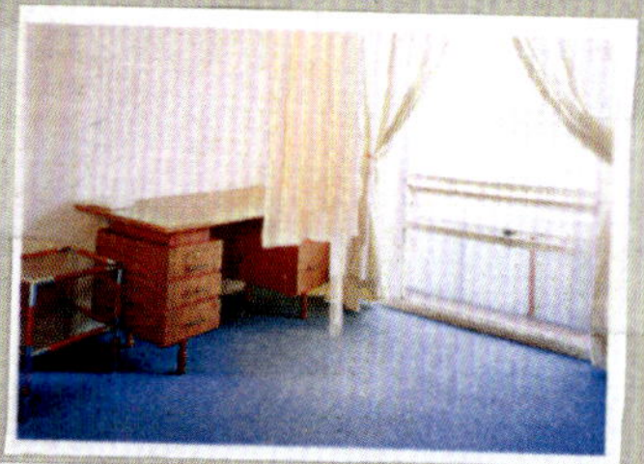

THE AIRBNB
IN POLANCO,
2022

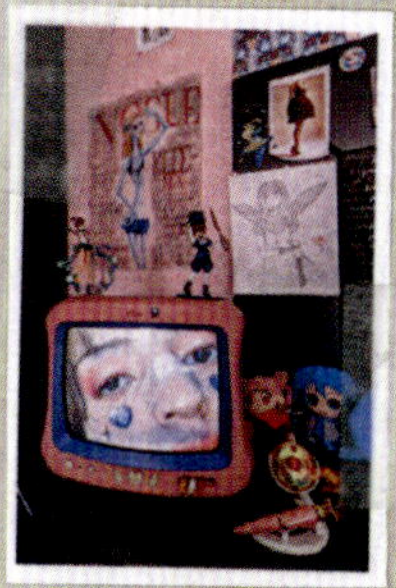

~~LA~~ LULA'S FANTASIA,
LINDAVISTA,
2020

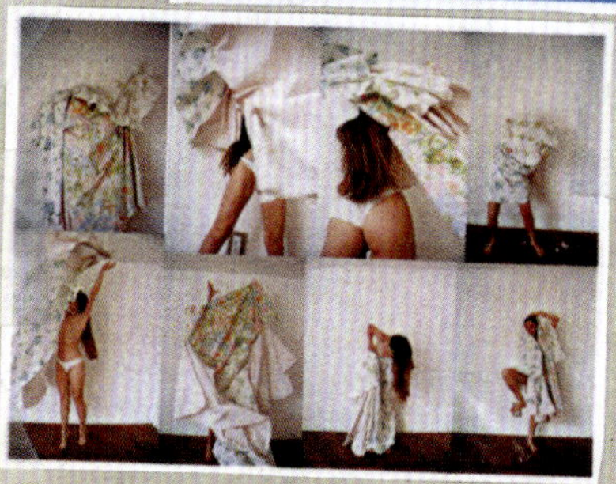

MARIA'S DANCE
IN SENTIMIENTO,
2019

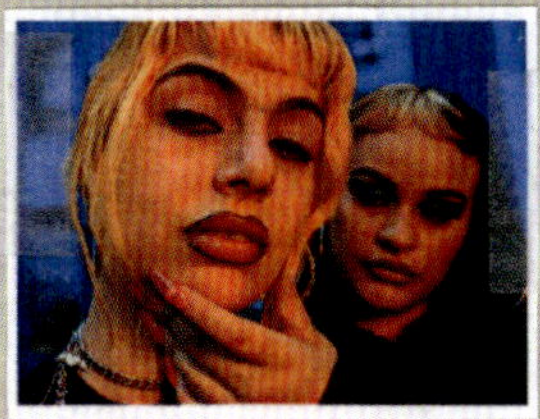

ANDREA AND SHEILA,
LOMAS DE CHAPULTEPEC,
2019

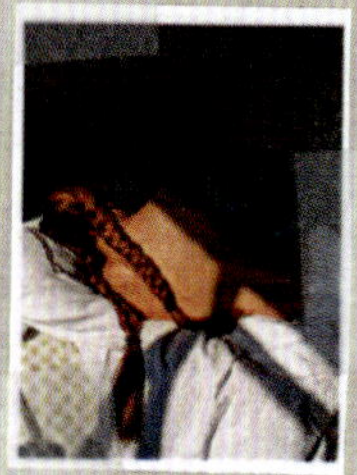

MARIA IN
HER BEDROOM,
SAN MIGUEL
CHAPULTEPEC,
2019

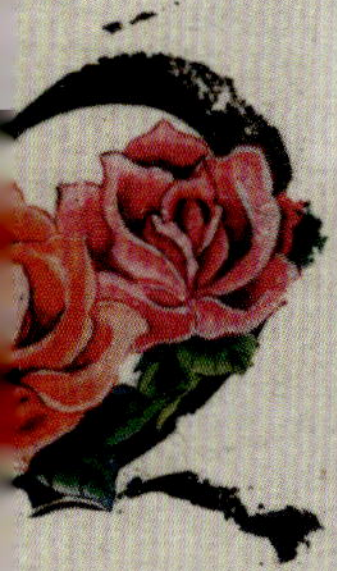

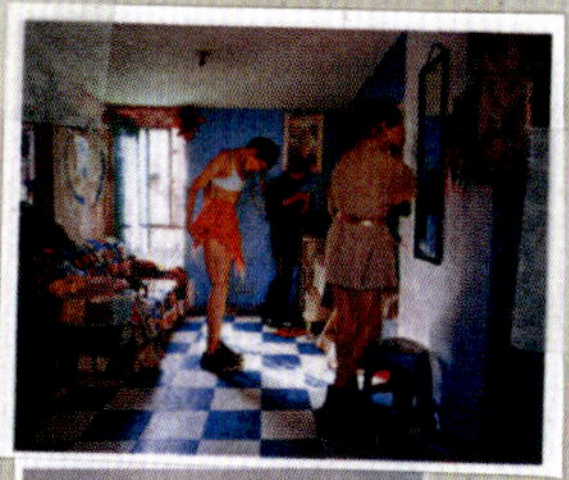

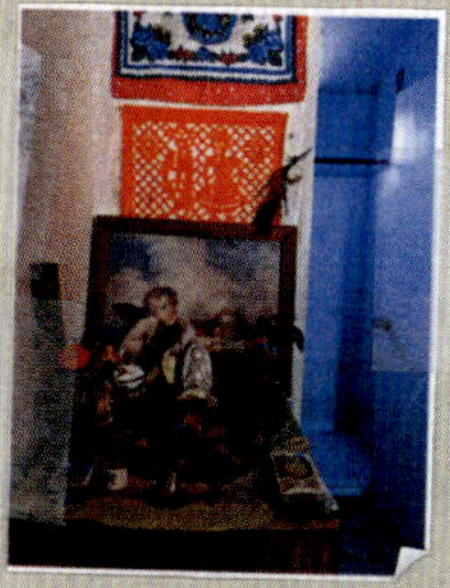

YUKKI,
AINE,
AND GRETA,
MAGIA ILEGAL,
2022

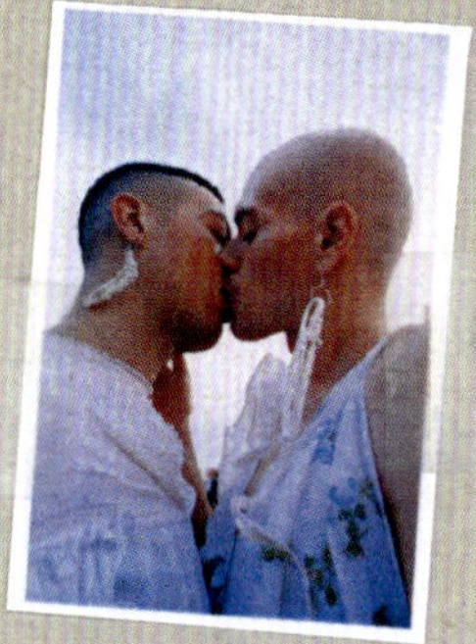

MANOLO AND ORLANDO,
TACUBAYA, 2019

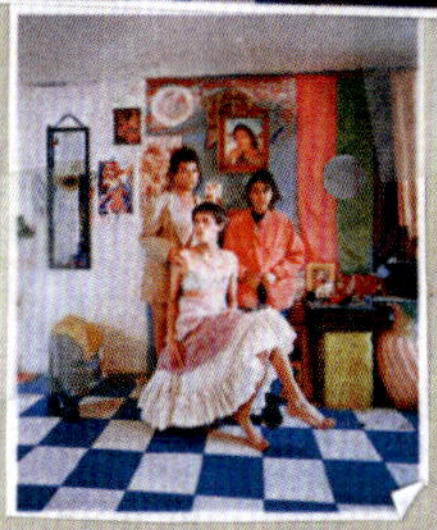

GRETA, AINE, MAR AND
ZURY ON THE WALL
♡ AT MAGIA ILEGAL ♡
IXTAPALUCA

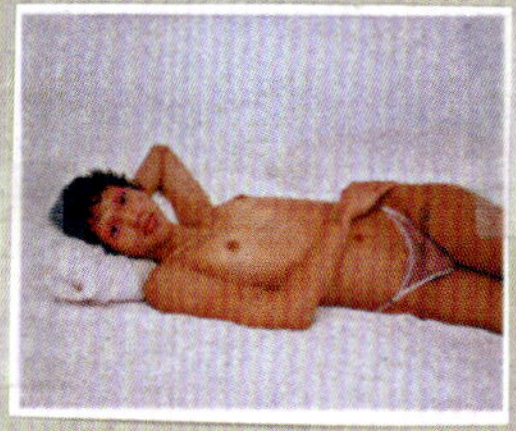

TATSUMI IN HER ROOM,
NAPOLES,
2022

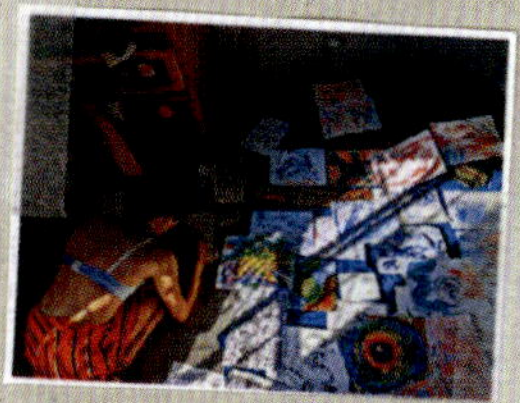

AINE WITH HER ARTWORK
DEDICATING A PROTECTIVE GIFT
FOR ME WHICH WILL LATER
GO ON MY WALL,
2022

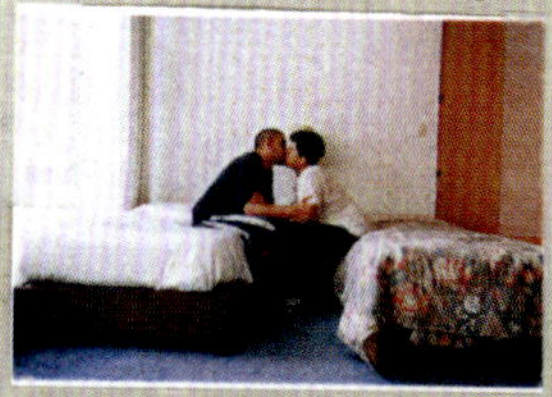

TE ARIKI AND ADRIAN,
2019

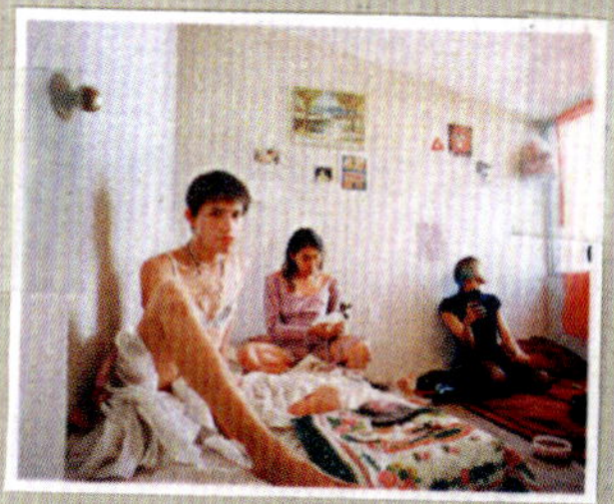

AINE, MAR, YUKKI IN ~~THEIR~~ THEIR BEDROOM, MAGIA ILEGAL,
2022

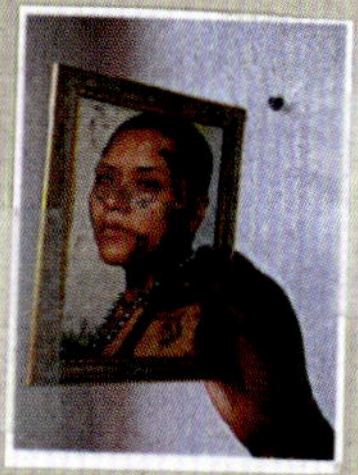

ANO,
CENTRO,
2019

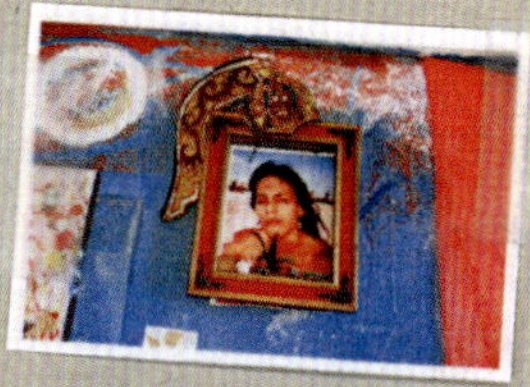

IN MEMORY OF ZURY,
AINE'S TRANS SISTER, 2022.

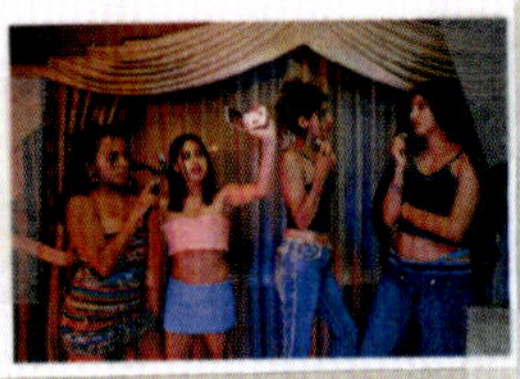

STYLED BY ZARA MIRKIN

DITZY GIRLS, 2019

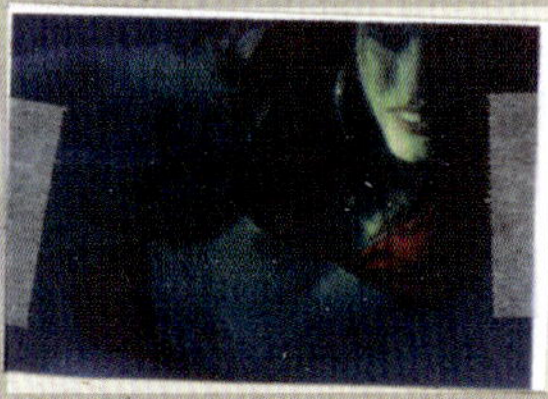

LORETO, 2020

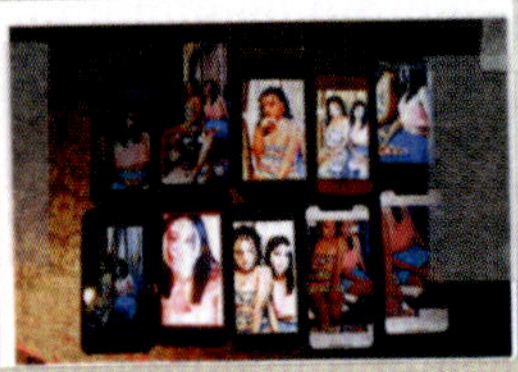

DITZY

DITZY IS A FASHION BRAND BY ADRIAN FIERRO LARA. STARTED IN 2019 AS AN ART PROJECT, DITZY IS A VISION OF MEXICO CITY WITH STRONG POLITICAL EXPRESSION, INSPIRED BY CHOCOMBIANOS, KANDI RAVERS AND PARIS HILTON FOR BROWN GIRLS.

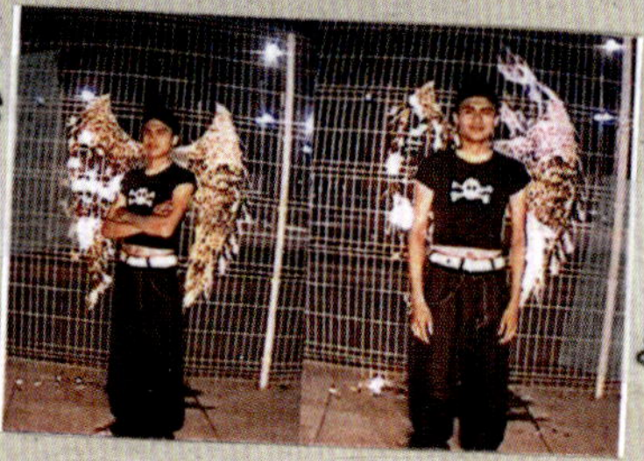

STYLED BY ZARA

DITZY ANGEL, CENTRO, 2019

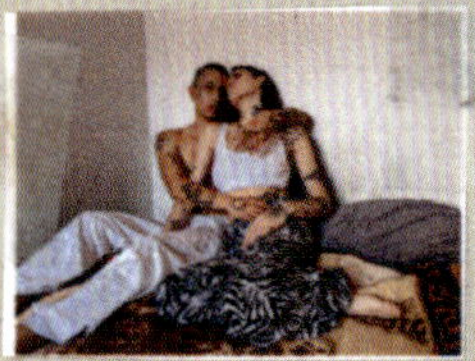

FER AND HAVI IN THEIR BEDROOM, CENTRO, 2021

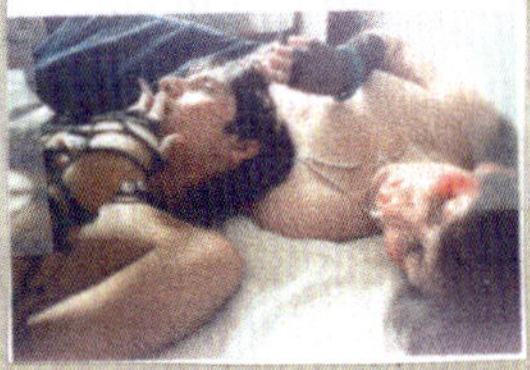

SEB AND SEBASTIAN, ROMA NORTE, 2022

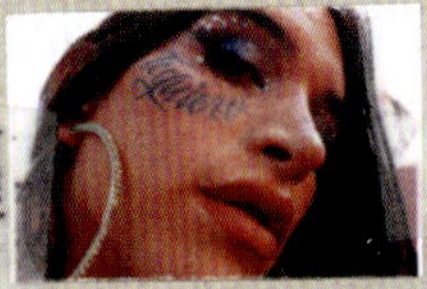

MAKEUP: KARLA

HAVI, 2019

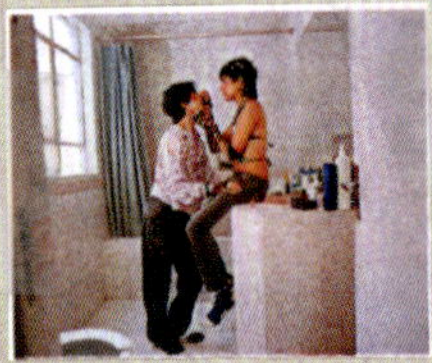

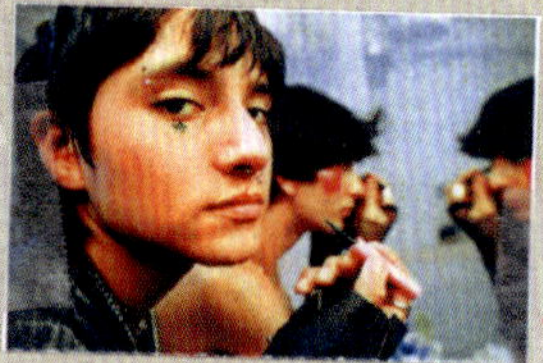

SEB AND SEBASTIAN, 2022

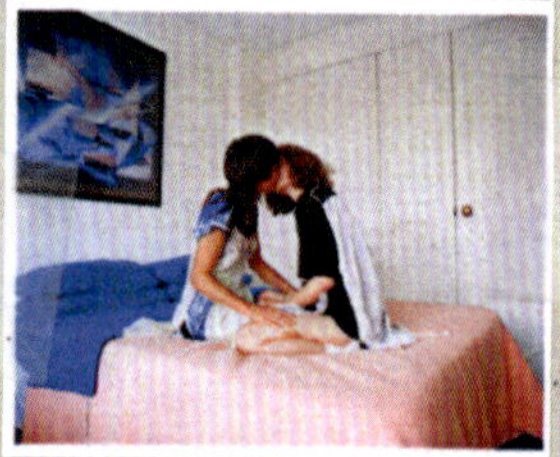

SENTI

UMA AND ADA IN SENTIMIENTO, POLANCO, 2022

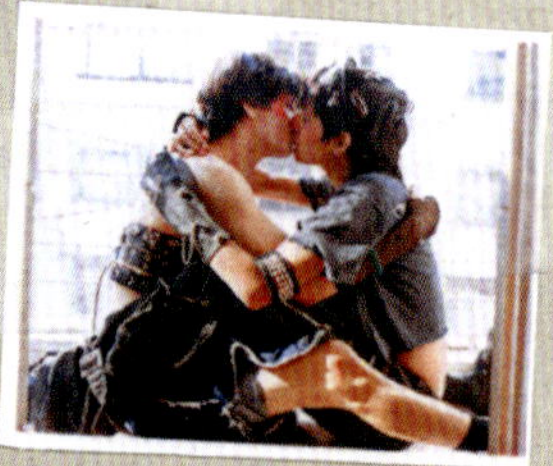

SEB

SEBASTIAN

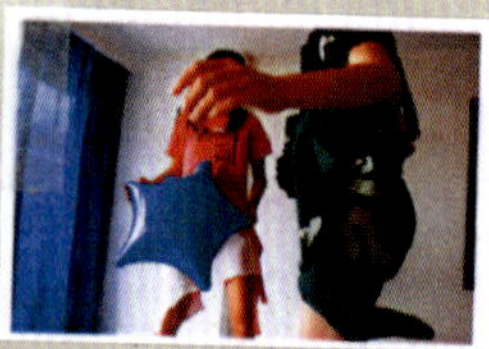

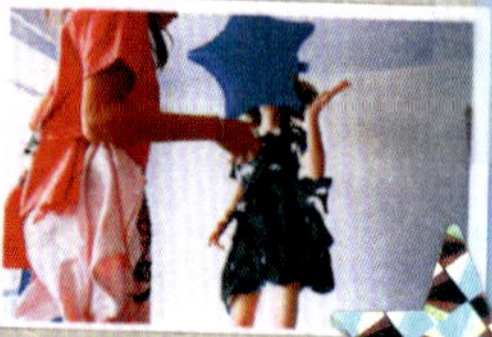

SENTI

SENTIMIENTO IS A MEXICAN SLOW FASHION PROJECT FOUNDED BY MARIA ISAS. FOCUSED ON RECYCLING WASTE AND FABRICS THAT ARE LOCALLY SOURCED, SENTIMIENTO CONNECTS PEOPLE AND OUR EARTH, COLLECTING, REPURPOSING AND POETICALLY STICHING POEMS AND WEAR INTO ONE.

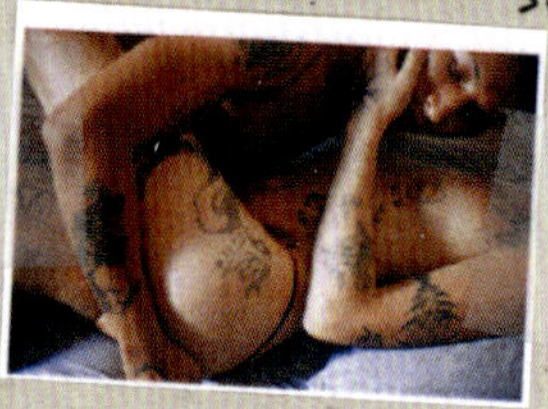

HAVI AND FER'S LOVE, 2019

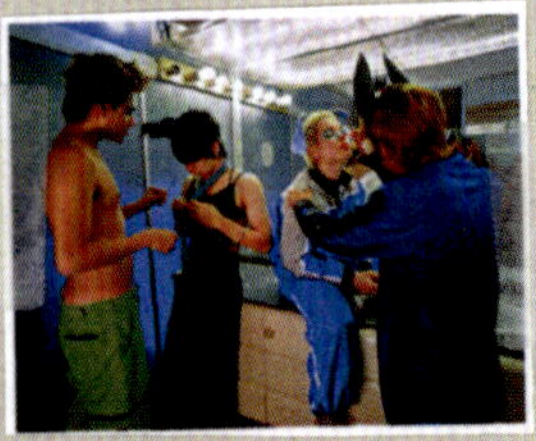

TIEMPOS PARTY, 2022
MAKEUP BY HUGO MATULA
STYLING BY SAMANTHA RODRIGUEZ

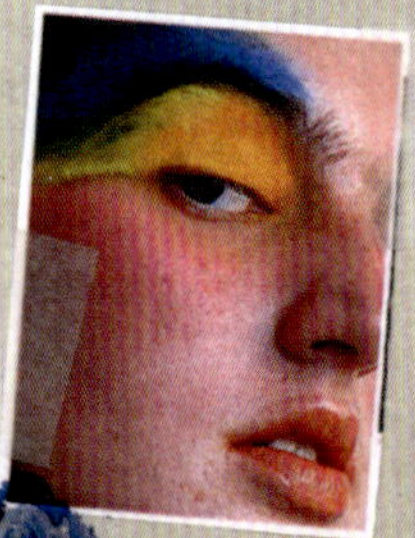

COSIMA, MAKEUP BY HUGO, 2022

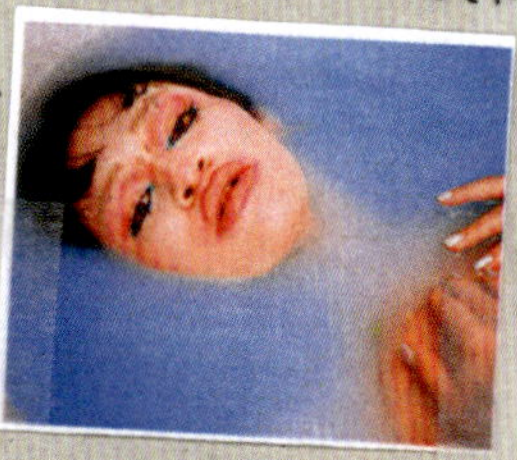

MAKEUP BY FERNANDA LUCERO RAMIREZ

VARON

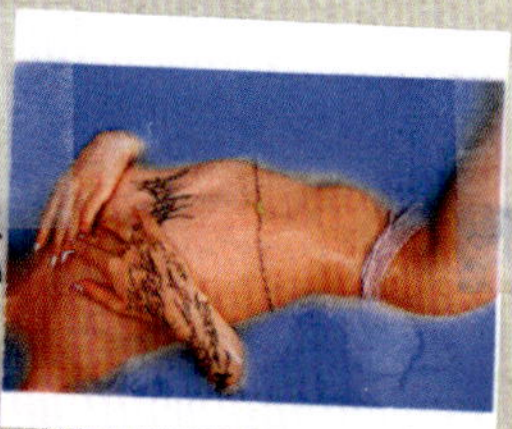

BLOBB

SALVIA IN VARON × BLOBB AT VORON'S STUDIO, CONDESA, 2022

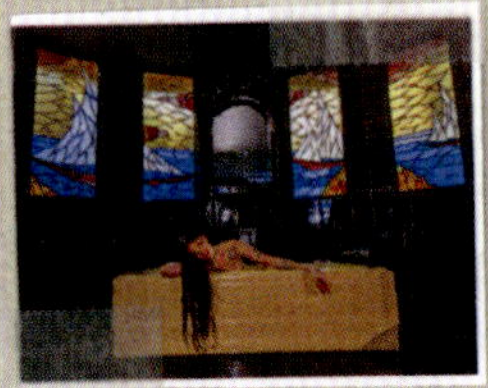

HAVI IN THE BATH, CONDESA, 2021

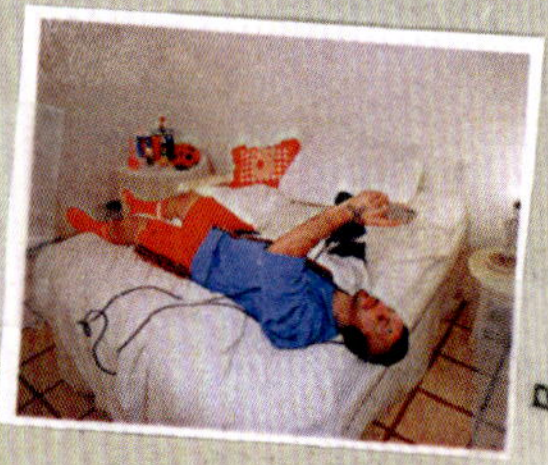

BLUE ROJO

BLUEROJO IN HIS ROOM WEARING SENTIMIENTO, GUERRERO, 2022

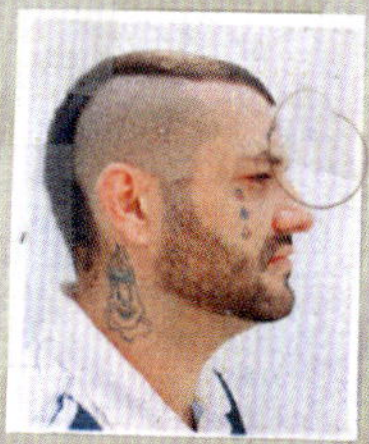
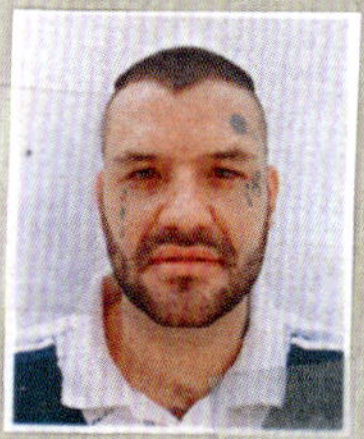

BLUE ROJO
IN SENTIMIENTO,
2022

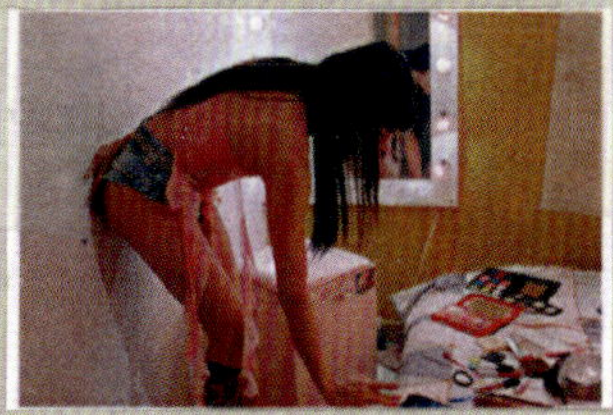

CAPULTITLAN

LORETO IN ~~HER~~ HER ROOM,
2020

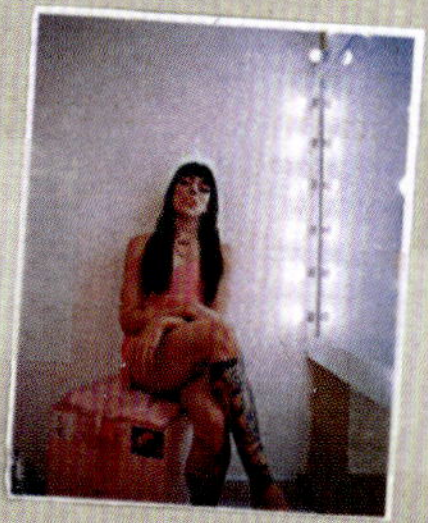

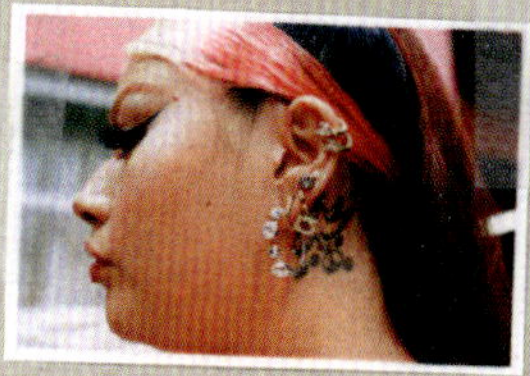

ROHO
KARLA ♡ JUAREZ, 2019

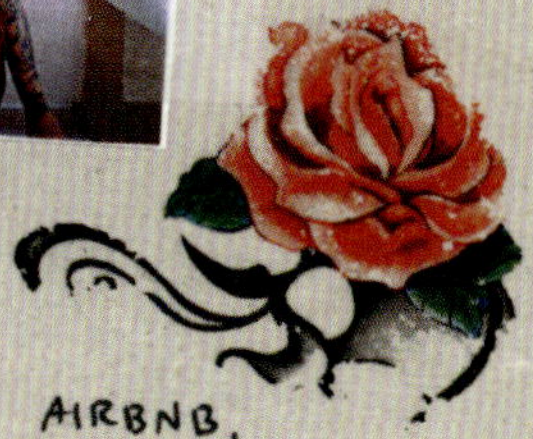

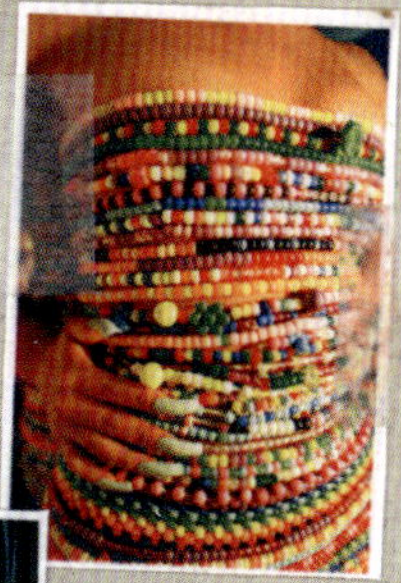

DITZY
DRESS,
2019

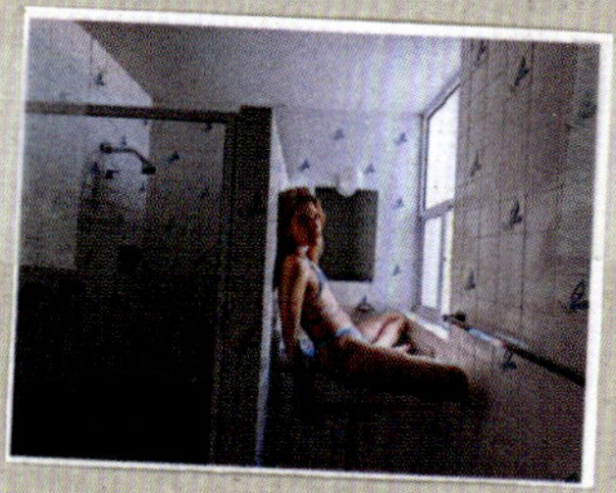

AINE AT MY AIRBNB,
CONDESA,
2020

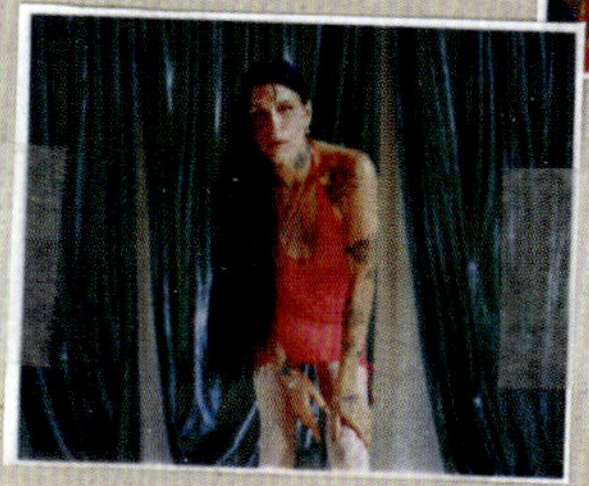

HAVI AT HOME,
2019

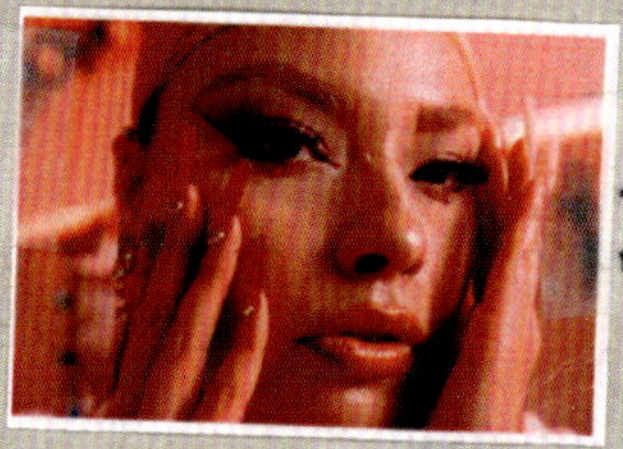

KARLA WITH NAILS BY HER,
ROHO 7, ♡
JUAREZ, 2019

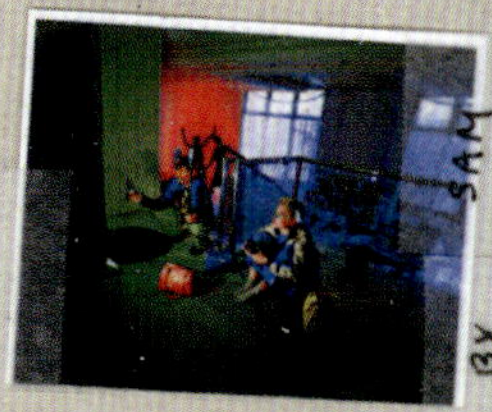

STYLED BY SAM
TIEMPOS PARTY,
2022

TIEMPOS IS A MEXICAN FASHION BRAND STARTED IN 2021 BY ESTEBAN TAMAYO, WHO DEFINES THEIR PRODUCTS LIKE PIECES OF EVIDENCE WITHIN FLEETING TIMES, AN AIM TO CREATE PUNCTUAL YET LASTING MOMENTS.

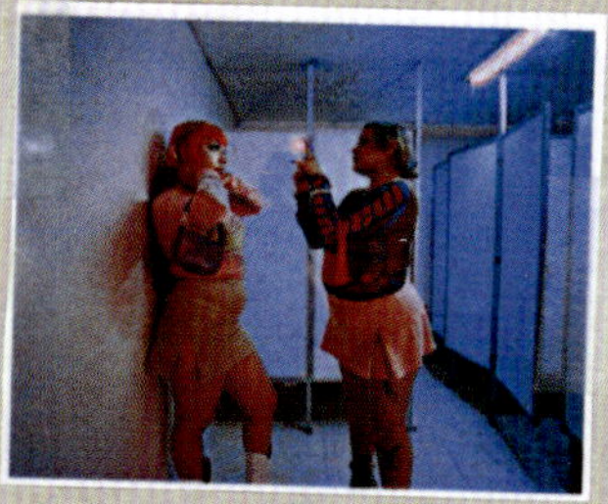

KARLA AND
SHEILA
AT LA FAENA
WEARING MADEME,
CENTRO
HISTORICO,
2022

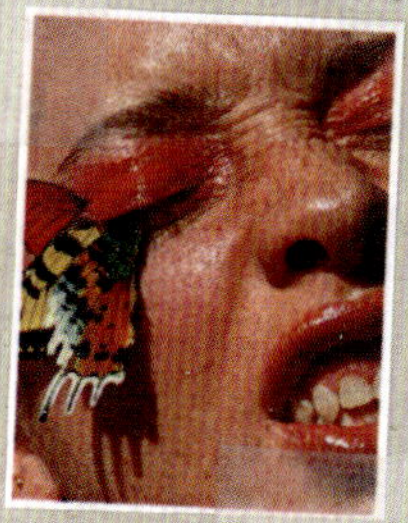

MARIA MARIPOSA FACE BY KARLA,
2019

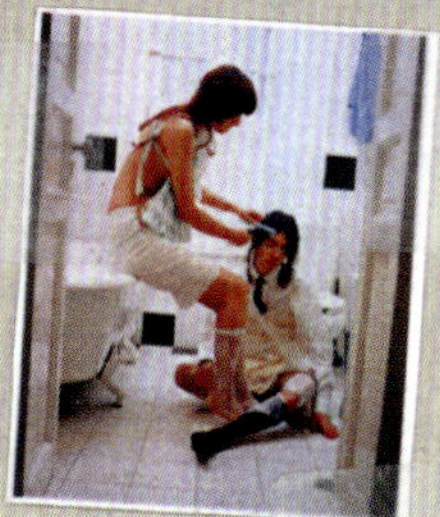
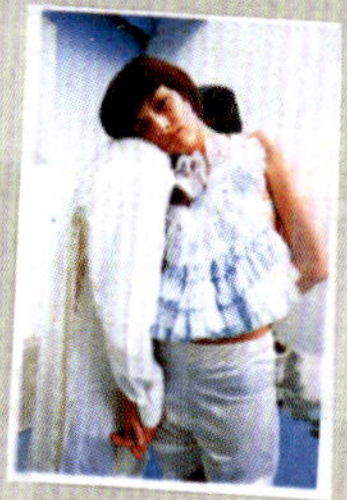

SENTI

DALZELL
AND
AURE,
ROMA
NORTE,
2022

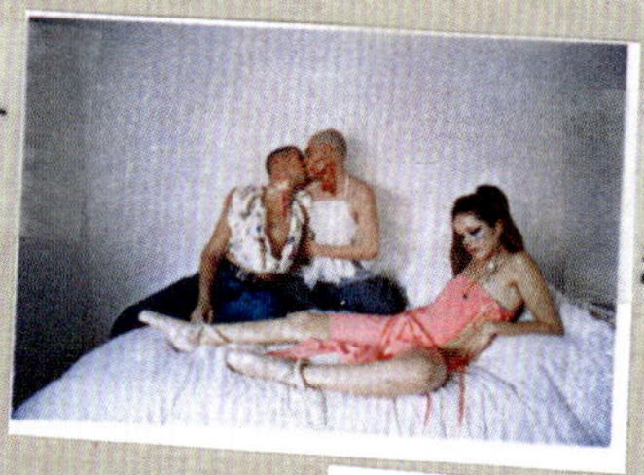

LICKY BY KARLA

ORLANDO, MANOLO, MARIA
ALL IN SENTIMIENTO,
2019
SAN MIGUEL CHAPULTEPEC

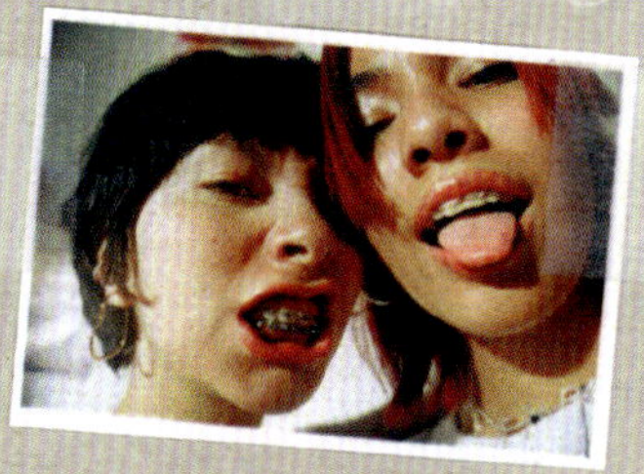

ZYANYA
~~AND~~ AND
VALERIA
JUAREZ, 2019

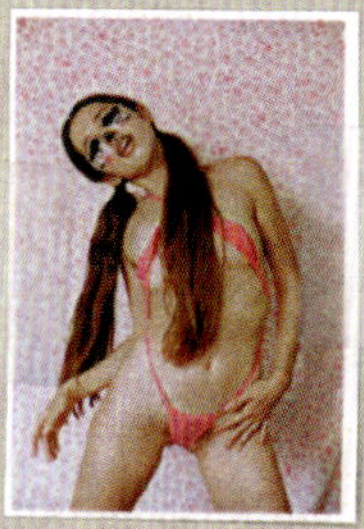
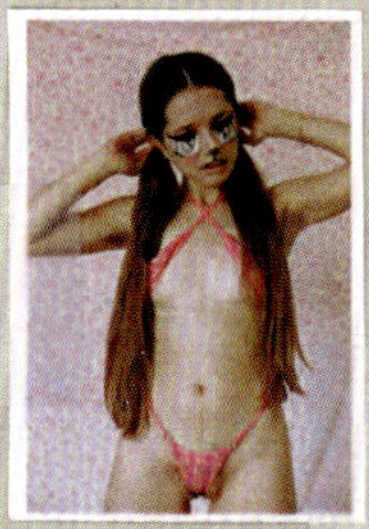
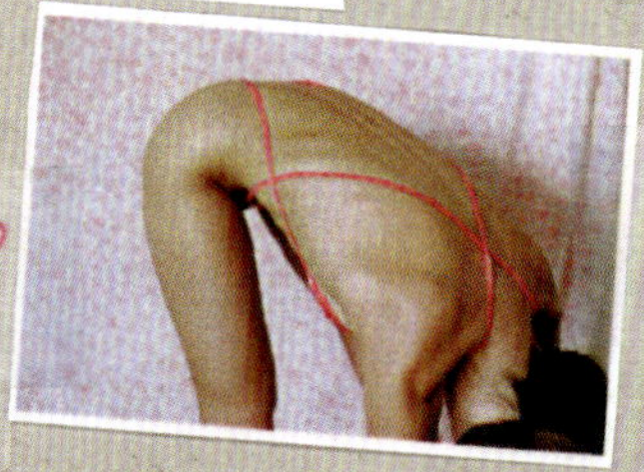

LICKY
LIU

MARIA AS
LICKY LIU,
MAKEUP BY
KARLA DONATO,
2019

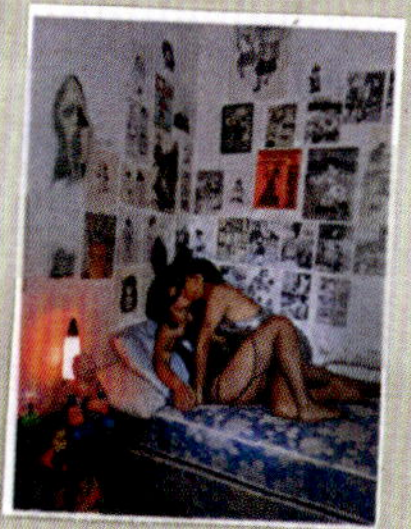

CUMI AND
CYNTHIA,
2019

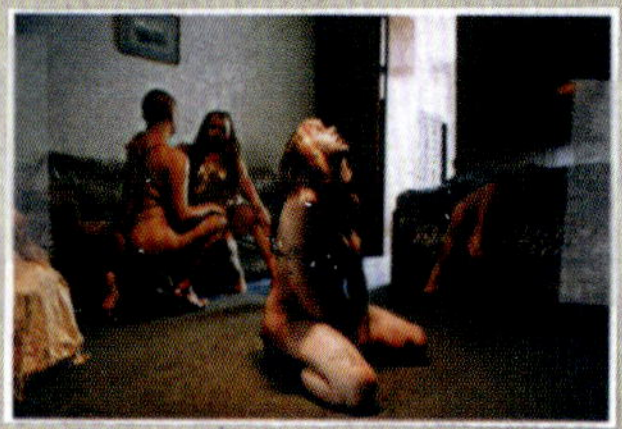

ANDREA

JOVANA, KARLA, SHEILA

2019

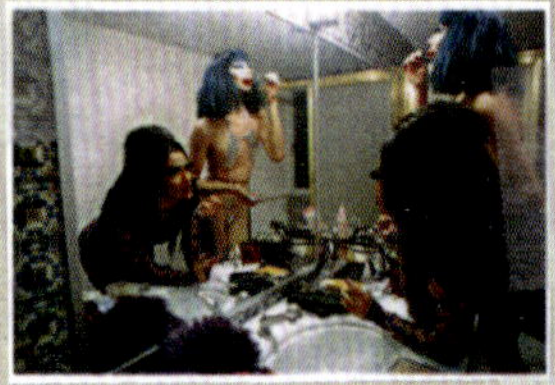

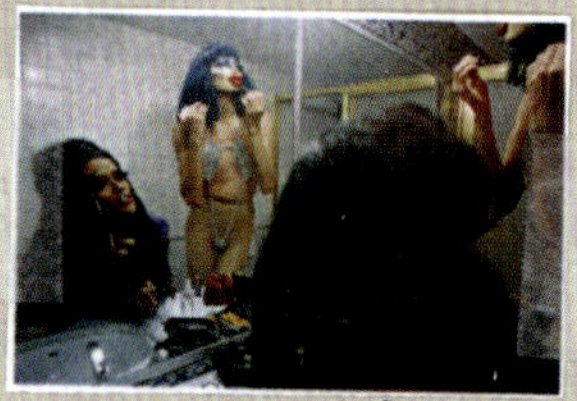

DOLORES AND POSSE,

2019

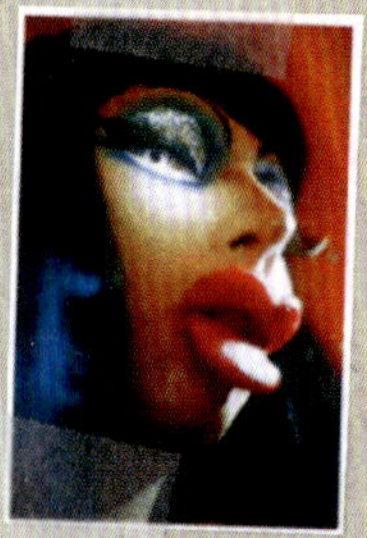

POSSE, 2019

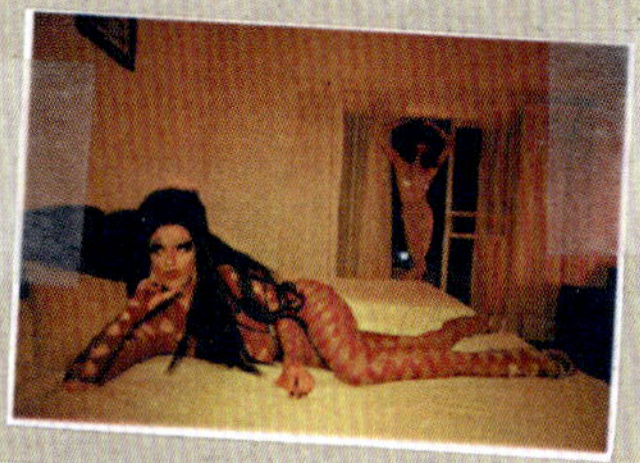

DOLORES AND POSSE,

2019

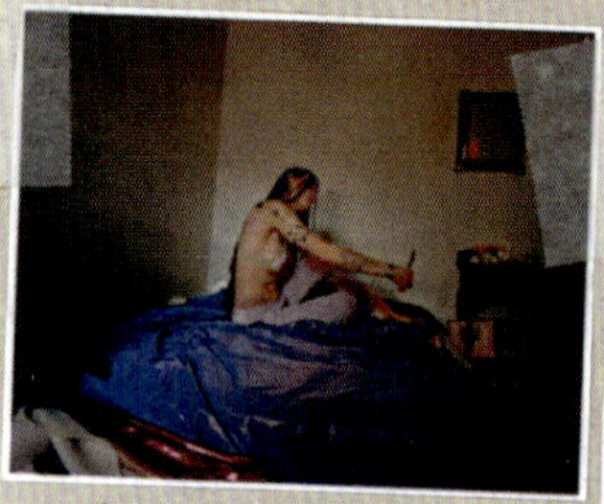

HAVI AT HOME POST SURGERY,

2022

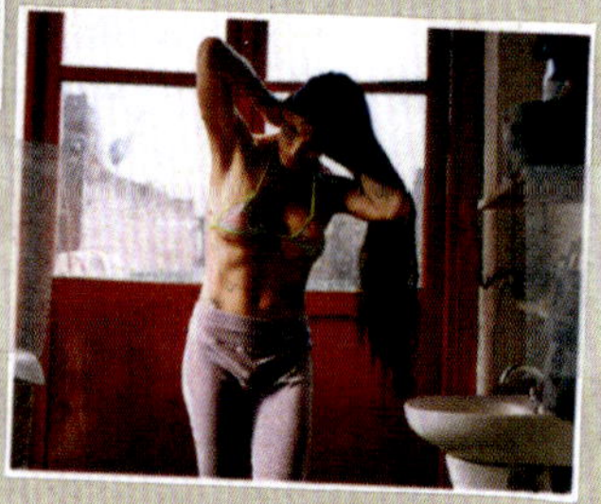

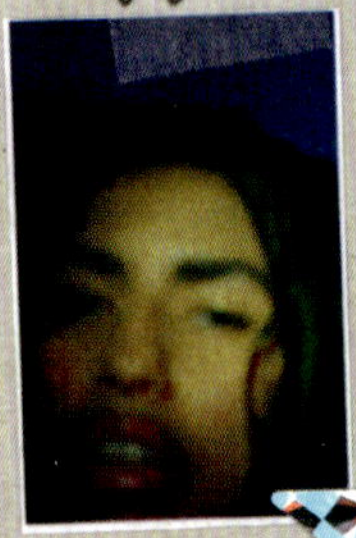

SAMANTHA FOREVER, AT MARIA'S,

2020

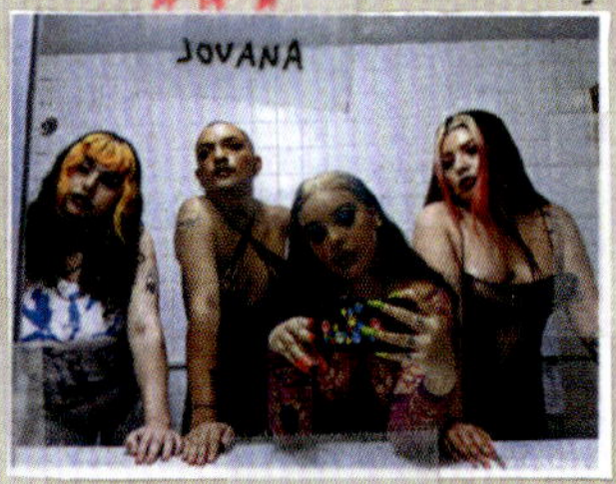

JOVANA KARLA SHEILA ANDREA

BATHROOM SELFIE, 2019

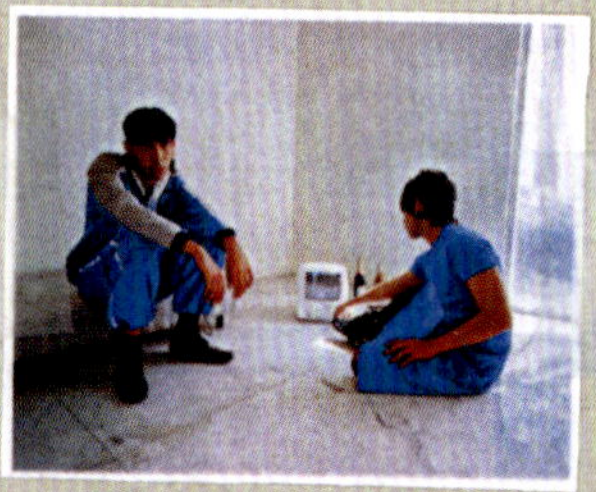

TIEMPOS BOYS STYLED BY SAM,

2022

AINE YUKKI SIETE SUNSHINE GRETA MAR

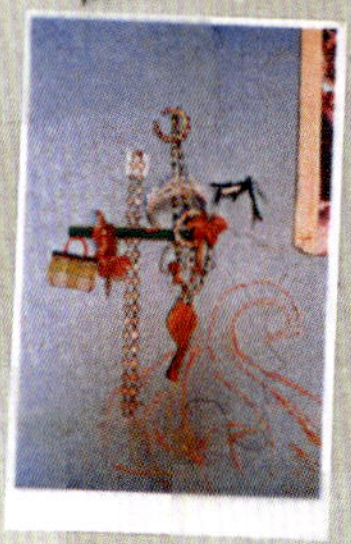

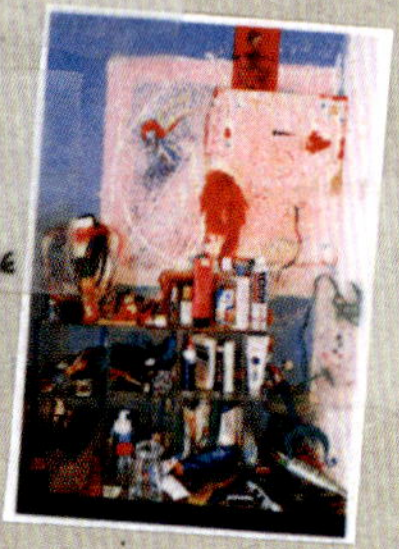

MAGIA ILEGAL,

IXTAPALUCA,

2020

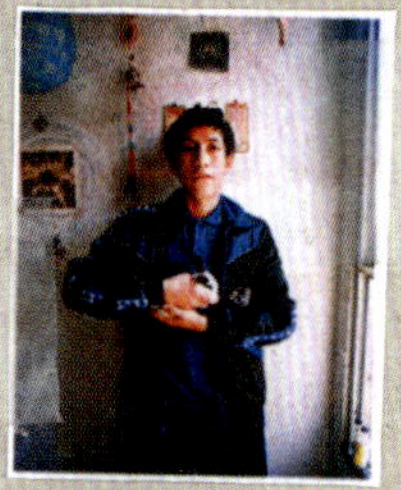

KEVIN MAYAHUEL AND SIETE THE BUNNY,

2022

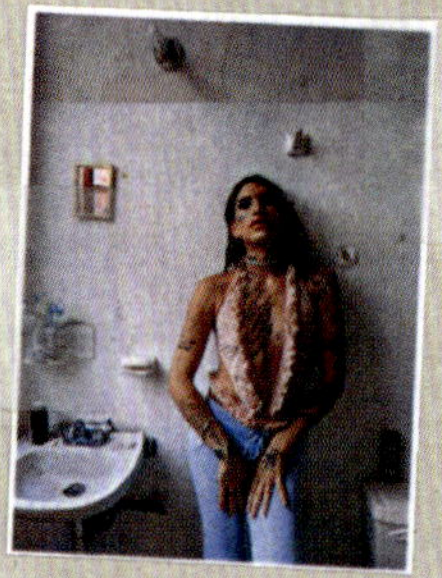

HAVI, CENTRO,

2019

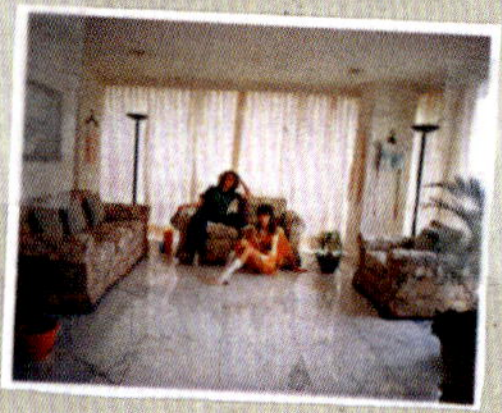

UMA AND ADA IN SENTIMIENTO,

2022

SENTI

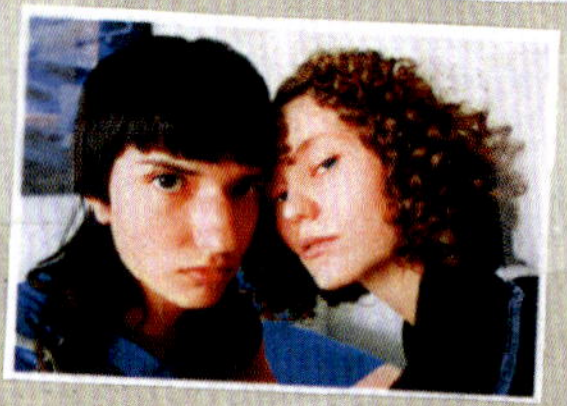

UMA AND ADA,

2022

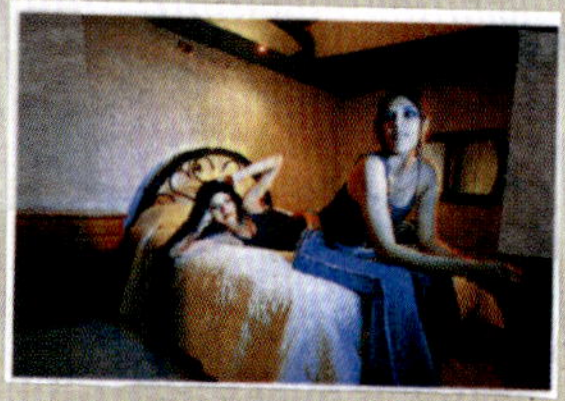

DITZY,

2019

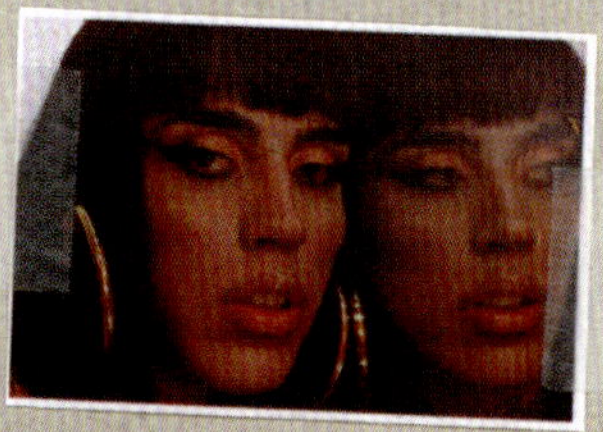

LORETO,

2020

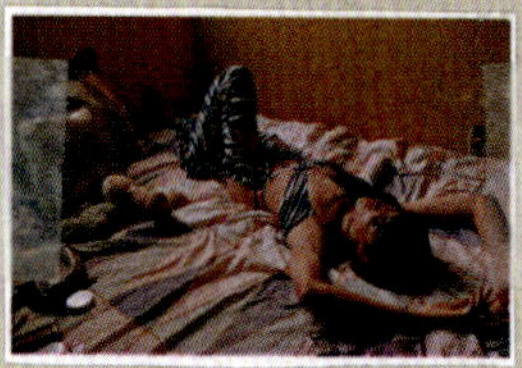

LORETO IN HER ROOM,

CAPULTITLAN,

2020

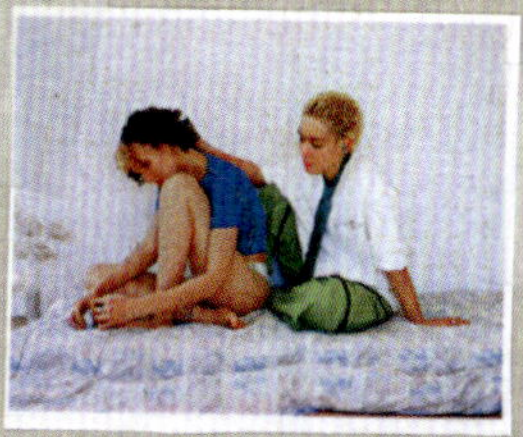

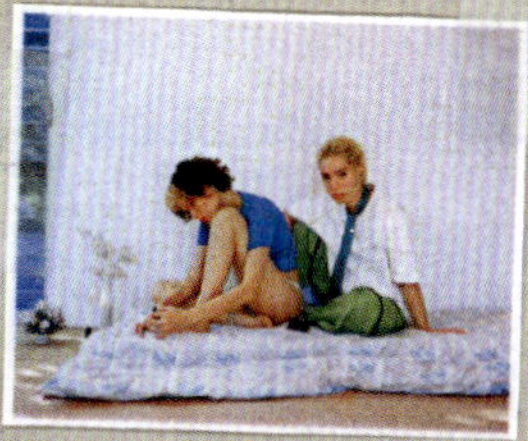

IT TOLD ME IT DOESNT HAVE TO BE PERFECT

ANGÉLICA AND CONSTANZA, 2022

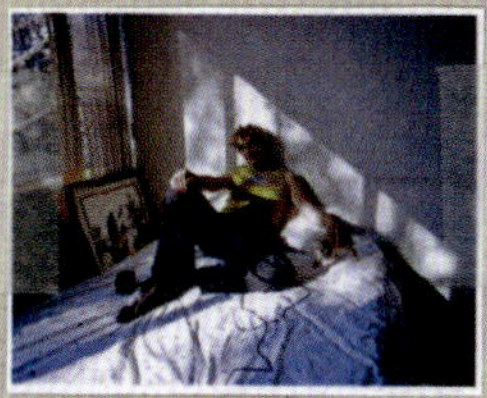

JOAQUIN IN TIEMPOS, 2022

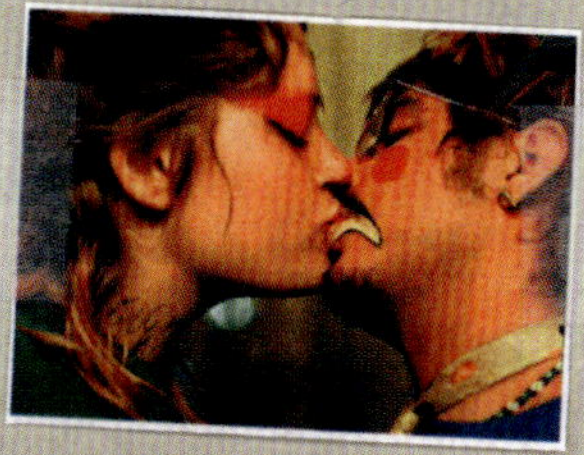

DANICA AND JORGE, MAKEUP BY HUGO, 2022

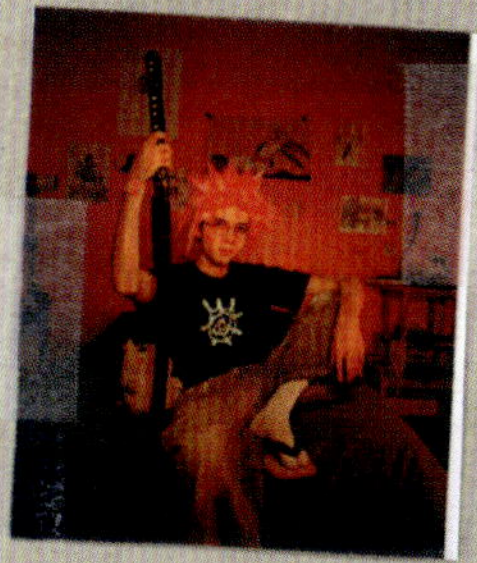

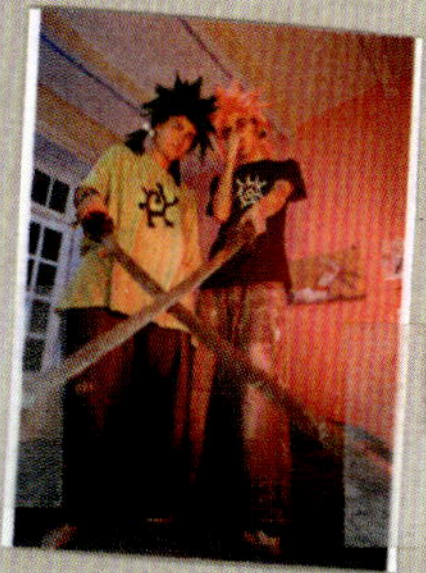

AURELIANO ALVARADO FAESLER MODOCHIKI AND TAMAYO D. OUMI, ROMA NORTE, 2019

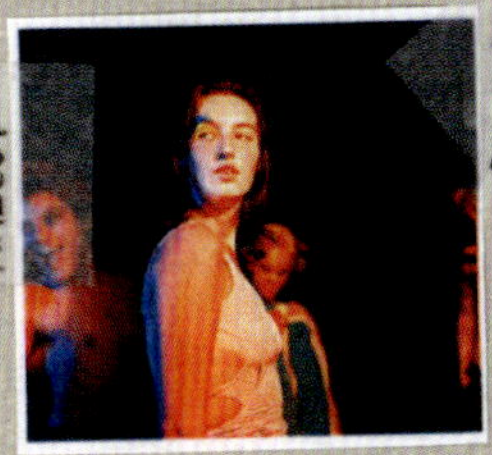

MAKEUP BY HUGO

JOAQUIN, COSIMA, CONS, ANGÉLICA, TIEMPOS PARTY, 2022

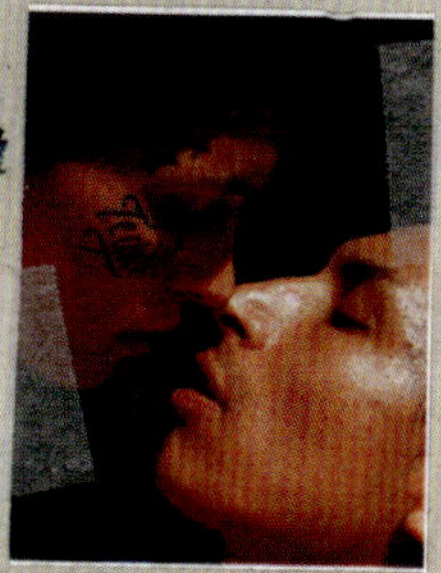

HAVI AND FER KISS, 2022

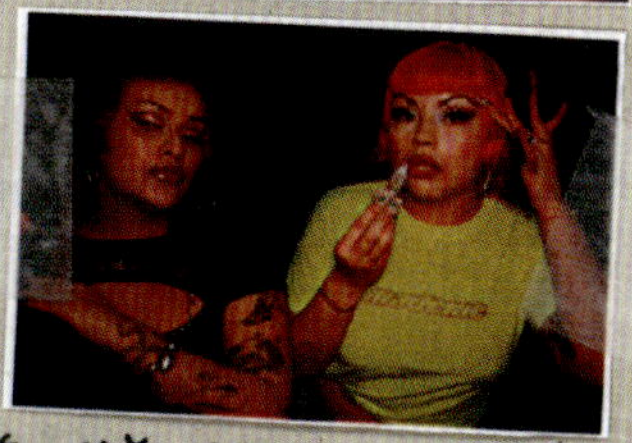

SHEILA AND KARLA, 2022

"I WOULD DEFINE MY STYLE AS KAWAII BUCHONA PUNK? I AM CHICANA, BADDIE, NAIL ARTIST, MAKEUP ARTIST, CURVY, BRUJA, FAIRY, FOREVER A SANRIO BITCH LOL"
-SHEILA

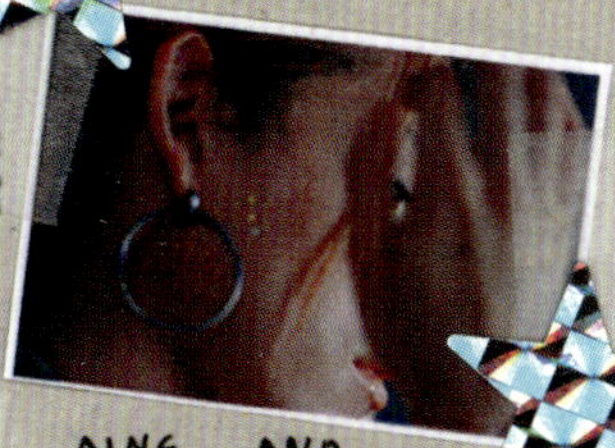

AINE THE RIVER, 2020

~~JOVANA~~ AINE TELLS ME: "THE COST OF FREEDOM IS EXPENSIVE BUT ALWAYS HAS BEEN"

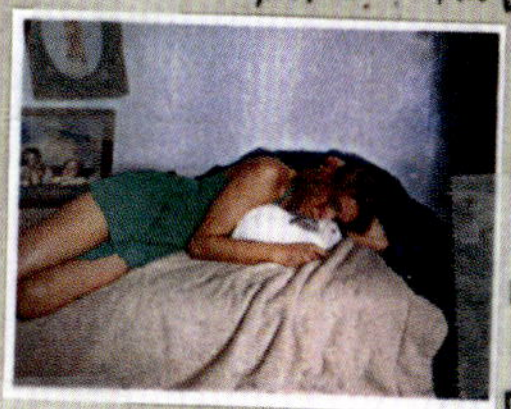

AINE AND SUNSHINE 2020

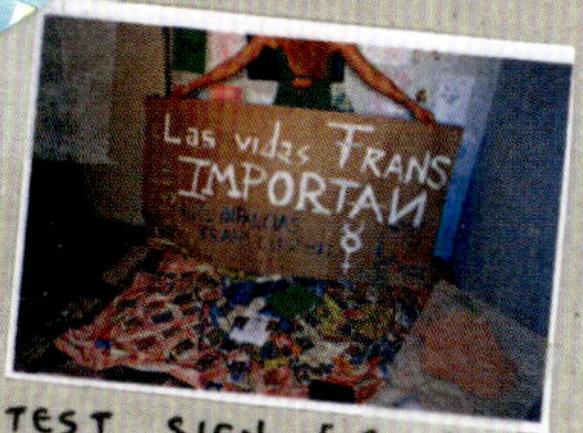

PROTEST SIGN FOR ANTIPRIDE 24 JUNE 2020

MAGIA ILEGAL

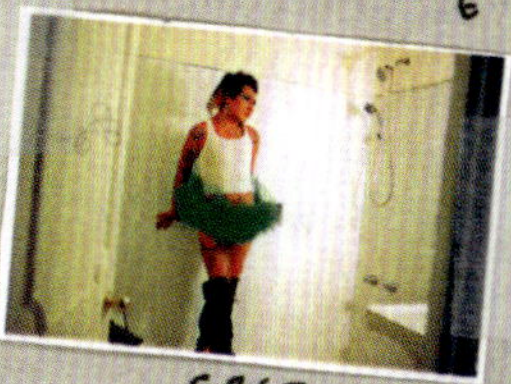

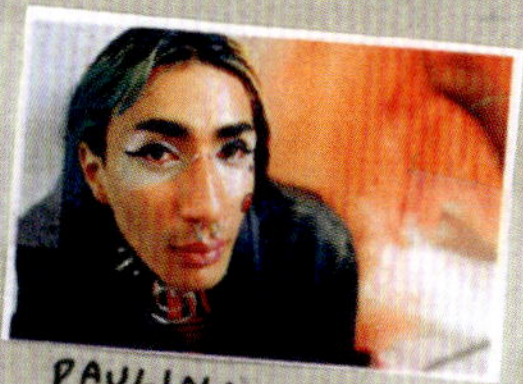

YUKKI

GRETA AT PAULINA STUDIO, 2022

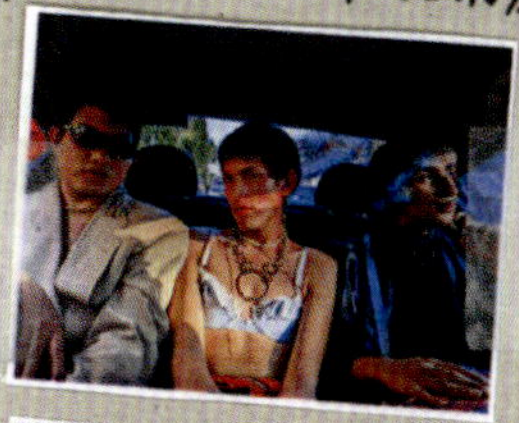

ON THE WAY TO INSURGENTES, 2022

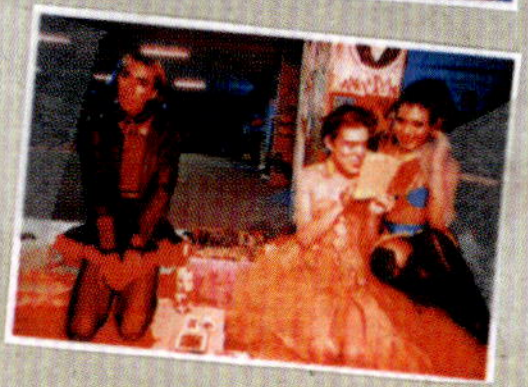

YUKKI, AINE, GRETA SELLING CLOTHES AT LA TIANGUIS, 2022

JOVANA

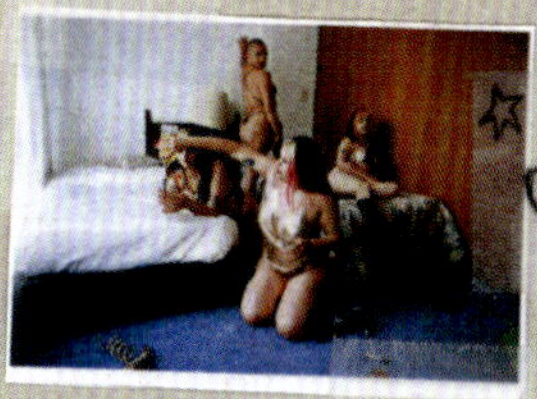

KARLA

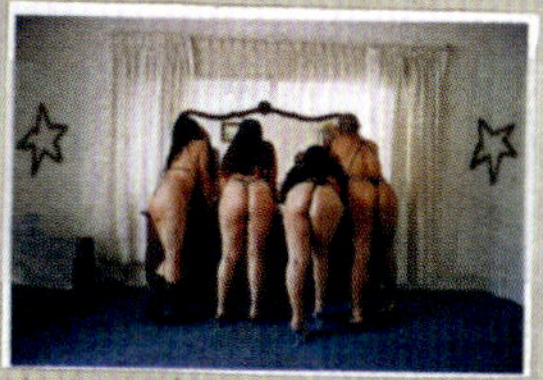

ANDREA

SHEILA

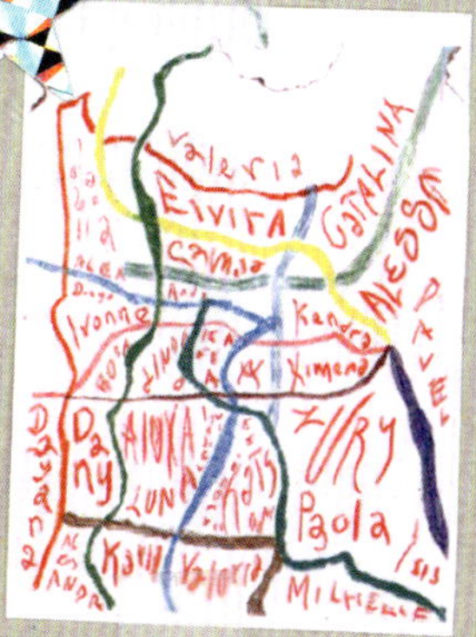

"MAP OF THE SUBWAY, THE GOLD REPRESENTS THE 45 DEATHS THAT RESULTED FROM THE 2022 ACCIDENT. IN CALLIGRAPHY, THE NAME OF TRANS PEOPLE WHO DIED DUE TO TRANSPHOBIA" ARTWORK AND WORDS BY AINE MARIN

MEXA HIDRA, BY AINÉ MARÍN

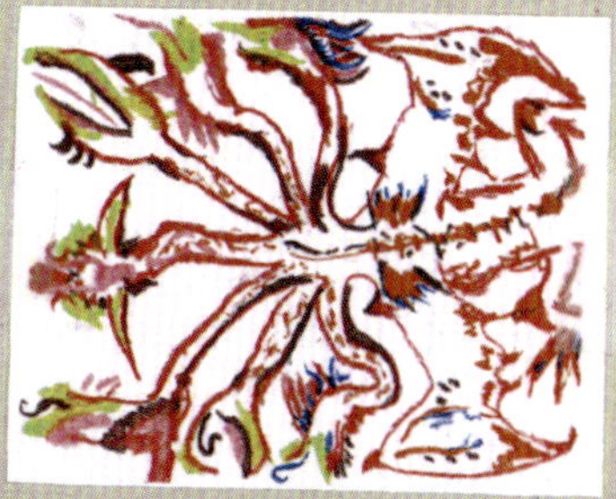

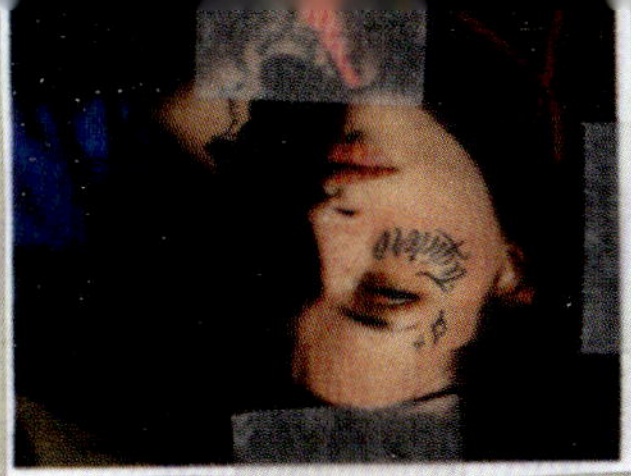
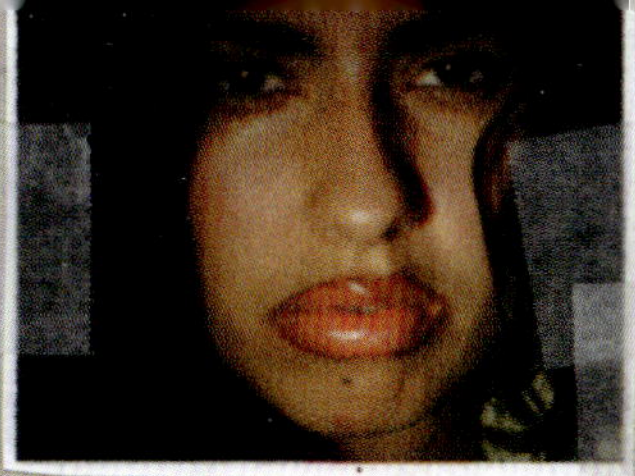
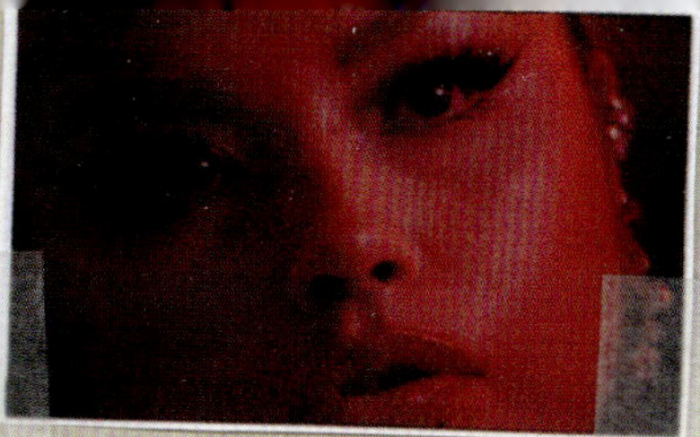
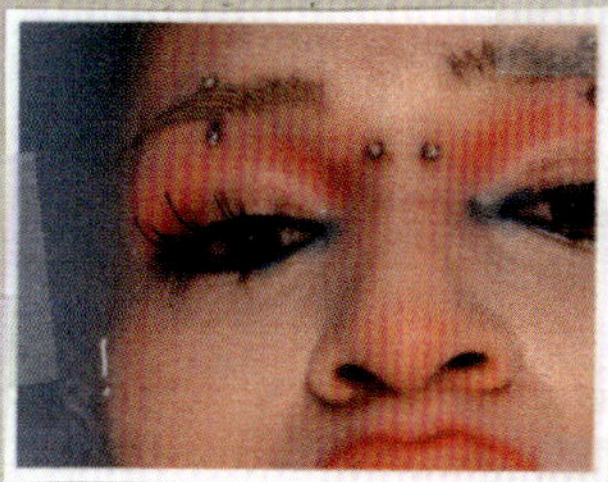
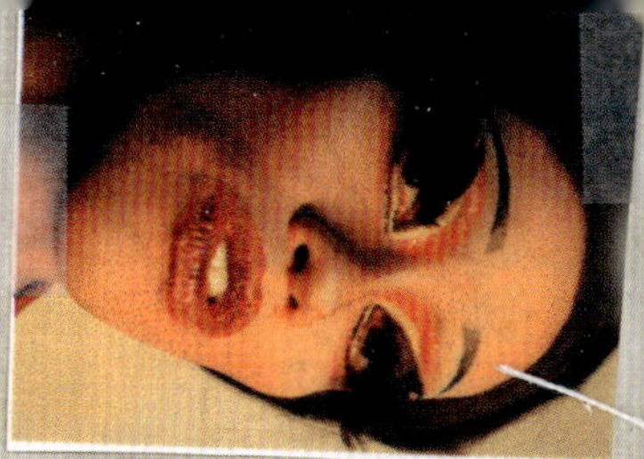
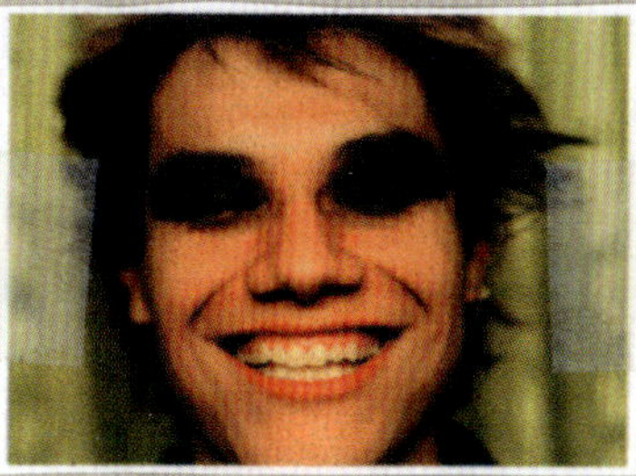
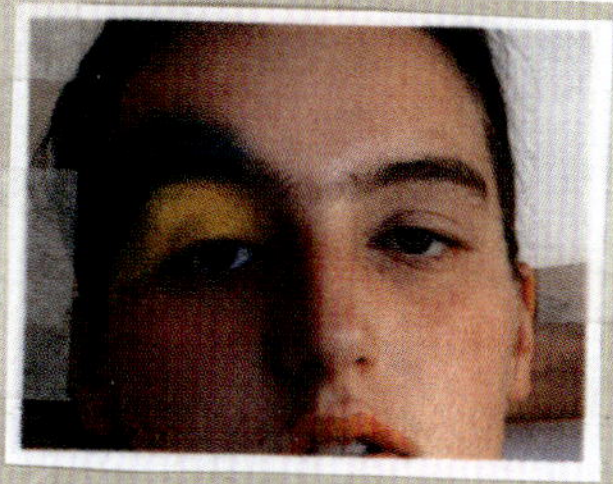
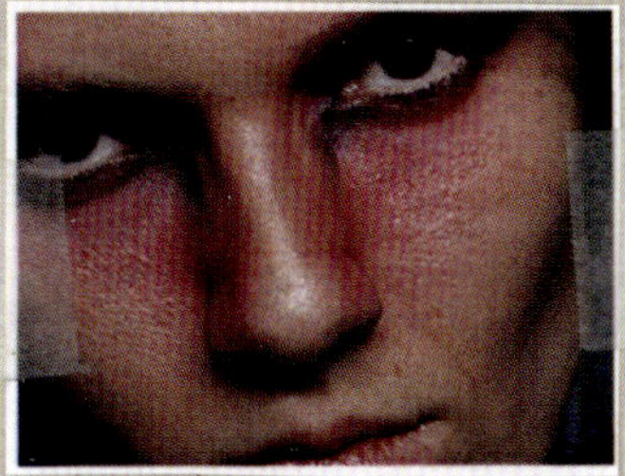
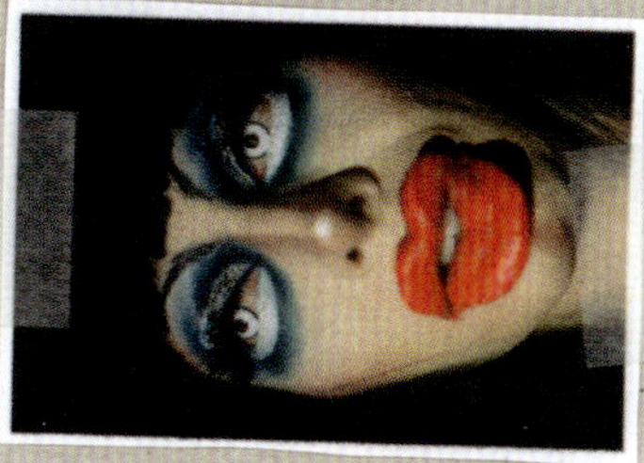
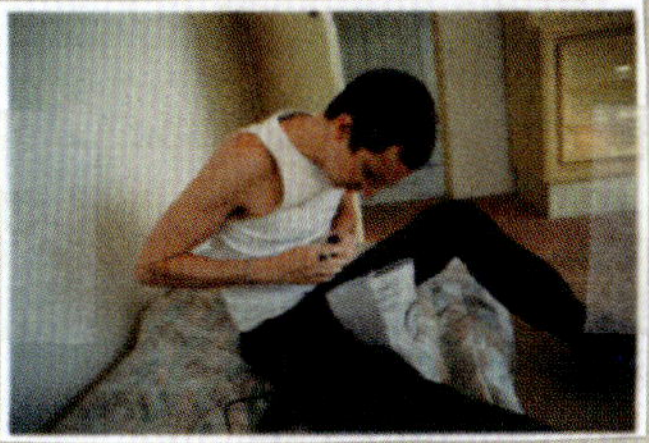
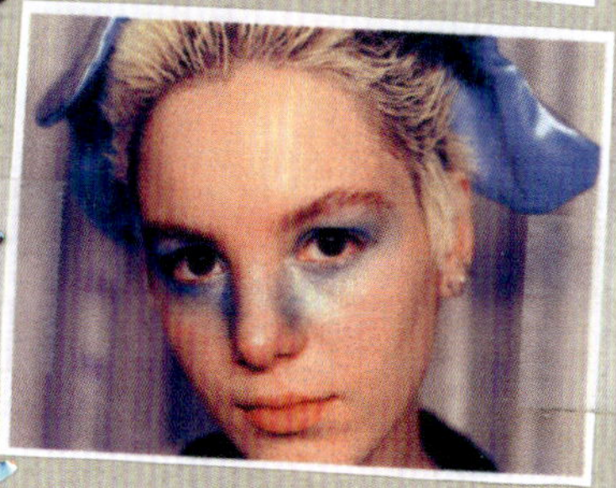

This book is a collection of images from 2019 - 2023 in Mexico City.
None of this would've been possible without the limitless love, generosity and opennes of the people in it. Thank you for being my collaborators and teachers, i'm eternally grateful for this time we shared and what we created together.
This book is dedicated to all of you~
Te Amo Demasiado,
Mayan

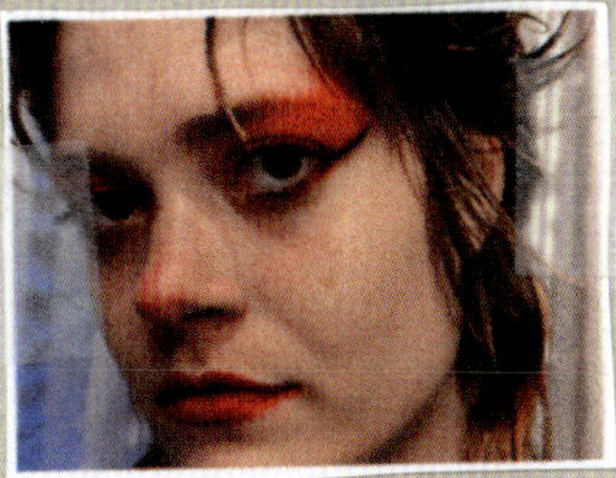
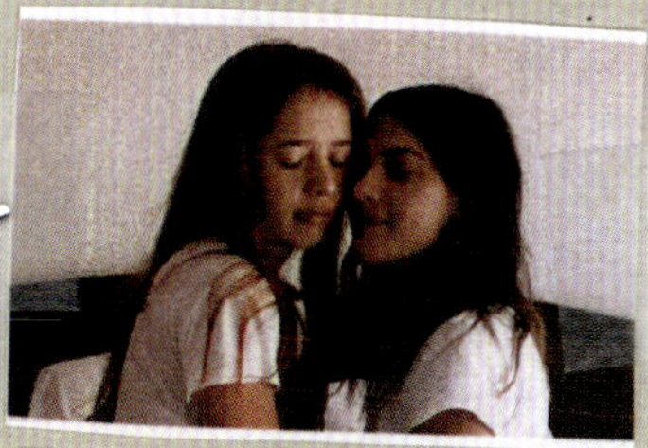
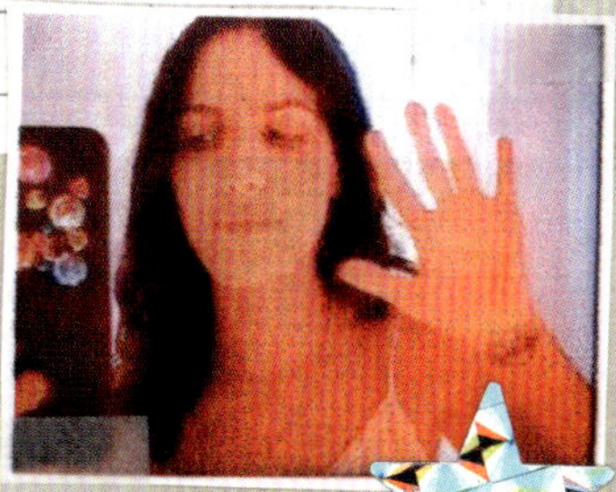
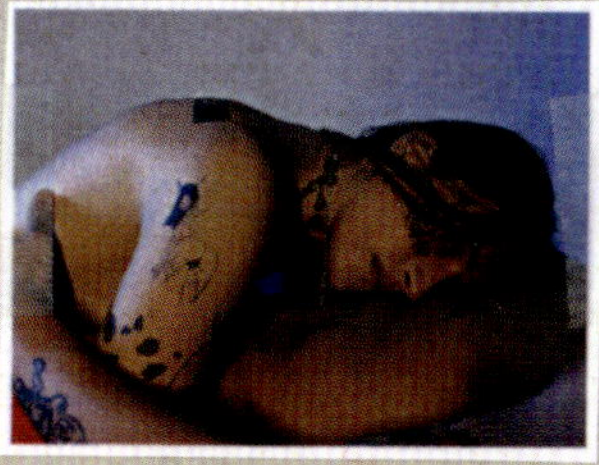
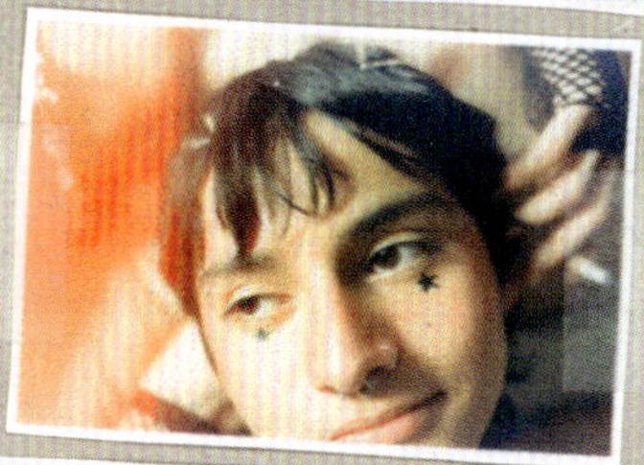
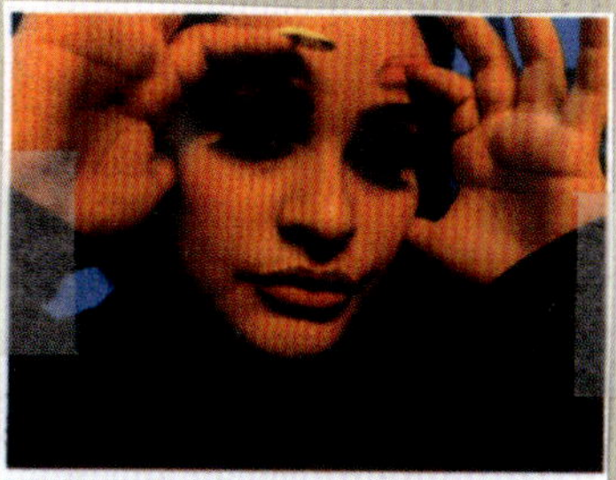
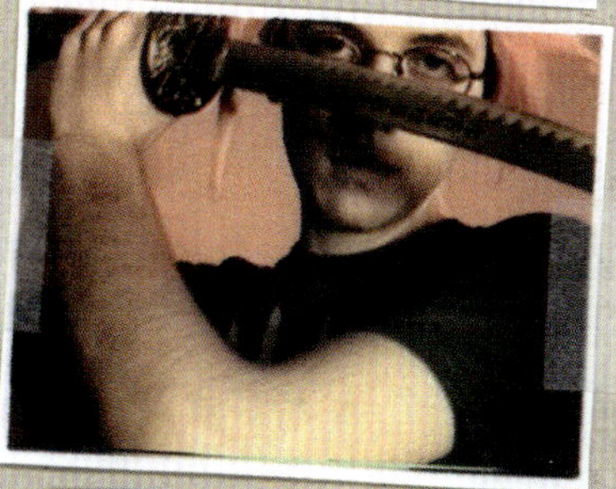
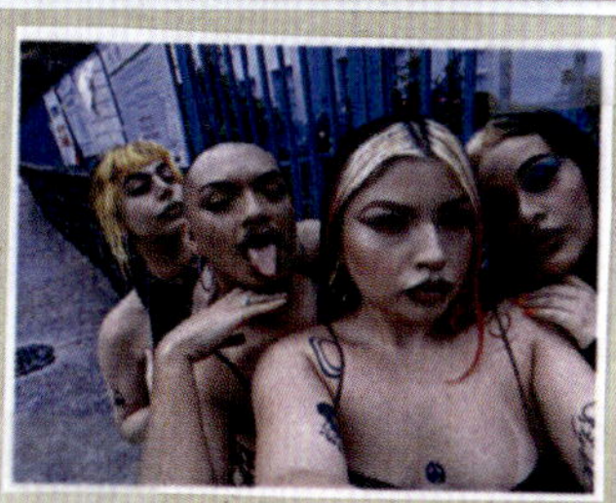
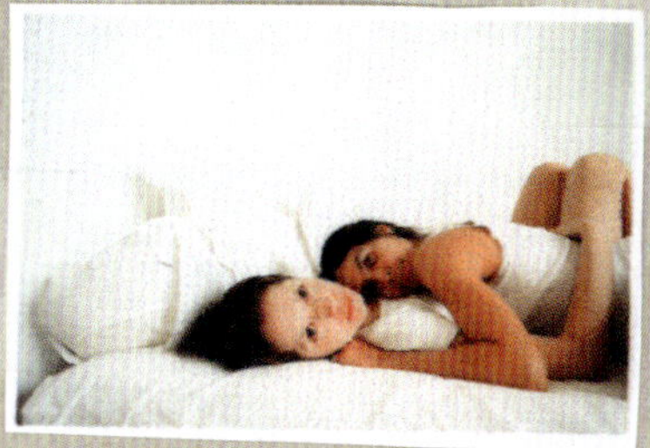
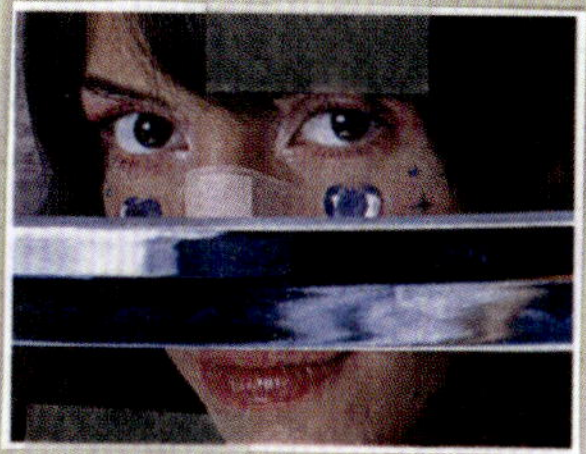
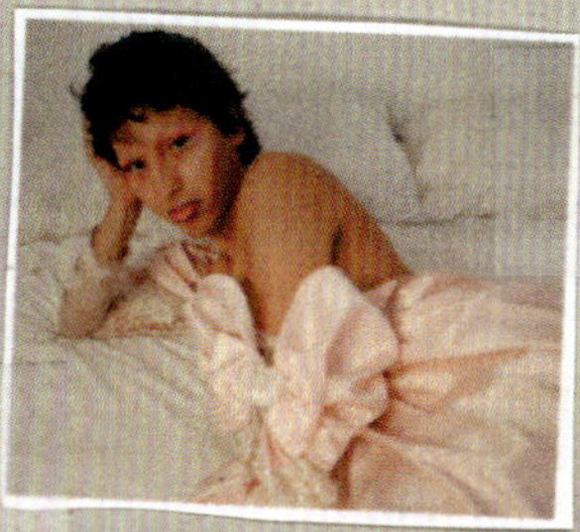
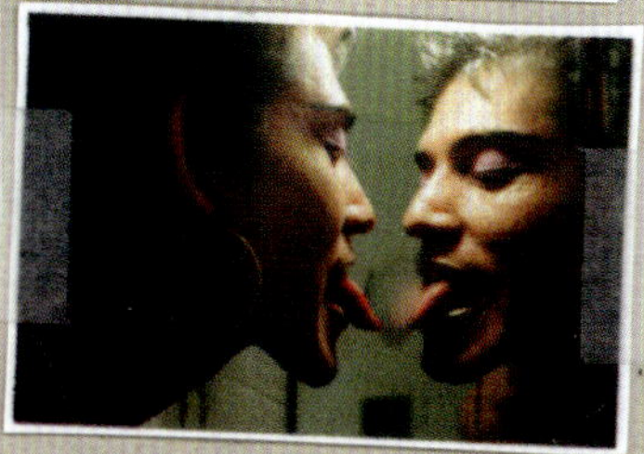